The Management of Bond Investments and Trading of Debt

The Management of Bond Investments and Trading of Debt

Dimitris N. Chorafas

ELSEVIER
BUTTERWORTH
HEINEMANN

AMSTERDAM • BOSTON • HEIDELBERG • LONDON • NEW YORK • OXFORD
PARIS • SAN DIEGO • SAN FRANCISCO • SINGAPORE • SYDNEY • TOKYO

Elsevier Butterworth-Heinemann
Linacre House, Jordan Hill, Oxford OX2 8DP
30 Corporate Drive, Burlington, MA 01803

First published 2005

British Library Cataloguing in Publication Data
A catalogue record for this title is available from the British Library

Library of Congress Cataloging in Publication Data Control Number: 2005924356

ISBN   0 7506 6726 5

For information on all Elsevier Butterworth-Heinemann publications
visit our website at http://books.elsevier.com

Typeset by Integra Software Services Pvt. Ltd, Pondicherry, India
www.integra-india.com
Printed and bound in Great Britain by Biddles Ltd, King's Lynn, Norfolk

Contents

Preface

With the democratization of lending and the socialization of risk, which started respectively in the late 1920s and mid-1930s but became a force after the Second World War, more and more people were able to borrow, and an increasing amount of outstanding debt has been federally subsidized. This combination has stimulated the financial markets, but at the same time created new types of wider and more diffused risk.

Unafraid for their government-insured deposits, people did not queue up to demand cash from their bank that had overlent in dubious deals, was imprudent in accepting substandard collateral, and finally went bust. Runs on banks attenuated, but resulting public complacency brought its own costs. By standing behind good and bad banks alike, the government in effect removed one of the most vital franchises in the banking industry.

In rapid succession, government guarantees of bank deposits, residential mortgages, farm loans, student loans, and other debt became widespread. This expanded the frequency and volume of borrowing and led to securitization of loans which have been sold to private and institutional investors.

■ People, companies, and institutions borrowed, and at the same time held other people's , other companies', and institutions' debt instruments as assets.
■ The democratization of lending and socialization of risk worked in synergy to enlarge the national income, creating a market for debt and requiring new, more effective methods for managing bond investments.

This is the subject of this present book. Written for professionals working in the debt instruments market, and also appealing to private investors who personally manage their assets, the theme of this book is the design, issuance, marketing, screening, and investing in bonds. Unlike total financing, debt financing excludes the issuance of shares and other equity – but the two domains have risk management in common, which is a key issue part of the present text.

Organization of the text

The book divides into four parts. Part 1 provides perspective into the dynamics of debt, leverage and globalization. Part 2 introduces the reader to bondholders' options, as well as risks and rewards attached to them. Part 3 looks into interest rates, inflation, yields, and duration. The theme of Part 4 is bond markets, credit rating, counterparty risk, market risk, and risk control.

Chapter 1 opens the dialog on debt instruments by restructuring under modern standard the concept of *credit*, which dates back to 1700 BC and the laws of Hammurabi, the great Babylonian emperor. Few people truly appreciate that *credit* is a financial term with a moral lineage, which goes beyond its meaning debt. Credit is trust given or received, typically in expectation of future payment for:

- Property transferred
- Fulfillment of promises given, or
- Other reasons, such as performance.

The democratization of lending, and therefore of credit, alters the centuries-old social landscape, down to basic economic rules which govern it. Because of it, more and more people have been able to borrow, but the resulting wider exposure led to an increasing amount of debt being traded under different forms in the market. As Chapter 1 explains, until this development took place, the working man in search of a personal loan was viewed as a case of philanthropy rather than of business.

Chapter 2 focuses on the trading of debt, in the globalized economy which we have experienced in the past three decades. Like the democratization of lending and social-ization of risk associated to it, globalization has been a force propelling economic growth by adding a macro-dimension to the financial market. Wealth creation, how-ever, requires transparency, reliable accounting statements, and open markets, which are far from being universal rules.

While the first two chapters provide perspective, Chapter 3 returns to the fundamentals – starting with the definition of fixed income instruments, their issuers, and the markets in which they are offered to investors. In the first years of the 21st century, easier monetary conditions and a greater willingness of private insti-tutional and corporate investors to bear risks in international capital markets, contributed to stronger growth in the world's economy.

The reader will find in Chapter 4 details of the principal types of debt instruments: Convertible bonds, zero bonds, junk bonds, credit derivatives, strips, and other bonds like high-high, Brady, Rubin, Chameleon, and Samurai – along with their unwanted consequences. Because the many different types of debt instruments pose the chal-lenge of evaluating them, and choosing among them, Chapter 5 guides the reader's hand on matters of choice, including price formation. This chapter also looks into certain markets and instruments, such as Euroland and Eurodollars.

As Chapter 6 brings to the reader's attention, securitization is the junction of bank loans and traded debt instruments. Without going into great detail, this chapter explains that there are a number of uncertainties in securitization which should condition investors' outlook. Somebody else's liabilities might make a portfolio volatile, because securitized instruments are the derivatives of loans. Chapter 6 also introduces the reader to capital adequacy requirements for banks under Basel II, while the dynamics of Basel II on the risk management side are discussed in Chapter 15.

While the notion of interest rates runs through the text from Chapter 1, it is essen-tially Chapter 5 which provides the reader with necessary linkage between interest rates, interest rate curves, bond markets, and investors' goals. This chapter also examines the economic aftermath of both high and rock-bottom interest rates, as well as introducing the reader to the concept of volatility in interest rate premium, and what this means in a portfolio's net worth.

Not only volatility in interest rates but also inflation can deliver a blow to bond-holders. Inflation sees to it that there can be a fairly significant difference between nominal and real interest rates, as Chapter 8 explains. The major engine behind inflation is government deficits, and of these we have had plenty in the first years of the new century. The text examines the aftermath of inflation and deflation on fixed rate debt instruments, convergence and divergence of debt patterns, as well as investing in inflation-indexed securities.

Chapter 9 is dedicated to the analysis of bond yields and use of credit risk-free government bonds for benchmarking. However, as a reviewer had it, math-phobes will be pleased to see that there are very few formulae throughout the book. Dr Stephen Hawking, the physicist, wrote in the introduction to his book *A Brief History of Time* that he was advised by his publisher that every time he uses math he cuts the readership population by 50%! Mindful of Hawking's experience, Chapters 9 and 10 have separated the mathematics of yield calculation, algorithms for computational procedures, Fisher parity, Macaulay's duration, convexity, as well as modified and effective duration, from the main text and concentrated it in each chapter's appendix.

Not only has it been a deliberate choice to limit algorithmic descriptions to a minimum, emphasizing instead the basic notions, but also the text is so written that the reader who does not care to go into mathematical formulae can skip the appendices altogether, and without a loss of content in the descriptive qualities of the text and its case studies. On the other hand, the analytics could not have been left out altogether because they are:

■ A common language, and
■ A fundamental part of human intelligence.

The theme of Chapter 10 is maturity and duration. Duration gives the investor an estimate on how much the price of a bond will change as yields change. In principle, duration is higher the lower is the coupon, the longer the maturity, and lower the yield of the bond. Convexity sees to it there is asymmetry: For a bullet bond, the price increase for a given decline in yield is greater than the price decrease for the same rise in yield.

Having elaborated to a reasonable level of detail the basic notions and tools for bond investors, with Chapter 11 the text changes its orientation towards the broader perspective – which could be seen as a continuation of the approach taken in Chapters 1 and 2. Chapter 11 talks of bond markets, money markets, and capital markets. It also presents to the reader a procedure for capital allocation in fixed income instruments, and provides principles for sound portfolio management, which should be of interest to all investors.

Chapter 12 addresses itself to credit quality and the contribution of independent rating agencies to identification of creditworthiness. This is a subject dear to all investors, and most particularly bondholders. The text explains the process of bond rating, gives practical examples, and it provides a frame of reference for loans quality, including the notion of risk-adjusted return on capital (RAROC). It is wise to remember that loans eventually morph into bonds.

The theme of Chapter 13 is case studies on credit quality, starting with large financial institutions and their assets, proceeding with bank failures (with a case study on Penn Square), and explaining how commercial paper and debt instruments can turn to ashes. On this, the case studies are Penn Central and Asia Pulp & Paper, and reference is also made to oil companies' financial statements.

Chapter 14 focuses on market risk; most particularly on interest rate bubbles and the bond market's meltdown. Specific issues are measuring exposure to interest rate risk, mismatch risk, reporting to regulators (with a case study from the Office of Thrift Supervision), risk points, exposure patterns, as well as hedging interest rate risk. Stress testing for interest rate and forex risk is another subject covered by this chapter.

Chapter 15 concludes the book by concentrating on Basel II and on the control of exposure. Basel II is briefly examined as a milestone in banking regulation bringing along fundamental changes such as risk-oriented capital adequacy for bank lending, additional disclosure and compliance requirements, more rigorous supervisory standards in banking, and introducing the notion of market discipline. All this obliges financial institutions to further develop their risk management processes, not only to cover the groundwork set out in Basel II but also to guarantee their own survival and growth.

Investors should appreciate that structural reforms in the financial industry are to their advantage. It is most vital to both shareholders and bondholders that a balance is achieved between safety and efficiency. Accurate evaluation of current financial conditions, reliable financial reporting, risk-based pricing of banking products, forward-looking estimates of exposure, and understanding of the degree of uncertainty surrounding credit risk and market risk, are at the core of investor protection.

*   *   *

My debts go to a long list of knowledgeable people and their organizations, who contributed to this research. Without their contributions this book would not have been possible. I am also indebted to several senior executives of financial institutions and securities experts for constructive criticism during the preparation of the manuscript.

Let me take this opportunity to thank Mike Cash and Karen Maloney for suggesting this project, Jennifer Wilkinson and Lona Koppen for seeing it all the way to publication, Deena Burgess, Melissa Read and Elaine Leek for the editorial work. To Eva-Maria Binder goes the credit for compiling the research results, typing the text, and making the camera-ready artwork and index.

Dimitris N. Chorafas
May 2005

Part 1
The dynamics of debt, leverage, and globalization

1 Democratization of lending and socialization of risk

1.1 Introduction

The financial markets have experienced several important developments in the years since the end of the Second World War. Two of them will concern us greatly in this book: The *democratization of lending* and the *socialization of risk*. Neither has happened overnight. The beginnings of the democratization of lending, and of credit, can be traced to a couple of years prior to the Great Depression, but its real impact started being felt in the 1950s and it became really evident in the following decades as:

- More and more people have been able to borrow
- Debt instruments became popular trades, and
- An increasing amount of debt has been federally subsidized.

Economic history teaches that in May 1928, on opening day at City Bank's personal loan department in New York, 500 applications for personal loans, by an equal number of individuals, poured in. The next three days brought another 2500. The way a bank officer related that event: 'The men outnumbered the women, and the married men outnumbered the single men. There are policemen and firemen and mail-carriers and clerks and stenographers – mostly office workers.[1]

Till then in New York banking, contrary to the policy followed with company loans, the working man in search of a *personal loan* was viewed as a case of philanthropy rather than of business. In 1928 a new epoch began, but because of the intervening Great Depression and the world war which followed it, it took another quarter of a century till personal lending became a respectable and profitable transaction.

The economic developments that followed the end of the Second World War saw to it that the sources of outstanding liabilities greatly multiplied. Personal lending now spanned across unsecured personal loans, mortgages, loans for home improvement, auto purchases, appliances, credit card receivables, and more – while the amounts involved in them reached for the stars. Moreover, these rapidly growing *personal liabilities* have been repackaged and sold to investors as *assets*. This:

- Expanded lending and borrowing, as well as magnified its aftermath, and
- Influenced the direction and behavior of investors, financial institutions and markets at large.

Governments, too, became deeply involved with the risks which confronted the voting population. An easily definable action characterizing the *socialization of risk* has been the salvage undertaken by governments, like that of Savings & Loans in the late 1980s in the United States, and of Crédit Lyonnais in the early 1990s in France. By standing behind good banks and bad banks alike, politicians and regulators have in effect removed the oldest franchise in banking: *safekeeping* – which started being chipped away back in the 1930s with *deposit insurance* (see Chapter 2).

Another development of the last decades of the 20th century, worth noting in debt trading, is the reinvention of unsecured paper in the form of *junk bonds* (see Chapter 4), which essentially means junk loans. These played an expansive role in the boom of the mid-1980s and late 1990s, as well as in the busts which followed them. With a junk loans policy and the socialization of risk,

- Creditors lend more freely than they had in the past, and
- Government intervened more actively than ever before, to absorb the inevitable losses.

It needs no explaining that taking risk is inseparable from lending and investing. The question is one of risk appetite: Which type and how much? No bond (see Chapter 3) and no loan (see Chapter 6) is ever fully secured no matter who is the issuer or the recipient. Therefore, at its most basic, every loan and every bond is a sort of speculation whose degree of exposure varies according to:

- Quality of collateral, if there is one, and
- Character and financial strength of the issuer or borrower.

This is precisely what the *risk of debt* is all about. With the socialization of risk associated to the lending business, the element of speculation has not been removed. Only its costs have been shifted while, at the same time, the public sector's credit increasingly supplanted the private sector's. Government guarantees became widespread and, as an after-effect, this expanded the volume of borrowing.

The globalization of debt (see Chapter 2) has magnified the pattern described in the preceding paragraphs, including its risks and rewards. But while globalization involves many governments and their private clubs, the Group of Ten (G-10) being an example, there is no global safety net for debt transactions. Experts suggest that this has often deceived investors, but as Johann Wolfgang von Goethe put it: 'We are never deceived. We deceive ourselves.'

1.2 The shift in economic activity

The references made in the Introduction highlight some of the aspects characterizing the evolution of debt in our society during the past 30 years. The 1980s, 1990s and first decade of the 21st century, contrast to the 1920s and 1930s when an abundance of lending was succeeded by drought, and an inflation of prices was followed by a deflation. The many forms of government guarantees that came along with the democratization of credit and socialization of risk succeeded in breaking this cycle; they did so by bringing every taxpayer into the frontline against the risks they themselves and many others have created.

To the opinion of cognizant economists, with the major shift of economic activity engineered by the democratization of lending during the 20th century, control of credit has moved from the private sector to the public sector. With this, counteraction to spikes in credit exposure has been increasingly characterized by administrative discretion followed by greater centralization of decision-making – all the way to the definition of reserves. Moreover, with demonetization of gold, the character of money has radically changed.

Paper money is, at least in theory, infinitely expandable, and the central bank is no longer constrained by the need for a reserve in physical values, such as represented by gold.

Today, central banks can create credit in the volume and at the price that the market will bear. Before the advent of a government-sponsored and -controlled central bank, commercial banks held their own reserves in their own vaults, or in the vaults of a trusted custodian. The central banking system took over this function, promoted on the ground that a government run monetary reserve is more effective than a decentralized one,[2] especially in a crisis.

The other side of this argument, of course, is that the duties of central banks loom large, and sometimes appear incoherent, in controlling inflation, deflation, and liquidity crises which hit the financial system (see Chapter 8). There is also a snowball effect. As credit expanded rapidly, companies and people applied more and more for loans at commercial and retail banks. Hard pressed to accommodate this transaction traffic, commercial banks applied for more money at the central bank – and they got it at a price.

But even the government cannot dispose infinite resources. Therefore, a fundamental investment question is whether the guarantor, be it the state or somebody else, is big enough to underwrite with good money the losses born from rapidly growing and widely ranging lending practices. In order to address this question, we must step back and take a look at the shift of economic activity during the past three or four decades.

A basic characteristic of this shift is that the epicenter of economic activity has moved from the real world of base metals, factories, railroads, and generally physical goods, to financial instruments, or virtual goods, representing the *virtual economy*. This is an event for which there is no precedent, and therefore no factual and documented evaluation can be made regarding the most likely results are we move further out. What can be said is that, on all evidence, the globalized service economy will probably give rise to business cycles characterized by swings in both:

- Credit volatility, and
- Market volatility.

The likely aftermath is more frequent but better controlled financial crises, which engender economic and social costs, opening the way to move socialization of risk. According to some studies, a financial crisis of some size claims about 9% of a nation's gross domestic product (GDP) – while the more severe ones, like those which afflicted Argentina and Indonesia, wiped out over 20% of GDP. The Asian financial crisis of 1997 pushed 22 million people in the region into poverty; a greater catastrophe than that endured as a result of the Great Depression.

It is unavoidable that in a free market system financial crises are taking place from time to time. To grow and keep growing, countries need deep financial markets which are liberalized. A market is liberalized and economic activity is deregulated if they are not under strict government control, with bureaucrats quite remote from the market itself

- Pulling the strings, and
- Improving the poor man's lot by making everybody poor.

The liberalization of market activity, however, has some important prerequisites. What makes a *market economy* is first and foremost the six freedoms: Freedom to enter the market, to engage in competition, to exit the market, to set prices, to make profits, and to fail. Other characteristics of the free economy are:

- Market sensitivity
- Customer orientation
- Rapid research, development and implementation, and
- A legal system supportive of individual and corporate accountability (see also Chapter 15).

Neither of these preconditions for a free market talks about avoidance of financial crises. In fact, the better way of looking at the likelihood of possible crises is to accept *a priori* that, by their nature, all financial instruments involve risk, including credit risk for non-performance by counterparties – either because of inability or because of unwillingness to face up to their obligations.

Exposure to credit risk is controlled through credit rating (see Chapters 12 and 13), credit approval, credit limits, continuous monitoring procedures, as well as reserves for losses. Eventually, mounting credit risk reaches the government's shore, and the question becomes one of how much of a salvage operation is affordable, and what is an acceptable level of regression in GDP. Also, whether the government has in place a damage control system so that this regression:

- Is temporary, and
- Is used as springboard for further economic advance.[3]

Well-managed entities seek to limit their exposure to credit risk in any single company, industry, country or region. Investors must, however, be aware that the maximum potential loss may exceed any amount recognized in a company's consolidated balance sheet. Moreover, banks, industrial firms and investors must effectively manage their exposure to market risk (see Chapter 14). This is done through prognostication, regular operating reviews of financing activities and portfolio positions. Also, when appropriate, through the use of derivative financial instruments (for hedging, see Chapter 2).

Prognostication is by no means an exact science. In a bull market, the most profitable mind is *faith* backed by *research*. But in a bear market, it is *doubt* even if the experts advise otherwise. Though there should be thoroughness of study and analysis in the background, both attitudes, faith and doubt, assist in qualifying the search for risks and rewards from market volatility.

Whether we talk of credit risk or market risk, thoroughness in analysis of disclosed financial elements and market behavior should never slacken. As advice, this runs contrary to what is suggested by the history of business cycles where, in general, the stage of prosperity is marked by an ever-increasing inefficiency in financial research – both on the side of the companies and at that of investors. This is counterproductive because the shift of economic activity towards the virtual economy requires more than ever:

- A significant amount of study and analysis
- The ability to turn on a dime (as Sam Walton said)[4]
- The strength to manage change, and
- The patience to go through the turbulence which accompanies a change in epochs.

An ancient Greek sage asked the Gods to give him three gifts: the strength to change the things he can, the patience to endure the things he cannot, and the wisdom to know the difference. This ancient wisdom applies exactly to present-day conditions because the transition to the virtual economy is characterized by both:

- Turbulence, and
- Business opportunity.

An example on how turbulence can be overcome and turned into business opportunity is provided by late 19th and early 20th century events in the United States, when scores of railroads went bankrupt during successive financial panics. To bring about order, J.P. Morgan, the top banker of his epoch, used a new and controversial technique, the Trust. He bought failing companies, reorganized them, made them profitable and brought back confidence to the market.

We actually live in interesting times. Credit risk and market risk in the virtual economy are more volatile than in the physical one, because they are influenced by heightened market activity and market psychology has become transparent. In all likelihood, the globalization of finance and invention of new instruments and trading patterns will see to it that, in the coming decade, volatility will reach new heights which are, at the present time, quite unfamiliar to investors. Precisely because there is no precedence to the twists to the globalized economy's ups and downs, both bulls and bears can make a point that is difficult to disprove.

1.3   Creativity, innovation, and tax incentives

In the virtual economy, which is based on debt rather than real assets, creativity is the best source of growth and of creation of wealth. Therefore, the value of education rises exponentially, particularly when it focuses on conceptual solutions and analytical thinking, or both. Creativity and innovation are the tools needed to address in an able manner the:

■ Design of new financial products for the virtual economy
■ Optimization of factors which increase the instruments' appeal to the market, and
■ Management of exposure, which becomes more polyvalent because of new ways of assuming risk (see Chapters 12 and 14).

The message these three bullets carry may seem to be quite apart from, or even irrelevant to, the democratization of credit. In reality, it underpins this process because credit and lending are no more limited to the working man in search of a personal loan, as was the case with the first personal loans offered by City Bank in 1928. In its most recent incarnation, the democratization of credit is *leverage* – and from there a way of gaining market edge.

People or companies find benefits in being ahead of the curve. In their search for market edge, 21st century companies must not only review their cost structure and trim it down, but also steadily look for new higher margin instruments and markets, as well as novel types of risks and their control. With the boom in debit instruments risk management has become the cornerstone of value differentiation (see Chapter 15) all the way to capital allocation, including identification of concentrations of risk across a company's assets and liabilities structure.[5]

To a very significant extent, training people for creativity and innovation is an issue novel to the educational establishment. Putting it in action requires massive changes in the curricula of schools and universities, steady faculty retraining, and refocused student objectives. Another prerequisite is efficient administration of a program aimed at providing new solutions to an economic environment characterized by the democratization of credit and socialization of risk.

Tax optimization provides an example (see also Chapter 5). One of the reasons, but only one, why companies and individuals favor debt over equity is that the laws making up the tax system have a pronounced positive bias for debt. Debt payments are tax-deductible and this has been enough of an incentive to provide a good part of the oiling of the economy through skyrocketing debt. The tax system favors debt financing over equity capital; which means bonds over stocks. If paid out in the form of a dividend to the stockholder, a dollar of corporate earnings is taxed twice:

■ First at the corporate tax rate, which is a high 50–60% depending on the country
■ Then at the individual tax rate, which can be as high as 90%, also depending on the jurisdiction.

Just as an example on how fast taxation grows, in 2003 an unmarried average wage earner in western Germany had to pay almost 64% of his or her additional gross income in tax and social security contribution. This is over 11% age points more than in 1990.[6] To this unwarranted high taxation should be added statutory health insurance and the social security burden.

The wrong tax incentives aside, there are other good reasons for companies to plunge into debt. In the early part of the 21st century interest rates have been low – in fact, the lowest in 46 years – and the prime rate on commercial loans is low too. Even junk bonds carry an interest which is far from being commensurate with the credit risk assumed by investors. This makes borrowing money an interesting way of achieving all sorts of things, including acquisitions.

In the first six or seven decades of the 20th century using borrowed money to buy a company was not unknown, but it was rather exotic. Big leverage (see section 1.4) did not find general acceptance in a population whose mind was set on ownership of assets; high gearing was the exception rather than the rule.

According to some experts this fixation on ownership of assets was rooted in the fact that attitudes from the Great Depression persisted, even in the 1950s. Furthermore, equities continued to have a better field, through reasonably good dividends compared to prime corporate bonds. At the low ebb of stock valuation in 1950,

- Stocks yielded nearly 7%
- By contrast, high grade corporate bonds yielded about 3%.

Tax considerations aside, in the decade that followed the Second World War investors were not ready to go for leveraging. They demanded safety and were even inclined to forgo capital gains for some assurance that their money was not at risk. This gave an impetus to high grade corporate bonds, even at a significantly lower rate of return than equities.

Part of the investor psychology was made up by the fact that in the go-go 1920s, banks had lent a high proportion of their deposits. Mid-1929, for instance, this stood at 80%. With war following the Depression, loans were replaced by government bonds, and by the end of the war the ratio of loans to deposits had fallen to 20%. Peacetime brought revival in the demand for credit, levels of new lending rose, and the ratio of loans to deposits climbed to 50% by 1955.

Contemplating what comes next, several financial experts suggested that in the longer term loans are bound to move upward because that is the trend of business. Some also prognosticated that new patterns of production and consumption would lead to increasing reliance on consumer credit. Those who had foresight and courage to say so were proved to be right, by the facts: the democratization of lending gained the upper ground.

Contrary to the pre- and immediate post-war years, in the last decade of the 20th century and early years of the 21st, the capital requirements of industrial enterprises have been largely determined by a sharp growth in financial assets which, in essence, are somebody else's liabilities. Based on statistics by the European Central

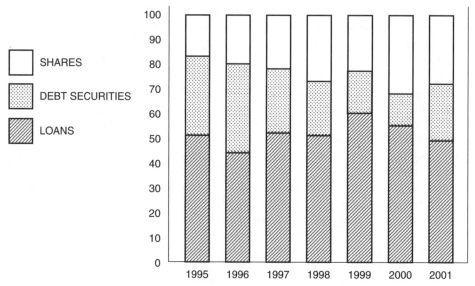

Figure 1.1 Financing of the non-financial sectors, excluding financial derivatives and
other accounts payable (as a percentage of total financing), 1995–2001.
(*Source:* European Central Bank)

Bank, Figure 1.1 demonstrates that in the 1995–9 timeframe loans to European
companies significantly increased, while financing through equity shrank. This situation reversed itself with the stock market collapse of year 2000, and the wave of
credit risk:

- By 2001 loans remained subdued, and
- The slack was taken by a rapid growth in corporate bonds.

The transition has, however, been from loans to bonds, not to equity. Within this
overall pattern, loans and bonds did the lion's share of industry financing. On average, loans and bonds outstrip equity financing by a ratio of nearly 4 to 1.

As is to be expected, exact statistics vary from country to country, but the trend is
general. The German economy provides an example. As Figure 1.2 shows, in
Germany the debt ratio has zoomed from 1995 to 2001, the timeframe of the previous example. But the net interest burden did not change appreciably because of interest rate decline.

In its monthly report of December 2003, the Bundesbank notes that while by late
2003 a generally more favorable picture emerged of the overall financing circumstances of German companies, there were also weaknesses. For instance, a sharp rise
in corporate insolvencies, indeed a 42% increase, has been a cause and result of an
accumulation of major corporate failures. As we will see in section 1.4, the amount
of leveraging and probability of default correlate – and this correlation is characterizing every company, anywhere in the world.

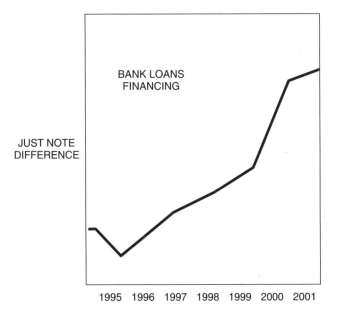

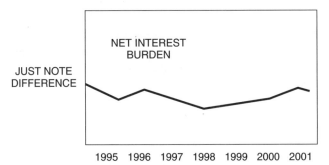

Figure 1.2 In the German economy, bank loans increased significantly in the boom years of the late 1990s. (*Source:* Deutsche Bundesbank)

1.4 Debt and unsustainable leverage

Debt financing is the trend, as section 1.3 has shown, but debt also means leverage – or living beyond one's means. The Bank for International Settlements (BIS) defines leverage as *a low ratio of capital to total assets*.[7] All banks are leveraged, but some are much more leveraged than others and these are the most exposed to a collapse of their balance sheet which leads to counterparty risk.

For evident reasons, the supervisory authorities are greatly concerned about leverage in the financial industry. The Basel Committee on Banking Supervision advises that when banks operate with very high leverage they increase their vulnerability to adverse economic events and boost the risk of failure (see also the discussion on Basel II, in Chapter 15).

In more general terms, on the one hand, a growing amount of debt propels the productive power of the economy as personal indebtedness filters mostly into consumption. However, when debt is incurred to cover shortfalls in income, the result is ephemeral because such money has only a very short-term aftermath. Economists say that most of the debt incurred over the past couple of decades has been for consumption, and they worry because of its exponential rise; the trend in US statistics is shown in Figure 1.3.

Behind this argument lies the fact that productive investments have a longer-term return. Spending today to build a technological infrastructure helps in increasing the productivity of the workforce. Far-sighted research and development (R&D) spending has similar effects. The drive to put a man on the Moon in the 1960s returned to the American economy an estimated $14 in benefits for every $1 that was spent.

On the other hand, financing through debt rather than savings and generally capital accumulation, has an important downside. Government indebtedness leads to inflation, as it is documented in Chapter 8. Breaking the so-called speed limit of the economy, discussed in section 1.7, is not without consequences. Corporate indebtedness weakens an entity's financing staying power, and excessive personal indebtedness can also lead to bankruptcy. About 2 million people have declared personal bankruptcy in the US, profiting from very favorable bankruptcy laws.

In one country after the other, within the Group of Ten greater details on debt levels, debt distribution and leverage underlying the economy substantiates worries associated with rapid growth of liabilities and their aftermath. In the US during the 1990s, within the financial sector of the economy the largest increase was the 661% rise in debt owed by issuers of asset-backed securities (ABS), which are derivative financial instruments.

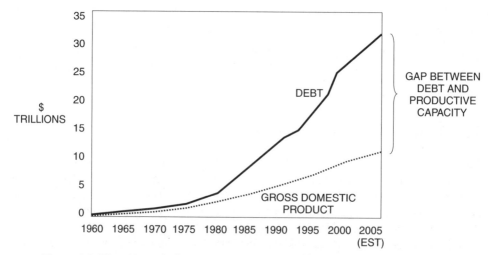

Figure 1.3 The US gross domestic product is outpaced by the growth of credit market debt

With ABS, securities are issued against the income stream generated from underlying assets. In liabilities growth, next to this figure, came the debt owed by real estate investment trusts (REITs) which, also during the 1990s, rose by 502%. Eventually, a bubble psychology carries the day, propelled by six factors which characterize a financial bubble:

- High liquidity
- Increased use of leverage
- Significant volatility
- Increased turnover
- A growing number of investors join in,[8] and
- New issuance of complex finance instruments, which are poorly understood by their investors and users.

The reader should appreciate that a significant increase in commodity prices is not among the factors mentioned in this list, because exponential price increases are the aftermath rather than a primary reason for bubbles. Are there any metrics which would permit us to measure how far a company is moving towards a level of leverage that is unsustainable? One answer is the *leverage ratio*, expressed as:

$$\text{Leverage ratio} = \frac{\text{Market Value of Debt}}{\text{Market Value of Assets}} \tag{1}$$

A proxy for the market value of assets is the company's capitalization. By contrast, it is not easy to measure the market value of debt, because this debt, or at least a large part of it, is not necessarily marketable and, therefore, it has no current price. Hence, rather than using equation (1) we can employ the *solvency ratio*:

$$\text{Solvency ratio} = \frac{\text{Liabilities}}{\text{Market Value of Assets}} \tag{2}$$

Again, in connection to equation (2), capitalization is proxy for market value of assets, but liabilities are taken at book value. The problem is that book value is based on accruals, and accruals do not really represent an entity's current financial situation.

Another important leverage ratio is that of *debt service coverage*. It is computed as earnings before interest and taxes (EBIT) over interest due (EBIT/interest due) and is considered to be quite predictive. As such, it is a good tool in discriminating between lower and higher gearing exposure – and therefore credit risk. The downside is that EBIT is proforma financial reporting, and proforma is often synonymous with 'cooking the books'.[9]

Leveraging, of course, has limits. A highly leveraged economy finds it difficult to carry forward because confidence in it wanes and investors as well as other market players run out of money – even borrowed money. This starts a process of *de-leveraging* characterized by defaults. For instance, there may be an increased density of debt problems, with people, companies and nations reaching or exceeding the limit of bankruptcy.

Default does not need to come only from the leveraged investors' side. In the area of business debt, companies that go bankrupt range in size from big entities to a swarm of smaller firms. In consumer debt, households have had difficulties paying off their credit card payments, doctor's bills, mortgages, and other financial obligations like credit card debt, which was virtually unknown before the late 1970s but today constitutes one of the main elements in securitized assets.

1.5 Leverage, common risk, and strategic risk

Leverage exists everywhere in the economy. Whether the investor buys bonds, purchases stocks, or does some other transaction, the instrument he gets has embedded in it a certain amount of gearing, and therefore of risk. Moreover, as we have seen in the preceding sections, practically every company runs on borrowed capital. Figure 1.4 looks at the assets and liabilities side of balance sheets of financial entities in Euroland. In many financial institutions the assets side of the balance sheet is essentially an exercise in leveraging.

In order to better appreciate this reference, it is proper to remember that even with the 1988 Capital Accord (Basel I), banks generally operate with an equity cushion of only 8%. In itself this means 1250% gearing approved by regulators. Alternatively, Basel II provides banks with the possibility to use the internal ratings-based (IRB) method to calculate their capital requirements.[10] Notice, however, that whether IRB, 8-percent or any other approach is used, this is a practical compromise; it is not a theoretically established limit based on a long trail of knowledge regarding:

- Credit exposure, and
- The aftermath of shocks.

As a reminder, when in the early 18th century John Law originally issued paper money through his Banque Royale, he kept gold and silver coin reserves at the level of 25% of printed money. This meant leverage by a factor of 4. Within a few years, however, gearing accelerated and it saw to it that the coin share of reserves decreased as leverage increased. In the aftermath, there was a run on the bank which was saved through intervention by the Regent of France. Later on, the Banque Royale again became overleveraged and finally it crashed.

In the opinion of regulators, under current conditions commercial banks can live with 8% reserves because, as far as their banking book is concerned, they are relatively long-term investors. Accidents do happen, however, as with the 1929 Depression in the United States and the Russian meltdown of 1998 – when there were runs on commercial banks and a number of credit institutions ran out of cash.

Things are different (not necessarily for the better) with the status of the trading book, and the derivative financial instruments in it. With the 1996 Market Risk Amendment the regulators require a daily measurement of exposure by banks, through the value-at-risk (VAR) model.[11] VAR numbers are supposed to give a snapshot of the bank's current market risk exposure through the computation of recognized but not realized gains and losses (see Chapter 14).

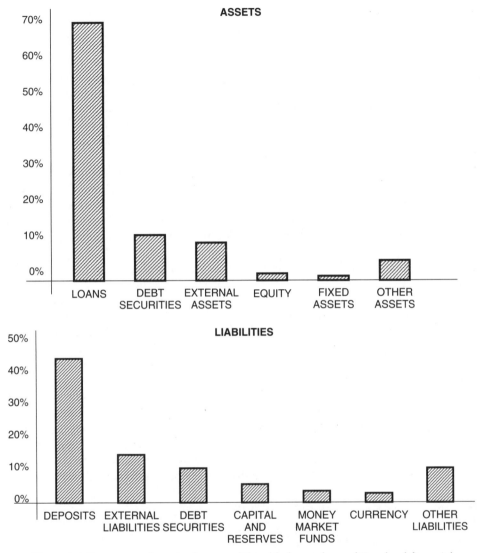

Figure 1.4 Percentage share in the consolidated balance sheet of Euroland financial entities at the end of 2000 (including the eurosystem): (*a*) assets; (*b*) liabilities. (*Source:* European Central Bank)

Aside from the fact that VAR is a weak and mathematically inconsistent model with several shortcomings,[12] under no condition should value at risk be interpreted as a predicator of future exposure in the bank's trading book; even less so of the institution's longer-term financial health. Moreover, VAR is not all-encompassing. It only answers one-third to two-thirds of market risk measurement requirements depending on:

■ The institution
■ Instruments in which it trades

- Composition of its portfolio, and
- Way it uses the computational results.

As any other algorithmic risk measure, value at risk is evidently open to model risk which can be aggravated by a near-sighted interpretation of obtained results. VAR could, however, help on an order of magnitude basis and for comparative reasons, regarding changes in exposure in the trading book. Table 1.1 presents a sample of six global banks whose VAR exposure increased most significantly between 2002 and 2003. How severe is this increase depends on several factors which do not cease to exist because they are not part of VAR.

VAR is, so to speak, a measure of *common* risk which says little about strategic factors. As a more realistic measure of exposure, given the stress developed by high gearing and other reasons, the more serious market players have developed the notion of *strategic risk* applied to market opportunities – as well as different instruments designed to respond to them. A strategic risk approach points out issues such as:

- Delays in defining and implementing innovative, compelling value propositions to answer market requirements
- Failure to recognize opportunities and threats from emerging technologies and/or exposure to emerging countries
- Inability to perceive the aftermath of ill-studied or poorly implemented business models
- Wanting risk management structures and solutions, as well as conflicts of interest.

These are major strategic challenges in today's competitive environment, which can lead to loss of market position, failure to retain important clients, the assumption of inordinate risk, a hemorrhage of money, or a combination of these factors. To meet such challenges, an entity has to develop and implement systematic and rigorous methods, processes and tools able to identify and manage the many aspects of strategic risk. One approach is the so-called *value drivers* serving as operational means for:

- Analyzing investment opportunities as they develop
- Measuring the extent to which current and projected performance contribute to sustainable value creation, and
- Putting limits to exposure so that potential losses are affordable.

Table 1.1 VAR exposure at global banks at the end of 2003 (US$ billions)

	2002	2003	Increase of exposure
UBS	180	260	50%
JP Morgan Chase	120	180	50%
Citigroup	50	70	40%
Morgan Stanley	50	60	20%
Goldman Sachs	45	60	33%
CSFB	40	50	25%

Both in terms of counterparty exposure and in the domain of assumed market risk, in a more precarious position than banks are hedge funds, which are not supervised by anybody and do not report even approximate figures of recognized gains and losses. Under these conditions leverage can take a totally different dimension, as will be demonstrated in Chapter 15.

One of the main issues which worries many experts is the pyramiding of borrowing. Hedge funds borrow to bet on the market. Funds of funds, which through banks commercialize the hedge funds produce to retail customers, also borrow and invest loaned cash in leveraged propositions. Finally, individuals borrow to invest in funds of funds. All this amounts to highly geared bets whose outcome is technical and obscure but mostly boils down to something simple: risk as high as Mount Everest.

Critics are rightly concerned by the fact that the hedge funds' and funds of funds' fee structure encourages their managers to borrow aggressively. Such fees are often calculated on the basis of all the money 'managed': equity plus debt. As a result, more borrowing means more pay – an enormous conflict of interest. 'It is a house of cards,' says one London fund of funds manager. 'Each level of debt amplifies the rest – and that is hard to manage.'[13]

This brings into perspective a downside of the democratization of lending, specifically the side where leverage has no limit to set and to watch. It is *as if* some of the players have lost their bearings in their high gearing exercises, and they depend on the socialization of risk (read taxpayers' money) to pull them out of their own miscalculations, and soften the heavy price of bankruptcy which comes further down the road.

The leverage of hedge funds is typically a medium two-digit number; 50 is not unheard of. Before it crashed LTCM had an exposure of $1.4 trillion with a capital of $4 billion; this means a leverage of 350 or 35 000%. LTCM's exposure is an extreme event, but when some hedge funds say that their leverage is 'only' 10 or 15, they usually fail to account for the fact they are mostly running on bought money, and this adds to the leverage factor.

The message the reader should retain from these references is how much personal skill counts in damage control when the bets being made turn on their head. In spite of advances with models, we simply do not have the means for modeling events like strategic risk and further-out exposure due to leveraging, even in a coarse way. Moreover, because the market changes and turns around intraday, there is lack of detail in the different geared financial plans – and as Mies van der Rohe, the architect, used to say: 'God is in the detail.'

Sparse data and algorithmic insufficiency prevent us from handling a great deal of detail through computers. Some people may dispute this argument. I would be the first to say financial engineering has made great strides,[14] but the complexity of the instruments and of the market's behavior has also increased by leaps and bounds. There is no evidence that even a minority of market players are able to identify in a factual and documented manner the aftermath of all value drivers in regard to:

- Revenue
- Cost, and
- Risk.

Indeed, it is easier to do so with classical business lines than with highly geared, illiquid instruments. For instance, we can estimate trend curves with net new money growth and average margins on assets, for products typically used in private banking and traditional asset management. But we are less able in computing the potential impact of derivative instruments used in complex investments deals, whether these are traded bank to bank, or sold by funds of funds to a growing population of retail investors – who should know that *their* future losses are not covered by the socialization of risk.

1.6 Debt management challenges

As we will see in Chapter 2, to a very large extent, globalization, economic development and capital flows work on the basis of debt financing. There is nothing awkward in this, because debt is easier to trade than assets. It is also easier to manipulate debt and create new financial instruments, as compared to assets. But debt handling should be subject to sound debt management practices.

The amount of debt by governments, supranatural organizations, banks and industrial corporations amounts to trillions of dollars, and this volume strongly influences the behavior of the global financial system – while at the same time it questions its long-term survival. To manage debt in an able manner, borrowers and lenders must have a clear understanding of *where* they want to base their financial strategy:

- Should they promote equity or debt, and why so?
- Should they prefer subordinated or non-subordinated debt?
- Is it better to contract loans on fixed or floating interest rates?
- What type of bonds should they issue to the capital market? Who should be the underwriter?
- What is the preferred currency denomination of debt instruments?

Both at national level and internationally, there are different ways to measure the costs and risks associated with a borrowing strategy. Discounted cash flow techniques are very useful,[15] and the same is true about marking to market the value of debt – though, as already stated, this is by no means an easy exercise since a good deal of this debt is kept to maturity (see Chapter 10) and will not be priced by the market at any early time.

Analytical approaches are important in pricing debt instruments, because they provide insight and foresight in a world where indebtedness increases at rapid pace. Research I carried out in the late 1990s documented that in nominal terms the issue of international bonds grew 25 times, in just 22 years, from 1975 to 1997: From $20 billion in 1975 to about $500 billion in 1997, while medium- to long-term syndicated loans also increased 20-fold.

A major reason in this trend towards greater debt financing has been the sharply rising government indebtedness, due to a shift toward major budget deficits and rather lax fiscal policies, but corporate and private individual debt also rises fast. Hence, it is most important for lenders and borrowers to steadily test the effects of changes in interest rates on anticipated cash.

For lenders, the focal point must be income stream commensurate to assumed risk and market prices.

For borrowers, the viewpoint concerning them the most is that of serving the debt.

Notice that debt financing by the different governments is contagious and has multiple-connect characteristics: governments, companies, and individuals tend to increase each other's leverage through synergy in borrowing. This can become biting because it is these same consumer households that are both borrowers and investors, as well as the same businesses are issuers of bonds and the also investors. Eventually growth of whatever:

- From earnings
- To leverage

might not be sustainable. When investments made along the lines discussed at the beginning of this section no longer give good returns, productivity, and with it profitability, start to decelerate and servicing of debt faces discontinuities which:

- Bring up the rate of defaults, and
- Lead to further profits recession.

No doubt, in a healthy economy, there will always be an element of debt and of doubt, which of itself, is not a problem. The problem comes when debt grows at unsustainable levels, most specifically as a substitute for financing what should be taken care of by income streams of households, as well as industrial, agricultural, and service firms – coupled with failure to control expenses and fostered by the speculative side of the economy. This creates the birthplace of *leverage risk*.

A leveraged economy wounded by a blown-up bubble takes long, painful years to return to normal economic conditions. For proof, ask the Japanese about their 1990 to 2004 experience, from the time the equities and real estate bubble burst until the start of a recovery based on a significant amount of deleveraging and increased return on equity (ROE) in business and industry – but also an unprecedented government indebtedness:

- In 1998 in the business sector, about half-way through the Japanese economy's depression, leveraging was nearly 70% and ROE 6.5%.
- In 2004 leveraging stood at an estimated 32%, while ROE seems to have zoomed to 65%.[16]

But government debt reached for the stars, zooming from about 65% of GDP in 1990 to an estimated 165% in 2004. Finland provides another example on how fast the national debt can grow. In 1990, the public debt to GDP ratio was a low 14.5%. But in the early 1990s, after the break-up of the Soviet Union, the Finnish economy experienced a severe economic recession, with a decrease in GDP and massive deficit which, by the end of 1995, had caused the debt to GDP ratio to jump to 60% – a 400% increase in only five years.

Just like individual people with their household budgets, governments find it difficult to keep a balance between receipt and spending. Banks loan the money to different governments for their wild spending, and so do investors who buy the government bonds in the capital market. Hence, in the last analysis, with the democratization of lending, the same people who benefit from entitlement programs lend to the government the money to spend lavishly on them.

When confronted with economic and financial problems, the stronger governments borrow a leaf out of the industrial corporations book and try to restructure the national economy. This is indeed a tough task, not only because imagination is in short supply but also because the measures to be taken are most frequently unpopular – since they are bound to hit:

- Some of the voters, and
- Many of the embedded interests.

As a result, rigorous restructuring measures are not being pushed through, and some are even being reversed. For instance, the 3-week strike of the French rail workers in November/December 1995 forced the Juppé government to dump a key measure in its plan to slash welfare deficits, that of extending retirement age. French rail employees continue to retire as early as age 50, which is clearly ridiculous.

Alain Juppé was also forced to scrap his plan to close uneconomic train routes, despite a rising rail deficit that, at the time, hit $6 billion per year. These concessions and cave-ins put paid to the planned reforms. They even obliged the French government to perpetuate state control of public services in a wholesale demonstration of socialization of risk, therefore:

- Dooming French taxpayers to subsidize inefficiency forever, and
- Keeping France's head in the sand as free markets were transforming the world economy.

Just as maddening in many countries is trying to reform other entitlement-type aspects of the deficit-plagued welfare state. For instance, up until the 2003 reforms of retirement age by the Rafarin government (for which Rafarin's party paid dearly in regional and European elections) successive French administrations did not bother to tell the citizen why changes mattered. They did not explain that in the last analysis it is the taxpayer who pays all, since the money must come from somewhere. Neither did the governments explain that, when it is properly managed, restructuring can be synonymous to job creation.

1.7 Controlling the speed limit of an economy

One of the characteristics of a leveraged economy is that the velocity of circulation of money, v, accelerates. This also happens when the central bank keeps interest rates low in an accommodating monetary policy. The aftermath is pushing the money supply (MS) so much higher for the same nominal monetary base (MB). For any economy, the fundamental equation relating money to money to the monetary base and velocity of circulation of money is:

$$MS = v \cdot MB \qquad\qquad (1)$$

Up to a point, but only up to a point, the acceleration of v makes everybody happy: Consumers spend in a big way, the housing market booms, the pace of business increases, bank failures diminish, and so on. But while consumers buy more on credit, this zooms their leverage – and there is a threshold on how much the velocity of circulation of money can accelerate. Past that *speed limit* comes inordinate monetary risk.

'There is no limit to the amount of money that can be created by the banking system,' Marriner Eccles, the chairman of Federal Reserve in the Franklin Roosevelt years , warned, 'but there are limits to our productive facilities which can be only slowly increased, and which at present are being used at near capacity.'[17]

When added to outstanding currency, the banking system's liabilities make up the basic component of the money supply (at M-1, M-2, M-3 levels which are not the subject of this book).[18] The money supply can grow and shrink depending on the velocity of circulation of money. A shrinking MS does not destroy any already issued money (which is the province of MB) it simply:

■ Erases billions of dollars (pounds, or euro) in credit from the *assets*, and
■ Takes away an equal amount of money from the *liabilities* side of the balance sheet.

It does affect, however, the gross domestic product. To better explain this issue, let me return to the fundamentals, taking as an example productivity improvements in the American economy which, during the late 1990s, have been elevated to the position of a national benefactor. In the United States, productivity improvements stand today at 2–3% per year. Experts believe that in estimating economic trends for the next 10 years,

■ This annual productivity growth should be coupled with a growth in capital spending, and
■ The effect, compound with an increase in labor force, should bring growth at 4% per year or better.

This 4% factor represents a growth in the economy's supply side known as *Potential Gross Domestic Product* (PGDP), which is an interesting metric because the growth of the economy's supply side is viewed as the Federal Reserve's *speed limit* for non-inflationary increase in GDP growth.

The concept is that as this speed limit rises, the probability of much higher price inflation (see Chapter 8), and of spikes in interest rates, diminishes. At least, this is the way economists think the joint effect from money supply and speed limit is supposed to work. Because nobody has studied it in a serious manner so far, the big unknown in this hypothesis is the huge leverage by derivative financial instruments. As Figure 1.5 suggests, the trend line of gearing is sky-high compared to the slow growth of other key variables in the Eccles statement:

■ Equity and reserves increase very slowly.
■ Loans are leverage, and up to a point help in generating assets.

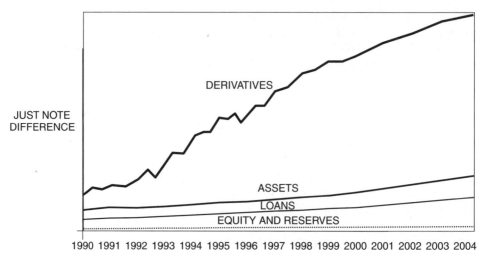

Figure 1.5 The rapid growth in derivatives versus the slow growth in assets, loans, equity, and reserves, 1990–2004

- What rises beyond control is exposure to derivative instruments, as well as their accumulation in the portfolio of banks and, more recently, in the portfolio of private investors and institutional investors. This exposure is 100% a characteristic of the virtual economy.

A major step towards the management of risk at national economic level is to define both synergy and contradiction which exists between the speed limit and gearing by derivative financial instruments. This is a study which has to be done economy-by-economy, therefore country-by-country, including the danger resulting from:

- Sky-high leverage, and
- The economy's overheating.

Such study must evidently include the known trade-offs between growth and inflation which apply in practically all cases, the risk of a derivatives bubble, as well as a number of unknowns not accounted for in old econometric models.

Some years ago, Grady Means, a partner at PricewaterhouseCoopers, argued that the United States can sustain 6–8% annual growth as business-to-business (B2B) applications of the Internet take off. 'People are just starting to apply B2B in creative ways,' said Means.[19] The bad news is that B2B applications have tanked in 2000/2001, as the interest bubble burst, and though they are now picking up they are a long way from delivering a miracle.

In the euphoria of the late 1990s, such estimates like the aforementioned one reflected the notion that new technology is creating plenty of opportunities to boost productivity, as companies use it to fundamentally change the way they organize and operate their businesses. Historically, new technologies have been introduced into an economy slowly; an example is plastics. But once or twice in a century, a transforming event takes place. In the last three decades of the 20th century microchips, computers, communications, and software:

- Generate a cascading effect, and
- Led to the hypothesis that the risks from high leveraging do not matter – which is wrong.

Even new terms have been invented in an effort to describe or explain economic puzzles. The *Nominal Gross Domestic Product* (NGDP) is an example. Today many economists prefer to focus on NGDP growth. If the desired inflation rate is, for instance, 2% and the long-term growth that can be sustained without pushing up inflation is about 2.5%, then the monetary authorities should aim to accommodate NGDP growth of about 4.5%. This, too, is a hypothesis which needs to be tested.

Nominal GDP and potential GDP tend to correlate. The latter is a prognosticator of the former, provided all goes well with the economy. Critics, however, say that this is not the way to bet. They also point out that, in their judgment, gross domestic product has never been a metric to measure real, physical economic growth. From the outset:

- GDP has been an accounting type measurement expressed in monetary terms, and
- There is no correspondence between what it is claimed that GDP measures, and what it actually expresses.

Neither is the definition of what is in and out of GDP a uniform one in the globalized economy. There are many differences in reporting standards. For instance, American statisticians count firms' spending on software as investment; in Europe it is treated as intermediate consumption. The surge in spending on software in recent years inflates America's growth statistics, but not Europe's.

To appreciate who may be right and who may be wrong, we should remember that during the period when GDP was developed, in the 1930s and 1940s, the economy of Western countries was much more industrially and agriculturally oriented. GDP was designed to indicate whether the economy was headed upward or downward. Today, the old GDP is a system based on axioms and postulates that downplay the mammoth service economy; it is as obsolete as the value added tax (VAT) invented in the late 1950s by the French taxmen to simulate the benefits the German *Konzern* derived from vertical integration – which happens to be another illusion.

Notes

1 James Grant, *Money of the Mind*, Farrar Straus Giroux, New York, 1992.
2 In 1951, while I was doing my training at Electricté de France (EDF), I was given exactly the same argument about the nationalization of power production and distribution, as well as of rail traffic.
3 Which is something the current leaders of Argentina fail to understand, let alone appreciate.

 4 Sam Walton, *Made in America: My Story*, Bantam Books, New York, 1992.
 5 D.N. Chorafas, *Economic Capital Allocation with Basel II: Cost and Benefit Analysis*, Butterworth-Heinemann, Oxford and Boston, 2004.
 6 Deutsche Bundesbank, Monthly Report, March 2004.
 7 Basel Committee on Banking Supervision: *The Relationship Between Banking Supervisors and Banks' External Auditors*, BIS, Basel, January 2002.
 8 With many newcomers being inexperienced, and easily carried away by a profits mirage.
 9 D.N. Chorafas, *Management Risk: The Bottleneck is at the Top of the Bottle*, Macmillan/Palgrave, London, 2004.
10 D.N. Chorafas, *Economic Capital Allocation with Basel II: Cost and Benefit Analysis*, Butterworth-Heinemann, London and Boston, 2004.
11 D.N. Chorafas, *The 1996 Market Risk Amendment: Understanding the Marking-to-Model and Value-at-Risk*, McGraw-Hill, Burr Ridge, IL, 1998.
12 D.N. Chorafas, *Modelling the Survival of Financial and Industrial Enterprises: Advantages, Challenges, and Problems with the Internal Rating-Based (IRB) Method*, Palgrave/Macmillan, London, 2002.
13 *The Economist*, 12 June 2004.
14 D.N. Chorafas, *Rocket Scientists in Banking*, Lafferty Publications, London and Dublin, 1995.
15 D.N. Chorafas, *The Management of Equity Investments*, Butterworth-Heinemann, London, 2005.
16 *The Economist*, 12 June 2004.
17 William Greider, *Secrets of the Temple: How the Federal Reserve Runs the Country*, Touchstone/Simon & Schuster, New York, 1987.
18 D.N. Chorafas, *The Money Magnet: Regulating International Finance and Analyzing Money Flows*, Euromoney Books, London, 1997.
19 *Business Week*, 10 April 2000.

2 Trading debt in a globalized economy

2.1 Introduction

Globalization and the trading of debt are pillars of modern capitalism, but there also exist unwritten laws. The **first law** of capitalism says money will migrate to the business environment it considers to inspire more confidence and/or the highest return is to be had. This promotes globalization. The pressure is relentless on money managers to care for assets entrusted to them, and always to do better than they have done in the past. There is also a parallel pressure on the most successful companies to continue their performance, such as:

- Fast growth, and
- Better returns

despite the increase in their size following years of rapid development. This demanding environment includes all entities benefiting directly or indirectly from globalization, innovation, and technology, including extensive usage of the most advanced systems, digitization, the Internet, and novel financial instruments.

Many cognizant people today think of the globalized economy and trading of debt as the latest metamorphosis of capitalism engineered by deregulation. Capitalism's newly found vitality is a novel combination of open markets, rapid innovation, personal incentives, as well as fiscal and monetary policies that help to keep inflation low and limit the cost of money. In this new economy, companies that care for their survival:

- Use financial strength to accelerate growth, while continuing to dominate the markets they serve, and
- Build quality products, seeing to it their facilities are furnished with the most competitive methods, equipment, and tools that are available.

They also do their best to respond to the globalized economy's planning period. Mid-December is the time when most US investment outfits – pension funds, mutual funds, insurance companies – sit down and make their new investment portfolio allocations for the coming year. That is when they decide to move ahead or significantly cut back on stocks, bonds, and derivative instruments in 'this' or in 'that' industrial sector or market.

In the relentless struggle for survival, *lean and mean* firms may lower prices to keep a competitor from entering a market, or use pricing power to buy market share. This is typically done when a company has financial staying power, because price wars require large sums of money. That's why liquidity is so important. Running out of money, or the ability to borrow it, means that the company cannot maintain its image or protect its business turf. This underpins the **second law** of capitalism, which is Darwinian: survival of the fittest.

The market, and therefore, the 21st century economy, will severely punish any industrial sector or any company that allows itself to become less efficient. The market players who count the most are those who know how to mine and analyze market data, how to spot productivity payoffs, how to see bottlenecks in the pipeline. One big difference with the old economy is that the penalties are swift. Companies can lose 90% or more of their capitalization at lightning speed, as Lucent Technologies, Nortel, Alcatel, AT&T, France Télécom, Deutsche Telekom, Sonera, and scores of others found out the hard way.

The **third law** of capitalism is post-Darwinian and states that there is no use for two sets of contradictory standards. When new rules of business are born, the old ones get discredited and disappear. The economy of the 21st century knows that it cannot overturn a pyramid of old habits, but it can undermine it until it collapses. In its place, it promotes *emerging industries*, but at the same time it is leveling the global playing field by speeding the flow of information through instantaneous communication.

Throughout the world, small local economies take advantage of this rapid succession of opportunities which would have been impossible without technological prowess. Ireland and Finland are example. But emerging industries, *emerging instruments*, and *emerging markets* also have major risks. Therefore, all entities will be well advised to do stress testing[1] in order to detect exposure at the edges of their operations and of their investments.

The **fourth law** of capitalism is that of flexibility and *adaptation*. Nothing is really predetermined or cast in steel. Though each epoch has its principles, these change over time as the financial and industrial system adapts to new conditions by accounting for market whims and drives, as well as to principles deriving themselves from the first three laws. Our epoch's principles are to:

- Keep costs of production, distribution and overhead very low
- Make business innovation instantly available to everyone
- Be ahead of the marketing curve at any time, everywhere, and
- Keep exposure under lock and key through rapid damage control.

The careful reader will notice that these four laws of capitalism reinforce the two basic changes of our epoch: democratization of credit and socialization of risk, of which we spoke in Chapter 1. Assisted by adaptation, globalization has expanded world-wide the democratization of credit, while rigorous competition has added the Darwinian touch. As for the socialization of risk, the most talkative reference is a Franco-German saying regarding nationalized companies which have been privatized and renationalized: 'When they are profitable we privatize them; and when they reach the edge of bankruptcy we nationalize them.' Taxpayers pay the difference.

2.2   Forces propelling economic growth

Globalization not only provides world-wide markets but also gives companies a major incentive to shift labor-intensive tasks abroad, where wages are so much lower. Socially speaking, this is part of the cost of globalization, while on the upside it deprives companies of their pricing power – and therefore it stabilizes the cost of goods.

The virtual economy adds to the drive to cut costs by igniting a race to execute labor-intensive jobs, like sales and purchasing, through the Internet, thereby cutting down on paperwork and accelerating the *time to cash* cycle. In terms of reducing costs, neither the Internet nor outsourcing recognize national borders. As a communications solution, the Internet has proved to be a revolutionary technology; a driver of global business transformation. The cultural change towards on-line dealing is being propelled by a series of self-reinforcing trends, as the Web:

- Enlarges the marketplace, cuts the fat out of business transactions
- Provides a pool of know-how, and
- Opens up new opportunities because people gain a direct pipeline into markets with innovative products and services.

As these examples document, the dynamics of global growth are changing as profoundly as they did with the advent of railroads, of electricity, of auto and air transport. The service economy sees to it that traditional factors of production and distribution are no longer the sole determinants of an economy's power, because economic potential is increasingly linked to the ability to use information immediately and effectively.

The change in market dynamics, however, is not doing away with some of the fundamentals which have characterized business since its beginning – for instance, the need for financial staying power, which is today served through debt rather than equity. Neither does it waive those factors that not only attract but also hold the attention of capital markets. If anything, it is reinforcing the variables that weigh most:

- On each company's performance and survival, and
- On each entity's individual solvency and credit rating.[2]

Experienced bankers, traders, and investment advisors appreciate that the markets' behavior and reaction should never be taken for granted. While novelty in investing can make people and companies run after new instruments and new opportunities, there is always a downside in following the trend – as proved by investments in Internet outfits in late 1990s. This says much about the risks involved in alternative forms of investments (see Chapter 1), because:

- Eventually the fundamentals of time-tested market behavior reconquer the upper ground,[3] and
- By so doing, they wipe out fortunes which were unwisely bet all the way on 'this' or 'that' trend.

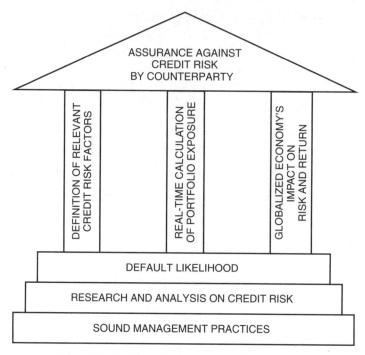

Figure 2.1 Trading of debt in a globalized economy

Both these points speak volumes about the care that should be exercised in trading debt and in investing in debt instruments. As shown in Figure 2.1, assurance against credit risk by counterparties rests on three pillars: the definition of relevant credit risk factors, prior to entering into a transaction; real-time calculation of credit and market exposure in the portfolio, coupled with willingness for corrective action; and the impact of a globalized economy on risk and return. Even far-away events can turn the most thoroughly studied portfolio structure on its head.

When major reverses are taking place, and reverses always happen in financial markets, what inevitably follows is a shakedown. Even companies at the cutting edge of technology or of financial innovation crash, and capital invested in them is no more to be seen. This is just as true of countries. In 1990, the glamour of Japan faded away and did not timidly start to come back until 2004. The meltdown of Internet companies is another example of the results that follow the bursting of a bubble.

As companies and countries do their best to capitalize on perceived or theoretical business opportunities, the challenge is to distinguish facts from fiction – of which there is plenty. One of the business models which gained the high ground in business planning in late 1999 assumed that by 2005 all US households would be on-line, at least half of them on high bandwidth connections. This:

- Implied radically different patterns of consumer behavior than those we already knew, and
- Built its hypotheses on the lowest common denominator of access to a high speed, media-rich Internet defining a new, global consumer space.

Companies that launched themselves to take advantage of such a model, as well as their investors and their lenders, hit a brick wall. Their merchandising viewpoint has been that of emulating amazon.com for a wide range of wares, while at the same time targeting the TV connection to expand the Internet audience. In their way, these companies and their advisors misinterpreted US statistics including:

- Convergence of the percentages of households with PCs, TVs, and on-line access, and
- Seemingly vast market of households with telephones and TVs whose synergy was supposed to revolutionize market penetration.

What whetted the appetite of the people who developed the aforementioned business model, is that there is a vast consumer market in the 103 million US households owning TVs. Of these, an estimated 85–95% will eventually be served through hybrid fiber-coax (HFC) solutions. Technically speaking, this might happen – but the hypothesis that interconnected consumers would spend lavishly in their virtual malls was a long shot that did not materialize.

People and companies who followed this type of reasoning bolstered their arguments with some other statistics. For instance, that 80% of US households live within 3.4 miles (5.5 km) of a telephone switching office and, therefore, they would not be able to imagine life without a digital subscriber line (DSL). Another study which I saw, along the same line of wanting reasoning, made use of a prediction by AT&T that by 2003 roughly:

- 70% of American households will have digital video
- 30% will have Internet protocol (IP) telephone, and
- 25–35% will have broadband Internet access.

We have long past the 2003 benchmark and these projections are still blue sky. People and companies who suffered most from daydreaming about the business aftermath of such predictions are those that have been unable to scale down their expectations and expenditures, and appreciate that not everything is as linear as it is thought to be.

One of the more articulate objections to the hypotheses supporting the business plans referred to here was that they paid no more than lip service to financing. With regard to the source of funds, money was supposed to grow on trees. As for return on investment, few senior executives noted its absence, because their plans were based on hopes rather than facts. It is therefore not surprising that the euphoria of the late 1990s was followed by major financial failures. Today, the booms and busts of the post-Second World War years are poorly understood. Yet, they have a common background of overexpansion propelled by:

- High leverage
- Followed by financial downturn.

This downturn has hit bond investors who bet on the expansionist scenario like a sledgehammer. Had they done their homework, they would have seen that the 19th century could teach some lessons. In the 1830s, with a tiny annual budget compared to its debt, the State of Indiana floated $10 million in bonds. A building boom followed and land values soared. Other states in the Union followed suit. By the early 1840s eight states and the territory of Florida had defaulted on their debts.

■ In a way similar to the Japanese real estate bust of the 1990s, land prices and the economy collapsed, and
■ In a way similar to the default by Argentina in late December 2000, debtors walked away from their obligations and creditors were left high and dry.

Another 19th century event, the crisis of 1873, was caused by a period of catch-up and overexpansion in railroad construction after the American Civil War. Periodic banking panics occurred because an expansion fueled by increasing leverage through an inordinate debt-issuance and debt-trading caused busts. In turn, failing banks meant:

■ Lost savings, and
■ Less credit.

On closer inspection, the busts of the late 19th/early 20th century in the United States have many of the characteristics of the Internet bubble of 2000–2002. In the early 20th century, the day was saved through the initiatives of J.P. Morgan. Then, in 1913, Congress created the Federal Reserve to prevent banking panics through better regulation of the economy.

As we saw in Chapter 1, the Great Depression brought the US Federal Government into the socialization of risk. Enacted in the 1930s, *deposit insurance* protects against lost savings, which is good, but also provides speculators with opportunities to make a kill, as demonstrated by the savings and loans (S&L) crisis of the late 1980s. These references are most relevant because of parallels between what happens in the present day and what has happened in the recent past.

Was it pure coincidence that the 2000–2002 bust of Western stock markets and economies followed the unrealistic assumptions we have seen, in repetition of 19th century events? Was the downturn an aftermath of the fact investors and companies (as well as some economists), placed themselves in the same untenable positions as the central planners of any socialist country? Or was it that the great expectations put on technology and globalization could simply not be fulfilled, because they were way out of anything that was reasonable?

2.3   Capital flows and impact of globalization on economic development

It is not at all surprising that globalization has both friends and foes. Its friends assert that integration into a world-wide market which knows no national frontiers is not only good for each country – and, by extension its companies and its citizen – but it is also the best way to enrich and empower the world's nations; particularly the so-called have-nots.

For the foes of globalization, who are by and large populist politicians, labor leaders, environmentalists and young activists, globalization makes the rich richer at the expense of the poor. To them, world trade and global finance lines the pockets of international conglomerates and of speculators. The victims are supposed to be working people, in factories and farms, as well as the majority of developing countries and the Earth as a whole.

Labor leaders and populist politicians in America rate globalization as being responsible for the loss first of blue collar jobs and then of white collar jobs, because of offshore outsourcing. Offshoring, they say, is a practice which imposes substantial social costs expressed, for instance, through the 'jobless recovery' of the US economy in 2003 and early 2004.

Populist politicians and labor leader in the less developed parts of the world have a different type of argument. From bankrupt Argentina to other countries at the edge of insolvency, they accuse globalization, and its huge financial flows, as having exploited them and of continuing to exploit them – all the way to depriving them of their national wealth.

Most of these arguments, however, are largely one-sided. For the better part of two decades, from mid-1980s to 2005, globalization has been the force which brought huge financial resources to the less developed countries. It also provided jobs for their people, while at the same time depriving Western companies of pricing power. This kept inflation low, at least in Group of Ten countries.

The globalization of finance and commerce has reached this outcome – which was not necessarily its goal – by making it possible for those developing countries best equipped in human capital to participate in the growing *knowledge economy*. Not only has the Western world been importing low cost standardized goods and services from the developing world, but also outsourced to those 'best equipped' countries a good deal of formerly inland jobs.

This rewrites the first law of capitalism, which should now read: 'Both money and jobs will migrate to the business environment which offers best returns.' As a recent example, in May 2004 a German cloth manufacturer was saying that the factory it had built in Romania was producing the same quality of garments as its factory in Germany at one-quarter the cost – and a rigorous swamping of costs it is not just the better solution, it is the only solution for this manufacturer's company to survive.

It is just as true, however, that not every country hoping to join the process of development is equipped to participate in the knowledge economy. As a result, the gap between rich and poor in the world continues to increase, with no signs of a reversal. Only those countries with first class human resources, like India, are able to emulate Japan's development in the post-Second World War years where the motor has been an educated, hard-working, low cost labor force.

The downside of rapid expansion is that it brings with it the human cost of galloping unemployment, and at the same time a shortage in skills. An example is provided in France, where there are millions of unemployed, but also 500 000 jobs that cannot be filled because the appropriate skills are lacking. India is now subcontracting to China some of the West's huge amount of outsourced work, which it cannot handle. And, to fill the gap in trained engineers created by massive migration of its best young scientists to the United States, India imports engineering skills from Vietnam.

Behind these facts lies the junction of the two most basic premises of globalization, which is rather poorly appreciated by its friends and by its critics. While the free movement of brains strengthens those countries which are ahead of the curve at the expense of the others, the rapid expansion of international private capital flows, that is investments and loans from capitalists of one country to those in another, brings along with it both boom and bust.

International private capital flows have brought significant economic benefits to their recipients, but they also have exposed several countries to periodic crises of confidence – particularly so when inflows of capital are suddenly reversed. Institutional investors who are behind a large part of these capital flows have short time horizons while, by contrast, the time horizon of commercial bankers who used to be the main lenders, was fairly long.

As the 1997 meltdown of the 'Asian tigers', 1998 Russian bankruptcy, and 2000 Argentinean bankruptcy document, crises promoted by the fast movement of capital rolled-in and rolled-out through globalization impose substantial economic and social costs. To avoid this happening, some economists call for constructive engagement among borrowers, creditors, and international financial institutions – while failing to specify how they will achieve that miracle.

The second law of capitalism which, as the Introduction stated, is Darwinian, suggests that such 'constructive agreements' cannot be done. Moreover, economic theory and practice refute the thesis that this is likely to happen, or that it is even possible. This is in no way a critique of globalization; it is a statement of facts in a world where:

- Credit has been democratized, as Chapter 1 has explained
- But somebody must pay for the socialization of risk – and this is the taxpayer country-by-country, not the 'citizen of the world'.

Trading debt has *its* prerogatives, and assuming the risk of bankruptcy is one of them. Risks have become socialized within one and the same country, not at a global scale. Crises do occur, and when they do, they hit hard the capital flows' recipients.

Transnational institutions, like the International Monetary Fund (IMF) and World Bank, do not have the resources to bear the full burden of covering every country's re-financing needs. Neither would it be desirable for them to do so. Indeed, one of the reasons why the international community has sought the involvement of private sector creditors in transborder financing is to help in easing, or even solving, financial crises when they occur. This is of course wishful thinking.

- Hedge funds and institutional investors are in for a fast buck.
- They are not babysitters of somebody else's economic and financial troubles.

When plans were laid for the creation of the IMF and World Bank during the Second World War, the architects of the new institutions feared that the global market for private capital had disappeared for good. But in the 1950s and 1960s crossborder flow among industrialized countries revived, and then it spread to developing economies. Subsequently, in the early to mid-1980s, capital flows into the so-called emerging markets were depressed as some of the heaviest borrowers, mainly in Latin America, had difficulties servicing their debts.

Economists say that Latin America suffered a lost decade of economic growth because of this crisis of confidence which also threatened to bring down commercial banks, especially in the United States. In the aftermath of financial earthquakes in the 1970s and 1980s the international community put considerable effort into resolving debt crises and, by 1997, gross private capital flows into emerging markets had risen to a peak of $290 billion.

The bad news has been that international money flows increased too rapidly relative to the size of national economies they served, and so did the risk. As I have already mentioned, exposure associated to global capital flows is not socialized, because no government picks up the price tag of that exposure. Thus private capital flows have become much more volatile than changes in the economic prospects of individual countries could:

- Explain, or
- Justify.

More than three decades of globalization of capital flows demonstrate that less developed economies have become increasingly vulnerable to crises of confidence. As investors and speculators try to get out through the same door, what takes place is akin to runs on banks. The psychology of nervous investors demonstrates that men and women think in herds – they tend to go mad in herds, and they only recover their senses slowly.

It is inevitable that post-bankruptcy some countries fared better than others. South Korea, for example, redressed its balance sheet fast because its people are hard-working and the government has been in charge. This cannot be said of Argentina, where the government itself procrastinated and tried to loot the lender. The after-effect has been that more than half of the country's population fell below the poverty line. Bondholders and other lenders, too, fared very badly, and IMF was caught in the middle between:

- Moral hazard, and
- Inability to apply its own rules.

This can be stated in conclusion. A fundamental characteristic of the global economy, and therefore of the debt markets, is that sudden reversal of big capital inflows, and shortage of foreign currency that this implies, inflict financial and economic pain. Just as the inflow of capital brings prosperity, the rapid outflow causes a major drop in the value of a country's currency, rise in the price of its imports, and zooming cost of servicing debts denominated in foreign currencies. It also brings an increase at poverty level.

2.4   The macro-dimension of financial markets

According to some economists, over the first two decades of the 21st century the change in global markets will dwarf what has occurred in the last forty years of the past century, or in any similar period of social and economic history. With the new millennium, the world's largest markets are undergoing a series of transforming events which increases both:

- Business opportunity, and
- The size of financial exposure.

This transformation obeys the third law of capitalism, which states that two sets of contradictory standards cannot stand. As the new rules of business, which have been outlined in sections 2.2 and 2.3 – as well as the principles of democratization of lending and socialization of risk, explained in Chapter 1 – come into play, the old economy's rules wane and disappear.

As an example, section 2.3 has explained how the barriers that separated national markets for goods, services, and capital flows have been increasingly breaking down. This has created larger and more dynamic regional markets, which in turn have added up to the globalized market – creating, in the process, a financial macro-dimension.

This macro-dimension is the product of interaction between what has become known as the *macro-markets*; for instance currency exchange, stock indices, bond futures, and all sorts of derivatives. Taken together, the macro-markets are large enough to accommodate lots of investors in their search for risk and return, including:

- Corporate treasurers
- Commercial and investment bankers, and
- The growing number of funds: pension, mutual, and hedge funds.

Nearly all of them are players in the macro-markets. Being present in these macro-markets, however, requires a macro focus – a process which has become increasingly important in recent years, as the typical investor's and trader's horizon has broadened in terms of:

- Global reach, and
- Asset diversity.

As we saw in Chapter 1, a growing number of investors are buying not only all sorts of debt, including structured instruments, but also other non-conventional products. All this has led to an unparalleled macro-influence on financial markets. It also demanded a great amount of adaptation, according to capitalism's fourth rule, in terms of both relative and absolute performance.

Though the different instruments which are typically lumped together in this macro-dimension are diverse, they have one important feature in common: they are part of the virtual economy (see Chapter 1). Plenty of other characteristics derive from this feature – including the ease of accommodating the risk appetite of investors. On the other hand, the most aggressive players start to find that, in the macro-markets, there is a significant difference between:

- Maintaining momentum, and
- Gaining momentum when the previous one has been lost.

A practical expression of this difference is that each big player's size is a hindrance in the process of regaining momentum in the aftermath of a profitless or outright downward period. Even for sharp operators, profitless periods are not uncommon, as the experience of many risk-taking institutional investors, treasurers, bankers and hedge funds managers demonstrated in 1994, following the debacle of a highly leveraged bond market in sequence to the Federal Reserve's raising of interest rates seven consecutive times (see Chapter 15).

As it will be recalled, when in 1995 this storm had passed by, practically all the big players in complex derivative financial instruments found it difficult to redress their balance sheet, recover very significant losses they had suffered, and create new business opportunities. The most challenging task for them has been to put their house in order, with a profit perspective commensurate to the risks they were taking.

Another common characteristic of macro-markets is that risk and return associated with them cannot be managed by seat the of the pants, or by paper and pencil. They require high technology, including on-line mining of rich databases, instantaneous communications, real-time computation, and fairly accurate mathematical models – both for business opportunity analysis and for effective risk control.

What the reader should appreciate in connection with this technology-oriented aspect of corporate life, is that while many applications domains benefit from the use of models, the majority require much more ingenuity than algorithms alone can provide.[4] I bring up this subject to caution that not everything is done through models, though algorithmic and heuristic solutions can help:

- In focusing attention on salient issues, and
- In prioritizing the list of exposures.

Policies and procedures make the difference between a successful use of technology and a trivial one. Top management policies are necessary both before the development (or adoption) of models and after their implementation and usage. As we will see in section 2.5, one of the crucial policies has to do with hedging against adverse market moves.

Hedging should be used by bankers, treasurers, and traders with all financial instruments, as an indispensable connection to the management of investments, and most particularly to activities connected to the macro-markets. Hedging, of course, is no financial penicillin. Many experts believe that even if hedging were adequately defined in connection to damage-control and everyone had a clear hedging policy, the majority of banks, treasuries and funds would not have systems in place to effectively use hedging policies.

One of the problems with macro-markets and other applications of hedging strategy is that many derivative instruments can be hard to value unless we have both skills and an array of analytical tools and high performance computers. Without appropriate supports, we may end up:

- Paying too much for what we buy, and
- Taking inordinate risks in making hedges.

As we will see in section 2.5, one of the first principles for understanding and following a hedging strategy is to be prepared and to be selective. We do not need to hedge everything. For instance, some oil companies protect themselves against swings in interest rates and currencies, but not in petroleum prices. Others, however, design their hedging program in a way to match their prevailing production profile a year or two forward.

2.5 Upside and downside of hedging

Some of the people I spoke to in my research suggested that accounting for gains and losses currently associated with hedges is incomplete and possibly misleading. While this observation is correct, it is beyond doubt that the first requirement in a hedging strategy is understanding of the instrument(s) to be used and of procedures associated to it (them). Any effective hedging policy rests on four pillars:

■ Knowing what we want to do
■ Understanding what we are doing
■ Having systems to support our policy, and
■ Making sure the senior management is in charge.

This is true of debt markets, equity markets, and macro-markets, but most particularly of the junction of debt markets and macro-markets because the two together get more easily superleveraged – and therefore, engender greater risk.

Moreover, hedging-related accounting should provide timely and accurate information for management, enriched with hedging-related disclosure. This should be done in a transparent manner (see section 2.6), enabling investors, creditors, government supervisors, and other users of financial statements to appreciate:

■ An entity's risk exposure, and
■ Its strategy for risk control.

To provide the reader with the holistic aspect of transparency requirements, Figure 2.2 gives a bird's-eye view of players contributing to production and distribution of reliable financial reports.

Alongside companies active in debt trading, hedging through complex transactions requires appropriate disclosures of the transactions themselves and of the instruments used to hedge anticipated moves, like compensation for assumed risks through derivative financial instruments. As for senior management's understanding of what hedging is supposed to do, and the risks it involves, this should include:

■ The period of time of firmly projected future financial action, and
■ The amount to hedging gains and losses realized, as well as explicitly deferred.

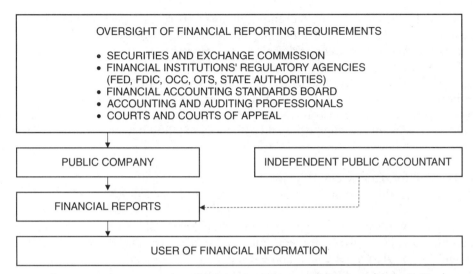

Figure 2.2 Players contributing to the production and distribution of reliable financial reports

Just as necessary is a description of transactions or other events that result in the recognition of gains or losses deferred by hedge accounting. This is not common policy, both because only recently has regulation begun looking into future gains and losses, and because few bankers, treasurers, traders, and investors take care to distinguish between speculating and hedging.

There exist, however, positive examples. In terms of currency exchange policy, for instance, some companies like Bechtel Corporation, the global engineering group, sometimes arrange to be paid in a basket of currencies that mirrors what they must lay out to cover costs. And in regard to interest rates, some companies guard against sudden spikes in currency exchange by hedging the maturities of their debt.

Sometimes management takes hedges by means of diversification outside the company's main business, but these hedges can turn sour. In the late 1970s/early 1980s, Merrill Lynch went into real estate brokerage, but lost money. In 1966, Nomura Securities was placed on Standard & Poor's CreditWatch list (with negative implications) after it said it would provide 371 billion yen ($3.39 billion) to help its Nomura Finance unit deal with bad real estate loans.

In other cases, the board micro-manages a hedge – doing so without allocating appropriate time, or even skill. Then a market gyration turns the hedge on its head. In late 1995, after the dollar's turnaround against the yen, Hirokazu Nakamura, chairman of Mitsubishi Motors, said that when the yen passed the 100 bar to the US dollar his company lost a torrent of money. Mitsubishi had hedged at 90 yen to the dollar, until 31 March 1996.[5]

Prognostication accounts for a great deal in the art of hedging, and market prognostication is a tough business. Therefore, while the calculations leading to a hedge may be sound and the hedge can initially work, as the market changes a hedge may become counterproductive.

A sound policy in debt markets and equity markets is that attention should also be paid to not losing the natural smoothing effect that the longer term can have on market prices. Another, parallel, principle is not missing the effects of an increase in volatility, either market-wide or toward the end of the life of an option.

Delta hedges and gamma hedges do provide an algorithmic approach to the implementation of a hedging policy, but also require real-time monitoring. Once the model of the derivative instruments we wish to control has been built, we can produce the means for handling delta and gamma in a skillful manner, provided that we have in place both:

- The skill for damage control, and
- Computers able to monitor exposure very carefully in real time.

If we adopt a hedging policy, then high technology should always be on hand supporting financial analysts, traders, and risk controllers. The bank's management should also be alert in judging *if* and *when* potentially risky positions are being accumulated, and whether they should be closed down.

The statement I have just made is an integral part of interactive computational finance, and is indispensable to every company doing hedges – though in the list of priorities the *first* basic rule in hedging is no different than the one Sun Tzu has written: 'If you know the enemy and know yourself, you need not fear the result of one hundred battles.'[6] Knowing ourselves begins with identifying our strengths and our weaknesses, as well as *where* our greatest risks are. This requires us to perceive, qualify, and quantify vulnerabilities in our portfolio, prior to advancing or recommending a hedging strategy. Good advice is always to remember that a hedge is similar to buying insurance. Before we buy the policy, we must decide how much we are willing to lose in relation to what the protection will cost.

The *second* basic rule in hedging is figuring out in advance not only the risk but also the cost. Both must be commensurate with what we aim to protect in terms of financial or other resources. Therefore, before choosing a strategy, we must perform a thorough examination of our company to unearth where its biggest vulnerabilities lie. We must also write down the goals we wish to reach through hedging, since it is not possible to target unspecified goals.

- Do we need to hedge revenues, cash flows, profits, or dividends?
- Where are our biggest foreign exchange risks (see Chapter 3)?
- What exactly are we hedging in terms of interest rates (see Chapter 7)?
- What is our target duration (see Chapter 10)?

The *third* rule guiding the hand of hedgers is the avoidance of fuzzy policies. Any self-respecting company needs to implement a clear corporate strategy on hedging. Do we have written guidelines? Do we know whether we hedge for profit or just to offset changes in market value? Have we decided on limits to hedging, commensurate with company goals?

In a way, the lack of such guidelines is not surprising if we take account of the fact that, in spite of lip service to strategic planning, few entities have a master plan against their opponents. Moreover, few companies are enthusiastic about setting their policy in black and white. Yet, doing so can eliminate a lot of confusion and ward off the traders' temptation to cross over into speculation.

The *fourth* basic rule is to avoid mixing up the treasury's legacy functions with hedging. This can be done by making sure traders have a separate pool of capital for hedging and that they have been given well-defined limits on how much they can risk. At the same time, the board should always know what each hedging operation is trying to achieve, and how far it succeeds or fails in its task.

Last but not least, hedging must be audited by an independent auditor that can examine the company's risk management policies and activities, as well as make recommendations for corrective action. This job is much more difficult when it comes to the macro-markets, because of the number of unknowns being involved; but it is doable.

2.6 Wealth creation requires an open and transparent financial market

A dynamic financial environment constitutes a precondition for sustained economic growth, which in turn is translated into a higher level of employment and a better standard of living. Section 2.5 also brought to the reader's attention that *transparency* is another prerequisite. It is impossible to effectively manage risks under conditions of secrecy, the existence of double books, and inability to audit financial reports in a fair but rigorous manner.

The business conditions prevailing in an open and transparent financial environment are at the junction of growth and a reasonable stability, with the economy's ups and downs exercising no disruptive force. Transparency allows traders and investors to be in charge of their exposure. Conversely, both risk aversion and too poorly calculated risks on the part of market players:

- Slow down the pace of economic activity, and
- Create adversity in the money market and capital market (see Chapter 3).

The accuracy and transparency of financial statements make it possible to assess the fair value of equities and of debt instruments, and they also impact the behavior of market participants. Dependable financial information allows us to test whether assets that are comparable and available trade at the same or similar prices. Reliable financial reporting also permits estimation of the degree of integration in the various financial markets, judging whether a common trading area like the European Union (EU) is homogeneous or heterogeneous. In the EU, for instance,

- Integration is quite advanced in many segments of the money market, but
- Contrary to expectations, integration is an alien concept in the bond market, and even more so in the equity market.

An example is the fact that yields on government bonds with similar, or in some cases identical, credit risk, maturity, and issuing characteristics have not entirely converged.

A possible reason may lie in differences in primary and secondary market liquidity, or the degree of development of derivatives markets connected to the various individual bond markets. There are, as well, persistent home biases often due to regulatory obstacles like bankruptcy law, as well as taxation.

Neither is the EU level of integration in the equity markets particularly high, although equity returns appear to be increasingly determined by factors common to Euroland. On the other hand, home-type bias in equity holdings, particularly investors' inclination to allocate a large fraction of their equity holdings to domestic stocks, has decreased, even though accounting standards vary from one country to the next. (This may change with the international accounting standard (IAS).)

Differences in accounting standards and in the quality as well as mandate of regulatory authorities are obstacles to transparency. They also make so much more difficult the control of risk in a transborder sense, thereby increasing investors' exposure. Alert investors appreciate that too much risk is as bad as lack of willingness to take any risk.

Eventually, the bubble bursts. In 1997 and 1998 the crises besetting some of the world's financial markets exerted dampening effects on the world economy, and hampered world trade. The aftermath ultimately hit every economy, though some were much more hurt than others. Under uncertainty, expansionary forces that might exist do not prove to be robust enough to provide an appropriate counterweight to negative market sentiment.

Overly restrictive monetary conditions, too, have a negative effect. Because financial environments do change over time, it is not surprising that the gross domestic product of the global economy has its ups and downs. The trend which has characterized the last quarter of the 20th century is shown in Figure 2.3. This trend line is an average. Some countries, like the United States have been doing much better than the average; others, like Japan and Indonesia, have been agonizing with negative growth.

The growth in GDP has an evident after-effect on personal wealth, though not everybody profits to the same degree. There is always an uneven distribution of

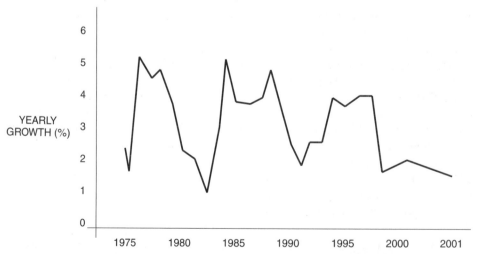

Figure 2.3 Average growth of gross domestic product in the global economy over 25 years (1975–2001)

wealth in the economy and the way to bet is that the rich get richer. In the 1890s Vilfredo Pareto, the Swiss Italian economist and mathematician, found that 1% of the Swiss population controlled about 35% of the nation's wealth. After more than a century of *isms* (Marxism, communism, fascism, nazism, fundamentalism), Pareto's law remains valid; the United States provides an example.

If anything, differences in wealth distribution tend to accentuate over time, as shown in Figure 2.4. In the late 1990s the average pre-tax income of the top 20% of US families was an order of magnitude (precisely 10.6 times) as large as that of the bottom 20% of families. In the late 1970s this multiple was just 7.4. Over two decades the gap between top and bottom 20% has grown by 43.5%. Figure 2.4 demonstrates the end result: the share of total personal income by the 40% of lower net worth individuals shrank from 17% to 13%.

Personal income and the creation of wealth correlate. The share of total personal income by the wealthiest 1% of the US population stood at 7.5% in 1980. Twenty years later, in 2001, this share had nearly doubled to 13%. The higher net worth individuals belonging to this 13% have growing investment needs, which will be answered through bonds (see Chapter 3) and equities.[7]

Because of the stock market boom but also for other reasons, the last five years of the 1990s were the most rewarding in terms of personal wealth. Defining net worth as including assets such as stocks, bonds, and equity in a home minus liabilities like mortgages and other debt, the median net worth of American families jumped almost

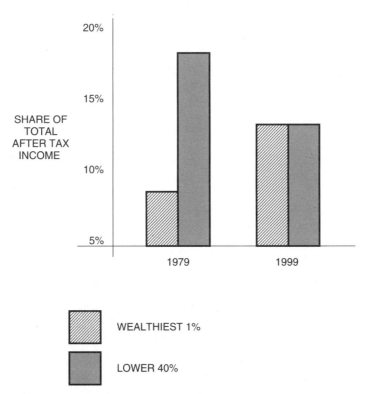

Figure 2.4 Pareto's law applied to the distribution of income in the United States

21.5%, from $60 900 in 1995 to about $74 000 in 2000. Presently in the United States, over 50% of families own stock, either directly or indirectly through mutual funds or 401(k) pension plans – up sharply from 40.4% in 1995 and 26.3 in 1989.

Since the higher paid persons tend to invest more than they consume, the silver lining of the creation of wealth is that a great deal of money passes into investments. The federal, state, and city governments also benefit, since the higher the income of a person, the more taxes he or she has to pay. These trends are an interesting aspect of the current investment environment.

Riding the wave of capitalization, however, involves the risk of a major correction, particularly when stock prices reach for the stars as they did in the 1995 to 1999 timeframe. With the rising wave shown in Figure 2.5, up to a point, but only up to a point, everyone profits. The day of reckoning comes later on with a major market correction, as it did in 2000.

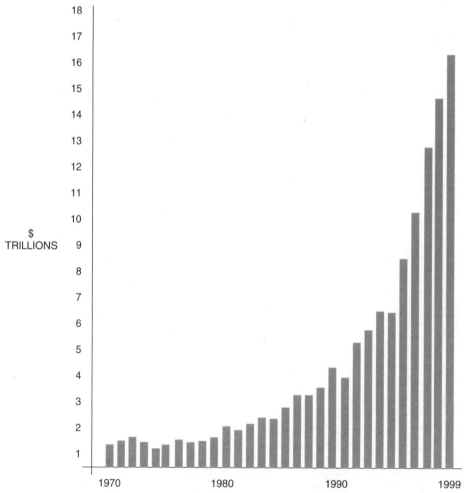

Figure 2.5 The growth of wealth in the US stock market: capitalization from 1970 to 1999

The portfolio of investors who know how to capitalize on the ups of the stock and bond markets gains in terms of asset value. For instance, after experiencing a rapid rise in its net worth during the late 1990s, Teachers Insurance & Annuity Association-College Retirement Equities Fund (TIAA/CREF), one of the largest and most successful pension funds in the world, expanded its offerings to include trust services and estate planning. The goal of the new offering was to cater to the 32 000 millionaires among its two million clients.

There was a time, in the not too distant past, when teachers were considered to be earning no more than wages permitting bare subsistence. Good fund management made some of them millionaires. TIAA/CREF and the other big pension funds today invest globally. Cross-border investments boomed as the 20th century came to a close. German statistics, for example, suggest that cross-border direct investments amount to 10% or more of the capital or voting rights.

In France about 40% of shareholder voting rights in big firms are foreign direct investments, most of them coming from pension funds and mutual funds. This is a different way of saying American and, to a lesser extent, British capital has taken hold of a big chunk of French industry. By contrast, with the exception of a couple of countries like Holland, pension funds in continental Europe are still in their infancy. This means that people depend wholesale on the state-run pension system, which in many countries is not far from bankruptcy.

2.7 Mercantilism is not a good strategy in an economy of mounting debt

In a memo to himself, Andrew Carnegie wrote: 'The amassing of wealth is one of the worst species of idolatry. To continue much longer overwhelmed by business cares and with most of my thoughts wholly upon the way to make more money in the shortest time, must degrade me beyond hope of permanent recovery.' Carnegie acted to solve his problem before it became worse. The answer was to sell Carnegie Steel for $480 million (which was big money at the time) to J.P. Morgan and become a philanthropist.

Andrew Carnegie spoke about the rat race for higher and higher profits. He did not speak about the amassed bad and doubtful debts that characterize our society and its institutions – maybe because in the first decade of the 20th century the trading of bad debts was not *en vogue*. Today the situation is totally different as many credit institutions and other entities securitize and sell to investors their bad debts. The pattern of charges for bad and doubtful debts in Figure 2.6 speaks volumes about the mountain of capital at risk, and the severity of a correction during a downtrend.

While we know that there will always be a business cycle with its booms and busts, such as has existed since the dawn of man as an economic animal, we are unable to predict when a growth wave will give way to a major correction, in contrast to the almost yearly minor corrections every economy is practically experiencing.

We are not able to prognosticate because capitalism's new form is quite different from the 600-year-old *mercantilism* which developed in Bruges, Amsterdam, and Hamburg (Hanseatic League, early 15th century). It is also quite different from the 150-year-old capitalism of the *industrial revolution* which first flourished in England.

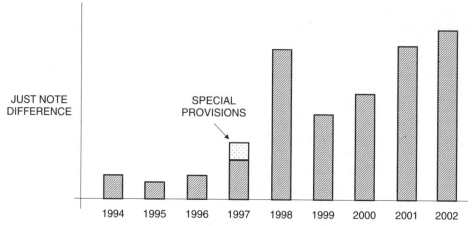

Figure 2.6 A money center bank's charges for bad and doubtful debts: capital at risk
skyrockets when the market goes into a tailspin

- Hedge funds and several banks nowadays try to reinvent mercantilism through
  alternative investments.[8]
- This is, however, the wrong attitude, one which can damage an institution's reputation and lead straight into legal risk.

One of the big differences in thinking dominating the 19th century industrial revolution as contrasted to the knowledge revolution of today, was that colonies should
serve the industrial country that owned them – as both producers of raw material
and consumers of manufactured goods. They must return profits by attracting
investments, provide useful materials, and supplement domestic markets when these
become saturated. The principle of *colonialism*, which has been a version of industrial
capitalism, has been that:

- Colonies should cost as little as possible to conquer and administer, but
- As far as possible they should raise revenues to cover their own expenses and leave
  a profit to their owner.

This was a *cost-plus* basis, much of the 'plus' coming from the fact that colonies
increased the prestige of the power that owned them against its international rivals,
securing benefits in the balance of power in Europe and other continents.
Furthermore, colonies had to contribute to the solution of some national problems
like absorbing excess population and disposing of socially undesirable elements.

Social reformers hoped that some colonies at least would provide homes for urban
unemployed and landless peasants. Moralists said the empire is a domain for the
exercise of youthful energies, the pioneering spirit, and other virtues. Sociologists suggested that people convicted of criminal or political offences could be transported to
the colonies (they were). Missionaries added that saving the souls of pagan natives
was an almost divine mission.

It is indeed quite instructive to remember that the big colonial drive started *after* the industrial revolution was well under way. In the 1880s, Jules Ferry, a French prime minister, said that colonial policy is the daughter of industrial policy. Ferry also stated that in rich states where capital abounds and accumulates rapidly, and the manufacturing system is undergoing continual growth, the establishment of a colony is tantamount to creation of a market. The field of action for capital and the demand for labor were measured by the size of the foreign market under control.

Does that not sound like the arguments for globalization some 120 years down the line? Superficially, it seems as if it is so, but there are also some notable differences. The industrial powers of the 19th century saw colonial acquisition as a way to expand their physical economy outwards. By contrast with today's globalization, the physical economy is imported rather than exported, moving from developing country to the Group of Ten, while what is exported is the virtual economy with:

- Transborder capital flows, and
- Mounting levels of debt world-wide.

Sometimes, an institution's senior executives endeavor to convey the impression they are in control of exposure through triumphal, bombastic, and hollow statements about future profits, but this does not do away with the Damocletian sword of doubtful assets. Few organizations can really pride themselves about an able, effective and steady management of their debts. While the forces propelling the new environment are usually associated to economic growth and development that appears to go beyond conventional economic thinking, they also involve a great amount of:

- New financial instruments with plenty of unknowns embedded in them, which must be analyzed and controlled, and
- Risk that is often associated with fast growth and lack of transparency, and which remains hidden till the bubble bursts.

To its proponents, the notions adding up to the economy of the 21st century can be found at the intersection of social systems, technology, physical assets, virtual assets, and financial liabilities that integrate into the activities of whole industrial sectors. To its critics, the growing risk approach to economic thinking does not make sense, particularly so because there is no comprehensive, coherent, and efficient economic theory to sustain it.

A theory which will do just that is not yet here, neither is the growing amount of risk appropriately managed. Increasing exposure is connected to all sorts of uncertainties, some of which have to do with financial issues and others with social forces. Economic growth, the redistribution of wealth (see section 2.6) and growing uncertainty about the stability of the financial system are propelled by:

- Exponential technology
- Increasing-return economics, and
- Derivatives financial instruments.

Exponential technology makes sure that companies that do not take seriously the need to steadily adapt to business evolution and re-invent themselves do not survive. This has nothing to do with mercantilism. The need to reinvent oneself has been present since the mid- to late 1980s. Look at the roster of the 100 largest US companies in 1991. Only 15 were still on the top 100 list in 2001. This falling from grace accelerates and it will continue to do so in the coming years.

One might wonder how is it possible that so many supposedly wealthy, well-managed, successful firms fail to hold, let alone improve, their standing? Evidently something has happened to make them unfit for the business environment in which they operate. As the previous sections documented, globalization, deregulation, and technology have changed the rules; but not everything is due to these reasons. More potent negative factors have been:

- Management that is incompetent, and
- A corporate culture which is falling behind in innovation, making the force of technology disruptive.

Globalization and technology evidently play an important role, but as Chapter 1 has explained, within the industrial economies themselves, the most important transformation is the democratization of credit, which leads towards mounting levels of debt repackaged and sold to investors as virtual assets. And while in the 19th century the assets were wholly physical, today, as Winston Churchill aptly predicted: 'The new empires are the empires of the mind' – but also the empires of other people's debt.

Notes

1 D.N. Chorafas, *Stress Testing: Risk Management Strategies for Extreme Events*, Euromoney, London, 2003.
2 D.N. Chorafas, *Economic Capital Allocation with Basel II: Cost and Benefit Analysis*, Butterworth-Heinemann, Oxford and Boston, 2004.
3 D.N. Chorafas, *The Management of Equity Investments*, Butterworth-Heinemann, Oxford, 2005.
4 D.N. Chorafas, *Modelling the Survival of Financial and Industrial Enterprises: Advantages, Challenges, and Problems with the Internal Rating-Based (IRB) Method*, Palgrave/Macmillan, London, 2002.
5 *The Asian Wall Street Journal*, 12 September.
6 Sun Tzu, *The Art of War*, New York, Delacorte Press, 1983.
7 D.N. Chorafas, *The Management of Equity Investments*, Butterworth-Heinemann, Oxford, 2005.
8 D.N. Chorafas, *Alternative Investments and the Mismanagement of Risk*, Macmillan/Palgrave, London, 2003.

Part 2

The bondholder's options, risks, and rewards

3 Bonds defined

3.1 Introduction

A *bond* is a loan; and as a loan it is an obligation on the issuer to provide one or more future cash flows to the buyer, and return the capital at maturity (see Chapter 10). The timing and size of these cash flow(s) may be pre-specified, or it may be dependent on an economic variable whose value is usually known a priori. Examples of types of bonds issued, for instance, by credit institutions are:

■ Flat rate bonds
■ Floating rate bonds
■ Convertible bonds
■ Deeply subordinated bonds
■ Callable bonds
■ Zero-coupon bonds
■ Convertible zero-coupon bonds
■ Flat rate euro medium term notes (MTN)
■ Fixed/flat rate euro MTNs
■ Step-up euro medium term notes
■ Index-linked bonds
■ Index-linked capital protected notes (CPN).

The primary critical variables of all bonds are: coupon (%), currency, face amount, maturity, credit rating of issuer, and credit rating of issue. There exist as well other important criteria, discussed in section 3.2.

The term *bond* is generally employed when speaking of long-term obligations, but there exist several variations in its actual usage. The more prominent features of a bond include the aforementioned definite promise to pay an interest and to repay the principal amount; an established maturity; a statement of the tender or medium of payment; and identification of currency and place of payment. Also, reference to the bond *indenture* for other rights and powers,[1] such as:

■ Limitations upon the issuance of additional securities
■ Action in the event of default of interest or principal payments
■ Curtailment of management prerogatives in the event of failure to meet prescribed conditions, and so on.

The choice of bonds versus equities has always puzzled investors. Though they do not participate in market upsides like stocks do, bonds have advantages. When in 1901 Andrew Carnegie sold Carnegie Steel to J.P. Morgan for $480 million, he also specified the means of payment: $160 million was to be gold-backed 5% bonds; $240 million in stock in the new company; and $80 million in cash. His own take was $225 639 000 – paid in 5% gold bonds and cash only. He wanted bonds to carry on his philanthropic activities rather than worrying about stock market volatility[2] – and he was right.

After Morgan brought the company public, the shares of US Steel, the consolidated firm, opened at $39 and within a month they were at $55. This was the largest company the world had ever seen, with $1.1 billion in common and preferred stock and $304 million in bonds, a ratio of $21.6 in publicly offered debt to $78.4 in public equity. At the time, no one thought in billions; this was a 'first'. However, from $55 in 1901 the stock slumped to $47 in 1902 and, following the first 20th century financial panic, it sank to $10 in 1903/1904 – a loss of more than 80% of its capitalization at its high water mark. (For an investor's holistic view see section 3.5.)

As we will see in section 3.2, there are many types of bonds characterized by degree of risk, rank of priority, secured or quasi-secured features, as well as bullet, callable, puttable, perpetual nature, and so on. Two of the main categories are registered bonds and coupon bonds.

Registered bonds obtain their name from the fact their owners are recorded in the proper company records, maintained by the issuing entity or by a transfer agent. On interest dates, the interest is mailed to listed holders.

■ The downside of this type of bond is that it is not as readily transferable as the coupon bond.
■ The upside is that it has the advantage of protecting the owner in the event of its loss.

A registered bond's owner will continue to receive interest and may in time secure a duplicate of the lost bond. The registered bond has some limited negotiability, in the sense that the owner may not endorse it over to any purchaser without the issuer's permission. Upon acquisition, however, the bond must be sent to the corporation, or its agent, for cancellation and for issuance of a new bond registered in the name of the new owner.

Registered bonds are usually held for the long term, and they seldom appear in the market for trading. The registration feature has a minor effect on the price of a bond since ownership can be traced, and taxes paid on interest income. (In some jurisdictions, like Italy and Austria, a similar bearer distinction exists with passbooks for savings.)

Coupon bonds are a different ballgame, they are also the most common, deriving their names from the coupon attached to the bond certificate: one coupon for each interest payment due during the life of the bond. In old times, on interest dates the holder of the bond would clip the coupon and remit it for payment. Collection was made through a bank, in much the same way as checks and notes are placed on deposit.

Coupons are nominal interest payments expressed as a percentage of the bond's notional, face or principal value. Most bonds feature coupons but zero-coupon bonds do not (see Chapter 4). The frequency at which interest payments are made varies between issues and across markets, but it is usually annually or semi-annually, though it may also be monthly. Bonds may be fixed income or floating:

- A *fixed-income* bond pays at regular intervals a predetermined percentage of its notional amount.
- The coupon of a *floating* bond is reset periodically, typically tied to a price index.

Coupon bonds are transferable by mere delivery. With *dematerialization*, which has eliminated paper as support, this transfer takes place computer-to-computer. The holder of the bond is its legal computer-registered owner, unless it can be shown that possession was obtained through illegal means. Today the administration of coupon bonds is done through a trustee – usually a bank. Still, because of the ready transferability of title, the trustee should notify the issuing entity immediately in the event of loss by theft or misplacement.

All counted, the registered bond feature is most important for long-term holding, while the quick transferability of coupon bonds lends itself to shorter-term investment. However, the dematerialization of securities handling, delivery versus payment, and automatic credit of interest to account of the bond's lawful owner, provide the advantages of both registered bonds and coupon bonds – as well as, quite evidently, the disadvantages of each.

3.2 An introduction to types of bonds

Bondholders are creditors of the company or any other entity issuing bonds, while stockholders are owners of the company. Funds invested in purchase of a debt instrument represent money lent to their issuer. Being merely creditors, bondholders ordinarily have no voting power to elect directors, and hence no direct control over the policies of the company.[3] In principle:

- Bondholders take less risk than stockholders, since interest on bonds must be met before any income is available for dividends to equity investors.
- But bondholders typically receive only the set rate of interest, even though the company may make huge profits and, as a result, its market value appreciates.

The main upside of bondholders is that, as we will see, they have a prior claim on the assets of the company in case of liquidation. Many debt instruments contain provisions that if the issuer fails to pay interest when due, voting power is automatically given to bondholders, so that they can protect their interests by having a voice in directing the policies of the business.

A different way of making this statement is that in some cases, if interest is defaulted several times running, stockholders may lose the right to vote and control may be transferred to bondholders until past interest defaults are cleared up and repayment of principal is assured. That privilege, however, is not associated with debt instruments issued by sovereigns. As the case of Argentina, in the early years of 21st century, documents, with sovereigns bondholders are at the mercy of politicians.

While, like every market, a bond market has its risks, it also presents considerable advantages to both issuers and investors. A well-established and dependable corporate bond market working in unison with:

■ A mature equities market, and
■ A sound banking system

is an important feature of a developed financial environment. Within the corporate bond market there exist different levels of creditworthiness, rated from AAA to BBB as investment grade, and below that as non-investment grade. These thresholds in creditworthiness help to smooth the financing of a greater number of corporations by providing a source of external funding in addition to bank loans and equity issuance.

The existence of below-investment-grade debt instruments is particularly useful to small and medium-sized enterprises as well as new, fast-growing firms with increasing financing needs which find difficulty in obtaining bank loans. In addition, from a macro-economic perspective, the low grade/high yield segment of corporate bonds can be a useful source of information on:

■ Current credit conditions, and
■ Future economic activity.

The reason underpinning this statement is that spreads of high yield/low grade over higher rated debt instruments are often valuable indicators of the market participants' perceptions – for instance, about future corporate defaults and bond yields justifying investment in debt instruments at large.

As the Introduction briefly mentioned, there are numerous types of bonds, and large companies often issue several types. Some are mortgage bonds, backed by specific pieces of physical property, others are backed by specific holdings of the issuer in securities of other firms. Still others are backed just by the general assets of the issuing entity, and so on. However, while in connection to *the same firm* bonds are a more conservative investment than stocks, it should be noted that this statement does not necessarily hold in comparing the securities of different companies.

Along with whether or not a given debt instrument bond has some specific backing. The important factor in determining its *degree of risk* is whether it has first, second, or third claim on the income and property of the issuer. In each entity there is a definite *rank of priority* of claims on earnings. For instance, first-mortgage bondholders ordinarily have 'first lien', that is, first claim to payment. Investors must be aware that:

■ Securities may be ranged in order of priority of claims on earnings and assets.
■ In the case of mortgages such classification is a continuous series, from first lien bonds to common stocks.

In principle, all bonds are supported by the general credit of the issuing entity. *Secured bonds*, however, have the added security of a preferred claim to a portion or all of the assets; the 'specific backing' to which reference was made in the preceding paragraphs. Its significance lies in the relative rights of creditors in the event of failure of the issuer, which has been implicitly stated in the second bullet.

A secured bond has better means of protection by enjoying prior claim to the property specified as security. If this property fails to be of sufficient value to cover the face value of all bonds plus accrued interest, bondholders with a secured claim would have priority on available resources. The last in that line of claims are the equity holders, who are the legal owners of the firm.[4]

Resources made available to a secured bond issue essentially represent the value of collateral originally pledged. For this to be effective, provisions must be made to have the collateral fixed for the life of the bond including, possibly, a privilege of substitution. Substitution of pledged security is a flexibility desired by management as a means of retaining control over hypothecated securities. From the viewpoint of bondholders, however, changes in collateral requirements may make it difficult to maintain the original relationship between:

- The value of collateral, and
- The par value of outstanding bonds.

Certain bonds may be designated as *quasi-secured*. These include guarantees, and assumed obligations by a third party, which provides coverage or alternatively has first liens on real property of the issuer. In other words, some party (or parties) other than the issuing company is (are) also liable for the bonds. Although the security being provided is not explicitly stated in the form of collateral, it does give added protection to bondholders – at least a better one than unsecured funded obligations.

Moreover, as the Introduction brought to the reader's attention, debt instruments can be classified by maturity: short, intermediate, or long term (see Chapter 10). They can be further segregated by type of issuer: corporate, the government, the central bank, municipal, mortgage-backed, or other securitized instruments. When an investor looks at a bond issue to make up his or her mind on whether to commit funds, he would typically follow an order of critical characteristics:

- Bond issuer
- Bond rating
- Interest paid
- Maturity
- Price
- Yield (which combines preceding bullets), and
- Taxation.

Municipals are not the only bond which may benefit from favorable taxation rules (at least in the US). There are plenty of tax-exempt issues: tax-supported general obligation bonds, revenue-supported bonds, bonds by educational and not-for-profit institutions,[5] bonds from health care issuers, tax-exempt housing bonds, debt issued by public power projects, as well as bonds by state governments, sovereigns, and sub-nationals.

Typically, but not always, coupons are taxed as ordinary income, and capital appreciation (or depreciation) of bonds as ordinary gains (or losses). Zero-coupon bonds (see Chapter 4) are taxed annually on the basis of imputed interest. This is true even if they are held over year's end. The taxation amount is based on the difference between:

- Initial purchase price, and
- Accredited price assumed to be the current price.

As these examples document, there is a significant variety of bond characteristics. Others can be created by altering the redemption method. If the debt's principal amount is repaid as a whole through a single redemption on maturity, the bond is a *bullet*. In the case of a *sinking bond* the issuer repays the face value in several terms, up to maturity, at pre-established future dates.

The bond's maturity may vary if option-type features are added to the issue. A *callable* bond gives the issuer the right to redeem the principal ahead of the due date. A *putable* bond gives the holder the right to sell the bond back to the issuer before maturity. *Extendable* bonds enable the issuer to extend the life of their debt instrument beyond the initially agreed maturity. With a *perpetual* bond, the issuer does not repay the principal but continues paying the coupons.

Bond investors should keep in mind that history, although helpful, does not provide foolproof clues to the future behavior of the issuer or of the instrument. Market interest rates may be rising because of inflation or other reasons, but the central bank may be sitting on its hands, raising the question: When does the period of officially rising rates begin? Interest rate changes have a significant impact on the value of fixed-rate instruments, or there may be a credit bubble with devastating effects on certain bond issues (more on credit rating in Chapter 12). Typically, bonds are not covered by the socialization of risk.

3.3   Markets and issuers of bonds[6]

The Introduction defined a bond as a loan made by an investor to a company, government body or other entity. Except zero-coupon bonds sold at a discount, other bonds may be bought above, at, or below par; and they pay interest over a fixed term. When the bond matures at the end of the term, the principal, or investment amount, is repaid to the investor unless the issuer has defaulted. Any entity, at least reasonably trustworthy, can issue bonds at a specific interest rate and maturity to raise cash. In principle,

- The higher the issuer's credit rating, the less the issuer must compensate investors with a yield, and
- The longer is the maturity, the more sensitive the bond is to changes in interest rates.

The price of bonds is volatile, though at a level less than that of equities. Still, if investors are not careful they could find themselves in a position of trading stock market volatility for bond market volatility. For this reason many financial advisors recommend sticking to bonds with 5- to 10-year maturities, but longer maturities with G-10 government bonds and AAA companies also make sense, to lock-in higher yields – when such yields prevail.

Investors should appreciate that the bond market is not regulated through an exchange, like the stock market. Issuers, and sellers in the secondary market, post their prices on an information provider network, such as Bloomberg, and/or ask for quotations, and typically trade over the counter in bilateral agreements. It follows that:

■ Investors cannot *post* a limit for buy or sell, as with equities, though they can give a limit to their broker, and
■ The transaction must be negotiated by the investor's bank with a counterparty, usually another bank which buys and sells or sells directly out of its portfolio.

This dealing may concern one of several kinds of bonds, each with its own risk/reward profile. US Treasury bonds, for instance, are free of risk of default because they are backed by the full faith and credit of the US government. For a US citizen an added advantage is that the interest on Treasuries is not subject to state income taxes. Even Treasuries, however, are subject to market risk because of ongoing change in interest rates. Market risk is expressed by volatility in bond prices.

For starters, *volatility* is a measure of the amount by which a given market price fluctuates over a given period of time. An implicit volatility is used as a prognosticator of expected fluctuation in market prices. Volatility is commonly defined as one standard deviation of price moves over a one-year period:

■ Expressed as a percentage of a commodity's standard price, and
■ Added or subtracted from current price, within specific confidence intervals, it describes the range of price variation.

US Treasuries and other Group of Ten (G-10) government bonds are a good example of market risk because for any practical purpose they are free of credit risk – but they are subject to price volatility, both historical and implied. (More on market risk in Chapter 14.)

As defined by Bloomberg, *implied volatility* represents volatility on the near-contract generic future, rolled over 20 days prior to expiry. In other words, 20 days prior to expiry of the contracts, a change is made in choice of contracts used to obtain implied volatility.

■ From the contract closest to maturity
■ To the next contract of a similar type.

Typically, but not always, implied bond market volatility is lower than implied stock market volatility. Both, however, are indicators of market players' uncertainty about future price developments (specifically, yield developments in case of debt instruments). When bond prices remain relatively stable in the major markets, the volatility drops.

Table 3.1 compares bond market and stock market volatility in the December 2003 to March 2004 timeframe. Figure 3.1 shows a pattern of bond volatility in terms of yield, in the 1990 to 2002 timeframe. The yields are those of 10-year German government

Table 3.1 Implied bond market volatility and stock market volatility in the United States, Europe, and Japan, December 2003 to January 2004[a]

	Instrument	Dec. 2003	Jan. 2004	Feb. 2004	March 2004
United States	Bonds	9.0%	8.2%	7.3%	7.1%
	Stocks	15.0%	13.0%	13.5%	16.5%
Germany	Bonds	5.4%	5.4%	5.0%	5.1%
	Stocks	NA	NA	NA	NA
Euroland	Bonds	NA	NA	NA	NA
	Stocks	17.5%	17.0%	16.0%	23.0%
Japan	Bonds	4.0%	3.4%	3.5%	4.3%
	Stocks	24.5%	22.5%	22.5%	24.0%

[a]Percentages per year; 10-day moving averages.
Source: Statistics for Bonds by Bloomberg, for stock by European Central Bank

bonds; therefore they are free of credit risk. It is interesting to notice that while in this timeframe the yield trend has definitely been downwards, there were three spikes in:

- 1989–90, when the corporates' credit risk zoomed
- 1993–94, as the bond market went into turbulence
- 1998–99, in the aftermath of the Russian bankruptcy and LTCM's meltdown.

Equally important is to note that the huge rise of bond markets is an aftermath of democratization of lending. The very act of employing debt instruments is synonymous to *leverage* (see Chapter 1). Investors should appreciate that, whether we talk of

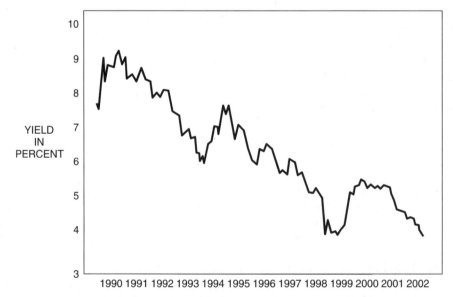

Figure 3.1 Volatility in the yield of 10-year German government bonds, in the 1990 to 2002 timeframe

government debt, company debt, or personal debt, the use of leverage can also increase volatility throughout the life of the investment. Moreover, under certain circumstances it may lead to deterioration of credit quality of the issuer (see Chapter 12).

Taking account of volatility characterizing bond markets and stock markets is the cornerstone to asset management, inasmuch as it has played a much bigger role in the past two decades than at any previous time. Intermediated by the market, debt and equity extend far into the future. While the size of bond markets differs across countries, and in many countries the government is the main issuer of debt securities sought after by investors,

- Bond markets are on the rise, and
- They are getting increasingly globalized.

For investors, the globalization of bond markets has its risks. Not only does every market for debt instruments have its own characteristics, but even government and government agency securities themselves may differ considerably in their creditworthiness, and in specifics related to maturity. For instance in the United States:

- Treasury bills are short-term debt issues
- Treasury bonds are long-term, and they used to go up to 30 years.

Federal agencies such as the Government National Mortgage Association (Ginnie Mae) also issue debt. The bonds of Ginnie Mae are mortgage-backed securities (MBS), which are made up of bundles of individual home mortgages, yielding more over time than Treasuries. In terms of credit risk, the US government has given implicit but not explicit guarantees against default, and Ginnie Mae's bonds carry other risks, such as early repayment.

If interest rates decline, some mortgages may be repaid early. As a result, the investor gets his money back earlier than he or she expected, and probably has to reinvest at lower rates. Conversely, if interest rates rise, mortgage payers are likely to continue their monthly payments since they benefit from a lower rate. The downside is that the institution which issued the securities is faced with *mismatch risk*, and may go bankrupt, as happened in the late 1980s in the United States with savings and loans (S&L).

Credit risk exists as well with municipal bonds, which are issued by states, cities and other local governments to pay for construction, sanitation work, road development, and other projects. Their risk tends to be lower than that of corporates, but they also offer lower interest rates capitalizing on the fact that (at least in the United States) they are exempt from federal and often state and local income taxes.

As we have already seen, corporate bonds are used by companies to finance expansion and other activities. They are riskier than government bonds; 'how much' riskier depends on the issuer's credit rating. Therefore, to compensate for credit risk and attract investors, they offer higher yields than government bonds. As corporate treasurers switch to bonds instead of loans for corporate financing, there is an acceleration of debt dynamics in regard to corporates (more on this later). Bonds from the corporate world may be issued by different industry sectors. Two of the earliest have been:

- *Utilities*: Electric, gas, and telecommunications services, and
- *Transportation*, such as railroads, airlines, air freight, motor vehicle companies.

The financial sector is increasingly tapping the debt market, particularly commercial banks, multi-line insurers and re-insurers, as well as property and casualty insurers. Another money-hungry sector of the economy is energy: Integrated oil and gas, oil/gas drilling, oil/gas exploration and production, oil/gas equipment and services, and so on.

Technology is another important industry sector in bond issuance. For instance, companies in (in alphabetic order): aerospace and defense, application software, biotechnology, communications equipment, computer hardware, electronic equipment, IT consulting, other IT services, semiconductors, systems software, and wireless telecommunications. The careful reader will notice that much of the market bubble, and associated defaults, of the 1990s came from these sectors.

Other industry sectors active in the issuance of bonds are consumer services and consumer staples. Examples of consumer services are casinos and gaming, health care distributors, health care services and facilities, hotels, managed health care outfits, movies and entertainment, publishing and printing, restaurants. Major consumer staples sectors are brewers, drug retailers, food retailers, health care equipment makers, manufacturers of household products, packaged foods entities, personal products firms, pharmaceuticals, soft drinks vendors, and tobacco companies.

With the democratization of lending and with so many issuers waiting for a favorable time to cap the market for debt, it is no surprise that the bond market has zoomed during the past ten years, as shown in Figure 3.2. It is interesting to observe

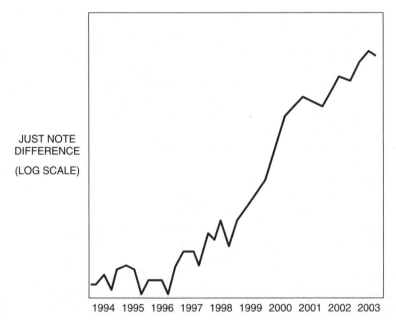

Figure 3.2 Bonds outstanding over a 10-year timeframe, including money market paper. (*Source:* statistics by Bank for International Settlements)

that the huge rise took place after 1998, practically in parallel to the stock market bubble. But contrary to the collapse of equity issuance,

- The rise in bond issuance went on after 2000
- Debt compensated for the lack of new equity's appeal to investors.

The default on interest payments also had an upwards trend, particularly in 1989 in Europe, 1992 in the United States, and 2002. Most exposed to a charge in insolvencies, which includes defaults in interest payments and capital repayments, have been investors who bought junk bonds, the lowest rated of the corporate bonds. As we will see in Chapters 4 and 12, junk bonds are high risk because there is a greater-than-average chance that the company will fail to face up to its obligations.

3.4 Bond market and equity market

Like good asset managers, successful investors are not running after the facts. From time to time, they step back from day-to-day business and take a philosophical look, which is conceptual in nature and takes into consideration a holistic investment perspective. As Figure 3.3 suggests, a holistic view in regard to investments includes bonds, equities, currencies, other commodities, and derivative financial instruments – as well as their risks and returns.

Each of these investment domains has its own subdivisions and its own market perspective, thereby posing an issue of choice. This is good news for investors, provided that they are prepared to confront issues associated with choice of debt instruments. Take the alternative of investing in government bonds versus corporates, of which we spoke in previous sections, as an example.

The way an article in *The Economist* had it, in March 2004 Berkshire Hathaway was sitting on a cash pile of $36 billion, much of it in government securities. Although, as Warren Buffett put it, these pay 'pathetically low interest' the pain of doing something stupid was potentially worse. 'I detest taking even small risks unless we feel that we are being adequately compensated for doing so,' the now legendary investor said.[7]

This is also a good example on bond versus equity investment choices. At the time Buffett was reportedly feeling bearish about the stock market, commenting that 'In recent years we've found it hard to find significantly undervalued stocks, a difficulty

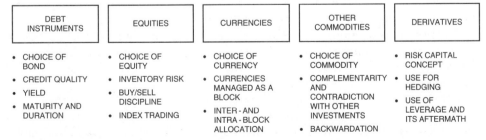

Figure 3.3 Computing domains in an investor's portfolio, each with its own risk and return

greatly accentuated by the mushrooming of the funds we must deploy.' And corporate bonds were too expensive for the risk they carry. Buffett bought $8 billion of them in 2002, when they were cheap, but the pendulum swung quickly, and 'this sector now looks decidedly unattractive to us,' Buffett said (see the discussion on credit spread in section 3.7).

With these and similar references in mind, it becomes evident that a most basic question an investor or investment manager should always ask is: 'Which are my alternatives?' As an example, in the following paragraphs we will consider the bond market versus equity market. The issue of choice in capital allocation between equities and fixed-income instruments is crucial. It is also the first major division an investor should consider in risk and return. In the past few years, capital markets have been characterized by a diverging trend in total returns – comprising price movements, interest, and dividends characterizing the:

- Bond market, and
- Equity market.

With some exceptions, between March 2000 and March 2003 the share index of major capital markets lost around three-quarters of its value. In the same period, the yields on 10-year euro-denominated government bonds fell from approximately $5\frac{1}{2}\%$ to below $3\frac{1}{2}\%$ (by the middle of 2003). In the aftermath, debt instruments' prices rose significantly and bond investors with high interest rates in their portfolio reaped significant profits.

The fact that the early years of the 21st century have seen a snowfall of profits for bond investors does not mean that there is no downside risk in these investments. As we will see in greater detail in subsequent chapters, bond investments have both interest rate risk – which is market risk – and credit risk; both must be taken into full account.

Investors seek refuge in debt instruments when they fear that all the air still has not been squeezed out of the stock market bubble. For instance, in 2002 alert investors noted that the Standard & Poor's 500-stock index was trading at 20 times projected 2002 earnings, well above the average multiple of 15.7 the index maintained over the past 42 years. That represented a 22% premium to the historical average, in spite of the stock market collapse.

The question 'Which are my alternatives?' comes up at this point, because also in 2002 bonds were trading at significant premium. Since 1960, the average yield on the 10-year Treasury note has been 7.25%. That made the yield of around 4.75% prevailing in 2002 more than one-third below this average.

The two references just made correlate. One reason for the premium were the stock market blues; another was low inflation. But bond yields respond to more than just the troubles equity investment face and experts said that interest rates could rise even as inflation stayed quiet, causing bond prices to plummet. Moreover, bond prices were swinging widely by traditional standards, which speaks volumes about the riskiness of bonds in the reference year.

In principle, but only in principle, as long as things are going badly on the equity market, there is a rush to high quality bonds. This is particularly true for G-10 government bonds, but the movement eventually spreads to lower quality bonds. A more complex view is that as long as investors are unsure about the prospects for growth in the economy and corporate earnings, they tend to favor lower yield but high rated debt instruments.

Investors who care for their capital judge the medium-term risk of capital losses on higher yielding but lower credit quality bond investments, to be greater than the interest which they gain. They are also concerned about the fact that perceived capital gains on volatile investments like stocks, may turn on their head. Investor psychology is, however, quite different when the equity market is in an upswing.

As these references demonstrate, investing in bonds and stocks has its ups and downs. These should be carefully studied because they help in building up the investor's defenses through diversification, as well as in capitalizing on market trends. By historical standards, a negative correlation between equity market and bond market tends to be an exception, though it happens from time to time.

Different studies tend to suggest that periods of negative correlation between equity markets and bond markets are often accompanied by significant volatility in stocks and a great degree of price uncertainty measured by implied volatility of options on the equity market. Other things being equal,

- In times of crisis investors shift their assets away from equities and purchase bonds, perceived to be safer.
- The negative correlation is often driven by high equity market volatility, leading to a flight towards fixed income instruments.

If a negative correlation prevails between the two markets, *then* rising equity prices are accompanied by falling bond prices, and therefore rising yield. By contrast, a positive correlation between stock markets and bond markets means that rising equity prices are accompanied by rising prices in the bond market and falling yields. Typically, when it happens, a positive correlation between equity market and debt market is rather *low*, with a coefficient of 0.3 or less.

If we make the hypothesis that equity prices reflect their future discounted dividends, and bond prices reflect their future interest payments, a positive correlation could be explained up to a point by the fact that the two markets depend on a common discounting factor which tends to come into play in the absence of change in inflationary expectations. However, the 0.3 correlation is relatively weak. Had it been a stronger one (0.5 or higher), then falling equity prices would be generally accompanied by falling bond prices, hence higher yields.

Moreover, sound investment principles suggest that bond yields must be high enough to adequately reflect the risk of an upturn in inflation. This is typically not the case when yields are near a peak. The silver lining is that when market participants remain quite wary about upcoming economic data and the next Federal Open Market Committee (FOMC) meeting, yields stay more-or-less in a trading range.

Finally, investors purchasing debt instruments in other than their base currency should pay a great deal of attention to foreign exchange risk (see section 3.8). This is also true of equity investors, but it is more pronounced with fixed income instruments because both the derived income and possible capital gains may be inadequate in compensating changes in currency parities. In other words, international investors are faced with the challenge of significant changes in exchange rates which may upset risk and return calculation relative to their portfolio.

3.5   Yield of fixed income instruments and the ECB model

This is only a preliminary discussion on yield (for a detailed discussion on yield and yield curves see Chapter 7 and Chapter 9) intended to bring to the reader's attention the fact that yield is not necessarily the same with nominal interest. Furthermore, publicly traded debt instruments may have a fixed interest rate or a variable one, the latter being known as floating interest rate. Because the fixed interest rate is by far the more frequently used, bonds are generally known as fixed income instruments.

Being active in the fixed income business means to originate, trade, and distribute a variety of debt-based instruments, including structured ones. It also means being responsible for loan syndication and for administering a loan portfolio – which may or may not be securitized. When it is managed at that broad scale, the fixed income business serves a wide client base of investors and borrowers, offering a range of fixed income services which:

- The underwriting of debt instruments, and their sale to individual investors, institutional investors, and other entities
- Principal finance, which involves the purchase, origination, and securitization of credit instruments, and
- A variety of derivative banking products, from structured finance to other leveraged financial instruments.

Interest rate-based credit products, from government bonds and corporate bonds to securitized loans, are subject to market acceptance and the market's mood expressed through implied bond market volatility (see section 3.4). This may be shorter term or longer term. Also short term and longer term may be the pattern of bond yields and rising or falling prices.

The *yield* of a security is a basic metric for valuation as far as its return to the investor is concerned. Fixed income securities are sold at a price which, to a significant extent, is established by the market. The higher (or lower) is that price for a given fixed interest rate through the maturity of the instrument, say 7%, the lower (or higher) will be the corresponding yield. As we will see in Chapter 9, yield is a metric which:

- Has internal consistency
- Is not contradictory to other measurement units, and
- Can be combined with risk measurements to present a holistic return pattern.

The investor's aversion to risk, or conversely his or her risk appetite, are crucial factors in the choices that have to be made. For instance, as long as risk aversion remains, the market regards G-10 government bonds as safe havens (see section 3.4). This increases the credit spread between government and corporate bonds. To the contrary, a greater risk appetite by investors sees the credit spread shrink (see section 3.7).

Because yield is all-important, the fixed income business is very sensitive to discount rates established by central banks. These define the cost of money to commercial bankers, and it has evident impact on loans and on the bond market. Reserve institutions closely follow the market's response to their moves both in the short term and in the longer term. The European Central Bank (ECB) has established a statistical framework defining long-term interest rates in the European Union, which takes into account:

- Bond issuer
- Maturity
- Coupon effect
- Taxation
- Aggregation
- Yield formula.

To weed out credit risk effects, only those bonds issued by central governments are being followed. The maturity is chosen to be as close as possible to 10 years' residual maturity, and any replacement of bonds is selected to minimize maturity drift. In this ECB model, there is no direct adjustment for coupon effect, and special feature bonds are omitted. Also, interest is taken gross of tax, because there are different taxation regimes for fixed interest instruments in the EU.

The choice of long-term government bonds rests on the economic assumption that these are the most secure type of debt instruments and, therefore, they are relatively less affected by credit risk considerations. As stated, ECB selects bonds with a residual maturity of close to 10 years; maturity typically varies in a bracket of 9.5–10.5 years. It also tries to keep drifting at a minimum. This, however, necessitates the regular issue of comparable bonds.

Another criterion used by the ECB in its model is that the bonds being considered should be sufficiently liquid – which government bonds more or less are – though much depends on the specific issue. This requirement helps in determining the choice between benchmark or sample approaches, depending on national market conditions. For yield to maturity the International Securities Markets Association (ISMA) formula is used (see the Appendix to this chapter). Moreover, where there is more than one bond in the sample, a simple average of the yields is employed to produce the representative rate.[8]

Account is also taken of the fact that, as mentioned in the discussion of a fixed interest instrument's yield, there is a positive relationship between coupon and price; while there is an inverse relationship between price and yield. For evident reasons, the ECB weights, by the coupon value, the extent to which changes in bond prices affect the yield:

- *If* the coupon is significantly different across countries,
- *Then* both the yield and its changes will not be comparable.

The structural liquidity of different markets is also considered. Statistically speaking, average yields calculated through samples are believed to be more stable over time, because the replacement of bonds in the basket is usually staggered, dampening the renewal effect. However, using a sample may not be meaningful when the range of variation in liquidity, among markets, is very diverse. Such diversity has a negative effect on the comparability of yields.

Use of the ECB algorithm (presented in the Appendix) makes it possible to adopt a portfolio approach which aggregates more than one bond included in the sample. This is seen as a better method than taking some form of average of the yields of fixed interest financial products. Through appropriate modeling, debt instruments can be:

- Treated as one series of cash flows, and
- Discounted together at the same rate.

Another alternative to the method which has been outlined is to use benchmark issues which are highly liquid. Typically, criteria for selecting averaging or benchmark bonds depend on market liquidity. The downside of this approach is that the risk of maturity drift is greater than that with the samples approach.

3.6　Credit spread risk and other risks[9]

Though related to the creditworthiness of the issuer and the rating, by independent agencies, of its bonds, *credit spread risk*, or simply spread risk, is basically market risk. The term denotes cases where the yield differential between risk-free bonds, such as Treasuries, and a debt instrument with credit risk, like corporate bonds (particularly of lower rating), can change – while the credit rating stays the same.

To a significant extent, changing credit spreads reflect investors' perception about implied volatility in the debt market. There is always a spread risk, because market perceptions change. Sometimes investors are so hungry for higher yield that they will forgo the prudential long hard look on credit risk which they assume with some types of bonds. In other times, they will dump these same bonds because of their lower creditworthiness.

A case in point is bonds below investment grade, rated BB+ or worse to which reference was made in Chapter 1 as junk bonds. By mid-March 2004, for instance, the index of junk debt spreads compiled by Standard & Poor's (S&P) had fallen by more than half since its high. Just how quickly the spread risk pendulum swung can be judged by the $1.1 billion in pre-tax profits that Berkshire Hathaway made on its junk bond portfolio in 2003.

The reader should not confuse the democratization of lending which characterizes a large cross-section of debt instruments with the forces propelling the ups and downs of spread risk. The latter has its own criteria, which are largely subjective. After the aftermath period of the great equity market bubble, by late 2003 and early 2004 bond defaults were falling. According to the experts, this was largely because:

- The economy was again becoming benign, and
- Interest rates were ultra-low, in practically all Western countries.

Very low interest rates meant that the resulting demand for yield made it feasible for the most speculative grade of issuers to have access to the capital market. For example, in January and February 2004, 46% of new junk issues carried a rating of B− or less. Over 2003 as a whole, the figure was 31%, which was in turn higher than in 2002.

But the fact investors sank money into junk bonds in exchange for a few basis points did not do away with credit risk. There is a sort of unwritten rule that when the share of lower grade issuance exceeds 30% of total debt instrument issuance for a sustained period of time, this generally serves as a reliable indicator of imminent default pressure two or three years down the line. We shall see if this proves to be true by 2006 and 2007, but in the meantime, in the second quarter of 2004 spread risk was shown up in connection to emerging market debt. Any investor or speculator who buys foreign debt issued by emerging countries takes separate but linked risks, which may haunt him or her for years to come.

- Risk associated to the market volatility of Western sovereign, credit risk-free bonds
- Credit risk proper connected to the emerging market sovereign issuing the bond, and
- Foreign exchange risk (see section 3.8), which is not negligible with G-10 currencies, but tends to be more pronounced with currencies of developing countries.

Because most bonds are denominated in dollars, what happens to American Treasury bond yields has a major impact on emerging market debt prices. That is, emerging market bond risk Type I. The Type II exposure reflects investors' perceptions of how likely the issuer of the bond is to default. This is precisely what is measured by the *credit spread* characterizing different types of bonds over US Treasuries. In principle:

- The greater the risk
- The higher the credit spread.

Investors should always ask to be compensated for Type I and Type II exposure, through an extra premium which should be looked at as a sort of self-reinsurance. Notice that while the reference made to Type I risk is universally valid, or nearly so, the basic currency used by the investor may require that both US Treasuries and gilts of the country in which the investor resides, as well as the basic currency he or she uses, should be accounted for. Interest rate curves are by no means the same from one sovereign country to another, as is shown in Figure 3.4 with an example on the pattern of Bank of England and European Central Bank interest rates.

Type III risk is taken by investors with all foreign currency investments, and most particularly those of emerging markets. Currency exchange volatility is not unwanted, but it must be properly managed. Paraphrasing what Thomas Jefferson said: 'Our liberty depends on freedom of the press, and that cannot be limited without being lost' – the readjustment of differences in sovereign economies is done through foreign exchange volatility, and rates cannot be permanently fixed without this flexibility being lost.

All three types of exposures with fixed income instruments should enter into risk and return calculations. In 2003, good money was made from falling credit spreads. From its peak in September 2002 to its trough in January 2004, an index of these spreads tracked by J.P. Morgan, known as EMBI+, fell from 1041 basis points over Treasuries, to 384 bps – but it rose to 596 by mid-May 2004.

The reason for the anomaly in this significant fall of credit spread is a fact many investors chose to forget: none of the top borrowers in emerging markets has a sound credit record. Brazil, the biggest borrower of all, defaulted in 1826, 1898, 1902,

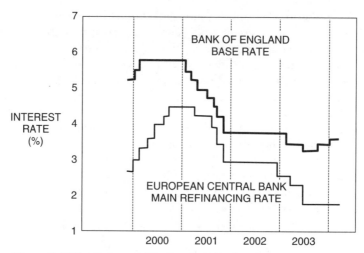

Figure 3.4 The patterns of Bank of England and European Central
Bank interest rate decisions, 2000–2003

1914, 1931, 1937, and 1983. Its neighbor, Argentina, another serial non-payer, is still
in default for $100 billion – the biggest in history. Russia last defaulted, albeit on its
domestic debt, in 1998.

In late 2003 and first quarter of 2004, the Type II case in bond pricing, to which I
made reference, had in the background the fact that while the creditworthiness of
emerging market issuers has not markedly improved, overall the credit spread significantly shrank – and it did so across the board. As a result, yields on emerging markets debt were ridiculously meager in the second half of 2003 and early 2004, given
the risks investors had taken by lending money to countries with a habit of:

- Eating up the interest, and
- Not repaying the capital.

Emerging countries are not alone in capitalizing on investors' greed and failure to
do their homework. A small yet growing group of major corporations is hawking
40-year and 50-year bonds to lock-in lower interest rates when central banks keep
them that way in an effort (often hopeless) to kick-start the economy.

No doubt, half-century paper is a good deal for the issuers. They pay, at most, a
quarter-point more than for a 30-year corporate bond and do not have to care about
paying the principal for one or two decades longer. But is the 50-year security a wise
move for buyers? The answer to this query is very negative, as holders are subject to
all sorts of risks. Not least among them are:

- The downgrading of companies and of their debt because of financial weaknesses,
  and
- The fact products die and get out of fashion, while vast technical changes may
  cause rapid product obsolescence weakening a company's market standing.

There is plenty of evidence on how easily business reverses can sink an issuer's credit rating. With the exception of gilts, there is a major question whether some borrowers will be around four or five decades later. That is the most pure sense of credit risk. With hindsight, all of the demi-centenary issuers of the early 1990s have been buffeted by one calamity or another, whether economic downturn, tough foreign competition, or major legal woes. And there is no reason to believe they and others will be exempt from future ill fortune.

3.7   A bird's-eye view of foreign exchange risk

With fixed exchange rates, which prevailed for more than a quarter century, from the end of the Second World War to 1971, the Type III risk mentioned in section 3.6) was practically non-existent in regard to bonds from Group of Ten and some other entities. But since 1971 things have changed; currency exchange rates have been floated, and this change made itself particularly felt after the oil shocks of the 1970s followed by currency market turbulence and stagflation (stagnation and inflation) characterizing the mid-1970s to early 1980s.

Moreover, in the immediate post-war decades currency exchange operations had in large part to do with international commerce. In 1970, the year before the collapse of the fixed exchange rate system, currency exchange trading around the world was about $12 billion a day, or less than $3 trillion a year. World trade (imports plus exports) totaled $593 billion in 1970 – which roughly means there was about six times more foreign exchange trading than there was actual foreign trade.

But after President Nixon took the dollar off the gold standard, in August 1971, foreign exchange trading increased eight-fold in just three years, to around $100 billion a day. Correspondingly, in the decade from 1971 to 1981, foreign exchange turnover increased four times faster than the increase in the value of world trade, leaving the share of international commerce in the dust.

The Federal Reserve was the first to attempt to measure the rapidly growing foreign exchange challenges. In 1977, it surveyed trading at 44 banks representing over 95% of all foreign exchange activity in the United States at that time. What it found is that there was $4.8 billion in daily foreign exchange trading in America alone – which on a yearly basis gives $1.2 trillion.

Foreign exchange volatility was significant in the 1980s, as with skyrocketing interest rates in the United States the dollar hit all-time highs, then collapsed following the Plaza Athene accord. By 1992 foreign exchange trading passed the $1 trillion a day milestone world-wide. By 2004, Swift, which links thousands of institutions in hundreds of countries, says that the nominal money flow exceeds $4 trillion per day.

It would be a considerable understatement to say that this is far in excess of the merchandise trade. The latter just amounts to 3% of aforementioned figures, according to some estimates. This means that foreign exchange is 33 times the world-wide merchandise trade, and on a daily basis it represents more than 35% of the gross national product (GNP) of the United States.

It does not take exceptional brain power to understand that, in reference to this huge forex volume, no central bank can act as lender of last resort or stabilizer of currency exchange markets. Hence, in the last analysis, everyone will be out on their own. No treasurer can leave that factor out of the equation when it comes to estimating the amount of assumed forex risk.

Furthermore, given the volatility in currency exchange rates, no investor with a multicurrency portfolio can leave out of their calculations the impact of forex risk. This statement is valid for both equity and debt investments, though bonds feel the forex risk more than stocks because, other things being equal, their price volatility is lower than that of stocks. Through 1999 statistics, Figure 3.5 dramatizes the impact of currency exchange changes in equity markets and debt markets.

A legitimate question is: since international commerce and foreign exchange operations have been decoupled, which is the driving force pushing the latter to aforementioned heights? The answer consists of three points which, a priori, correlate among themselves:

- Cross-border direct investments
- Investments in securities (bonds and stocks), and
- Speculative cross-border money movements, including derivatives products.

Currency plays a crucial role in all investments. For instance, the introduction of the euro right after the turn of the millennium has brought significant change in the European bond markets. The former national markets, especially for government bonds, became more integrated. There has also been increased activity in both the primary and the secondary markets. Also, various market segments were, and still remain up to a point, underdeveloped in terms of:

- Depth
- Efficiency, and
- Completeness.

Notice that the integration of bond markets is not an instant development, but greater market maturity is helped by the disappearance within Euroland of currency exchange risk – which has been one of key factors constraining cross-border investments.

Currency integration has also helped Euroland investors to substantially increase the diversification of their portfolios, particularly of their bond portfolios, which classically had a rather significant domestic orientation. An interesting observation is that investors in smaller Euroland countries have diversified more quickly than those in larger ones.[10]

Demographic risks, country rating, current account deficit, and other variables, all the way to rising and falling interest rates, do play a key role in foreign exchange risk. Therefore, not only currency investors should be concerned about what makes a currency exchange tick. One particularly important factor is the weight of speculative positions.

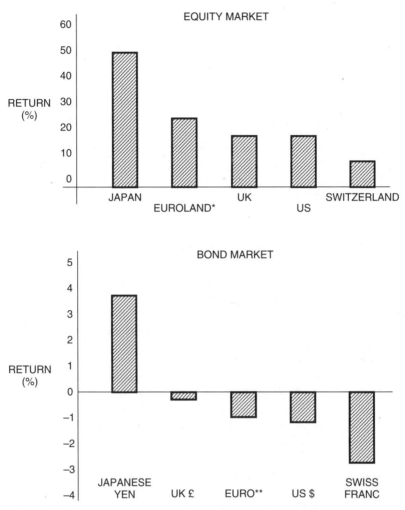

Figure 3.5 Return on investment from equity markets and bond markets in different countries and currencies in 1999. *Average figure between equity returns in France, Germany, Italy, and Holland. **Euroland average

An example on speculations connected to currency exchange in the 2001–2004 timeframe has been the practice of using the yen and the dollar as funding currencies for *carry trades*. For instance, borrowing at low US interest rates to buy higher yielding assets – a very popular speculative operation, indeed.

In 2003 the dollar was hurt because of very low interest rate compared to other major currencies, like the Euro and the British pound. Experts suggested that beyond position-squaring, the 2004 support for the dollar from higher nominal US interest rates is uncertain – but, other things being equal, rising real interest rates are an important source of support for a currency. Historical comparisons brought evidence that the equity market's reaction to interest rates increases also plays a role.

■ Tightening by the Federal Reserve in 1999 was accompanied by a rising dollar as equities rallied.
■ But in 1994, equities were unsettled by the pace of policy tightening and the dollar also fell.

Higher interest rates exacerbate problems connected to structural balance of payments. The rise in bond yields could increase a country's current account deficit as a percentage of its gross domestic product. Furthermore, higher oil prices and fading fiscal stimulus tend to reduce an economy's growth prospects, and they undermine the currency. All these considerations are of significant interest to bond investors, because of their potential impact on portfolio position, new investments, and risks associated to both of them.

3.8 Bond restructuring and arbitrage

Bonds issued for the global capital market are usually in strong currencies: US dollars, British pounds, euros, and to a lesser extent yen and Swiss francs – though there are also emissions in other currencies like Canadian dollars and Australian dollars. Developing-country bonds denominated in their own currencies are typically for their internal market. Only those investors with a huge appetite for foreign exchange risk will be interested in them.

The careful reader will recall that currency risk aside every fixed income instrument has embedded in it credit risk which weights on investor preferences. An example of credit risk preferences by investors is provided by the Luxembourg bond market, which roughly accounts for 3.4% of Euroland issues. In this market, on the average,

■ About 30% of the volume issued features AAA rating
■ 25% an AA rating
■ 12% an A rating, and
■ The remaining 33% BBB and BB ratings.

(There will be more on bond ratings in Chapter 12.)

Bonds default because their issuer goes bankrupt or seeks protection from bankruptcy by gaming the system. The majority of these cases arise among companies characterized by BB or lower ratings. For bondholders, bankruptcy does not necessarily wipe out all claims. Some time down the line the issue arises of restructuring the defaulted party's bonds.

A good example on difficulties connected to restructuring of bonds comes from Telecom Argentina, which defaulted at about the same time as the whole of Argentina, as a sovereign state, was declared bankrupt by its appointed president. Having been rebuffed in connection to its first two debt restructuring plans, which were unacceptable to investors, on 11 May 2004, Telecom Argentina advanced a third proposal at the $2.63 billion dollar level – which can be taken as a typical example of how investors can be defrauded.

This latest offer to the telecommunications company's bondholders has been more advantageous for investors than those which preceded it. Apart from a higher rate of recovery for the principal, it covered part of matured interest to be capitalized: for every 1000 dollars or euros of debt 1058 were recognized prior to the discounts. The plan proposes three options to bondholders:

- Option A, requiring at least $300 million, suggested an interest rate of 4% to 7%, with step-up corresponding to maturities of 2008, 2014, and 2017.
- Option B was changed from previous 'plans' by eliminating tranches paid in cash. In the new offer it consisted in only one step to 2011 with an interest rate of 9% to 10%.
- Option C offered a cash payment of $740 and $850 for every $1058, depending on debt instrument conditions – but on the average it practically meant a heavy discount of about 25%.

As the reaction of shareholders to Telecom Argentina, and to Argentina's sovereign debt demonstrate, restructuring may be an option, but it is not a *carte blanche* in debtor's hands. This is particularly true if the debtor hopes to be able to issue more bonds in the future, and find investors for them. There are moreover legal and administrative constraints.

For instance in the case of the aforementioned telecommunications company, the whole bond restructuring operation is subject to an Argentinean procedure of debit management, involving an out-of-court agreement reached between the debtor and the numerical majority of creditors who control at least two-thirds of nominal value of bonds subject to restructuring. This majority has been difficult to obtain because:

- The aforementioned options were unfavorable to creditors, and
- The very slow pace of this procedure has shown a debtor unwilling to face up to its obligations.

The looting of investors by companies and sovereigns who find through bankruptcy an easy way out of their obligations, should be a lesson to bondholders and potential bondholders. Credit quality matters, and this in a dual sense:

- The debtor's *ability* to pay the interest and repay the principal, and
- The debtor's *willingness* to face up to obligations he has assumed as issuer to the debt instrument.

The risks behind these two bullets are not the same. The grade given to the entity and its debt by independent rating agencies addresses the first bullet. The second is a matter of ethics, and the best guide is historical evidence. As Abraham Lincoln said, one who did something wrong will do something wrong again.

Seen from a different perspective, ratings below AA, and even more so below A, may be (sometimes) subject to a significant spread risk (see section 3.6). Moreover, as we have seen, all bonds are exposed to interest rate risk, including the AAA-rated.

Many companies argue that the ups and downs in the price of their bonds do not affect them. This may be true of old issues traded in the secondary market, but not necessarily of new underwritings.

The 'do not affect' argument rests on the assumption that even if a $500 million issue is trading at, say, $550 million, the firm is obliged to repay only the face value when the bonds mature. This hypothesis, however, wrongly implies that firms exist in isolation. The bonds in this example will have moved to $550 million because interest rates have fallen. Lower rates, in turn, increase the burden of the bonds because:

- Future payments to service and redeem them are fixed, and
- Those payments have become more valuable in terms of today's money.

Investors provide the answer to how much more expensive a bond issue may become to its issuer, through change in the market value of the debt – in this example, $50 million. Account should also be taken of the fact that financial markets influence the value of a company's assets and of its obligations. For instance, changes in exchange rates affect the entity's income if costs and revenues come in different currencies.

For these reasons, not only must all pertinent market changes be tracked, but also market risk should be properly calculated in all its aspects. When this is done in a consistent, timely, accurate and sophisticated way, it makes possible *bond arbitrage* – which involves spotting apparently unjustified differences, the so-called 'anomalies'.

Anomalies characterizing the price of bonds with similar characteristics and risks do happen from time to time, because the market is not efficient.[11] When they detect such anomalies, speculators place huge bets that the price(s) will revert to its (their) 'normal' relationship. Because bond arbitrage is speculative, it involves significant risks. One of them is that many traders start making the same bet, the result of which is that:

- This bet becomes less profitable
- It is characterized by increased volatility in profits
- Sometimes there is no liquid market for the assets, so that the anomaly is hypothetical.

Bond arbitrage is also done 'on the news' and, as such, it is illegal. While the advice is to leave bond arbitrage to speculators, all asset managers and all major investors should have on hand consistent, timely, and sophisticated ways of tracking market risk (see Chapter 15). Measuring the shifting value of assets is, however, a demanding business.

To find prices for assets, in their portfolio, or those they propose to buy or sell, investors often have to devise their own financial models able to show how shifts in interest rates, currencies or market demand affect the present value of their positions. This is the domain of rocket science, using algorithmic and heuristic approaches.[12] Amazon.com has become the first company known to have instituted a new position – that of the *chief algorithmic officer*.[13]

Finally, in connection to new bond issues investors must be aware of the likelihood of overpricing or even outright fraud. In the early 1990s, Salomon Brothers – the investment bank who at the time led in Treasury sales – came down in flames because of having manipulated the market in US government bonds. One would have thought this has been an expensive lesson to be remembered by financial institutions; but it was not so.

About ten years down the line, on 4 February 2003, a former top economist at Goldman Sachs was indicted on seven counts of illegally trading on confidential information about the Treasury Department's plan to end sales of 30-year bonds. The defendant, John Youngdahl, was charged with conspiracy, wire fraud, and securities fraud, among other charges. Youngdahl pleaded not guilty and was released on $800 000 bail pending a trial. He also faces a lawsuit by the Securities and Exchange Commission. The lesson these references provide is that all parties – issuers, underwriters, traders, and investors – will be well advised to be and to remain on their guard for all sorts of mishappenings.

Here is a further reference on how far a scam can go. Federal prosecutors in Manhattan also charged a Wall Street consultant, Peter Davis, with illegally providing the information to Youngdahl, so he could pass it on to Goldman traders. Davis pleaded guilty to conspiracy and wire fraud, prosecutors said. Goldman itself agreed to pay more than $9.3 million to settle charges by the Securities and Exchange Commission that it had failed to stop traders from buying on the news. It neither admitted nor denied any wrongdoing.[14]

Appendix 3.A   The ECB algorithm

The European Central Bank algorithm for computation of yield-to-maturity:

$$P = \sum_{i=1}^{n} CF_i \cdot V^{T_i}$$

where:

P = gross price, representing purchase price plus accrued interest
n = number of future cash flows
CF_i = cash flow at payment i
V = annualized discounting factor, $1/(1 + y)$
T_i = time in years to the i-th cash flow
y = annualized yield

Notes

1 The word 'indenture' stems from earlier times when agreements were written on one side of the original sheet, after which the page was torn and the separate pieces given to the parties involved. Indentures are important issues to company financing. Essentially, they are the contract, or agreement, between the issuer, trustee, and bondholders.
2 Peter Krass, *Carnegie*, Wiley, New York, 2002.

3 Theoretically, small shareholders have an owner's power over the company in which they invest. Practically, they have no more such power than bondholders.

4 D.N. Chorafas, *The Management of Equity Investments*, Butterworth-Heinemann, London, 2005.

5 D.N. Chorafas, *The Management of Philanthropy in the 21st Century*, Institutional Investor, New York, 2002.

6 A more detailed discussion on markets of bonds, including more market, capital market, and repo market, will be found in Chapter 11.

7 *The Economist*, 13 March 2004.

8 ECB, Bond Markets and Long-Term Interest Rates in EU Accession Countries, Frankfurt, October 2003.

9 Credit spread risk is further discussed in Chapter 7.

10 *ECB Monthly Bulletin*, January 2000.

11 D.N. Chorafas, *The Management of Equity Investments*, Butterworth-Heinemann, London, 2005.

12 D.N. Chorafas, *Rocket Scientists in Banking*, Lafferty Publications, London and Dublin, 1995.

13 *The Economist*, 15 May 2004.

14 *International Herald Tribune*, 5 September 2003.

4 Convertible bonds, zero bonds, junk bonds, strips, and other bonds

4.1 Introduction

Chapter 3 has explained that, in the general case, fixed interest debt instruments represent borrowing by the issuer who promises to pay the buyer an interest at certain established dates, and the principal at maturity. But there are exceptions. For instance, with *zero-coupon* bonds (see section 4.3) the interest is deducted from the purchase price at time of sale, while the principal will be paid at maturity.

Chapter 3 has also given a bird's-eye view of other variations characterizing debt instruments. For example, they may be *bullet*, also called 'straight', or *callable* at the issuer's discretion (see section 4.2). The latter permit the originating entity to repay a bond at a time prior to maturity, which is favorable to it, and at a specified price (usually at par).

Prepayment is usually done at the most inopportune time for the investor, as the issuer benefits from lower interest rates. One of the risks associated to prepayment of callable bonds, is that it can hit the investor hard if he has bought the bond above par value. Another risk associated to prepayment is that it interrupts a projected cash flow necessary to face, for example, an institutional investor's obligations such as annuities.

Convertible bonds (see section 4.4) are a hybrid between fixed interest instruments and equity. With them, the holder has the right to convert his or her investment into shares at a predetermined price. But while these bonds which represent debt can be converted into equity, convertible bonds do not offer their holder the best of two worlds, as is often said to be the case.

Other bonds are designed to present their owner with preferential tax treatment. An example, from the United States, is municipal bonds, which are general obligations backed by taxes, or revenue bonds issued to finance a specific project and paid by the receipts the project generates. Both benefit from tax advantages, but of the two the revenue bonds are riskier.

There are plenty of other types of bonds, like junk bonds (introduced in Chapter 1 and discussed in section 4.6) or high interest, which is a misnomer because it fails to signal out embedded credit risk, Rubin bonds and Brady bonds (see section 4.9) and more. With derivative financial instruments innovation in the debt market has been unstoppable,

- Exploring new and untested sources of funding, and
- Entering uncharted waters in terms of assumed risk.

'Clothes and automobiles change every year,' Paul M. Mazur of Lehman Brothers once said. 'But because the currency remains the same in appearance, though its value steadily declines, most people believe that finance does not change. Actually, debt financing changes like everything else. We have to find new models in financing, just as in clothes and automobiles, if we want to stay on top. We must remain inventive architects of the money business.[1]

But we must also be ahead of the curve in terms of estimating, monitoring and controlling assumed risk; appreciating that everything that shines is not gold. As an old proverb has it: 'Value like beauty is what catches your eye.' Our eye, however, may not catch the unwanted consequences connected to a new financial instrument, making our portfolio vulnerable to crises and even to malfeasance.[2]

An example from the motor vehicle industry helps in making the point that innovation is *always* welcome, provided that *we know the risks* which we assume. This example concerns a very important finding connected to the now popular special utility vehicles (SUVs); it is a research result that nobody seems to want to talk about: A heavy car, like the SUV, exhibits during crash tests a deceleration of the dummy's head of about 42 g. By contrast, smaller and lighter cars exhibit only 20 g or better.[3]

This high level of exposure to head injuries has been established through experimentation on head injury criteria defined by the so-called FMVSS crash test 208. Similar types of exposure, albeit of a financial nature, exist with untested new debt instruments, particularly those of a derivative nature. Though in this chapter we will concentrate our attention on the better-known variations of fixed interest products, starting with straight and callable bonds, the reader must be aware that there are plenty of debt instruments with risk characteristics way above those we will consider.

4.2 Straight and callable bonds

Chapter 3 has explained that bonds are issued by governments, companies, institutions, and other parties. These may be investment grade (BBB or better) or non-investment grade (BB or worse, see Chapter 12); they feature a fixed or a floating rate coupon (for instance adjusted to inflation or to an index); and they may be straight (or bullet) or, alternatively, callable at issuers' choice. The percentage of bullet vs callable, fixed vs floating rate, convertible, zero-coupon, and other bond characteristics varies from market to market and year to year. As an example, Table 4.1 presents statistics from two consecutive years of bond issuance in the Grand Duchy of Luxembourg.

Table 4.1 Statistics from two years of issuance of debt instruments in Luxembourg

Type of bond	Number of issues	Year 1%	Year 2%
Straight	914	57.0	62.1
Floating rate	408	25.4	23.1
Zero-coupon	213	13.3	9.7
Convertibles	3	2.7	3.4
With warrants	26	1.6	1.7

As can be appreciated from the statistics in Table 4.1, in both years the majority of issues have been bullet bonds, but the number of floating rate debt instruments is also fairly significant. These statistics are interesting because Luxembourg is an international financial platform, competing as an off-shore for global investors' money with other known names like Jersey, Bermuda, and the Cayman Islands.

A good reason why fixed income straight bonds are favored by investors is that they are the best positioned to benefit from an upswing in the bond market, if interest rates fall. In 2002–2003 with rock-bottom interest rates for dollars, yen, pounds, and euros, 20-year bonds with a nominal rate of 6–7% have been selling at 122% or more of their issue value, providing their holders with hefty paper profits.

By contrast, floating rate and callable debt instruments did not experience significant capital appreciation. Investors must be aware that when the price of a callable bond exceeds its call price, that bond will not fully participate in any further rally. This could be expected as:

- The debt instrument becomes vulnerable to a call and,
- *If* purchased above the call price, then a loss of principal would ensue.

In addition, not all call features are the same for all issues. Different issues tend to provide alternative call provisions. Therefore, bondholders must carefully review the call features of each issue they plan to purchase (or have in their inventory), and be careful not to get confused by terminology which sometimes is twisted or obscure:

- One of the most common areas of confusion is a bond's *non-refundable* feature.
- Some investors believe that this term is synonymous with *non-callable*, but it is not.

Non-callable provisions prohibit the call of the bond for any reason until maturity; or, alternatively for a specified time. In general, the non-refundable feature only restricts the calling of the bond during a certain time period with *borrowed funds* obtained at a lower cost than the current bond – which is a cheat for the investor.

The trick is that during the non-refunding period, the company which issued the debt instrument may utilize excess cash or even funds raised through the sale of equity securities or some other holdings, to call the bonds. While this does not happen frequently, it has happened in the past – and if rates continue to decline the potential for retiring such debt through different means becomes greater.

The above-mentioned features apply to virtually all corporate debt issues, but the public utility sector presents additional concerns. Most electric utilities issue mortgage bonds under complex indentures which allow for the call of bonds under certain circumstances, and often at special redemption prices; for instance, at or near par. Of the alternative ways for electric utilities to call bonds, the three most commonly found in indentures are:

- Maintenance and replacement funds: This provision requires a company to spend a certain amount of funds (usually set by a formula) for maintenance and replacement. Should there be a deficiency of spending, cash can be deposited and at times used to retire bonds.
- Funnel sinking funds: Some utilities are allowed to calculate the gross amount of their sinking fund requirements for the total amount of debt instruments, of all

series outstanding. They can then use the total requirement and retire bonds of any series they choose.

■ Property sales: A lot of indentures provide that funds received from sale of different properties may, or even in some cases must, be used to retire bonds. Investors should therefore be very careful with their choices and acquaint themselves with the past history of different industry sectors, even better of the issuer, to avoid future unpleasant surprises.

Notice that these three ways to call bonds are being presented as an example; they are not meant to be all-inclusive. Indentures vary from company to company. In fact, even individual issues of the same company may contain different restrictions, with regard to the call feature associated to them. Therefore, it is up to the investor to:

■ Properly identify and understand the special features of bonds in his or her portfolio, and
■ Search the terms of each issue, in order to ascertain the risk of an unfavorable call.

The Luxembourg statistics presented in Table 4.1 have also shown that roughly a quarter of bond issues in that country are floating rate. It would have been more precise to call them *adjustable rate* securities, which permits one to make a finer distinction between two different types of debt instruments.

In the general case, adjustable rate bonds have interest rates that are adjusted periodically, according to a set formula, to minimize fluctuation in the principal value of investments. The maturity of such securities may be shortened under certain specified conditions.

■ *Variable rate* securities are domestic certificates of deposit which provide for the establishment of a new interest rate at predetermined dates, or whenever a specified interest rate (such as the bank prime lending rate) changes.
■ *Floating rate* securities are corporate, bank holding company, asset-backed notes, or Eurodollar certificates of deposit, with *reset* provisions similar to those for variable rate instruments.

The myriad of differences in basic type features and in provisions by indentures suggests that to properly analyze risk and return associated to debt instruments discussed in this section, as well as those presented in the following sections of the present chapter, investors need much more than a simple interest discount model which permits them to evaluate the value of a bond. The first requirement is understanding of *conditions* characterizing the debt instrument, and

■ These are not presented automatically by the broker.
■ Instead, the investor must specifically ask for them, read them, and appreciate their impact – prior to committing funds.

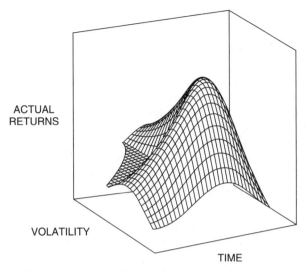

ACTUAL
RETURNS

VOLATILITY

TIME

Figure 4.1 A three-dimensional presentation permits
more variables and describes better the changing risk
and return patterns

Provided the conditions associated to a debt instrument are acceptable, the next prob-lem is that of using an interest discount model. As we will see in Chapters 7 and 9, there are plenty of yield algorithms, ranging from simple to complex. Professionals should choose a sophisticated approach able to give fairly accurate yield estimates; by contrast, a relatively simple equation would answer the average investor's 'need to know'.

In a nutshell, evaluation of the value of a bond typically takes into account the equivalent to present value of all future expected cash flows, including callable fea-tures, adjustable rate and so on. Usually, this discount rate of return required by the investor is not made up of a risk-free interest rate for the period under consideration, therefore requiring adjustment for credit risk – through a premium which reflects uncertainty connected to counterparty exposure.

A three-dimensional visualization like the one presented in Figure 4.1 is most helpful. The required return on investment (ROI) should correspond over the longer run to the cost of capital, plus risk premiums for holding debt instruments positions and a profit margin. Within this frame of reference can be tracked short- and medium-term deviations from longer-term yield targets.

4.3 Zero-coupon bonds

From the investor's viewpoint, zero-coupon bonds have certain advantages over coupon-bearing bonds. One of them is that they have only one payment at final matu-rity, relieving their holders of the problem of reinvesting coupon payments. They also respond to the need of investors who wish to manage future payment flows exactly. On the downside, investors who depend on regular coupon payments are being deprived of them through zero-coupon.

For instance, zero-coupon instruments may serve the case of insurance benefits or of a pension plan which has to be paid on a one-off basis on a fixed date. They may also be attractive to domestic investors from a tax perspective. Typically, the investment income which is relevant to personal income tax, and tax on interest income, is ascertained from the difference between the buying and selling price, or *redemption account*.

By buying a zero-coupon bond with the appropriate maturity, or by selling it, investors can optimize their tax bill, by allowing investment income to fall in a period which is favorable to them in terms of tax treatment. In a way, they are capitalizing on a tax deferral effect which is embedded into the instrument. There is also the fact that with coupon-bearing bonds an accurate evaluation of effective yield can be made, at time of investment, only by using imputed assumptions concerning the reinvestment of coupon payments.

- Since the reinvestment yield is not known in advance, the yield to maturity calculated at the time of purchase will deviate from actual yield, which can only be determined ex-post.
- By contrast, with zero-coupon bonds the yield computed at time of purchase will also be actually realized, if the bond is held until maturity.

In computational terms, in the case of zero-coupon bonds the duration (see Chapter 10) is always equal to the residual maturity. Therefore, its price reacts a good deal more to interest rate changes than the price of coupon-bearing bonds of same residual maturity. The latter have a shorter duration on account of the recurring interest payments.

Because there is both an upside and a downside, opinions are divided in regard to the market benefits of zero-coupons. The pros say that, because such bonds are available over a maturity spectrum, they provide the market with a term structure which exists in addition to the yield-to-maturity structure of coupon bonds. For comparative purposes, Figure 4.2 shows two yield curves, one each for:

- Estimated zero-coupon yield curve, and
- Yield-to-maturity for coupon-bearing bonds.

Both are presented with residual maturity of up to 20 years (more on yield curves in Chapters 7 and 9). Zero-coupon yield curves can be computed theoretically on the basis of data on coupon bonds. However, the actual zero-coupon yield will usually deviate from the estimated values, depending on:

- Maturity, and
- Interest rate trend.

As an example from market reaction, when interest rates are expected to rise, demand will be higher. Because zero-coupon bonds show greater convexity (see Chapter 10) than coupon bonds, in case of a decline in yields the relative price increase of zero-coupon debt instruments is higher than for a coupon bond.

This also has a counterpart. If there is a rise in yields, the relative fall in the price of a zero-coupon debt instrument is less than that of a coupon-bearing instrument.

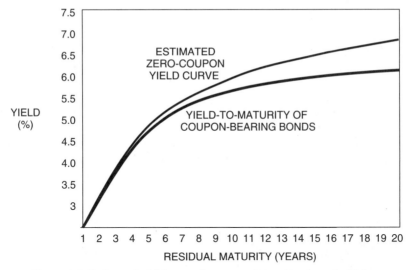

Figure 4.2 Estimated yield curve for zero-coupon bonds and yield-to-maturity for coupon-bearing debt instruments

Knowledgeable investors use this asymmetry to help themselves in managing their assets. (See also the use of zero-coupons as proxy in a Bloomberg mode, in section 4.5.)

As the aforementioned features suggest, zero-coupon bonds are particularly attractive to investors who are prepared not only to take risks, but also to manage them in an able manner. The interest sensitivity of portfolios can be handled rather effectively with zero-coupons because, given the same maturity, they have a longer duration and hence greater convexity than coupon-bearing bonds. On the other hand, zero-coupon debt instruments require greater risk management skill than the classical bonds.

A variation of zero-coupon bonds is the liquid yield option note (LYON), which is a convertible instrument (see section 4.4). The concept behind zero-convertible bonds is that investors buy it at a large discount from face value. It gives zero interest payments until it matures, typically in 15–20 years, when it is redeemed at face value, but it can be converted into stock at any time.

The profit concept underpinning liquid option notes is that if the stock goes up, the LYON becomes a lot more valuable. But more than investors, it is issuers and traders who love them. For brokerage houses, these instruments can mean handsome fees. Issuing corporations are interested in them because:

- They raise money from the public at below-market rate, and
- They are able to defer the interest payments for years.

On the other hand, this particular product is not universally appreciated. Critics say buyers can be disappointed while from the issuer's point of view it is almost a no-lose proposition. For instance, to profit with LYONS, the equity of the issuers has to keep going up at a rapid rate. And there is always the risk that the company issuing a LYON may file for protection from bankruptcy under Chapter 11.

4.4 Convertible bonds

Convertible bonds are hybrid securities involving both debt and equity. They pay a periodic coupon but also contain an embedded equity option. This permits the investor to convert them into a pre-established amount of shares of the company issuing the convertible bond.

Convertible bonds are not to be confused with bonds with warrants, which are also hybrid securities but consist of an underlying bond which pays a coupon and have as well an attached warrant allowing the investor to exercise his or her right regarding a pre-established amount of shares of the issuer. This warrant is often equity-based, and it can be detached and traded separately from the bond.

Exchangeable bonds are another variety that can be swapped for a company's shares and cash, if the company's share price rises above a certain level by a given date. This knock-on feature sometimes leads to gaming the market. Therefore, it is not surprising that, in Tokyo, Japan's Securities and Exchange Surveillance Commission (SESC) has focused its investigations on large sell orders placed by brokerages in an effort to drive down the share price of companies in which they hold exchangeable bonds, to avoid reimbursement.

Several banks have been referred by SESC to Japan's Financial Services Agency (FSA) for penalties related to this practice. Nevertheless, leaving aside issues connected to lust, greed and capital market manipulations, at the positive end convertible bonds offer what several experts say with some hype is 'the best of both worlds':

- Steady income like conventional bonds, and
- Potential capital gains to the investor, like stocks.

That's the thesis of the 'pros', which is not bought by the convertible bond's critics. Indeed, critics suggest that there is a different way of looking at the issue of convertible bonds – examining them as a class of their own. As such, convertible bonds are risky investments, characterized by:

- Interest-rate volatility
- Equity price fluctuations, and
- Changes in foreign exchange rates (for foreign issues).

Notice that these three bullets are not negatives in all cases, but investors must be aware of the message which they carry, and be able to exercise timely and effective risk control. As and when this *is* the case, convertibles may have appeal, particularly at a time when many traditional gauges of global stock values indicate that normal equity is expensive – though this is often factored into the price of convertible bonds.

In terms of their mechanics, convertible bonds are issued on large as well as on small capitalizations, and with a few exceptions, they are found in nearly every major market around the world. Convertible bonds have been particularly popular in Japan. In other markets, outside Japan and the United States, there are strict rules on how such securities are sold to the public, making it difficult to popularize them.

Though design characteristics may vary from one market to the other, and from one issue to the next, some of the terms of classical convertible bonds are fairly similar the world over. For instance, the securities are typically issued as 5–10-year bonds with interest rates that are 1–2 percentage points (100 to 200 basis points), lower than yields on bullet, fixed rate corporate bonds.

- To attract buyers and to compensate for the lower rate, investors are allowed to exchange such bonds for a fixed amount of the issuer's stock if its price climbs.
- While prices on a classic convertible are influenced by interest rate trends, often appreciating as rates fall, they are more sensitive to changes in the underlying shares' value.

To get the most from convertible bonds, investors must pay close attention to the prospects for the underlying shares. They must also consider whether they are protected from calls for redemption. For instance, on older convertible bonds with particularly high interest rates, issuers may be tempted to redeem the debt instrument and refinance at lower rates, if terms allow it.

On the other hand, the fixed yield of a convertible bond sees to it that it falls less than the underlying stock, when the price of the latter declines. But since a convertible bond is typically issued for a sum that is 15–25% higher than corresponding stock value, it often moves more slowly as the stock appreciates.

As a general rule of thumb, investors should avoid issues that sell for more than 30% over par in the United States and Europe, and issues that sell for more than 40% over par in Japan. *Par* is equivalent to the value of money, or principal, investors receive when bonds mature. When bonds sell over par by a large margin, the yield will probably be insignificant when compared with stock dividends, therefore eliminating downside protection.

Investors should also be wary of certain covenants unfavorable to them. An example is US, Japanese, and European bonds that can only be converted profitably if shares rise more than 20%. Even in a rising market, in other times than bubble years, stock prices are unlikely to catch up with high bond premiums, thereby eliminating the chance for capital gains.

What has been outlined in the preceding paragraphs is part and parcel of the investor's risk control systems and procedures. Models can allow estimation of the likely effects on portfolio positions of relatively small market changes. But since convertible bonds are a derivative instrument, for whole portfolio risk due to large market movements standard tests of exposure are not enough. Investors will be well advised to do stress testing.[4]

4.5 The Bloomberg model for portfolio value-at-risk

Bloomberg has developed a model known as Portfolio Value-at-Risk Report (PVAR),[5] which calculates worst-case risk by first mapping a given portfolio to a new structure. This consists only of *primitive assets*, which are the assets whose volatilities and correlations are estimated daily by Bloomberg.

According to its developer, the Portfolio Value-at-Risk Report can be used with both bonds and equities. Its mapping of callable bonds is to the same primitive assets as bullet bonds distinguishing benchmark-maturity of 3-month, 6-month, and so on; and using as proxy zero-coupon bonds.

Because cash flows of callable bonds are not fixed, and depend on the yield curve, they cannot be mapped in a simple way like the cash flows of bullet bonds. For this reason, Bloomberg's PVAR maps the change in price of a callable bond as a function of a parallel shift in the yield curve. This approach incorporates:

- An option adjusted spread (OAS) duration with linear component, and
- An OAS-convexity model with quadratic component.

PVAR addresses 16 maturities on the yield curve, and therefore the yield curve's shift must itself be mapped to these 16 primitive assets. This is accomplished by generating a fictitious par bond, having approximately the same duration as the original callable bond.

Because the parallel shift in the yield curve is not a primitive asset, modeling the dependence on the yield curve is not enough. Duration and convexity of this proxy bond relate its price to shifts in the yield curve. Since the proxy is a bullet bond, it becomes possible to map its cash flows to the benchmark-maturity, zero-coupon (see section 4.3) primitive assets.

The careful reader will appreciate the sophistication characterizing component parts of this model, as well as the need for hypotheses characterizing the sequential steps which have been taken. Hypotheses are being made particularly in connection to:

- Price change of the callable bond, as a function of a parallel shift in the yield curve
- Proxy par bond as a function of yield curve shift
- Par bond as a function of the returns on its cash flow, and
- Returns on the callable bond's cash flow, in function of returns on the benchmark-maturity primitive asset's cash flow.

Taken together, these sequential steps constitute a model of the callable bond's price change as a function of returns on primitive assets. For currency risk purposes, a dual-currency bond is handled by using two yield curves and the implied forward exchange rate(s). This is largely based on a parity relationship.

PVAR calculates the partial derivative of the bond price with respect to foreign exchange rate of the equity, using a simplified approach. The model assumes that the only effect of foreign exchange rate on convertible bond price (see section 4.4) is in converting the equity price to the bond's currency. Other indirect effects of changes in foreign exchange rate are not accounted for, because they are considered to be small compared with the aforementioned direct effect.

Bloomberg suggests that modeling the market risk of equity in PVAR is simpler than modeling the market risk of cash flows. The equity security is mapped to the equity index by using the volatility of the equity, through the equity price's sensitivity to the index. The equity also needs to be mapped to cash in order to preserve the market value of the original security. Through volatilities and correlations of the primitive assets, PVAR computes the value at risk of the original portfolio.

4.6   Junk bonds and credit derivatives

Junk bonds is the name Wall Street has attached to credit risk-exposed, high yielding, often unsecured debt graded BB or lower by independent ratings services. In the not-too-distant past, debt instruments below investment grade were issued by the so-called 'fallen angels'. These were rather well-to-do companies which had fallen into hard times:

- Lost their credit qualification
- Found it difficult to secure bank loans, and
- Came to the capital market for financing, paying significantly higher interest than going rate.

But their bankruptcy record was low, something in the level of 2%, as Michael Milken found in the early 1980s in his research. Starting with the 1984 Drexel Burnham High Yield Bond Conference in Beverly Hills, Milken launched the credo that: 'It is profitable to believe what others doubt.'[6] There were many takers and the market for junk bonds boomed, but this tremendously changed the fallen angels default probability for the worse.

Today, one of the definitions of junk bonds is that of risk capital masquerading as debt financing. Non-investment grade debt instruments are bought by investors willing to ignore substandard credit ratings in exchange for better yields. Their holders also bet on a permeability between the BBB and BB compartments of independent rating agencies, but without adequately considering the downside possibility.

Warren Buffett dismisses junk bonds as weeds priced as flowers.[7] The way *The Economist* has it, it is hard to think of a surer way to lose money than buying lowly-rated bonds by US companies at their present yields. When this chapter was written in November 2004:

- The credit spread of junk bonds was a mere 220 basis points.
- This was way down from a peak of nearly 1000 basis points in March 2002, when their default likelihood stood at 10.5% in a year.

True enough, risk-taking is inseparable from lending and investors can profit more by taking credit risk than market risk. That is precisely what debt is, and just as precisely what credit is. As cannot be repeated too often, every loan, even if fully secured, has embedded in it a certain level of speculation. With the democratization of lending and socialization of risk in the banking business (see Chapter 1) the element of speculation was not removed; only its costs were shifted.

- Junk bonds are one of the engines of this shift.
- Credit derivatives are another, more modern example of risk shifting.[8]

'The market with credit derivatives might become FUBAR [fouled up beyond all recognition] if there are many bankruptcies in manufacturing and merchandising,' said one analyst during my research, adding that 'There is considerable speculation over if and when this will happen; but it might happen.' Two decades of experience with junk bonds demonstrate that, indeed, it does happen and imprudent investors pay the bill.

Plenty of companies are in the perilous situation of huge debt and overcapacity. Some financial analysts are worried that many loans which have found their way into the credit derivatives food chain are way down in creditworthiness rating. In the simplest of terms, the trouble with highly leveraged companies, whether through junk bonds or through loans, is that:

- They owe too much, and
- They own too little.

Japanese firms, for example, are deeply indebted, with an average debt/equity ratio of 4 to 1. This situation might be bearable if everyone did not know about it, but it is wretchedly hard to fix reliable numbers that permit investors to watch credit risk carefully. In the United States, the unraveling of weak companies in the financial industry started in 1985 with the collapse of firms such as Drysdale Securities, Lombard-Wall, E.S.M. Government Securities, and Bevill, Bresler & Schuman Asset Management.

While the bankruptcy of these brokerage companies menaced the apparently safe world of government bond trading, hundreds of millions of dollars have been lost by banks, pension funds, municipalities, and state agencies under the impression that they were making perfectly safe investments backed by government securities. All this is part of the process that brought to the market the torrent of junk bonds, made Michael Milken a billionaire, and propelled Drexel Burnham Lambert to stardom – until it crashed.

The up, down, and up again of junk bonds (till a new down) makes an interesting case study not only on its own merits but also, if not primarily, because it serves as proxy and prognosticator of what will happen in the credit derivatives market – only on a much bigger scale. In terms of management insight and foresight, the common element is inability, or unwillingness, to study the after-effects of a financial instrument that:

- Leaves the niche market where it was born, and
- Rolls on to assume global proportions.

Absent from the simplistic algorithm of the 2% bankruptcy rate of the fallen angels has been the fact that, just as a stream of travelers change something of the land through which they pass, a swarm of traders and a torrent of trades have a major impact on default statistics. With access to nearly unlimited funds through junk bond issues, the market for low credit rating debt instruments gets magnified, with such players as:

- Corporate raiders
- Buyout specialists,
- Fast-track businessmen, and
- A minority of serious entrepreneurs with limited finances.

All these folks could pick up money to spend in pursuit of their goals in the junk bond market. In the 1980s, for investors, as well as for banks, this was uncharted territory. Milken and his Drexel associates took the pro-debt cause much further than commercial and retail banks alone would ever have dared to do.

- Junk bonds were highly speculative not from the moment they were issued, but after their market's fall.
- Quite similarly, credit derivatives became highly speculative after insurers and other investors went for them in droves.

This becomes a self-feeding cycle as more professionals join the business bandwagon and hybrid instruments come into the mainstream. Since the mid-1990s, billions in junk bond collateralized obligations have been issued, underwritten by investment banks like Morgan Stanley, Goldman Sachs and Credit Suisse First Boston. Exactly how much of that already has gone down the drain is not known, but analysts estimate that real losses and paper losses to investors such as hedge funds and insurance companies stand at many billion of dollars.

4.7 High-high risk bonds

Milken-type junk bonds are not the only high credit risk game in the global financial village. Another even higher bet on lack of creditworthiness have been the *high-high bonds*, a term coined in Japan where they originated (by all evidence) at the beginning of 1994. In just six months after their introduction Nikko Securities alone underwrote around 300 billion yen of them (US$3 billion).

High-high bonds got this name because they have a high coupon, giving the impression that their yield is high. But they are also sold at a high price, which makes the real yield lower than average. Not only Japanese entities but also the World Bank and Sweden were among the borrowers that took advantage of this cheap source of money at investors' expense (see also the discussion on Samurai bonds, in section 4.10).

Subsequently, some of Nikko's rivals have claimed that mutual funds run by its investment management affiliate were forced to swallow plenty of high-high bonds. Others suggested that the indifference of small investors to risk explains why such high credit risk bonds can be sold. Indeed it seems that smaller Japanese investors, including:

- Regional banks, and
- Municipal pension funds

are not too fussy about what they buy. They simply don't look at the bonds' overall return (plenty of other investors follow the same rotten policy). Moreover, these yen-denominated bonds look relatively attractive to Japan's small investors because, with interest rates near zero, returns on other investments are even lower – given Japan's dismal economic performance from 1990 to 2004.

Junk bonds, high-high bonds, and other superlatives fail, and since this has become known, sharp operators have tried to make a profit by repackaging them. In the late 1990s and the first couple of years of the 21st century, a new venture has been promoted: buying up a lot of bonds issued by companies in trouble, and turning them into new instruments with sugar-coating. Debt by telecommunications, health care, and other companies facing troubles is the raw material. The ingenuity is in the fact that:

- Even if all the underlying bonds carry junk ratings
- The 'new' securities offer investors a range of risk options.

As with high-high bonds, this trick seems to work. Investors, even some of those generally risk-averse, have bought 'investment-grade slices' of repackaged offerings, giving them first claim on cash from restructured junk bonds, but lower interest rates. Others took a bigger gamble and bought slices with junk-junk ratings at higher interest rates. Some even brought the riskiest slice, offering interest rates of 20% and more, known as *toxic waste* in the market, which were not even rated.

Private investors, pension funds, insurance companies and many others were caught in that game. American Express is an example. Flush with money from insurance and annuities premiums paid by its customers, it plunged into this very high risk market. Not only did the firm buy plenty of securities from other issuers, but it also began packaging its own securitized junk bonds for sale through other investment firms, keeping some of the toxic part for its own account.

Experts at Wall Street suggested that American Express entered into this sort of security in roughly 60 separate deals, including 12 created internally in exchange for management fees. Yet, the company has plenty of experience with losses resulting from dubious financial deals and questionable instruments. In 1989, Shearson Lehman Hutton Holdings, an American Express subsidiary, suffered millions of dollars in losses on loans partially backed by junk bonds.

4.8   The stripping of bonds

Stripping stands for Separate Trading of Registered Interest and Principal of Securities (STRIPS). The stripping of a bond implies the separation of the certificate representing the principal amount from that associated to the interest coupons. Following this, principal strip and individual coupon strips are traded separately. In financial terms, these are zero-coupon bonds with residual (staggered) maturities. A Treasury bill, guild or Bund running, for instance, for 10 years may be broken down into a:

■ Stripped bond (principal strip), as a zero-coupon bond with a maturity of 10 years, and
■ Ten coupon strips as zero-coupon bonds, with maturities ranging from 1 to 10 years.

Stripping of a bond also implies the corresponding possibility of reconstructing the underlying original bond from the coupon strips and the principal strip. Such reconstruction of the bond is a prerequisite of arbitrage between the underlying bond and its components.

Theoretically, it is possible for the entire issue of a bond to be broken down into strips. In practice, however, this will probably not happen because quite likely there will be demand for the underlying bond in the market, not only for its strips. Typically, coupon strips with the same maturity are grouped together under a single securities identification number, with the same price and yield. This is done:

■ Irrespective of the bond from which they are stripped, and
■ Irrespective of its coupon.

The result is that the differing coupons will no longer be of relevance. The reason for combining coupon strips of the same maturity is to achieve liquidity that is as high as possible, throughout the entire maturity spectrum, which may range beyond the limits of the above example – such as up to 30 years.

Still, ultimately, it is up to the market players themselves to determine liquidity in the individual segments. Therefore, for any practical purpose, the financial market sets the price for STRIPS, and anticipation of market response is instrumental in influencing stripping activities, as well as in the bond's reconstruction.

Moreover, *synthetic bonds* could be constructed if principal strips are rebundled either with other principal strips, or with coupon strips of the same maturity. But in the interests of correct disclosure of debt, regulatory authorities are not looking with favor towards this sort of synthetic bond.

While, in the general case, the Group of Ten reserve banks are not averse to stripping, because this tends to create investment opportunities in all maturity categories, they are concerned about complex arrangements that make it difficult to appreciate embedded risk. They are also concerned about possible scams that might be engineered through stripping.

Moreover, one should bear in mind in all this the fact that new structured instruments can be made from STRIPS if one is careful enough to choose two parts that appear to be the same value but actually are not. Frank Partnoy[9] describes such an instrument where:

- The big value part is called the *premium* piece, and
- The other part is the *discount* piece.

The trade to which Partnoy makes reference (an instrument specifically designed for Japanese investors by Morgan Stanley) requires both a premium and a discount part. In the case of this particular trade, the more valuable premium piece was called an *IOette*. The less valuable discount piece was a zero-coupon, simply representing a single payment at some defined future date. Design-wise, however, the IOette has been much more complex, a sort of collateralized mortgage obligation (CMO), based in mortgage payments by house owners.

The name IOette comes from the common practice of stripping mortgages by interest and principal. IO is the *interest-only* part with a claim on the home owners' payments of interest. The principal only (PO) part has a claim on just the payments of principal. The problem with IOettes is that they are among the most volatile CMOs. As such, they have caused big unexpected losses to their holders. Because the IOette blends IOs with a little bit of POs:

- A new structured instrument can mix these interest and principal payments in a way fitting some special purpose, and
- If one mixes IOs and POs according to a self-devised formula, one can create new IOettes from a pool of mortgages.

In most cases, however, the greater value of IOettes comes from the IO part. Because it uses only a very small amount of PO, when the investment bank makes an IOette it is left with lots of PO, which it needs to hold separately. This leads to interesting but risky structured instrument properties.

Because its interest payments are huge in relation to the principal, an IOette has a very high price relative to its nominal amount. Since the IOette has only a little bit of principal, the bond's interest payments are great by comparison to the PO face amount. In theory, there is no limit to the size of an IOette coupon, except that the regulators might find out about this asymmetric risk and become inquisitive, which creates a practical limitation.

If an IOette with $1.000 face amount paid interest of $800 a year for, say, 20 years, *then* the investor would receive $16.000 of interest in total, though one might receive interest for a shorter time period if the underlying mortgages were prepaid. As a result of such a highly skewed cost and benefit margin, an IOette with a $1000 face value might be worth many times more than that amount.

The possibility for scams comes from the fact that the aforementioned highly skewed cost and benefit makes the IOette a first-class candidate for twisting the P&L statement through imaginary, if not outright fake, profits. On the one hand, the zero-coupon strip qualifies as the discount part, as it is worth much less than its face amount. On the other hand, taken together IOettes and zeros become a sort of modern financial alchemy which can deceive practically everybody – even the experts.

4.9   Brady bonds and Rubin bonds

Named after former US Treasury secretary Nicholas Brady, who invented them in the late 1980s, Brady bonds represent the restructured bad debt of Latin American and other emerging countries that overborrowed from US credit institutions all the way to default. These bonds were designed to prevent financial meltdown for lenders and borrowers:

- Bradys are normally collateralized by US zero-coupon bonds of various maturities.
- Hence, their principal is guaranteed but most bonds' coupons are not.

The algorithm is that if a country cannot make its interest payments, investors can at least collect 100% of their principal when the bonds come due. The risk is that investors lose out on interest, and they have tied up their money for years instead of putting it into a yield paying investment. That's the downside.

Because defaulting Brady bonds no longer pay interest, their value in the secondary market plummets to only a fraction of their face value. This makes the Brady bonds market highly volatile, reacting to moves in US bond prices and especially to bad news from emerging nations, such as the Mexican peso devaluation of late 1994.

In spite of the aforementioned risks, insurance companies and other institutional investors as well as hedge funds, have been willing to take that chance. According to the management of US open-end mutual funds dedicated to emerging-market debt, Brady bonds have gone mainstream and they are trading cross-country.

In September 1996, for instance, JP Morgan launched an issue for German investors based on Ecuadorian Brady bonds but denominated in German marks. The rationale for this offer was that investors 'wanted' exposure to exotic Ecuadorian debt without the currency risk of a dollar-denominated asset. That DM150 million seven-year issue:

- Carried a coupon of 12.25%, and
- It was structured by swapping the dollar cash flows from the Ecuadorian debt into German marks.

Rubin bonds, named after the US Treasury secretary for the majority of the Clinton years, are a different ballgame; they are inflation-indexed bonds touted as risk-free to be sold to millions of not-so-sophisticated investors. Yet while indexed bonds hold certain virtues, they also present major risks.

By issuing long-term bonds that guarantee a fixed interest rate over inflation the politicians think they can finance the government's huge debt at lower interest rates. Investors may like the concept because they tend to believe they will be able to stash away savings for retirement without having to worry about inflation – but this is precisely the problem with the Rubin bonds.

Several experts think that, in the longer run, diluting the discipline of inflation worries for individuals is a big mistake. Inflation risk is inseparable from bond investing, as we will see in Chapter 8. Back in the 1970s, when most salaries were linked to cost-of-living allowances (COLAS), people were theoretically insulated from inflation. But the practical result has been that:

- Inflation fed on itself, and
- The high borrowing costs were borne by taxpayers.

Investors, too, have to lose. British investors in inflation-indexed bonds have lost out in a big way. Between 1985 and 1995, indexed bonds provided a good annual return in nominal amounts, but because of high inflation the British pound fell like a rock. As a matter of principle, inflation-indexed bonds mark a wholesale transfer of risk from investors to taxpayers if the government has to pay higher rates – and it does not really give investors much of an advantage.

If public demand for inflation-indexed bonds runs as high as some experts predict when inflation picks up again, *then* government-sponsored inflation indexed bonds could turn into another unfunded liability for the government. This different sort of socialization of risk adds up to the woes characterizing social security, health care, and federal pensions' deficits.

As an example of the acceleration effect, France (and the French taxpayer) suffered a debacle with gold-price-indexed bonds offered in 1972 by Giscard d'Estaing, while the future president of the Republic was still minister of finance. When the money became due, the French taxpayer had to cough up about 500% of the bonds' original worth – with the few profiting at the expense of the many.

4.10   Chameleon bonds, Samurai bonds, and unwanted consequences

As the last example in section 4.9 helps to demonstrate, there can be unexpected consequences with new bond versions, which have not been thoroughly studied in terms of their aftermath. This is not a one-off phenomenon, but a case of frequent occurrence, particularly at times of rapid acceleration of investors' appetite for debt instruments.

This acceleration is shown by the curve in Figure 4.3, representing the rapid rise of credit debt in the Unites States over nearly five decades. In the global economy, both governments and companies capitalize on the leverage made possible through rapid increase in investors' appetite for other people's and entities' debt, particularly in liquid markets.

Liquidity and the growth in market appeal of debt instruments correlate. The most common solution to enhance liquidity, dealers suggest, is public issuance with buy-back guarantees. Sovereigns of the Group of Ten can offer that. Others capitalize on idiosyncratic structures such as chameleon and neutralized notes.

- *Chameleon* bonds allow issuers to change the structure of the note according to investor perception of market risk.
- *Neutralized* notes are sold by the dealer to a broad base of different investors.

Given the freedom to develop new debt instruments, it is not surprising that a variety of specifications prevails. Some are fairly settled, such as basic buy-back guarantees; others are still in the developmental stage, as new features are added to the bonds, which means that their exposure is fairly unknown.

New futures may look attractive to buyers, but when their risks are not well known there may be a lot of unwanted consequences. As an example, one of the popular but highly risky fixed income securities is the *Samurai bond*. These are

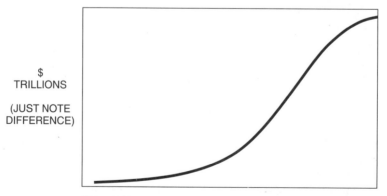

Figure 4.3 The rapid rise of credit market debt in the United States, 1955–2004

yen-denominated, issued in Japan by foreign governments and foreign companies in reflection of the fact that with rock-bottom yen interest rates lasting for a decade and a half:

- Different foreigners have been raising money at trivial interest, through the Samurais, and
- They are helped by big Japanese securities firms that have brought borrowers to this market.

The Samurai market experienced a fast growth in the 1994 to 1997 timeframe. For instance, in the year to 31 March 1995, foreigners issued bonds worth 1.3 trillion yen (US$12 billion) and this grew to 3.8 trillion yen (nearly $33 billion) in the year ending 31 March 1997.

The irony is that few of these borrowers actually wanted to borrow yen. Most wanted dollars. But with the trivially low yen interest rates it has been much cheaper to borrow yen and swap the proceeds into dollars than to borrow dollars directly (till the dollar, too, reached a 46-year low interest rate). The issuers of Samurai bonds capitalized on the fact that most investors have no idea of the bonds' true worth, because they are financial newcomers. Moreover,

- Samurais are not listed on an exchange, so there is no official price for them, and
- The only real secondary market is provided by foreign firms, who have been profiting nicely, not by Japanese issuers.

Two sorts of issuer, each associated with different types of risk, dominate this market. The one is emerging countries, which have raised billions worth of Samurais at the expense of Japanese investors – who probably don't know that most of these bonds are not even deemed worthy of investment-grade rating by Moody's and Standard & Poor's.

The other major issuer in the Samurai market is richer, more creditworthy countries and their companies. As an example, in the first quarter of 1997 there have been issued 2.7 trillion yen ($24 billion) worth of Samurai bonds. This has been a 2671% increase from two years earlier, explained by the fact that as the bait caught unsophisticated Japanese investors, many issuers, companies and sovereigns, could profit.

Knowledgeable analysts think that Samurai bonds are the nearest thing to junk bonds, and there is the added risk of the whole Samurai market coming down in flames. In 2003 and 2004 interest rates finally started rising in Japan, and the whole Samurai investment gamble could be turned on its head.

In 2004 interest rates are also starting to rise in the United States, propelled by a pick-up in consumer prices (see Chapter 8), and this means other complex debt constructs, too, may come unstuck. At Wall Street experts say there will be no repetition of the 1994 bonds debacle because the Fed learned a lesson and will not raise interest rates too rapidly. This may be true, but another crucial element is the unwinding of fairly complex bond positions in the mortgage-backed and other bond securities markets as, for instance, emerging market debt.

■ Unwinding of complex transactions always affects in a significant way the rest of the credit markets.

Bond traders in droves have hedged their positions by shorting Treasury bonds to buy other fixed-income securities. When nearly everybody tries to liquidate the same positions, particularly leveraged ones, liquid markets turn to illiquid with disastrous effects. Moreover:

■ Portfolio managers who own these bonds on margin meet their margin calls by selling what they can sell, namely Treasuries.

With few buyers to take out the sellers in instruments and markets under stress, prices simply go down sharply. The question astute financial analysts have been asking as the dust of the bonds earthquake of 1994 settles is: 'Will further pressure be put on the bond market?' The answer hinged on the following queries.

■ How fast, how far the Federal reserve will go in raising interest rates?
■ How many more highly leveraged portfolios of various kinds of bonds are yet to be unwound?
■ How much potential these have to put further pressure on the entire credit market?
■ How many brokerage firms' trading desks are going to cut back their bond positions, and further pressure on the bond market?
■ Will investors who lost their appetite for buying bonds now start to sell bonds, putting the bond market under further stress?

A different but related question is what will make investors and speculators come back to the bond market. For instance, what is the threshold that short-term interest rates must reach before bond market participants can be satisfied? And what is the level of confidence below which it will be virtually impossible to make money in stocks and bonds?

Notes

1 Joseph Wechsberg, *The Merchant Bankers*, Pocket Books/Simon and Schuster, New York, 1966.
2 D.N. Chorafas, *Managing Risk in the New Economy*, New York Institute of Finance, New York, 2001.
3 *European Automotive Design*, April 2004.
4 D.N. Chorafas, *Stress Testing: Risk Management Strategies for Extreme Events*, Euromoney, London, 2003.
5 The VAR model has been discussed in Chapter 1. It will come into perspective again in Chapter 14.
6 James Grant, *Money of the Mind*, Farrar Strauss Giroux, New York, 1992.
7 *The Economist*, 6 November 2004.
8 D.N. Chorafas, *Credit Derivatives and the Management of Risk*, New York Institute of Finance, New York, 2000.
9 Frank Partnoy, *F.I.A.S.C.O.: The Truth About High Finance*, Profile Books, London, 1997.

5 Choosing bonds

5.1 Introduction

The apple-pie and motherhood principle of the investment industry is that having in one's portfolio different types of securities, which essentially means practicing diversification, helps in reducing risk. If one falls in value, others may rise in value at the same time, potentially making up for some of the loss. The way such logic goes, this should guide the hand of investors in choosing bonds. Or, isn't it quite so?

Starting with the fundamentals, during periods of volatility, a portfolio that includes investments in both equities and debt instruments may not decline in value as much as one that is focused only on stocks or only on bonds. At the same time, however, effective diversification requires much more than just adding different investments to one's portfolio. On the bonds' side, for instance, it will be wise to differentiate among different types of debt investments – government and corporate bonds, for example.

Often, though not always, government debt is a rather conservative investment option, *if* backed by full faith and high credit of the issuing sovereign. But also government bonds offer lower yields than those of other issuers, therefore the portfolio's rate of return will tend to be low.

Usually, corporate bonds pay higher yields than government debt, but they are also riskier than the latter. For instance, credit risk may be high, as with junk bonds, because the issuer company may not be able to continue paying interest and on maturity repay principal to the investor. Moreover, the issuance of corporate bonds tends to be concentrated on a relatively small number of industries.

Among corporates, frequent debt instrument issuers are the motor vehicle and air transport industries, followed by telecommunications, information technology, and the energy sector. Some of these industries, like air transport, are risky because they are too much leveraged, their products are aging or alternatively too new and untested. In other cases, mismanagement has taken the upper hand, and for other reasons.

Investors should therefore carefully weigh advantage and disadvantages of one alternative against the other – for instance, more attractive income against the downside of greater counterparty risk. Up to a point, protection of principal can be obtained by concentrating on higher credit quality of debt instruments, and by practicing a policy of diversification among:

- Bond issuers
- Maturity dates, and
- Quality ratings.

This brings into perspective some of the criteria regarding choices to be made, which indeed go well beyond government debt and corporates. There are many segments in the bond market, and all of them are affected by different factors. Neither will these segments always perform the same way over a longer timeframe. A dynamic financial market has many twists of which the investor must be aware.

As the careful reader will recall from Chapter 3, no matter which may be the debt instrument, and who is its issuer, an investor is a creditor of the issuing entity, *not* an owner like a stockholder. The upside is that the bondholder must be paid any principal and interest due, before stockholders receive any dividends. But to assure themselves their investment is worth while, investors should carefully watch four most significant characteristics of a debt instrument:

- Quality, characterized by the issuer's creditworthiness (see Chapter 12)
- Interest rates and their margin over projected inflation (see Chapters 7 and 8)
- Yield, which represents the return one expects to receive on his or her investment (see Chapter 9)
- Maturity or how long the investor must wait before the issuer repays (see Chapter 10).

The issuer of debt instruments should also observe certain principles which are fundamental to business success: being a low cost producer helps in having money to pay one's debt, and being steady innovators sustains market appeal.

In the case studies they conducted with their graduate students, Dr Neil Jacoby and Dr Louis Sorel, my professors of business policy at UCLA in the early 1950s, downgraded those of the participants to their seminars who came up with financial issues as the *salient* problem. Sorel used to say that a company can always find financing *if*:

- It has first-class management
- Is in control of its costs, and
- Has products appealing to the market.

Corporate mismanagement, high cost structures, and product obsolescence were at the top of the list in salient problems for corporate failures. Indeed, time and again industrial history shows that well-managed companies win by delivering products and services that many others can also deliver, by providing them cheaper, faster, more efficiently. The alternative model is seizing market leadership by innovating to create unique value, new technology, and new intellectual capital. In this case, innovation is the differentiator which gives these companies an edge in the market and provides the cash flow necessary to face the entity's debt obligations.

5.2 Investors can never be too careful

A couple of decades ago choosing a good investment-grade bond was relatively simple. Today, there are scores of basic, hybrid, and derivative debt instruments masquerading as 'bonds', as well as simple bonds from frail issuers. As a result, the act of investing in them faces many pitfalls. Those investors keep ahead of the curve, who:

- Do their homework
- Subject all claims to rigorous research, and
- Exercise great care in making bond choices.

Beyond the message carried by these three points, the investor should be asking: 'Are my skills right for the challenges I am facing in the selection of investments and in the management of my assets?' If the answer is 'No!', *then* he or she should get the proper training to be able to reach a factual, documented, and *independent* investment selection decision.

Selection of the proper investment is a function of market factors but also, if not primarily, of the investor's own income-and-risk profile. It is also part of the art of portfolio management – a task to which this book hopes to contribute.

Ego-rich personalities end up with great disappointments in the investments they do. The *ego* is the wrong sort of counselor. The right counselor is humility, and attention to detail. Serious investors are always interested to read the fine print of the issuer's claims, understand what it says, and challenge even the most 'obvious' statements or 'positive' market opinions. Here are two practical examples on how something which looks 'obviously good' may be *awfully wrong*:

■ Fame, based on smoke and mirrors, and
■ Quantitative information that might have been massaged.

A high-flyer of the go-go 1990s has been WorldCom, one of the largest US carriers. Its stock was reaching for the stars and practically no investment advisor questioned the dependability of its debt instruments. But the company was over-leveraged and burdened by billions of dollars in debt from an acquisition spree and multiple fraud. In July 2002, WorldCom sought Chapter 11 bankruptcy protection.

■ Equity holders lost practically all of their capital, and
■ Much of the bondholder debt was converted to equity, following the bankruptcy.

As part of its emergence from bankruptcy protection, MCI, the renamed WorldCom, settled fraud charges by the Securities and Exchange Commission (SEC) and paid $750 million cash and stock. Subsequently the SEC asked MCI for information regarding state tax shelters; and in early July 2004, two years after the bankruptcy, it issued subpoenas from members of the WorldCom official committee of unsecured creditors – the court-appointed bondholder committee.

According to an August 24 filing in the US bankruptcy court in New York, the subpoenas demanded 'thousands if not millions of pages' regarding communications between WorldCom and its bondholders, including confidentiality agreements and meeting notes. (This information comes from the court filing by Akin Grump, which requested funds from MCI to cover the costs of complying with the SEC document demands.)[1]

The second example is the price–earnings (P/E) ratio from equity analysis. Few investors appreciate that the P/E is flawed. During the 1950s and 1960s, when the economy was relatively functional, most of the reported earnings were real, derived from productive output in manufacturing, mining, construction, and agriculture. This is not the case today. In the second quarter of 2004, financials represented one-third of all profits by the S&P 500 – and this, as the reader is aware from Chapter 1, is the virtual economy loaded in paper profits.

Experts suggest that during the 1960s stocks had a higher price–earnings ratio than in previous decades, partly because of speculation. In the 1970s and 1980s the price–earnings ratio averaged 12:1. Several people knowledgeable in the equity markets say that if P/E gets to 18:1 or much above, as it does, there is no way that the earnings stream of the company can support such a high price. Something will have to give, and the way to bet is that the price will slide.

Of course, a company may boost its earnings by creative accounting, significant downsizing (Lucent today has about one-third the employees it had in the late 1990s), selling off divisions or playing lottery in the derivatives markers, which many of the bigger companies do. All this however ends by weakening an entity's financial position and its creditworthiness. P/Es are not customarily used in the choice of bonds, but maybe they should be employed in a negative sense, in connection to their issuers:

■ An issuer with high P/E, in the range of 30–80 or beyond, is most likely one with financial troubles brewing, and
■ An issuer's P/Es in the range 12–15 is providing, other things being equal, a certain level of confidence in his ability to survive.

Notice, however, that this relation is not linear. While a P/E ratio out of range on the high side signals a potential bubble (in the late 1990s some Internet stocks had infinite P/E ratios selling at high price but having tiny earnings), a very low P/E ratio is also an indicator of current or potential trouble. Some experts say that among old economy companies P/Es between 2 and 4 indicate the entity is worth no more than its book value.

Prudence in bond selection also advises that, because since the 1980s, and most particularly the late 1990s and early years of this century, otherwise reputable companies have invested in junk bonds (see Chapter 4) is no reason to follow their example. Investing in deep discount corporate debt is fraught with hazard. Investors should never believe, even if they are told so, that:

■ Deep discount securities are worth buying when they sell significantly below their par value
■ Because junk bonds are largely bought by speculators, they fluctuate more sharply with interest rate changes than investment-grade instruments.

It needs no explaining that greater market volatility increases most significantly assumed exposure. Moreover all 'advice' and all 'standards', time-honored or otherwise, should be subject to critical review. It is indeed incomprehensible that institutional investors and many others buy 20- or 30-year corporate bonds because they want to lock in a nice rate, without paying attention to the fact that:

■ The bond is callable, or
■ It has other bells and whistles attached to it.

Particularly perilous, when the bond is called, is the case of the investor who paid above par to acquire it. Over and above this loss he or she faces the prospect of reinvesting the money at lower rates prevailing in the market. Associated to this statement is the choice of maturities. With short maturities, a callable feature will not make that much difference because even the paid price is contained. On the other hand, if the rates go up, the bonds are not going to depreciate that much because the investor will be getting back his or her capital at par, at maturity date. The message is: Buy longer maturities, but watch out.

The globalization of debt markets and other markets (see Chapter 2) also poses interesting challenges in terms of choosing bonds. Other things being equal, investors in any given country know its government, and the companies based in it, much better than foreign governments and foreign companies. With globalization, however, the trend is to invest abroad without appropriate research, even if:

- The number of unknowns increases, and
- Information about securities is not always up to standard.

Information about securities issues, and the way the market treats these issues, is an important element in investment analysis. While holders of financial assets (correctly) view bond investments as a more rewarding alternative to bank deposits and negotiable instruments issued by banks like certificates of deposit (CDs), scarce information about the issuer and the issue can make that greater return a poisoned chalice.

Legal issues are of particular relevance to the writing of covenants that are supposed to contribute to the investor's own protection. This fact alone makes it necessary to have full transparency with regard to legal risk.[2] Making mandatory due diligence helps to inform investors in regard to:

- The exposure they assume, and
- The guarantees they are given.

But due diligence is not a universal principle, and investors who believe that it should be taken for granted are deceiving themselves. Everyone confronted with choices in investments should appreciate that different jurisdictions have laws that sometimes contradict those in the home country – and in other cases are impossible to enforce because of corrupt police and judiciary.

Take mergers as an example of information bottlenecks and juridical problems. For all the talk about globalization, transborder acquisitions, and companies with operations around the world, it does matter *where* a company's management is based. The realization that DaimlerChrysler was not a combination of equals, as originally advertised, but was being run from Germany led to serious litigation in the United States. But this reference is by no means a statement against globalization; no serious party would argue for rolling back the carpet of world-wide commerce and finance. Rather, the DaimlerChrysler example and a long list of other similar references to imprudent interpretations of statements being made, should be seen as calls for exercising much greater care when:

- Investment decisions are reached, and
- Choices of debt instruments are made.

Savvy investors would use globalization to their advantage, as means for providing for diversification – and not to their disadvantage by augmenting assumed risk because of substandard homework. Investors must learn to diversify not only between debt and equities (and sometimes other instruments) but also within the bond market.

5.3 Price formation for bonds

Let's start with denominations. Corporate debt instruments are usually issued in $1000 face or par amount. Each security is, in effect, an IOU representing the issuer's promise to repay the loan face amount in a stated period of time, and pay interest at established intervals. This loan must be priced and sold to the market. The question is *how* the price formation process will operate.

Contrasted to a financial system dominated by relatively steady lending by commercial bankers, the price of bonds must satisfy two further requirements which, up to a point, contradict one another: It must be appealing to investors whose role is not that of acting as financial intermediaries, and it should be advantageous to the company as source of financing. For both reasons, senior management must always compare the cost of bonds, loans, and other financing forms like share issuance. Nearly, though not always,

- A higher stock market valuation tends to lower the issuance volume of bonds, and
- A weak equity market tends to encourage the corporate sector in issuing bonds and convertible bonds.

There are also projects for which equity issuance is no option. One of the earliest bond offerings in the capital market, back in the mid-19th century, was by the St Louis and Illinois Bridge Company, which was constituted to undertake the construction of one of the longest bridges built at that time. The contract was awarded in February 1870, but financing a project of more than $5 million could not depend on bank loans alone. Hence, the board's decision to sell bonds, just like the railroads did.

When Andrew Carnegie, who later became the king of the steel industry, read the published reports that $4 million in first-mortgage bonds were to be sold in New York and London to finance the completion of the St Louis bridge, he approached the chairman of the bridge company's executive and finance committee, William Taussig, with a proposal that he sell the bonds for a commission of $50 000 payable in St Louis and Illinois Bridge Company stock. With this, Carnegie proved he was willing to sacrifice a short-term gain in cash for a higher long-term benefit.

With the company's agreement and with letters of reference, Carnegie sailed for England for a meeting with Junius Morgan, who operated out of London, and was known to excel at selling US investments to Europeans. Using bonds to pay for a bridge was an entirely new concept, but Morgan is said to have been intrigued with this novel project, and submitted the papers to his lawyers for review.

After the legal advisors scrutinized the terms of the project, Junius Morgan requested a number of changes before he would agree to handle the floating of the bonds and set a five- to six-week time period for confirmation of requested changes. Carnegie, who had worked in his 'teens for a telegraph company, made good use of the transatlantic cable, which was laid in 1866. Two days later he surprised Morgan by having the approved changes in hand.[3] This is some of the earliest available evidence that advanced technology gives a boost to financial transactions.

Critical factors in management's choice between alternative forms of financing are prevailing interest rates, maturity of the loan, covenants and their influence on pricing of new debt instruments. Most often, opposing factors are affecting bond yields. On the one hand, market optimism on the strength of the economy pushes them higher. On the other, the fact that market participants appear to perceive inflationary risks puts upward pressure on bond yields over and above the aftermath of creditworthiness. Nowadays price formation for bonds also centers on:

■ The rating agencies' assessment of default risk, and
■ The cyclicity of yields in the secondary market.

Both have a critical impact on corporate financing conditions. Excessive yield fluctuations of corporate bonds which go beyond movements in the general interest rate level, plus the premium needed for higher credit risks, can lead to both too much bond issuance and mispricing.

■ Overinvestment is a specific risk at times when yield premiums are very low.
■ To the contrary, when yield premiums are very high, the high cost of money can lead to underinvestment.

There may as well be transborder effects. For instance, in the 1980s and 1990s the spillover of short-term yield volatility between markets increased independently of correlation between capital market rate levels. Moreover, because of the size of its financial market, the United States created strong stimuli to interest rate movements in European debt securities markets. Particularly significant has been the impact of yield movements in the US bonds market on the German bond market.

Changes in credit rating beyond a certain level add to these effects, but also there can be noticeable fluctuations over time in interest rate premiums for debt instruments within a given rating category. For example, in 2002, for European companies rated BBB differences in inbound premiums were much more than 200 basis points (bp), though such a figure fell to below 100 bp at the end of 2003.

The aforementioned decline in yields in 2003 has an evident impact on price formation, which has been even more significant in the case of junk bonds with a high default rate. As an example, the interest rate premium of C-rated European bonds declined from over 3000 basis points in 2002 to less than 1000 bp in the following year – a very sharp fall.

There are many more differences between bonds impacting on price formation than told by the foregoing examples. An issue that has attracted significant attention during recent years is the pricing of redeemable bonds versus bullets. The same is true of zero-coupon bonds and convertible bonds, as well as derivative financial instruments.

Mathematical tests can be instrumental in making factual and documented comparisons between pricing structures. Taking bullet bonds as the control population, that is the reference level against which all other types of bonds are tested, statistical tools like chi-square tests can be effectively used to investigate:

- Bond design, and
- Pricing of new bond issues, post-mortem.

(Specialists should notice that the advantage of chi-square in comparison to other statistical tests is that the distribution function depends solely upon the degree of freedom, f. This is a statistical measure which has not been so far properly exploited in financial analysis – yet it is a powerful tool as several applications domains help demonstrate.)

A bond design test would concentrate on market prices of similar instruments, aiming to evaluate the appeal of certain features, as well as identify and size up their associated risk; also, evaluating market prices of similar instruments to uncover hidden trading and investment opportunities.

In the secondary market, too, steady pricing tests are most important, and this includes debt instruments of sovereigns, even if there is no immediate bankruptcy risk. Take the Italian public debt as an example. 'Italy's finances are slipping,' says Fitch Ratings;[4] let's see why.

While on 26 May 2004 Fitch reaffirmed Italy's AA credit rating, it also warned the republic that its public finances are not what they should be. Indeed, yield spreads on Italy's government bonds suggest the sovereign remains under threat of a downgrade, which would be the first such move on a Euroland government since the launch of the euro in 2001. In mid-2004, yields on Italy's 10-year bonds were just 1 basis point above those of Greece, which Fitch rates two notches lower at A+.

If this characterizes the debt of a sovereign who is member of the Group of Seven (G-7), and is also the third largest economy in Euroland, think about price formation and its risks connected to bonds of less developed countries. This is dramatized by the events of May 2004, which can be summed up in one short sentence: Emerging markets' debt fell out of favor.

Let's start with Brazil, which is the biggest debtor among the so-called emerging countries. Brazil's 11% bond, which matures on 17 August 2040 and is highly volatile, has become the benchmark near-junk-status bond for all emerging markets, as the American 30-year Treasury used to be for Western investors interest in AAA debt instruments.

As a much-favored play for investors fleeing tiny yields on US Treasuries and continental European government bonds, the price of *Brazil's 11% '40* rose from 43 cents per dollar of face value in late 2002 to 120 cents in January 2004. This has been dragging yields from 26.7% to 9.5%. From January to May 2004, however, this bond's price fell by 30% – which speaks volumes about its volatility.

A pricing structure that turns on its head sends the message that investors have been getting cold feet with highly risky bonds. Another major factor for the fall has been the fact that, following a sequence of strong economic statistics from the United States and associated inflationary stirrings, the Federal Reserve let it be known it would put up interest rates much sooner than the market had expected. With globalization,

- *If* US yields start climbing
- *Then* emerging markets' yields are falling.

One of the investors' major worries has been that a rise in US rates will withdraw crucial investor support for emerging markets' debt around the world – bonds that have risen beyond any investment reasons other than greed. Suddenly, investors have begun to fear they have been doubled because many, and most particularly hedge funds, have taken advantage of ultra-cheap borrowing to leverage their paper profits.

5.4   Euroland and lessons from Eurodollars

The launch of the euro as the common currency of 12 countries in the European Union (out of 15 at the time) has led to the gradual integration of an equal number of national markets for debt instruments, issued by both sovereigns and corporates. This took place under legal and other transborder constraints discussed in section 5.2 – since there has been only a currency integration, but not a political, fiscal, and juridical one.

The pros say that the introduction of the euro as common currency has offered the market increased depth and liquidity. This process gained momentum from the late 1990s technology boom, which resulted in a significant increase in financing needs, particularly among the large listed telecommunication enterprises. According to the pros, the investment trend has been reinforced by corporate mergers and acquisitions.

There are two key points here in this reference to the effect of introducing a unique currency in Euroland: removal of currency exchange risk (see Chapter 3) and greater market liquidity. A third factor that should be added is a somewhat better diffusion of financial information. This is important inasmuch as the price of corporate debt securities reacts much more to:

- Credit risk, and
- Interest rate trends

than to a company's earning performance and other variables that typically influence equity prices. Wider diffusion of credit information means that changes in a company's perceived credit quality, and actual credit rating, more rapidly affect the price of its debt instruments, and can be instrumental in making their market more (or less) liquid.

As for the second point, the removal of foreign exchange risk in bond investments in Euroland increased the importance of the effects of interest rate changes. It needs no reminder that like the price of all fixed income securities, that of corporate debt tends to rise when interest rates drop and to decline when interest rates rise.

The liquidity argument, too, has substance. In the opinion of several experts, a one currency wider market promotes liquidity, and therefore it impacts trading in debt instruments in a positive way. Market liquidity is all-important because, among other reasons, new issues are announced daily in the corporate debt market, providing investors with ongoing opportunities to meet their portfolio targets.

A wider market allows that, on any business day, investors can select from a variety of issues that may suit specific criteria, purchasing debt securities at par with new issues and therefore avoiding the payment of premium and/or accrued interest. There is no doubt that a unique currency spanning a dozen economies, three of which are members of the Group of Seven, helps in enlarging the frame of reference in:

- New bond offerings, and
- The secondary market.

Still the lack of polished, fiscal and juridical interpretation among Euroland countries is a handicap, and it is too early yet to say how far the benefits may go, and which will be the potential pitfalls. Therefore, I have made the deliberate choice to take the Eurobond (essentially Eurodollar) market of the post-Second World War years as an example. What can we learn from the nascent Eurobond market of the early- to mid-1960s that could be a helpful input 40 years down the line?

The Eurobond market has been fed by tax incentives. It was principally created for issuers eager to avoid the interest equalization tax in the United States (see also in section 5.8 tax optimization by German companies). For over three decades, the Eurobond market has been dominated by dollar issues, with some 60% of debt instruments sold to American investors, while securities in sterling accounted for only 5%.

The market in Eurocurrencies was not very active, except perhaps in German marks, with other currencies mainly used for various types of arbitrage. Paul Einzig brings to attention that, from time to time, the market in German mark deposits was indirectly supplied with funds by the Banque de France. French banks employed marks bought from the Banque de France for lending in the Euromark market.[5] This is a role the euro now plays, without the need for such convoluted operations.

However, even under the conditions that have been briefly described, the Eurodollar system constituted an improvement over past practices because it reduced friction which was handicapping the smooth operation of the market mechanism. Eurodollars were not a special kind of US dollars, and there was absolutely nothing to distinguish them from ordinary dollars – except the fact that they had to be redeposited with a European bank. In fact, as Einzig points out,

- The placing and taking of Eurodollar deposits has been a loan transaction, and
- Because of this, it was argued that the Eurodollar market is part of the money market and not of the foreign exchange market.

In a sense the Eurodollar market had already created a continent-wide money market which worked in parallel to the local money markets. With the euro, these local money markets have disappeared in the 12 countries, which adopted the new currency – and the euro itself has taken over functions already established through Eurodollars.

It is, however, appropriate to notice that, to a substantial extent, Eurodollar deposits came into being because they were able to offer the foreign holder advantages he or she could not obtain through time deposits in the United States, or in types of short-term dollar investments with a comparable degree of:

- Liquidity, and
- Security.

The Eurodollar market offered investors liquidity and security over and above the higher yield than what was then (mid-1990s) offered by the low interest rates in the United States, since then as now (first quarter of 2004) the US government had adopted a policy of cheap money. This particular advantage of higher yield is not sustained by the euro, since Euroland's interest rates are only slightly above those of the United States – and as of mid-2004 US rates are rising but Euroland's rates are on hold.

Paul Einzig also points out another interesting fact. While the Eurodollar market significantly increased the global use of the American dollar and reduced the role of British sterling in international financing, at the same time it strengthened London's global financial role at the expense of New York. This suggests that:

- The international financial role of a currency, and
- The international role played by a big banking center

have been essentially decoupled. It is interesting to note that this experience has been repeated with the euro. The choice of a global banking center by counterparties is largely conditioned not by the currency that is used in transactions, but by who gives these counterparties:

- Lower overheads
- Wider range of facilities, and
- A better choice of skills.

This is a lesson also taught by globalization at large. The internationalization of finance has demonstrated that the four laws of capitalism discussed in Chapter 2 remain valid and applicable. Indeed, what has happened with globalization is capitalism in action. At least in the European financial landscape, the stronger and better-managed financial center becomes stronger, though there may always be room for small *boutiques*.

5.5 Euroland and bond market compliance

Though political and fiscal integration in Euroland, and in the larger European Union of 25 countries, is still a chimera, some effort is being made to take care of juridical rough corners. On the compliance side, securities issued in euros, as well as those issued by euro area residents in any currency, will have to conform to both European and international standards. The former have been set out by the European System of Accounts 1995 (ESA 95). International accounting standards have been elaborated by the International Accounting Standards Board (IASB).

In March 2004, IASB unveiled new rules, which will most likely be used in some 90 countries around the globe. In Europe, 7000 or so listed companies are scheduled to begin implementing them in 2005, in spite of a long-running dispute between the European Union and IASB over how to account for derivatives, swaps, options, and other instruments, whose gains and losses can be easily manipulated.

This controversy has primarily revolved around International Accounting Standard 39 (IAS 39), which compels companies to account for financial instruments at market values rather than through accruals. European banks and insurers have insisted that this would result in too much artificial volatility, and it would contrast to the fact that European accounting rules have allowed firms to value derivatives at historic cost (read: at totally irrelevant values).

This has been a curious argument indeed, because already, according to the EU Capital Adequacy Framework of 1998, derivatives that are placed in the trading book due to management intent, and that fulfill the necessary requirements, are marked to market. It is only normal that with the IAS Regulation, which aims to provide a level playing field, from 1 January 2005 *all* listed companies in the EU are required to publish their consolidated accounts in accordance with International Accounting Standards/International Financial Reporting Standards (IAS/IFRS) issued by the International Accounting Standards Board.

According to IAS 39, a *derivative* that is classified as held for trading – except for a derivative that is a designated and effective hedging instrument – must be carried at *fair value* through profit and loss. Moreover, a good deal of International Accounting Standards, and more specifically IAS 39, reflect US regulation on recognition and measurement of exposure (US GAAP, SFAS 133) already in place. There exists a long-term convergence project between the IASB and the US Financial Accounting Standards Board (FASB) towards a single set of high quality financial reporting standards. In an age of globalization, this is the minimum one should expect and ask for.

Correctly, IASB has been standing firm on this point of convergence with US accounting rules and regulations, but it has given ground on an amendment to IAS 39, making it easier for companies to use macro-hedging. Originally, IASB proposed that institutions match every derivative to a specific asset or liability whose risk they are hedging. The aforementioned amendment, however, has permitted hedging out the whole exposure. Even if IASB accepted such amendment, the argument can be divided into two parts:

■ For reasons of good governance, companies should use the more detailed matching method IASB originally wanted.

The results of this more analytical and more accurate approach must be reported to the board, senior executives, risk managers, and all other authorized persons through the company's Internal Accounting Management Information System (IAMIS).[6] Such information may well be eye-opening in terms of distribution and gravity of assumed risks.

■ By contrast, report to regulators and stockholders could reflect an integrative approach, at a level of confidence that provides a margin of safety.

Another uncertainty in terms of how dependable the accounts of debt instrument issuers will be revolves around the European Parliament, which has not yet authorized

IAS 39 and IAS 32. (The latter deals with insurance accounting.) With politicians having a the final word on approval, outright rejection of IAS 39 is still possible, leaving Europe without coherent accounting standards, and at the same time significantly damaging the market prospects of euro-denominated bonds.

I would add one more issue whose lack of proper settlement is a downside for euro-denominated equity and corporate debt, because at the bottom line it has to do with companies' creditworthiness. On 31 March 2004, in the United States the Financial Accounting Standards Board published its second proposal to force all firms to deduct the cost of employees' share options from profits. Straight afterwards, a score of technology executives lobbied legislators against the FASB rule, and a new bill was devised meant to derail FASB's new initiative. But the Congressional Budget Office has openly supported FASB.

European companies, too, have had an unfavorable reaction to the new rule in the making. They fear that costing options would lower reported profits and, therefore, ultimately the firm's stock price. Given the lavish way in which executive options are distributed, there is no doubt that expensing them would lower the profits of many companies, while some may even show a loss rather than a profit. But the answer to this challenge is to be less generous with other people's money – instead of trying to fake the numbers.

European and US companies who react so negatively to the costing of executive options should appreciate that it is not creative accounting that makes them look good.[7] Since the bubble years of the late 1990s, this unwarranted shrinkage of corporate resources through outrageous generous options:

- Has thrown doubt on their usefulness, and
- Has made nervous both shareholders and bondholders.

According to ex-fund manager Paul Myners, the amount of wealth transferred via options from investors to executives in the S&P 500 index has amounted to $1 trillion.[8] This is an unacceptable practice bordering on outright fraud (more on this in section 5.7).

Sovereigns, companies, and private investors in Euroland can only benefit from rules that promote transparency and dependability of accounts. The rules should be stricter than in the United States because of the diversity which exists among EU member states in economic terms, in legislation, and in jurisprudence. Business is based on confidence, and a sound, transparent accounting system can help a great deal in economic and financial integration.

Moreover, the financial integration of the 10 newcomer countries to the EU holds some interesting surprises, which some experts call 'disruption forces' – a misnomer. The first is that with the exception of Slovenia, their wage costs are significantly lower than those of the 15 in the old EU On average the difference is 1 to 6. Anything that costs only 16% of another's product's price, produced with about equal skill and quality, is going to sell like hotcakes.

- Germany, already facing 10.5% unemployment, will see this number sharply rise.
- No wonder that in France and Germany there is a growing sentiment against the newcomers to the EU.

Not only jobs but also companies may move east. This is what experts call 'the second disruption force', which is another misnomer. Ireland has already shown how successful tax breaks and low corporate taxes can be. Now comes Estonia, which has a corporate tax rate of 0% versus Germany's 38%, the Netherlands' 35%, and France's 33%. What will dissuade companies from the old EU to incorporate in Estonia – as in the United States where so many big companies have incorporated in New Jersey?

5.6   Return on capital for bondholders

While *bond issuers* should be sensitive to the price formation process in the their market and regularly update their approach to be ahead of the curve, *bondholders* will be well advised to do their calculations prior to commitment, as well as including the risk they assume. Risk-free return on capital essentially means capital income, and it is the sum of:

- Interest corrected for inflation distortions, and
- Capital appreciation or, alternatively, depreciation of each bond holding.

This sum must be divided by the yield (see Chapter 9) the investor gets for allocating his or her capital to secure (read: credit risk free) instruments like US Treasury bonds, adjusted for these same two bullets. Notice, however, that while inflation will hit equally an investment in, say, an emerging country's bond and US Treasuries, capital appreciation and depreciation will be much more pronounced in the former than in the latter.

The ratio to which I just referred tells the bond investor what is the extra margin he or she gets for the credit risk being taken. The crucial question is: 'Is it worth it?' To answer this query the investor should think in terms of risk-adjusted return on capital (RAROC): Would the extra yield be enough to buy a reinsurance for assumed credit risk?

Return on capital should not be confused with return on total equity (ROTE). Both measure effectiveness in investments, but for leveraged investors from the ROE calculation must be subtracted the part financed by debt. Therefore, ROTE is higher than ROC, or nearly equal to it when the entity is very little leveraged. A real-life example over a 2-year period is shown in Figure 5.1.

While in this example the investor has been able to maintain return on equity above return on capital or equal to it, this does not need to be always the case. The careful reader will take notice that, with two exceptions, at the beginning of the first year and second year the bond portfolio mapped in Figure 5.1 has not been leveraged too much.

Clearly such evaluations should be steady and able to bring to the attention of the asset manager every deviation from goals and limits. The basic principle is that the return on capital should always exceed the cost of capital, yet it is surprising how often the concept is ignored and investments are made and held without due attention to ROE, ROTE, and RAROC.

In terms of asset management the good news is that there is now focus on returns on capital as opposed to just growth. This has been an ongoing trend in the financial industry. At corporate level, for example, during these first years of the 21st century

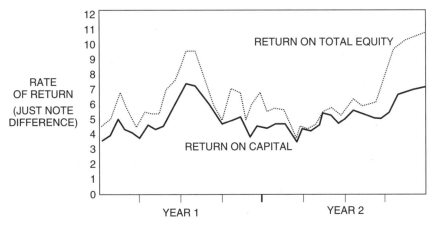

Figure 5.1 Return on capital and return on equity of an investor's portfolio over a 2-year timeframe

much of the free capital has been used to repair balance sheets damaged by the excesses of the late 1990s. The discretionary use of the next year's projected profits helps to test the ROC mantra.

Every investor, asset manager, or corporation has developed its own benchmark. Though those used by other entities may help in focusing one's attention, they should not be used *as is*. Even within the same industry sector return on capital can vary considerably from one class of entities to the next as well as within the class itself. Based on statistics by the Deutsche Bundesbank from the 1997 to 2001 timeframe, Table 5.1 presents these differences in ROC between big German commercial banks, regional banks, and other institutions.

Often, though not always, companies with high return on capital turn in considerable stock market gains. Since ROC includes profits flowing from all the money a business uses in its operations, it captures the firm's ability to deliver total returns to shareholders. This is important inasmuch as a critical measure of increasing efficiency in company operations is improved profit margins.

The problem with many companies is that return on capital is not part of the management culture, though this seems to be changing. For instance, until the mid- to late 1990s Deutsche Bank did not think return on capital should factor into its investment decisions.[9]

Return on net worth (RONW) is another metric, which differs from the previous ones in the sense that net worth is marked to market and the return is corrected for distortions created by inflation. This contrasts with typical book-accounting measures that are based on the historical cost of assets (which means very little) and resulting depreciation changes.

Measures like book accounting, essentially accruals, are inaccurate because they ignore current market value of assets, as well as distortions by inflation. In addition, at least in the manufacturing industry, impacts of big write-offs and shifts in depreciation rules can significantly affect book figures.

While the examples I have been giving in the preceding paragraphs concern company performance rather than returns on an investor's portfolio, they do help in

Table 5.1 Return on capital of German commercial banks and other institutions (1997–2001)

	1997		1998		1999		2000		2001	
	Before taxes	After taxes	Before taxes	After taxes	Before taxes	After taxes	Before taxes	After taxes	Before taxes	After taxes
Big commercial banks	7.38	5.44	39.51	19.24	6.23	5.48	6.34	7.23	4.96	5.69
Regional banks	11.52	7.48	16.75	11.54	16.51	10.08	11.58	7.41	4.13	1.27
Savings banks	19.37	6.66	17.82	6.52	15.18	6.12	13.39	6.02	9.22	5.08
Credit cooperatives	14.94	5.82	12.84	5.05	10.70	4.74	8.59	4.09	7.76	4.58
Mortgage banks	15.92	8.93	17.81	10.42	15.62	8.87	5.89	2.37	8.92	6.48
All banks	12.75	6.47	19.34	10.20	11.22	6.51	9.32	6.07	6.23	4.59

better understanding the latter because they emphasize the importance of investing in the winners' debt and equity, rather than championing the losers – as many governments do with taxpayers' money. Here are some examples.

Consider first the long list of corporate disaster stories in France, including Alcatel, Alstom, Bull, Crédit Lyonnais and the Eurotunnel. These are companies which, by being awfully mismanaged and sustained through taxpayers' money in the twilight between life and death, have deceived both their shareholders and their bondholders. Their whole strategy is based on false premises that:

- Size and government support equate strength, and
- Their survival through handouts increases their chances of hitting the jackpot.

Such hypotheses make a mockery of the fact that, to a significant extent, the role of return on investment and that of industrial policy coincide. This role is to create the economic conditions in which competition can flourish; according to the laws of capitalism (see Chapter 2), it is not to preserve or manipulate established but dying big corporate structures.

While making up their mind in choosing bonds, investors should appreciate that one of the first casualties in the corporate bond market's reversal in fortunes are those entities which are surviving on life support. In terms of credit risk they are followed by companies belonging to an ever-saturated industrial sector and/or loaded with debt.

At time of writing (in May 2004), it has been the motor vehicle manufacturers whose debt has been losing its appeal as higher oil prices and interest rates threaten to weaken demand for vehicles. Wavering in the corporate bond market is an important barometer of change in credit risk.

To appreciate the impact of change in market sentiment towards a whole industry sector, the reader should recall that among themselves motor vehicle manufacturers comprise the biggest sector of the corporate bond market. Therefore, the fact that yield spreads tightened by some 175 basis points in 2003 provides an important message to investors. The same is true of the fact that in the first five months of 2004 yield spreads widened by some 24 bp, indicating that investors are demanding to be paid more for the risk of owning the vehicle industry's bonds.

A more detailed way of looking at the debt instruments of motor vehicle companies is that this is a sector facing an increasing number of question marks, down to company level. Yield spreads on some of Ford's 10-year bonds widened 44 bp between January and the end of May 2004, to 232 bp. Moreover, at the end of 2003 Ford Motor Credit had $130 billion in unsecured term debt.[10] Correspondingly, GM's securities have widened 74 bp, to 222 bp. These considerations should be integrated into investors' calculations of return on capital.

5.7 Disincentives in holding bonds

A cushion for major declines in bonds is the fact that, aware of credit risk embedded into debt instruments, more and more individuals seem to be satisfying their need for income by buying Treasuries with the idea of holding them in the longer term. However, rather than promoting this strategy, legislation has built in disincentives. For instance, US financial institutions no longer buy and hold bonds as they used to do, because accounting rules have made it less and less interesting for banks to be investors in bonds.

- When bonds go down, they could impair a bank's book value as they mark the bonds to market under FAS 115, and
- As loan demand grows, banks are selling bonds in order to lend the money out to borrowers: commercial, industrial, real estate, and consumer.

Behind FAS 115 lies the fact that instead of being investors in bonds, financial institutions use debt instruments for trading. Bonds are sold short through reverse repurchase agreements, with the short sellers lending money and taking the security they want to short as collateral. This leads to the concept of *reverse spread*, defined as the difference between:

- The lending rate on general collateral, and
- The lending rate on specific collateral.

This is the rate available when only any Treasury bond will serve as collateral minus the rate available when only a specific Treasury bond will serve that function. Such spread is usually positive because the difficulties in finding the owner of a particular bond and the likely attempts of other would-be shorters to find the same bond, translates into an opportunity loss on the money lent through reverses.

These are games for financial institutions, and not particularly for speculators – not for investors. The latter, however, are often frustrated by the fact that bondholders do not have as much clout as shareholders in terms of asking tough questions. Bond investors feeling that way should recall that equity investor activism is fairly recent and generally reserved for the big firms, usually institutional investors. For example, CalPers, the giant California pension fund, has been instrumental in lifting investor protection and transparency standards through its activism. One of its latest policies is that of screening emerging markets countries against a range of criteria, including:

- Political stability
- Labor market practices
- Market liquidity, and
- Proficiency of stock market settlement.

Bondholders can learn a great deal from this CalPers initiative, which is most commendable. Careful screening constitutes a form of engagement with the counterparty in which one invests, because it involves careful evaluation and sets clear criteria for a company or a country to meet. In fact, whether the investment is equity or debt, such criteria should include standards for:

- Management policies
- Sound accounting standards
- Financial transparency
- Shareholder and creditor rights
- Dependable stock exchange listing for equities, and
- Handholding with bondholders to emphasize the debtor's responsibilities.

To better appreciate CalPers' initiative, it is necessary to recall that this is a pension fund that has often demonstrated its accountability, with a defined investment strategy that is longer-term and active. Pensioners who trust the CalPers board with their savings are well served by such due diligence.

Neither is CalPers the one and only example of investor activism, which has been a response to the fact that in the past 15 years shareholders, and to a lesser extent bondholders, are in revolt. The corporate scandals at Enron, Global Crossing, WorldCom, Parmalat, and scores of other firms, as well as the long bear market of 2000–2003, have stripped away the mark of the CEO as Superman. People and entities who put their trust and their money in companies are challenging their executives on a whole range of issues from:

- Composition of the board, to
- Lavish executive options (see section 5.5), and
- Relationship with internal and external auditors.

In the go-go 1990s, when corporate profits were soaring, almost every manager looked as 'great'. Since investors were earning returns of 20% or more per year, why should they mind if the image of a CEO as business genius was true or false? By contrast, the bear market brought home that executives skimmed the cream from the companies during the good times, but did not share investors' pains in bad times.

It could be argued that such happenings are dreadful for equity investors but not for bondholders. Such a concept, however, is not true. Though in specifics concerning their investments shareholders and bondholders may have different goals, in terms of general principles their interests are the same:

- Shareholders want the company in which they invest to prosper in order to get capital appreciation and pay dividends.
- Bondholders want the company whose debt they buy to survive in order to pay interest to its bonds and reimburse the capital.

When companies are eaten from within through fat executive options and outrageous perks, they cannot prosper and they may not even survive. Along with mismanagement, looting from within the shareholders' equity and the bondholders' credit is one of the major disincentives for not investing in companies and for not holding corporate debt. What looks like security at the outset can appear to be a reward for failure when the executive departs. It is good advice for investors when making bond choices to pass by companies with fat stock options. Other things being equal, these are more fragile than their peers because they divert their resources to self-gratification of managers rather than, first and foremost, fulfilling their obligations to investors who bought their debt.

5.8   Taxation and debt instruments

Taxation is sometimes a matter of invention, and in many cases it has long-term effects. Broadsheets, characterizing the larger size newspapers, became popular in Britain after the Tories introduced a stamp tax in 1711. This taxed newspapers per sheet of newsprint and its effect was that papers were thereafter published as single sheets with huge pages.[11] It has taken almost 300 years for the broadsheet size, which became traditional, to change. This is proof of two things:

- The power of taxes to influence behavior, and
- The delays in any associated change of behavior once a certain de facto standard takes hold.

There are several methods of tax optimization in connection to bonds; some serve the issuers, and others the holders. For instance, at the originator's side German companies issue bonds mostly through foreign financing subsidiaries. This provides tax advantages in German trade earnings tax. The reader may also recall that in the 1960s US companies patronized the European market to avoid interest equalization tax in the United States.

In the case of German firms, when computing trade earnings tax, 50% of the interest on long-term debt, which means debt with a maturity of over one year, is included in the assessment basis. By contrast, interest on short-term loans remains tax-free. This trade tax burden, however, may be circumvented by lending the financial resources short term to the domestic parent company.[12]

On the bond investor's side, in Switzerland, taxation at the source for shares and obligations, from Swiss emissions only, amounts to 35%. Shares and obligations from foreign issuance are partly tax-free at the source, particularly titles subject to Luxembourg law, but the Luxembourg law may be changing (more on this later).

Italy has a tax at source for interest paid by bonds, at 12.5%, applicable to private investors, whether residents or not, but not to companies. There is a policy of generalization of withholding tax in the European Union, with the associated procedures having gone through prolonged and extensive negotiations, partly aimed to eliminate tax havens and partly to improve the deplorable financial situation of some governments.

Under the paying agent system targeted with the new EU directives, the withholding tax is collected by the bank that pays the interest to the bondholder. In this sense, the deduction of withholding tax cannot be avoided by selecting bonds free of withholding tax, if the safekeeping account is held at a bank located in a country where paying agent tax applies.

To the contrary, under the *debtor system*, on which the Swiss withholding tax is based, tax is withheld by the debtor rather than by the paying agent; that is, by the company which issues the coupon-paying bond. This contrasts to taxation of interest income in the EU, where the *paying agent system* is applied with regard to the levying of a withholding tax.

The paying agent system makes an interesting case study because, for several years, finance ministers of the European Union have been discussing, disagreeing, and finally agreeing on measures to curb cross-border tax evasion. The original concept has been characterized by attempts to make member states share information on taxable income from cross-border savings accounts and bond investments – with, in the background, an EU-wide withholding tax of non-resident savings.

This plan has been vetoed by Luxembourg, Austria, and Belgium over several years. All three countries, which make significant profits from foreign accounts, refused to exchange banking information unless Switzerland, which is not an EU member, agreed the same measures. The excuse has been banking secrecy. Subsequently, under a compromise put together by the EU's Greek presidency, the three countries were allowed to retain their banking secrecy laws until Switzerland and other non-EU countries, including the US, Monaco, Andorra, Liechtenstein, and San Marino, agreed to exchange information on EU residents' savings – a vast and asymmetric plan, which included on one side a financial colossus and lilliputians on the other.

The compromise has been that luxembourg, Austria, and Belgium will impose a withholding tax on non-resident savings, starting at 15% and escalating to 35% in 2011, while other EU members will exchange information on non-resident accounts. Liechtenstein, San Marino, Monaco, Gibraltar, and Andorra accepted the exchange of information. The 10 new EU countries were not asked their opinion; they will be obliged to adopt the exchange of information system from the start.

- Legal entities are not affected by the EU paying agent tax, but
- All individual clients who are domiciled for tax purposes in an EU country are subject to the one or the other of these regimes.

Both the exchange of information and withholding tax solutions can only be applied, however, if the paying agent is located in a EU country, or in a country which has signed agreements with the EU to implement the Savings Directive. Evidently, there are loopholes. Geographically speaking, the Bermudas do not actually belong to the Caribbean and were able to successfully oppose inclusion in the Savings Directive in contrast to the British Virgin Islands (BVI).

The Bahamas are in the Caribbean, but they form an independent state, and for this reason are also not subject to the EU Savings Directive. The Cayman Islands do not consider themselves a dependency or overseas territory, and they are therefore vehemently refusing to adopt the rules made by the EU, and so on.

Other financial centers such Singapore, Hong Kong, Japan, Canada, and Australia are also not included, although recent reports suggest that negotiations have commenced with Singapore and Hong Kong in this regard. The entry into force of the EU Savings Directive will not be affected by the result of negotiations with Singapore and Hong Kong, and at the present time it is completely unclear whether these two states will be interested to continue such negotiations.

Moreover, while the United States seems prepared to exchange a certain amount of information with the EU, it no longer belongs to the group of countries, like Switzerland, with which separate agreements on inclusion in the directive are planned. In an age of globalization, the EU withholding tax is faced with strong head winds and its loopholes will no doubt be exploited by all interested parties.

5.9 The camel is a horse designed by a committee

The European Union withholding tax is nothing else but a compromise among diverse and characterizing conflicting interests of EU members. Between the lines, it means in effect that there will be no automatic exchange of banking information between European Union member states before 2011 (or some postponed date), while Luxembourg, Austria, and Belgium will apply a withholding tax on non-resident accounts.

The revenues from this withholding tax will be shared with the EU citizens' home countries, while account holders' identities will remain secret. Contrary to physical persons, juridical persons are not concerned by this deduction at the source and exchange of information. If the EU Savings Directive had included companies, it would have raised a revolution, and at the same time it would have been a hammer blow to globalization.

Even the way it stands, it will hit some of the EU countries hard. For instance, Luxembourg, whose financial sector accounts for more than 40% of its gross domestic product is the EU member most hurt by this new measure. As for the UK, Chancellor Gordon Brown had vetoed earlier plans for a withholding tax in favor of an exchange of banking information, but then agreed to the compromise in order to get legislation on the statute book. When this was announced, a UK Treasury spokeswoman was quick to inform who would listen that 'There is no threat to the City, or the eurobond market.'

In short, what the EU governments and politicians managed to reach as an agreement is best described by the old joke that 'A camel is a horse designed by a committee'. Buried in the details of the Savings Directive are hilarious contradictions, throwing doubts on its usefulness as a taxation model – let alone the fact that taxing savings is a very bad policy indeed.

The bottom line is that it has all been a game of give and take – and of conflicts of interest. Switzerland is hurt by the EU Savings Directive, despite assurances by the Swiss Bankers Association (SBA) there would be no changes to the country's secretive banking laws. In fact such assurances proved inconsistent, when the Swiss government agreed to major concessions to the EU. But Switzerland does not want to be left out of European Union commercial agreements, and most particularly its privileged relation with Germany in terms of exports.

To appreciate the possible harm to Switzerland by the European Union's withholding tax, it is necessary to bring into perspective that its banks have built a more than US$3 trillion wealth management industry, capitalizing on the prevailing secretive approach. It is no wonder that the Swiss have steadfastly refused to sign up to the automatic exchange of information about cash held by EU residents in Swiss bank accounts. Based on statistics by *The Financial Times*, Table 5.2 shows that two of the six global private banks – and by far the biggest – are Swiss.

As a frame of reference, in Table 5.2 Swiss banks hold the No. 1 and No. 3 positions, the No. 2 and No. 6 are US banks. Moreover, the United States is also the country with

Table 5.2 Top 10 global private banks
(by assets under management)

	US$ bn
UBS	1030
Merrill Lynch	935
Crédit Suisse	394
Deutsche Bank	183
HSBC	169
Citigroup	145

Source: Financial Times, 27 May 2004

the most billionaires and millionaires, both in absolute numbers and in annual increase. Capitalizing on that base, and the references which it provides, Merrill Lynch and Citigroup may well be the winners of what UBS and Crédit Suisse lose because the EU Savings Directive lifts their veil of secrecy.

In a globalized economy, unless taxation rules – including deduction at the source and any other gimmicks – are universal, investors and savers will always find ways to game the system, or, to put it mildly, to exercise tax optimization.

Price setters, investors, and risk managers should appreciate that taxes are among the *major imperfections* in the securities markets. For instance, the practice of taxing dividends more heavily than capital gains has raised questions about the pricing of securities with different payouts. The existence of imperfections along with the rapid development of new instruments serve to make the landscape of investments more complex because of the:

- Investment options that differ in terms of tax treatment of their dividend income, and
- The virtual impossibility of a total lack of tax harmonization in the global financial environment.

This problem (or more precisely opportunity to investors) did not arise only yesterday, as the following quotation documents. The author is Dr Henning Schulte-Noelle: 'Increasingly, the high tax countries in EMU [European Monetary Union] are calling for harmonization of corporate taxes among member states. They fear that otherwise there will be a spate of tax dumping combined with the transfer of jobs to low tax countries and a corresponding loss of state revenues.'[13]

That is precisely the problem, and it brings up another crucial issue, which does not seem to have been given the attention it deserves by governments. Not only is capital highly mobile, in a transborder sense, within a globalized economy (which, as we saw, is the first law of capitalism), but also labor is mobile within regional groupings, like the European Union. Companies are free to outsource their work to wherever there prevails:

- More favorable taxation laws, and
- Low wages for skilled labor.

In his aforementioned article, Dr Schulte-Noelle (correctly) disagrees with this tax-and-tax policy of many governments, and its background reasons. He makes the point that rather than trying to pass over the landscape of Euroland with a tax bulldozer, like the French and German governments try to do:

- Tax competition is wanted because it helps to fulfill the goal of a *lean state*, that politicians often like to endorse but do nothing to reach it, and
- As far as the taxpayers are concerned, it is precisely through *tax competition* that greater efficiency and value are achieved in the provision of services in which they participate as producers and consumers.

These notions provide more food for thought in relation to a model of investor behavior in regard to tax treatment. Such a model is further complicated by the fact that adverse changes in the pattern of particular securities are often accompanied by *grandfather clauses*, which shield existing holders from the changes in the tax law. In other cases, however, new tax laws close loopholes on which a whole investment strategy was based; or, alternatively, open new ones.

In conclusion, taxation should be one of the crucial variables in pricing debt instruments, and in choosing them for an investment portfolio. On the issuer's side, senior management must always be keen to audit the pricing and repricing of financial instruments, weeding out weak assumptions or wishful thinking and at the same time assuring compliance with prevailing laws and regulations. This mission can be effectively assisted through stress testing, not only scenarios and sensitivities but also rigorous statistical analyses using historical data and hypotheses – as well as drills.[14]

Notes

1 *Financial Times*, 17 September 2004.
2 D.N. Chorafas, *Operational Risk Control with Basel II: Basic Principles and Capital Requirements*, Butterworth-Heinemann, Oxford and Boston, 2004.
3 Peter Krass, *Carnegie*, Wiley, Hoboken, NJ, 2002.
4 *Financial Times*, 27 May 2004.
5 Paul Einzig, *The Euro-Dollar System*, Macmillan, London, 1967.
6 D.N. Chorafas, *The Real-time Enterprise*, Auerbach, New York, 2005.
7 D.N. Chorafas, *Management Risk: The Bottleneck is at the Top of the Bottle*, Macmillan/Palgrave, London, 2004.
8 *Financial Times*, 27 May 2004.
9 *Business Week*, 23 March 1998.
10 *EIR*, 19 December 2003.
11 *The Economist*, 12 June 2004.
12 *Deutsche Bundesbank*, Monthly Report, April 2004.
13 Lettre d'Information, Association Internationale pour l'Etude de l'Economie de l'Assurance, Geneva, August 1999.
14 D.N. Chorafas, *Stress Testing: Risk Management Strategies for Extreme Events*, Euromoney, London, 2003.

6 Bank loans and securitization

6.1 Introduction

The careful reader will recall that the company that needs to raise money has three alternatives: Issue bonds (including convertible bonds), issue equity, or take a bank loan. Both bank loans and the issuance of debt securities have associated fixed costs. In the case of loans, the costs faced by the credit institution, which will eventually be paid by the borrower, include client rating, analysis of several years of financial statements, and examination of the prospects of the project or operation to be financed.

In connection to bond issuance, the costs are those of study of the prospects of a capital market offering, preparation of the term sheet and prospectus, as well as a roadshow presentation for institutional investors. A significant cost is the fees of the investment bank that will act as consultant and/or as underwriter. Because capital markets are more efficient than commercial banks, the way to bet is that bond issuance will be the more effective alternative – a major reason why in the United States bank lending is sharply down, as industrial and merchandising companies tend to issue bonds.

Whether financing is done through bank loans or debt instruments sold in the capital market, an interesting question is: Who is more indebted, the European or the American industry? As Figure 6.1 shows, if corporate debt is considered as a percentage of gross domestic product, over nearly two decades European companies have been borrowing more heavily than US ones. But Table 6.1 demonstrates that the pattern of borrowing is not even. While between the 1980s and 1990s in Germany bank lending has increased, in the UK and France it shrank, and in Japan it decreased only slightly.

Financing via the bond market has prerequisites associated to rules established by regulators, as well as requirements imposed by the market so that an offering of debt instruments attracts the investors' attention. Companies contemplating a bond offering must appreciate that this has associated to it issuance procedures. They should moreover understand that bonds and bank loans differ in many respects, among major differences between the two forms of financing being:

- Insolvency, and
- Restructuring.

As far as the creditor is a commercial bank, it is easier to adjust the terms and conditions of lending, because the bank that has given the loan is quite often ready to renegotiate. This is not true of the capital market, which typically includes a large number of bond holders, often with diverse interests. On the other hand, as already

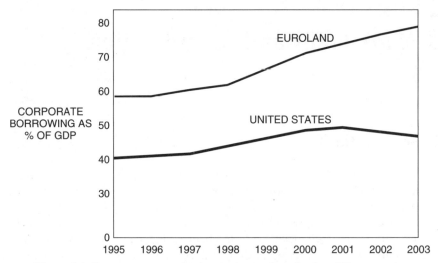

Figure 6.1 European companies borrow more heavily than US companies and do not put the brakes on after 2000

Table 6.1 The decline of bank lending *vs.* the issuance of debt securities[a]

	1980s	1990s
United States	34.5	18.0
France	44.0	21.5
UK	84.0	73.0
Japan	94.5	90.5
Germany	51.0	57.0

[a]The balance of financing requirements is covered through debt securities.

mentioned, the capital market is much more efficient than the banking industry in terms of costs, interest rates, and conditions.

The risks are also asymmetric, often in favor of banks. While scrupulous borrowers may try to game the system, the way to bet is that because of their regular contacts with the debtor, and ongoing monitoring of credit, relationship bankers have better information on the state of solvency of their borrowers than do bondholders. Another asymmetry, this time in favor of capital markets, is that it is easier to sell a bond portfolio than to sell loans – though this has changed with securitization (see section 6.6).

Holders of debt instruments can dispose of their paper comparatively easily in the event of a deterioration in the debtor's credit rating – albeit at price loss. Banks are typically stuck with the loans, unless they have already securitized them and sold them to investors. This is another reason why bankers have an incentive to maintain a fairly strong linkage between their institution and the company to whom they have lent.

Moreover, the ongoing development of prudential regulation, and especially the rules of Basel II (see sections 6.4 and 6.5, as well as Chapter 15) have led the banks towards improving their procedures for measuring and controlling credit risk. This has led to the recent trend towards risk-based pricing of products, evidently including loans.[1] As this brief introduction demonstrates, there is ground for careful analysis of the case of bonds versus loans, just as senior management should be doing a careful study of:

- The cost of debt, and
- The cost of equity.

The *cost of debt* can be determined through the firm's current borrowing rate and interest rate mix. These reflect the expected return of debt holders. One way to compute the cost of debt is to first project the expected interest expense that an entity expects to pay on its outstanding debt each year. This being done, the cost of debt is the discount rate that equates:

- To the current market value of debt, and
- The present value of the stream of expected interest payments.

In a way similar to the cost of debt, which reflects the expected return to debtholders, the *cost of equity* represents the expected return to shareholders. Different models are available for this computation. One is the Capital Asset Pricing Model (CAPM), which calculates the cost of equity as the sum of:

- The risk-free interest rate (such as US Treasury bonds), and
- The risk premium on the company's shares, projected in the coming years.

Expected risk premium is based on the sensitivity of a share's price to overall stock market movements. This approach has been consistently used by financial analysts, so that there is a body of knowledge in its regard. Cost of debt and cost of equity are references to balance sheet capital. But the securitization of loans is off-balance sheet (OBS) capital, accessible through derivatives or by means of transferring risk to other firms.

6.2 Determination of bank lending rates

Several factors play a role in determining bank lending practices and rates. The trend in interest rates and interest rate changes in all types of deposits, lending and the central bank's discount rate is one of them. The administrative cost of bank–customer relationships and the handling cost of loans is another. Bank-specific characteristics, like the market to which it appeals as well as the interplay between the credit institution's profitability and refinancing conditions, are more factors helping in the determination of bank lending rates.

It is only normal that prevailing lending rates are driven by developments in the money market and capital market (see Chapter 11). Banks have to refinance themselves by buying money in these markets, and moreover their deposit rates should reflect trends in these markets in order to attract funds. This leads to a close relationship between:

- Negative interest paid for saving, time deposits, CDs, and so on
- Positive interest gained for company loans, personal loans and other lending activities, and
- Interest rates with comparable maturities which prevail in the money market and capital market.

It is fairly normal that prevailing interest rate on loans to households for mortgages has historically tended to move in tandem with 5-year government bond yields, but the correlation is not equal to 1. Each credit institution must also consider the degree of prevailing competitive forces within different segments of the credit market to which it appeals.

No credit institution dominates the financial market the way General Motors used to control pricing in the auto industry, or IBM in computers. A bank's power to influence interest rates depends not only on what other banks are doing but also on the availability of alternative sources of funds available to its customers, within each customer's class of creditworthiness (see Chapter 12) – both in general terms and when the bank grants a loan.

Experience, however, shows that in the general case bank lending rates tend to react with a delay to market interest rate developments, though eventually bank lending rates do adjust to prevailing market interest rates. In Euroland, for instance, after May 2002 there was a rather sluggish adjustment of some long-term bank lending rates to companies, in line with the declines in market interest rates, which may have been due to growing concerns about creditworthiness as bankruptcy rates rose.[2]

Moreover, the capital market shares the banks' concern about credit risk; this concern is expressed by a widening of corporate bond spreads, over rates for gilts. As an example, the differential between yields on BBB-rated corporate bonds and government bonds with comparable maturities rose from about 190 basis points to around 220 basis points between May and December 2003, with a peak of about 260 basis points in October of that same year.

On the supply side, restructuring of banking lending practices and rates tends to promote higher efficiency and more competitive pricing. This is a necessary adjustment as credit institutions face increased competition from other financial intermediaries like insurance companies, pension funds, and non-bank banks.

The reader is already aware that the ongoing increase in the availability of alternative non-bank sources of finance, through commercial paper, corporate bonds, household mortgages, car loans, and more, impacts most significantly on the lending perspective as well as on market liquidity. This is tantamount to saying that changes in banking practices are welcome, as at the demand side customers become more sensitive to the interest rates on bank loans compared with those charged by:

- Other financial institutions
- Acceptance corporations of auto manufacturers

- Other capital financing arms of industrial companies, and
- Capital markets for corporate bonds.

There is both a demand and supply side to this issue. In the money market and in the capital market, credit institutions trying to assure their supply of funds compete with many of their own clients in terms of liquidity. The margin on which both banks and their clients were betting is the one between interest received (positive interest), and interest paid (negative interest). The trend lines for both, for continental European banks, over a 20-year period, are shown in Figure 6.2 (more on positive and negative interest in Chapter 14).

The better margin of profits between interest received and interest paid does not always go to the swift and most creditworthy, but this is the way to bet. Swiftness is related to both management effectiveness[3] and to a clean balance sheet; also to the bank's control over increases in funding costs.

The study of borrower behavior in Euroland, in the first years of the 21st century, can be revealing in terms of changes taking place in the banking sector. Careful analysis demonstrates that for a single currency area like Euroland, interest rates are affected not only by the now common monetary policy but also by remaining national particularities such as:

- Demand and supply side dynamics, and
- Structure of financial relationships in a given country.

Both prove to be major factors determining lending rates. As we have seen above (Table 6.1), compared with most of the EU member states, German banks play a

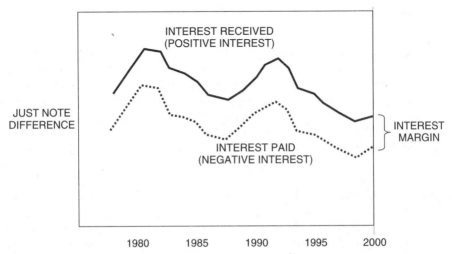

Figure 6.2 Positive and negative interest respectively received and paid by the banking sector in Euroland, 1980 and 2000

more important role in the financing of the country's industry. Moreover, in the area of corporate financing, the generally longer-term credit relations of a company tend to be concentrated at one or a few banks.

Steady handholding leads to a good flow of information. Other things being equal, relationship banking enables loans to be granted at more favorable conditions with respect to interest rates and volume. A study by the Deutsche Bundesbank documents that this is particularly important and for loans with long maturity.[4] On the downside, such close connection fosters dependence on the borrower's preferred bank, with the result of:

- Lowering competitive advantages, and
- Often leading to higher borrowing cost.

Another negative of relationship banking is that the so-called house bank does not fully adapt its lending conditions in spite of changing market parameters. House banks hold the upper ground in limiting adverse selection of credit institutions by borrowers, and might as well assume greater credit risk than their competitors by continuing to finance 'favored customers' whose creditworthiness is in a slide.

A lack of adaptation, or very slow adaptation, by the banking sector to changing market conditions also leads to a certain lull in modernization by the borrowers. Unless older plants, marketing channels, procedures, technology, and the personnel's skills are steadily updated and closely integrated with newly developed competitive solutions, and unless they are readjusted to effectively meet the needs of corporate strategy as well as the market's whims and drives, growth and indeed business survival will be in doubt as backwater thinking brings increasing:

- Problems
- Strains, and
- Inefficiencies.

This is another aspect of benefits brought by greater competitiveness and efficiency in lending, including the growing competition by money markets and capital markets through their purchase of commercial paper and bonds offerings by industrial firms. All else being equal, companies that appeal to the market for their funding rather than to their house bank are more conscious of the urgent need for steadily improving efficiency and cost-control to assure their survival.

A recent example is given by Delta Air Lines, which, in May 2004, warned that it would seek Chapter 11 bankruptcy protection unless it could reduce costs and improve competitiveness. The United States' third-largest carrier has been seeking to cut pilot's pay by 30%, though pilots have offered to take 9% less as an alternative.[5] Contrast this to Alitalia and other government-sponsored airlines who benefit from house bank loans guaranteed by taxpayers (against their best interest). Having taken the taxpayer to the cleaners, these 'too dear to fail' entities go on strike rather than cutting costs and slimming down in order to become more competitive.

6.3   Panics and their aftermath

Part of the margin between the positive interest rates charged by banks to their clients, and the negative interest rates which represent the average cost of capital – from rates paid to depositors to bought money – goes to cover the risks of lending and to assuring the credit institution's financial staying power. Financial staying power is necessary because the way to bet is that, from time to time,

- There will be adversity, and
- There are going to be panics.

For example, over the second half of the 19th century till a few years prior to the First World War, a span of about six decades, there were six major panics in the United States, at the average of one per 10 years:

- Panic of 1857
- Panic of 1873
- Panic of 1893
- Panic of 1901
- Panic of 1907
- Panic of 1914.

The 1873 and subsequent two US market panics were connected to the railroad building boom which followed the American Civil War. The functions of a transcontinental railway are polyvalent but foremost, in the American case, has been that of integrating the USA, coast to coast, from the Atlantic to the Pacific. The money was lent largely by banks, although the railroads are also at the very origin of the creation of the capital market.[6] The financing of such vast projects did not come without major surprises.

The year 1873 saw the scandal of the Union Pacific Railroad and of Crédit Mobilier, followed by a depression that damped US industrial growth for several years. Confidence came back and in the 1880s railroads comprised 60% of all issues in the US capital market. A new bust came a few years later.

In 1900, Barings failed because of overexposure to financing US municipalities. This did not lead to a crisis because in 1890 Barings was rescued by the Bank of England. (The Bank of England, however, did not repeat its rescue initiative when Barings went into bankruptcy again in 1995, following its speculation with derivative financial instruments in the Japanese market.)

Scores of railroads went under during the 1893 panic. To save the day, James Pierpont Morgan reorganized the industry and used what was then a controversial new technique, the *trusts*, to bring about financial order. Another issue which fed into the 1893/94 panic was the crisis of bimetallism (silver and gold standard for the dollar supported by mining interests), bringing the United States to the brink of financial chaos and leading to a depression.

Then, on 9 May 1901 came the biggest crash known till then in the United States, with Northwest Pacific and the railroads takeover struggle at its epicenter. J.P. Morgan again intervened. When he was later criticized for having profited on depressed equities he uttered his famous remark: 'I owe the public nothing . . . I feel bound in honor when I reorganize a property, and I am morally responsible to its management to protect it, and I generally protect it.'[7]

No politician could have put it in better terms. When some years ago Charles Pasqua, a French party leader, was challenged in a public interview that neither he nor his political opponents honored their promises, he answered: 'The promises oblige only those who listen to them.' Investors take note!

More than one hundred years have elapsed since the big railroad earthquakes, and there exists a striking similarity between then and now: in 1901 the railroads were the high tech of their time, in 2001 the epicenter has been the telecoms and their financial woes – to the tune of more than 70 billion euro (US$84 billion), counting France Télécom and Deutsche Telekom together. On the other hand, there is a positive chain reaction.[8]

- The railroads gave rise to the steel industry, because of the materials they consumed.
- Similarly, the boom of the telecoms promoted the telecommunications supplier industry – Alcatel, Siemens, Nortel, Lucent, Nokia, and others.

But there are also significant differences. The most important is that of leadership. In 1901 J.P. Morgan put together an unprecedented rescue operation and with this brought confidence back to the markets. Today, such a giant has not yet shown up. The nearest thing to a rescue mission has been the socialization of risk by governments, which spend taxpayers' money lavishly in an effort to bring the economy back on track.

As the railroads' and telecommunications' examples demonstrate, acting as intermediaries commercial banks are an important element in the functioning of an economy, channeling funds from households and companies that are net savers to those that are net borrowers, thereby bringing together supply of and demand for funds. But to continue to function properly, credit institutions must be well capitalized.

Strong capitalization and rigorous as well as timely damage control correlate. The banks' senior management must manage risk in the most effective way. *If* the board and CEO expect a worsening of the general economic outlook, *then* bank policies should become more restrictive in providing credit to prospective borrowers, tightening the:

- Credit standards, and
- Conditions and terms.

This would have an impact on general availability of financing, as at least some borrowers may experience difficulties in finding alternative sources of funds, but in spite of the democratization of lending (see Chapter 1), banks are not welfare institutions. An example of what happens when loans are given philanthropically for political reasons rather than subsequent to rigorous financial analysis, is provided by post-communist China.

6.4   China's credit policies: a case study

Available information points to the fact that China's banking system, which is virtually all state-owned, not only does not allocate credit efficiently, but also poor credit
judgment gets amplified through political favors. In a way reminiscent of late 19th
century US lending practices, the misallocation of credits and risks gets worse with the
country's rapid economic growth. According to some estimates, in China's case bad
debts may already be at the level of 40–50% of loans – which makes the banking
system virtually bankrupt.

Experts suggest that the Chinese government is aware of this but, by all evidence,
is concerned by what will happen to the economy if it experiences a *credit crunch*.
In a broader sense, a credit crunch is a significant decrease in the supply of credit;
more narrowly it means interruption in the pipeline of bank loans which are given
regardless of whether borrowers qualify for them or not. As the 1991–2004 credit
events in neighboring Japan demonstrated,

- A credit crunch has potentially serious repercussions on economic development, and
- A sudden change of lending regime, necessary as it might be, can lead to a rash of
  defaults.

Moreover, the lack of a capital market, which might provide an alternative source
of financing, makes matters worse. China practically does not have a capital market
to finance its boom in the first years of the 21st century. The fact that its companies
are highly leveraged with loans means that a torrent of money has been advanced by
the country's credit institutions which:

- Carry all of the risks of lending, and
- Will experience all of the aftermath of a potential financial panic.

Forty to fifty percent of the loans being bad debts is an awesome figure, able to wipe
out the 4% capital requirements of credit institutions a dozen times over. One wonders
how things got that bad, but pulling out of the trap will not be easy.

There are exceptions to this statement, as not all banks are exposed to that high
level. For instance, the way a recent news item had it, the non-performing loan rate
of Bank of China, one of the country's biggest credit institutions, has fallen to less
than 6%.[9] This is:

- Still more than the bank's capital adequacy ratio, and
- It came in the aftermath of a government-organized auction of problem assets in
  early 2004.

Also, this covert salvage operation poses the question of whether the Chinese
government can repeat the gesture with all of the troubled banks. On the other hand,
according to experts, because of high gearing and interlocking debt relationships
among borrowers, the risk is real that a sudden contraction of credit could precipitously
trigger cash flow problems for a significant number of Chinese companies.

Should such an event take place, the Chinese banks will end up bearing the brunt, to the point that the whole banking sector will have to be recapitalized. Indeed, recapitalization at the taxpayers' expense is an option. *If* it is properly managed, it could be a successful operation, as the reader will see in Chapter 11 with the case study on Japan's Shinsei, the reborn Long-Term Credit Bank of Japan (LTCB).

As it will be recalled, LTCB collapsed in 1998; renamed as Shinsei it now has a clean balance sheet – an exception among Japanese credit institutions. Like most Chinese banks, LTCB was a huge bureaucracy which, under political patronage, provided low-margin corporate loans. After default, and after having been recapitalized through taxpayers' money, it was turned around by a new capable management.

China's central bank has a most crucial role to play in recapitalizing and restructuring the country's commercial banking system, while at the same time keeping a tight lid on inflation. Dr Paul Volcker, who as chairman of the Federal Reserve launched the successful fight against the ruinous inflation of the 1970s, once said that 'The truly unique power of a central bank is the power to create money, and ultimately the power to create is the power to destroy.'[10] All reserve institutions fall under this dictum.

LTCB's example fits China's current banking crisis because the country's banking industry has been dominated, for long years, by the so-called Big Four national banks: the Agricultural Bank of China, the Bank of China, the China Construction Bank, and the Industrial and Commercial Bank of China. All four credit institutions still draw enormous deposits, and play a major role in lending, albeit a declining one:

- Accounting for about three-fifths of nationwide loans, and
- Carrying along with it an accompanying very significant exposure.

China's dilemma is one of the clearest examples of the important role of credit in the business cycle, and of what will follow when it is disrupted. Chinese policy-makers are also faced by the fact that it is very difficult to determine when a situation of restrictive bank lending behavior should be classified as a major financial stress in the economy, and how far they can go in providing market liquidity before the banking system busts and the public panics, as happened in August 1998 with Russia's bankruptcy.

As a precautionary measure, at time of writing (2004) China's Big Four national banks have become more cautious in their lending, but many other Chinese credit institutions have not, even if they are facing rising burdens of problem loans. These smaller banks are mostly state-owned enterprises, often belonging to municipalities that are playing a growing role in dictating the banks' lending decisions, especially loans to local projects, many of which are pork-barrel type.

According to estimates made by independent rating agencies, credit risk continues building up, with China's banks not receiving timely payments of interest and principal on the aforementioned huge percentage of their loans. This is a gap very difficult, if at all possible, to bridge – twice the proportion acknowledged by Beijing and far higher than in other countries, like Japan, that have also struggled (and are still coping) with bad debt problems.

But at the same time, politically speaking, cutting off credit to insolvent state-owned enterprises is near to impossible, even for other reasons than prestige and 'losing face' which is an important decision-making criterion in the East. Most of these companies employ too many workers, and shutting them down would lead to major social troubles. The good news is that, as China watchers have been suggesting, there is a broad awareness that the country's banks need to:

- Improve their governance
- Learn to assess risk better, and
- Take measures to contain their sprawling exposure to credit risk.[11]

The bad news is that abiding by these three messages means adopting processes that could lead to the feared credit crunch. This is precisely why a case study on China's banking mess is so interesting. The current banking problems started in the post-Mao years, with China's rulers giving too much weight to the advice of different 'experts' and not enough to the evidence that:

- The economy was growing well beyond an affordable pace, and
- Neither the politicians themselves nor the central bankers were really in charge.

It is not the intention of this text to give advice. Nevertheless, generally speaking, to improve the function of its banking system, and its loans structure, a country needs financial reform, risk-based pricing of loans and other financial products, as well as rigorous transformation in corporate governance. In the most absolute sense, it also has to:

- Train its commercial bankers and central bankers in risk management, and
- Equip them with the technology which permits them to effectively exercise this function.

Altogether that will take years. In parallel to this, to avoid another wave of bad loans, China's banks have to introduce – and without loss of time – better organization, training and empowering their loans officers to say no to potential bad debts, in spite of the borrower's political patronage. It will also be wise if the government ensures that the country's banks abide by international capital adequacy standards promoted by Basel II (see section 6.6), because these represent a long experience compressed into some crisp guidelines.

6.5 Bank regulation and risk control

One of the curiosities of a leveraged economy is that while the party lasts bankruptcies of credit institutions hit a bottom; but then there is a spike as the bill becomes due. The American banking system came under stress in the late 1980s because of the real estate and junk bond bubbles. Not only did the savings and loans industry collapse, but also commercial banks have been feeling the heat – the bankruptcy of the Bank of New England is an example.

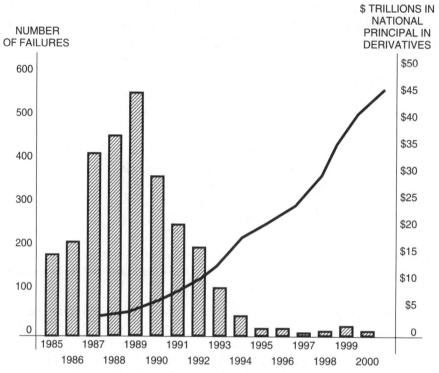

Figure 6.3 An interesting trend in bank failures and the growth of derivatives in the US markets

On the other hand, as Figure 6.3 shows, the banks' failure rate significantly dropped in the 1990s. This may seem curious, but according to experts the reason lies in the fact that the derivatives market built itself up. What were then the new financing instruments created a striking pattern, with the flight into derivatives giving the wrong message that the banking system had recovered. The trouble is that:

■ Derivatives are not a cure but a process for rolling over the unpayable claims of the banking system, and
■ These claims accumulate into larger and larger unpayables which one day reach explosion point and somebody has to foot the bill.

Statistical evidence beyond Figure 6.3 suggests that using derivatives in a big way has turned the global financial system into a highly geared environment in which, up to a point, bank failures indeed became hidden. The gearing, however, has continued and as the ongoing exposure accumulates, it eventually shows up as a bubble. This, in a nutshell, is the financial story of the late 1990s. The silver lining is that:

■ A market with no bank failures is often one in which financial services are expensive and consumer choices are limited.
■ Or, alternatively, one in which risks are compounded to explosion point, which comes after a critical threshold is exceeded.

Many events might serve as the trigger, one of them being the fact that global regulation is still wanting, though slowly it is coming into place. The new economy did not redefine the nature and framework of risk, even if it changed its frequency and magnitude. It has been essentially the business failures and the regulators (in that order) who have done the redefinition through the:

- 1988 capital adequacy accord (Basel I)
- 1996 market risk amendment, and
- New capital adequacy rules (Basel II), which started as a discussion paper in 1999 and will be implemented at the end of 2006.

Basel II (see section 6.6 and Chapter 15) has promoted important innovation in risk control, such as the internal rating-based (IRB) method for dynamic computation of capital requirements. Basel II has also contributed to the globalization of credit risk measures by promoting rating by independent agencies.

Notice that the new regulations in risk control are not motivated by risk aversion. Rather they are projected to keep risk-taking within prudent limits. Taking risks is healthy as long as the appropriate internal controls are in place and senior management is in charge. Therefore, regulators have worked diligently to identify risks to financial stability and to provide guidelines about them. Risks to financial stability include:

- An inordinate amount of bankruptcies
- Financial crime and market abuse
- Market malfunction due to a number of reasons
- Mismanagement of companies, which end by destroying financial and other resources.

Many risks are associated with lack of appropriate investor protection, inadequate understanding by investors of financial products and services, and convoluted wheeling and dealing which does not allow the market to perform its functions. Both financial stability and consumer-oriented risks can arise not only from individual firms but also from world-wide economic trends and conditions, including:

- Asymmetric developments in social policy
- Abrupt changes in consumer behavior, and
- Introduction of financial products which are only partially understood or lead to unintended consequences.

The issue has already been raised in previous chapters that because of the financial market's globalization, regulatory action must work crossborder; it cannot be confined within national frontiers. Homogeneous global regulation is very important, not only due to the diversity of risks which may be punching this or that financial bubble, but also for the reason that regulatory diversity impedes the continued internationalization of financial services, as well as it:

- Increases transactional costs
- Reduces transparency in a significant way

- Magnifies the negative effects of market failures, and
- Provokes restrictive domestic trade-related regulation.

Barriers to markets exist when governments restrict the number of competitors, limit the functioning of free price-setting mechanisms, decide single-handed on exchange rates, and stiffen innovation; also, when governments try to swamp competitive advantages through restrictive practices weeding out potential entrants. All these factors work to the detriment of the economy's growth and its sustenance.

In principle, market access alone does not guarantee the globalization of financial services. A vital ingredient is the development of a regulatory structure based on efficiency, simplicity, transparency, and risk control within a framework of appropriate prudential rules. It is in the interest of the various sectors of the economy to be supportive of effective regulation and of supervisory activities in the areas of:

- Ethical behavior
- Reliable financial reporting
- Financial solvency, and
- Investor protection.

As an example, the practice of alternative investments, addressed to individual investors,[12] and the management of risk associated with them, should be seen within this perspective. All four bullets contribute to the proper functioning of markets and of the economy. Therefore, the management of risk is indivisible from their observance, and any regulatory system that bypasses one or more of these issues is not going to keep the eventual bubble under control.

Moreover, the more complex a financial instrument, old or new, the more difficult it is to develop and maintain a prudential supervisory environment, particularly one that tries to establish and maintain a level playing field. The right sort of competition laws should regulate the scope and nature of the global market rather than targeting individual competitors. Well-structured rules should underpin the authority given to supervisors to prevent:

- Collusive price setting
- Market sharing arrangements
- Aggressive off-loading of risk to investors, and
- Excessive exposure which lessens the financial staying power of the banks assuming it.

In principle, the more dynamic and more competitive a market the more important is prudential regulation, but also the more complex and difficult are the issues to be addressed. For a regulated industry such as banking, the inclusion of specific principles like those described by the above four bullets is critical in setting the pattern of globalization.

Financial institutions, and other companies, are right to worry about prescriptive regulation but, at the same time, rules should be in place to protect the interests of all parties. Any regulation that does not treat all market players in a fair but rigorous way, throws doubts on its usefulness as a model.

In conclusion, it is the duty of both regulators and governments to assure that business confidence in a globalized economy is neither misplaced nor undermined, that asset quality is enough to satisfy capital requirements and provide for financial staying power, and that the needed policy provisions are in place. Also that corrective action will be taken anytime something happens which dents business confidence.

6.6 The confirmation of Basel II

On 11 May 2004, following almost five years of negotiation, the Basel Committee on Banking Supervision reached agreement on new international rules which link capital more closely to the riskiness of a bank's assets. Basel I, the old capital adequacy system of 1988, had no risk-based formula; Basel II, the new one, does and also provides the framework for its further evolution. (See Chapter 15 on the analytics and risk management requirements associated to Basel II.)

From the end of 2006, in Europe but not in the United States, Basel II capital adequacy rules will apply to smaller, less sophisticated banks that follow the standard method. In the United States only big, international banks will be subject to Basel II and they will have to apply the advanced internal risk-based (A-IRB) method. Both European and US banks using A-IRB won an extra year in which to comply – a year which should be used in simulations and benchmarks between a flat 8% capital adequacy and A-IRB.

Notice that US banks are subject not only to Basel rules but also to *prompt corrective action* (PCA) requirements, which were introduced in the early 1990s to strengthen the banking system. And there is, with Basel II, a second pillar which strengthens the supervisors' discretion and authority, as well as a third one which brings market discipline into play (more on this later).

The market can be a tough critter. Whether in the United States, Europe, or Asia, to be considered *well capitalized* a bank must have *tier-one* capital of at least 5% of its unweighted assets; below 4% it is believed to be undercapitalized. This is not exactly what the regulators say; it is what the market wants.

As the experience with Basel II rules and models is new, there can always be surprises. For instance, the Federal Deposit Insurance Corporation (FDIC) estimates that Basel II banks can expect their capital requirements to fall sharply over a business cycle. *If* so, this will drag the Basel II minimum below the level needed to keep equity ratios above 4% for some of the economic cycles. Therefore, FDIC wants US banks to maintain the 8% capital ratio (established by Basel I) no matter what the models say.

Fundamentally, capital adequacy rules under Basel II convert into capital charge the probability that a borrower will default, the size and maturity of the loan, and a bank's exposure at default. Other things being equal, the higher the probability of default, the higher the charge. If recession deepens, every company's chances of default will be affected and charges will be rising across the board. Banks will also need to tighten their lending conditions (see in section 6.5 the example of China). Some experts fear that, for this reason, Basel II might make business cycles more severe

- Causing banks to tighten credit during recessions, and
- Loosening their credit rules too much during booms.

These are, of course, hypotheses, and pessimistic ones for that matter; only time will tell, and there is no doubt that regulators will watch closely to take the needed steps if the case arises. No new system – particularly one with many unknowns – works perfectly the first time around. There is no doubt that it can be made better, after commercial bankers and regulators gain experience with its results.

A great deal of the challenge with Basel II, particularly in connection to the advanced internal ratings-based (A-IRB) method, would be the implementation of risk-weighted pricing for banking products and services. As one of the regulators put it, even if you are a small but specialized bank, and know your business, you can go for A-IRB.

In the UK, the Bank of England expects that credit institutions representing more than 80% of the banking industry's assets will adopt A-IRB; the rest will more likely adopt the standard method. Not many are expected to choose F-IRB – which stands for foundation internal ratings-based approach, and fits between the other two in terms of sophistication.

In the United States, John Hawke, head of the Office of the Comptroller of the Currency (OCC), one of the main bank regulators, says that an extensive process remains before Basel II can be adopted, including input from Congress and a fourth quantitative impact study (QIS). This extensive process requires concentration and hard work, as it simultaneously involves:

- Learning Basel II's more complex aspects
- Changing the bank's culture towards risk-based pricing, and
- Putting in place a technology-based system of real-time management control.

Moreover, the majority of the work so far has focused on Basel II's Pillar I, whose aim is capital adequacy. But as discussed in the preceding paragraphs, there is also Pillar 2, which allows national supervisors the discretion to adjust regulatory capital levels; and Pillar 3, which compels banks to disclose significantly more information to financial markets than they usually do. The market discipline that will be exercised through greater transparency is likely to have a much bigger effect on capital requirements, and on the banks' behavior, than A-IRB's models and procedures.

Commercial bankers should appreciate that a great deal of attention must also be paid to high technology, and most importantly data collection, mining, and analysis as well as modeling and simulation. Data must be handled fully on-line from point of origin to point of destination.[13] The Internet may help, by facilitating the bank's ability in reaching on-line clients and its own outposts, collecting information.

Credit institutions will be well advised to exploit the possible benefits of using the Internet as a data collection channel for new and old services, an example of the latter being claims adjustment. For instance, business-to-business (B2B) Internet transactions offer an opportunity for credit insurers because by providing lines of credit to buyers on the Internet, they:

- Enhance their fee-based revenues, and
- Leverage their proprietary information on the creditworthiness of their customers.

From loans to trading and securities sales, several business lines present opportunities and challenges in terms of on-line deals. One of the challenges is the development and use of model-based real-time systems that can make a significant contribution to credit enhancements; for example, real-time evaluation of fair value of asset-backed commercial paper, trade receivables and liabilities incurred by insured parties.

Because of its capillarity, the Internet helps credit insurance companies to deliver more personalized information to their clients, as well as reducing paperwork costs related to processing information – a good deal of the work being done on-line. The Internet also assists insurers to improve efficiency in underwriting, distribution, administration, and claims settlement. Similar statements can be made about banking.

These and similar activities help the bottom line because they are reflected in lower costs. It should, however, be kept in mind that information technology requires leadership, skill, and expenditures – and many institutions do not fulfill the requirements for leadership and expertise. Whether we talk of A-IRB and its models, of database mining, or of the use of a capillary network like the Internet, technology is an enabling tool. It is not a substitute for human ingenuity and know-how.

6.7 An introduction to securitization[14]

The process of *securitization* generally refers to borrowing backed by securities. In addition to the issue of debt securities by final borrowers, securitization includes bank debt securities to fund lending. Owing to its wider and wider acceptance as a financial instrument, and the fact that since the late 1990s securitization is used to arbitrage the capital requirements of Basel I, this process is changing the nature of financial relationships both:

- For the lender, and
- For the borrower.

In the general case, securitization increases the degree of liquidity of loan portfolios in commercial banks, retail banks, and savings and loans. Tradable loan agreements enable individual investors to manage their portfolios more flexibly; they also give them an array of options in their choice of bonds. But, as we will see, there is also a downside.

To start with a brief historical reference, Samuel W. Straus is credited with originating, in 1909, the first mortgage security with a senior claim. Securitization of mortgages prospered during the following two decades, but second liens made these instruments fragile; credit quality tends to suffer as securities issuance rises. Moreover, the Great Depression took them off the financial map.

Securitization of mortgages restarted in 1970, when the US government-sponsored National Mortgage Association invented the 'Ginnie Mae passthrough'. This has been a mortgage-backed security that over three-and-a-half decades has grown into a huge market. After savings and loans (S&L), or any other institution financing mortgages, establishes the contract with the homeowner, it usually:

- Brings it into a mortgage pool, and
- Asks investment banks to make an offer for securitizing the mortgages in the pool.

Subsequently, payments received from homeowners will service these securities, which are often sold to investors throughout the world. Like any other instrument, however, securitized products have several risks for the holder. For instance, if interest rates decline, home owners could decide to refinance their current mortgage, by prepaying the principal and taking out a new mortgage at a lower rate. But

- *If* every homeowner in a pool, or nearly so, prepaid their mortgages
- *Then* holders of mortgage-based securities would be hurt.

Holders of securitized mortgages would not receive interest payments once the mortgages in a pool were prepaid, though they will get their principal, unless the home owner has defaulted. Prognosticating prepayment of mortgages is tough but necessary because investors want it, and it is also the basis for pricing these securities.

- Pricing is based on option-adjusted spread (OAS), and
- The likely decay of mortgages is studied through the Monte Carlo method.[15]

In spite of these and other exposures associated with securitized products, the securitization of lending in global financial markets has progressed quite significantly during the past 35 years. Its scale and pace have had far-reaching implications for the role of banks, as well as for monetary policy in different countries. Furthermore, in many cases broad secondary markets provide the basis for derivative instruments through which microeconomic risk positions can be controlled selectively. The possibility of large-scale portfolio switching:

- Makes the financial system potentially more sensitive to swings in sentiment.
- But, at the same time, it becomes more difficult for the central bank to assess the effects of monetary policy measures on the financial market.

As a relatively new direction in investing and trading, securitization calls for monetary policy-makers counteracting, to a greater extent than ever before, on uncertainties and shifts in market expectations. They also need to watch not only their own macroeconomic models but also prognostications of financial market players. This is absolutely necessary in order to develop a credible and predictable counterinflationary policy stance.

Critics say that to make matters more complex, massive shifts of funds may result in destabilization if they lead to sharp fluctuations in a portfolio's estimated profitability. There may also be liquidity shortages on the markets as a whole. The pros answer that securitization opens new vistas in financial transactions.

Because it permits the development of innovative financial instruments securitization has become one of the principal transactional elements in the international financial market, and a popular one. The strength of the trend towards securitization is highlighted by the increase in bond issues in OECD countries and in Euromarkets.

The use of debt securities for raising funds and for investing has now become common practice in most Group of Ten countries. This is part of a wider development (promoted by deregulation) which, since the early 1980s, has seen the securities markets undergoing a fundamental change because of the:

- Availability of customized instruments
- Growing globalization of financing and investment activities
- Innovation in the securities markets, and
- Development and use of new risk management tools and methods.

Investors should be aware that the buyer of securitized assets assumes the full default risk of securitized mortgages or other loans which, in the case of a classic bank deposit, is reduced by the dissemination of credit risk and the bank's assumption of liability. Also, up to a certain level, for instance:

- $100 000 in the United States
- 20 000 euro in Euroland

depositors are protected by deposit insurance, a guarantee provided by state-supported organizations like the Federal Deposits Insurance Corporation (FDIC) in the United States. That's part of the socialization of risk. Investors of securitized mortgages don't benefit from such protection.

Moreover, with the growing importance of liquid, securitized assets, and the globalization of financial markets, the banking system tends to be more strongly exposed to shifts in market sentiment. Indeed, one indication of the greater volatility of the financial markets is the rise in turnover of domestic debt securities.

Part of the downside is the fact that proactive securitization of the better loans may lead to a possible deterioration of the quality of the banking book. If so, this will have significant effects on the bank itself and on securitization. Also, as a matter of principle, an effective financial system cannot simply be equated with securitized financing.

Despite shortcomings in individual cases, discussed in earlier sections, relationship banking can be an instrumental process because it provides the credit institution with an incentive to monitor the debtor on an ongoing basis. Such an incentive does not exist for individual creditors if the securities are spread over a wide range of investors (see also Chapter 5).

Conservative bankers who are not enthusiastic about securitization also point out that through relationship banking the flow of information is channeled between the bank and the debtor. Therefore, it remains restricted in terms of disclosure. By contrast, the capital market should always be open and transparent, because this is the only way to gain investor confidence, and promote market discipline.

6.8 Securitization as a mechanism for risk transfer?

Basel II has addressed issues relating to securitization for the dual reason that it is so important to the modern economy (and for that matter to the whole of the banking system) and because credit institutions use it to arbitrage their capital requirements.

The arbitrage of capital adequacy is one of the forces that work to promote securitization. Others are:

■ A growing demand for securities on the part of domestic private investors
■ A pronounced increase in institutional savings which have to be invested, and
■ A parallel drive by financial institutions to unload to third parties risk embedded into their banking book.

When in the early 1990s the US economy was in difficulty, one of the industries badly bruised was banking. Between 1989 and 1993, US supervisors closed 1418 banks with assets of $554 billion. Also, Citibank was thought to be at risk of going under. By contrast, in the recession of 2000–2003, the US banking industry has suffered only some rather minor knocks.

One of the reasons for this significant difference in recession effects is thought to be that the early 21st century recession was much less deep than that of a decade before. But several experts think that it is more likely banks have become more resilient because they securitize and sell their credit risks.

To a greater or lesser extent, this is true of most of the Group of Ten countries. The United States is the best example even if, as Table 6.1 has shown, US banks now directly supply less than 20% of the money companies raise each year, compared to a much greater percentage in other countries.

Investors should appreciate that, to a significant extent, with securitization the main sufferers from credit risk are bondholders rather than banks. By securitizing their loans credit institutions transfer their exposure to these other investors. Banks love this risk transfer, and as statistics document during the 1990s and the first years of this century, the growth of markets for spreading risk has been remarkable. Most:

■ Mortgages
■ Credit card receivables
■ Auto loans
■ Other personal loans, and
■ An increasing number of corporates are securitized.

This way they are taken off the books of originating banks. There are also risk-sharing schemes, such as syndicated loans, in which one bank, or a small group of banks, brings together a large number of lenders. These are sometimes strange bedfellows. Syndicated loans might include pension funds and insurance companies, not only other banks.

Another significant increase in financial transactions aimed at risk transfer has been in the value of loans sold to other financial institutions on the secondary market. The volume has grown five-fold in the 1990s, to over $100 billion.[16] Add to these statistics the rise of credit derivatives, especially credit-default swaps which are being bought by big banks, and the result is a pattern of the financial market's transformation.

It may sound iconoclastic to say that this is not necessarily a change for the better, but there are reasons for this statement. One of the basic reasons is that *risk sold* (or insurance purchased to cover risk), and *risk bought* tend to balance each other – making the motion of risk transfer questionable. It sounds like (the now illegal) broadband communications swaps between WorldCom, Enron Broadband, Global Crossing, and other subsequently defunct players.

- In the third quarter of 2003, American banks held more than $400 billion-worth of credit-default insurance.
- But, at the same time, they were guarantors of almost $350 billion-worth, a high multiple from the mid-1990s when this market barely existed.

The pros say that the outcome of all this turning around of financial contracts has been to soften the effect of corporate defaults on the banking system. When companies default on their bonds, or when bond prices are marked sharply downwards, all bondholders suffered, including hedge funds, pension funds, insurers, and private investors – not only the banks. The critics answer that too much smoke and mirrors helps nobody; and some of the regulators seem to side with the critics.

6.9   A bridge too far in democratization of lending

If banks act as the main financial intermediaries, and loans rather than bonds are the industrial sector's preferred channel of financing, *then* in case a company defaults on its loans, the cost hits its house bank. Based on this fact, which cannot be disputed, the pros say that credit institutions are more willing to lend if they are able to securitize and sell their loans. And they are even more willing to lend if they know that they can buy insurance against default through derivative instruments.

This is advancing the democratization of credit so much further; but it is also a way of looking at modern finance which has its detractors. Critics say that an easy securitization of bad loans, the finding of willing counterparties in credit-default swaps and other similar risk-transfer transactions, end by making the banks trigger-happy and *less prudent* with their loans. Thereby,

- They poison the whole financial system, and
- They bring nearer the day when the global financial fabric will be torn apart.

Critics also question the reasons for the apparent change in private savers' and institutional investors' behavior, characterizing as rather simplistic the explanation that this is associated with the rise in incomes and financial assets. There is some value in this questioning attitude, though the view that the demographic trends, and the resultant burden, impose penalties on public pension schemes and lead private investors in the aforementioned direction, also has its worth.

Annuities and pensions, including private pensions, relieve – up to a point – the burden imposed on public pension schemes by an aging society. They also boost indirect securitized lending through the intermediation of insurance companies, pension funds, and investment funds. Such an underlying trend has been evident for some time, and it is most likely to persist.

■ *If* direct private investments, private pensions, and other annuities are to be successful,
■ Then there must be reliable outlets providing investment opportunities, at easy reach and at reasonably good yield.

The pros say that securitization of other people's companies, and sovereign's liabilities, provide precisely this outlet. It may be so. The problem however is that this answer does not consider the term *reliable*, which is a keyword. *If* the pensioners' assets are the consumers' liabilities leveraged *n* times, *then* these assets hang dangerously suspended. Who will provide the safety net? The state supermarket?

Among critical factors on the downside are not only the possible tidal wave of credit risk, but also market unknowns associated with a highly leveraged economy. There also exist hidden correlations among risk factors, which may turn the financial system on its head. And there is the fact that, with globalization, the supervisory responsibilities and duties, not to mention the making and testing of monetary policy, have become so complex.

To a fairly significant extent, the accelerating securitization trend has been accompanied by the erosion of formerly stable relationships between total deposits, banks' loan portfolios, and the money stock variables derived from their relationship. Securitization has also altered the overall price movements in a free market, and the process of their correction.

As a result of securitization's effect on the money supply (see Chapter 1), some of the major central banks had to abandon the strategy of monetary targeting, focusing instead on interest rates. An example here is the policy now followed by the Federal Reserve.[17]

Several other central bankers also mentioned that in terms of monetary targeting, the advance of securitized lending, and of different deposit vehicles, is a particular challenge. Part of this challenge is the impact securitization has not only in the jurisdiction of a certain central bank but also in other countries, particularly those of the Group of Ten. This impact affects the stability of underlying monetary relationships.

■ Securitization in short maturity ranges may impede a definition of monetary aggregates that is empirically meaningful, and
■ The extent to which this may impair the quality of the money stock as an indicator depends to a large extent on the pace at which new securitized instruments develop and spread.

Problems of this sort have primarily become manifest where administrative interest rate restrictions have prevented bank deposits from carrying market-related interest rates. Also, they have encouraged large-scale securitized innovation to circumvent these restrictions.

According to some expert opinions, the controllability of monetary aggregates may also be hampered by decreasing interest rate sensitivity to the demand for money. This is particularly true if, as a consequence of securitization, the specific interest earned by money holding increases. Another challenge is that the growing integration of markets; and the trend towards splitting financial services into their individual components, can further blur the dividing lines between banking and market intermediation, as well as the national and international financial platform.

Notes

1 D.N. Chorafas, *Economic Capital Allocation with Basel II: Cost and Benefit Analysis*, Butterworth-Heinemann, Oxford and Boston, 2004.
2 European Central Bank, Annual Report 2002.
3 D.N. Chorafas, *Rating Management's Effectiveness with Case Studies in Telecommunications*, Macmillan/Palgrave, London, 2004.
4 Deutsche Bundesbank, Monthly Report, February 2004.
5 *The Economist*, 15 May 2004.
6 D.N. Chorafas, *The Management of Equity Investments*, Butterworth-Heinemann, Oxford, 2005.
7 Ron Chernow, *The House of Morgan*, Touchstone/Simon & Schuster, New York, 1990.
8 D.N. Chorafas, *Rating Management's Effectiveness with Case Studies in Telecommunications*, Macmillan/Palgrave, London, 2005.
9 *Financial Times*, 15 July 2004.
10 *The Economist*, 19 June 2004.
11 D.N. Chorafas, *Managing Credit Risk*, Volume 1: *Analyzing, Rating and Pricing the Probability of Default*, Euromoney, London, 2000.
12 D.N. Chorafas, *Alternative Investments and the Mismanagement of Risk*, Macmillan/Palgrave, London, 2003.
13 D.N. Chorafas, *The Real-Time Enterprise*, Auerbach, New York, 2005.
14 The process of securitization is very important to modern finance and it deserves a full book, not just a section. This is only an introduction aimed to link loans to bonds.
15 D.N. Chorafas, *Chaos Theory in the Financial Markets*, Probus/Irwin, Chicago, 1994.
16 D.N. Chorafas, *Credit Derivatives and the Management of Risk*, New York Institute of Finance, New York, 2000.
17 D.N. Chorafas, *The Money Magnet: Regulating International Finance and Analyzing Money Flows*, Euromoney, London, 1997.

Part 3
Interest rates, yields, and duration

7 The dynamics of interest rates

7.1 Introduction

Bondholders are creditors. It is therefore only normal that they receive an interest in exchange for the money they have lent to an entity, whether government, company or any other issuer of obligations. As has been discussed in Part 2, apart from the promises to bondholders to repay the borrowed funds, this entity assumes the obligation to pay the lender, at specified future dates, a set rate of interest for the period over which the bond is outstanding. This is the *interest rate* of the bond.

Theoretically, the interest rate is the bondholder's profit. Practically, this profit tends to be less than the previous sentence might suggest – for various reasons, inflation being one of them (see Chapter 8). Prior to examining the practical differences, which are largely determined through the distinction between *nominal* and *real* interest rates, as well as the definition of *yield* (which has been introduced in Chapter 3), it is appropriate to bring to the reader's attention facts regarding the concept of 'profit'.

In finance and economics, the definitions of profit and of interest differ significantly from those of accounting practice, which is based on regulatory rules and conventions. The term *profit* is typically considered to mean a residual income. This is the portion of income that remains after all costs, implicit as well as explicit, are met.

- *Common profit* is the part of such residual return arising because of uncertainties and associated assumed risks.
- *Profit of exclusive position*, also known as monopoly rent, results when, for any reason, an entity exploits monopolistic position; for instance, in the aftermath of an exclusive patent.

Generally, though not always, economic *rent* is return received from property or service that cannot be duplicated. The difference between the income a worker receives in his most advantageous employment and what he could get in other alternatives is a form of rent. This term has, however, been degraded because of too many people 'seeking rent' through nepotism, lobbying, entitlement programs, and wild strikes.

In economic terms, *interest* is defined as the price paid for the use of loanable funds, whether these funds are borrowed or owner-invested. A first bifurcation between 'common interest' and 'exclusive interest' is similar to that of profit. Common interest reflects risk being assumed, while interest from an exclusive investment position is the result of conflict of interest – all the way from favoritism to gains achieved through covert influence, of which there is sometimes plenty, and the abuse of one's position, as in the case of executive options.[1]

(The theoretical definition of interest is that of price paid for temporary provision of funding in a state of equilibrium, which aligns supply and demand on the capital market; this will not be dealt with in this text. Other reasons aside, this is too theoretical, because the savings and investments behind supply and demand for funds are never really in equilibrium.)

Two important points should be made in connection to *common interest*, which is the theme of this book. The first is that economic theory tends to associate interest to substantially riskless investments, such as US government bonds and guilds. This is a little too restrictive (if not outright theoretical) because, as we will see, there is credit risk (Chapter 12) and market risk (Chapter 14), as well as operational risks associated to a bond position held by an investor.[2]

The second is that only at time of issue, and in cases not even then, is the stipulated (quoted, posted) *nominal* bond interest rate synonymous with its yield. In the secondary market, unless the bond sells at par, the nominal and *real* interest rates differ – with the actual price of the bond accounting for this difference. As we will see in Chapter 8, *yield-to-maturity* (see Chapter 8), or internal rate of return, is calculated from the instrument's market price and nominal interest rate.

Because difference in terminology can be confusing, let's follow a couple of examples that explain how the actual rate of interest may not be the same as the nominal rate. As a simple example, if one goes to the bank to borrow money, one finds that the bank ordinarily deducts its interest on the loan in advance. As a result, the borrower will sign a note promising to pay the bank, say, $10 000 in one year, but if the rate charged is, for instance, 8%, after deducting the interest upfront, the bank gives the borrower $9200.

This practice of deducting interest in advance of the loan is known as *discounting*. Strictly speaking, the bank charges a discount rate rather than an interest rate. Notice, as well, that the borrower is actually paying more than 8% interest on the funds he receives as a loan, since he is charged 8% on $10 000 but receives only $9200.

Let's now look into *bond yields*. Bonds are usually issued in amounts of $1000 and feature a set rate of interest. If a $1000 bond bears 6% interest, this means the issuer will pay the bondholder $60 in interest annually, whatever the debt instrument's market price happens to be at the time; and he will repay the $1000 face value at maturity.

Suppose, however, that an investor is now contemplating the purchase in the secondary market of a nominal value $1000 6% bond due in 2015, which is selling for $1050. The real interest rate is less because the bond is selling above par. By contrast, *if* the fixed rate instrument was selling below par – say, at $950 – then the investor would have received more than the nominal 6% rate of interest on it, having bought it at discount. The way to bet is that in the majority of cases, the nominal and real interest rates will not be equal.

7.2   Who sets interest rates?

The nominal, or quoted, interest rate is written by the issuer but it is not really decided by him. What the issuer basically does is read the currently prevailing interest rate in the market and currency of the projected bond, take account of the company's credit rating, outstanding debt and other factors, and come up with a nominal interest rate (and sometimes covenants) which will make the debt instrument appealing to the market.

If the issuer does not *really* decide on the interest rate of the bond, then who does? Theoretically, interest rates are manipulated by governments and by central banks, but practically, interest rates are set by the market, which might judge the government's and central bank's decisions as being heavy-handed, light-hearted, or simply insufficient.

What the central bank (or the government, depending on jurisdiction) really sets is the discount rate for loaning money to the banking system. This influences the market rate, particularly the short-term rate, but does not really cast it in stone. In fact, the market might judge the government 'set' rate as too low, or too high slowing growth needlessly. Monetary authorities:

■ May lower the discount rate to boost the equity market, or make the medium-term market's interest rate fall.
■ In other cases, they may raise the discount rate to cool the equity market, or burst a nascent bubble.

Discount rates are a monetary policy instrument of the reserve institution. The only interest rates that central banks and governments can directly affect are nominal, short-term ones. In a free economy, longer-term interest rates, which matter much more for investment and growth, escape the authorities' control.

■ The market decides what is to happen to them, and
■ The market shapes the yield curve (see section 7.6).

This is not the only perspective that is important to investors in order to appreciate what happens with interest rates. Even the quoted interest on a bond instrument, as well as the yield being computed, are not fully an investor's common profit. Nominal bond yields should be split into two main components:

■ A real yield (see Chapter 9), and
■ The expected rate of inflation (see Chapter 8).

Even the real yield is not truly 'real', because it should be thought of as the sum of a desired rate of return and risk-premium. Among other things, the latter reflects uncertainty about exposure taken with the bond – in terms of credit risk, market risk (including interest rate risk, currency risk, *et al.*), and operational risk.

For debt instruments issued in any major currency, real yields are determined by the balance of demand and supply in the increasingly global market for capital. They are likely to rise if investment rises or if savings as well as other factors, representing the supply of capital, fall. An increase in risk premium, caused by an increase in uncertainty, will also push real yield upwards.

For instance, in the 1970s real interest rates averaged close to zero, and over several years they were negative. This happens from time to time, one of the reasons being that investors see inflation as a temporary problem and fail to demand nominal yields that are big enough to compensate them for future inflation. As a result, they lose money.

In the 1980s, real bond yields averaged 6%, partly because investors, having lost heavily in the previous decade, had learned their lesson. As a result, they demanded a much bigger risk premium than they might have done otherwise. But also in the late 1980s, as investors became more confident that inflation would stay down, the risk premium fell – though heavy demand for capital kept up real yields.

Reference to the 1970s and 1980s provides an excellent example of the way the market works. In the 1980s the market was helped by several governments which carried out supply-side reforms, raising the rate of return on investment, and hence the demand for capital. The 1980s were also a decade of financial deregulation, which:

- Boosted the demand for private credit, and
- Reduced net personal savings.

One of the criteria the market uses in setting medium- to longer-term interest rates is the volume of transactions done in debt instruments. This has a counterpart in the equities market, and often it is more appreciated with stocks than with bonds. Other events may also have a significant impact on volume of transactions. For instance, in September 2001, right after the September 11 (9/11) terrorist attack, the $18 trillion US bond market was operating at well below normal volumes.

Both market psychology and technical factors, in the aftermath of the destruction of the Twin Towers in New York, combined to swamp market volume. So great were the difficulties of settling and clearing trades when the bond market reopened two days after 9/11, that the market had to extend the time for settling bond trades to five days in an attempt to clear up the backlog. Still:

- Corporate bond trading was only 50% of normal, and
- Spreads between dealers' buying and selling prices widened with benchmark US Treasury bonds.

Moreover, longer-maturity issues were dropping in price as the market demanded higher interest rates to compensate for bigger risks. Indeed, bonds were facing their old nemesis: a return of federal deficit spending that:

- Revived fears of inflation, and
- Stepped up competition for capital.

Had there been a crash in the market precipitated by the 9/11 events, nobody could have accused high interest rates of being responsible. As shown in Figure 7.1, 2001 was a year of very low interest rates in the three major currencies – the US dollar, the British pound and the euro – while interest rates on the Japanese yen were for all practical purposes submerged.

In that difficult market, underwriters were called on to raise capital for insurance companies who – as it was thought at the time – had to pay out anywhere from $30 to $100 billion on property and life claims. And there were other *ifs* that weighed on market sentiment, and had an impact on both:

- Volume of transactions, and
- Interest rates demanded by investors.

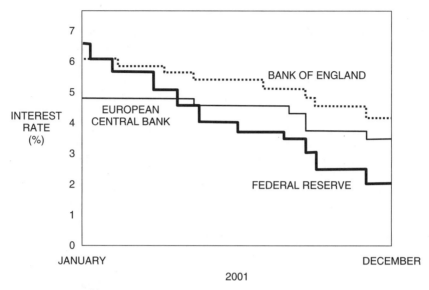

Figure 7.1 The aggressive cuts in interest rates to turn around the economy

For instance, *if* the Federal Reserve were not providing capital and if Congress were not crafting a bailout to prevent the airline industry from defaulting on more than $35 billion of debt, experts said that there would be virtually no way the capital market could raise funds. Wall Street never likes having to count on Washington for help, but in this particular case there was little choice.

In fact, the Fed and the central banks of Western Europe did engage in a global campaign of raising liquidity to keep the financial markets operating smoothly after 9/11. In the following week they flooded the money markets with cash. The Fed also cut interest rates by 50 basis points, and led central banks around the world into concerted action to avert a world economic crisis.

The aftermath of 9/11 in the financial market provides an interesting response to the question posed in the heading for this section, broadening the answer to include different parties. These parties (who make up 'the market') not only come into contact with one another, but also anticipate – or at least try to guess – each other's:

■ Expectations
■ Hopes
■ Fears, and
■ Likely response.

In the United States, securities firms asked the Fed if they could tap the discount window, a step that had not been taken since the 1930s. And in addition to the billions the Federal Reserve lent through the discount window, it also pumped tens of billions into the money market through securities repurchase agreements (repos). This cash deluge peaked on September 14th, when the Fed flooded the banking system with $81.25 billion, many times the $5 billion or so it normally adds, and then acted to limit the fallout overseas.

On September 13th, just prior to this US liquidity spike, after a series of transatlantic phone calls, the Fed announced that it had set up a $50 billion currency swap with the European Central Bank (ECB) to make sure the ECB had enough dollars to meet cash demands of the banks it oversees. According to some reports, getting the ECB's president, Wim Duisenberg, to go along with interest-rate cuts was tricky, because for the European Central Bank price stability is a priority.

All this helps in documenting in no uncertain terms that the way central banks interact with the market, and vice versa, is far from being linear. In essence it is an interplay between a myriad of factors, the most important being supply and demand, uncertainty, push and pull by monetary authorities, and the market's own appreciation of facts and figures – as well as prevailing psychology. The interest rate can thus be seen as an end result, encapsulating so many factors into one number.

7.3   Effect of interest rate hikes on the market

Section 7.2 stated that by easing on interest rates central banks are pumping liquidity into the market; with lower interest rates, money costs less. As a commodity, it becomes more generally available. The result is that the velocity of circulation of money accelerates (see Chapter 1). Another way of doing so is to reduce the reserve requirements of banks.[3]

Both strategies have risks, a major one being that of igniting inflation (see Chapter 8). But what about if the central bank hikes the discount rate? It is clear that this makes money more expensive, but what will be the effect on the market for debt and equities? Historical evidence provides some of the answers.

For instance, by early June 2004, the Federal Reserve announced that it would begin to raise interest rates 'soon' – and this for several practical reasons. Thereafter, rates on money market funds began to creep higher, with the increase in money market yields roughly matching the projected increase in the Fed funds rate.

It needs no explanation that when interest rates move north the price of fixed coupon debt instruments goes south. That's the only way for the yield to match the new, higher rate. The question is how orderly such transition may be, and a good part of the response depends on:

- Whether or not the central bank's rate increases are expected in terms of their size and frequency, and
- How highly leveraged at the lower interest rate are the different market players, particularly big speculators and hedge funds.

In 1994, when the Fed raised interest rates seven consecutive times, there had been a blood bath among geared-up speculators in debt instruments. These had probably thought that the very low interest rates of the early 1990s could last forever, and they gambled in that direction.

With this in mind, confronted by a new series of interest rate hikes by the Fed, in June 2004 financial analysts debated what might be the result this time around. One frequently heard opinion has been that things will not be so bad because for all the worries about the parallels between 1994 and 2004, the futures market in 1994 was only priced for 100 basis points worth of tightening. By contrast, in 2004 that figure is closer to 300.

In addition, many analysts suggested, one should recall that inflation expectations were quite high in 1994. Core inflation heading into 1994 was 3% versus 1.7% in 2004. The statistics may be right, but such an argument forgets that in 2004 total inflation in the United States has also been 3%, while in France and in the UK it stood at 2.8% – in all cases thanks to huge government deficits (see Chapter 8).

These different assurances by the governments and some of the analysts have been non-starters with investors, and most particularly with speculators. By mid-May 2004, hedge funds were liquidating positions with long-term fixed coupon debt instruments, as well as emerging countries and other overpriced bonds. At the same time, sophisticated private and institutional investors concerned about an income stream during the next couple of years have been locking in the yield on 2-year Treasury notes.

Mid-June 2004 the yield of a 2-year Treasury was about 2.75%, roughly 225 basis points more than a money market fund. Some analysts suggested that for a money fund to match that income stream, its yield would have to rise enough to compensate for the initial shortfall. But:

- If yields were to rise steadily, money market rates would have to climb to about 5% at the end of 2005, and
- Short of this, investors could not wind up with more income from a mid-2004 2-year Treasury.

This speaks volumes about the extent to which a right or wrong guesstimate in interest rate direction can make the difference between black and red ink. Merrill Lynch suggested that in light of Fed rate hikes and projected further increases in long-term yields, investors should be wary of leveraged closed-end bond funds – because most closed-end bond funds borrow at short-term rates to finance purchases of longer-term bonds.[4] If yields rise as we expect, both sides of that position would suffer.

- A fund's borrowing costs would rise as short-term rates move higher, and
- The value of a fund's bond holdings would decline as long-term rates rise.

What about the effect on equity investors of interest rate hikes by the Federal Reserve? The optimists said that, as financial history suggests, equity investors do not need to fear: stocks have risen in the 12 months following the first Fed move, even if bonds tend to lose ground after the central bank begins tightening.

According to at least one opinion, the economic environment that leads the Fed to begin tightening includes a positive background for stocks. Some analysts suggested that, in both the stock and bond markets, lower quality issues tend to outperform those of higher quality in the 12 months following the first rate hike, even if:

- The disparity is more clear-cut for bonds, and
- Low quality stocks may outperform only for the short term.[5]

A basic hypothesis behind this advice has been that of guesstimated size and frequency of Fed rate hikes, starting with the 25 basis points decided at the Federal Open Market Committee meeting of 30 June 2004. Some analysts spoke of another 50 basis points worth of tightening by the end of 2004 – with a cumulative result of a 1.75% interest rate, and an expected funds rate of 3% at the end of 2005. Other analysts saw a rate of 2% or more at the end of 2004, and between 4 and 5% at the end of 2005 (more on this later).

This is a good example of guesstimates about size and frequency of rate hikes, as well as of tentative conclusions regarding the net value of assets in an investor's portfolio. The careful reader will notice that when these hypotheses are made nobody, including members of the Fed, is sure on how high interest rates will go so far ahead.

7.4   Interest rates, net asset value, and present value

The theme of this section can best be explained through a short case study, starting with the fact that in 1994 interest rates were about the same as they were eight years earlier. This being the case, since the value of a bond remains practically the same if rates are unchanged, a bond mutual fund's principal, or net asset value (NAV), should have been little changed, if at all.

This, however, was not the case. The question then arises, why have the NAVs of bond funds dropped between 7.6 and 26.6% during 1994? This reference to an entity's sinking net asset value indeed included some large and well-known bond funds, which are not known for taking hits because of exposure in derivatives investments.

The answer to the puzzle is that, over the years, many bond funds paid out interest income that seemed well in excess of the going rate in the bond market. By all likelihood, these did so because of the drive to attract investors by showing great returns – which led them to an investment strategy that:

- Paid out a higher current yield than the real yield of their investments permitted, and
- Did so at the expense of the fund's capital as well as, to a significant extent, future yield.

In the aftermath, the NAVs of these entities have suffered a large decline, with losses being noticed by investors who withdrew billions out of bond funds in 1994. This brings into perspective the issue raised in section 7.2, that with fixed income instruments investors must account for, and separate from one another:

- The real yield, and
- The expected rate of inflation.

Even if inflation is benign, there is always some part of the instrument's interest rate which must go to compensate for the loss of the purchasing power of money. Another part must be set aside to cover administrative and other costs and leave some profit to the asset manager. When the payout is higher than the real yield minus the aforementioned factors, the difference is covered by reduction in net asset value.

In the 1986 to 1994 timeframe, bond funds were able to hype their yields by invest-ing in what are known as *premium bonds*. These debt instruments were issued in the early 1980s when interest rates were very high, because inflation was stellar; but in the late 1980s they were selling way above par. Such strategy of buying premium yield but highly expensive bonds has many risks, because:

- With repayments the premium paid above par is lost, and
- A hike in interest rates sees to it that such a premium shrinks, or altogether disappears.

Rare has been the case of bond funds that had the foresight of factoring these risks into their investment equation. But even if the highly paid professionals running invest-ment funds don't do so, the individual investor should be more sophisticated for the sake of his net asset value. The trouble is that the investor does not necessarily know about the need to compensate for inflation and administration expenses, as well as for interest rate and prepayment risks, in order to keep the portfolio's net asset value intact.

Moreover, it simply is not enough to make an adjustment for inflation just once. A rational approach demands that, starting with nominal interest rates, real interest rates are adjusted for expected inflation over the corresponding time horizon. Only a full maturity perspective can provide a realistic measure of real return on an investment – as well as of the real cost of financing.

Notice that in computational terms the calculation of real interest rates based on nominal interest rates is subject to some practical and conceptual difficulties. First and foremost, a reliable measure of expected inflation over the relevant horizon is normally not observable, and it can only be estimated. Also, it is not too obvious which price deflator is most relevant.

Under these conditions, the simplest (but not necessarily the best) approach to the computation of short- and long-term real interest rates is to use the latest available annual consumer price inflation (CPI) rate as a proxy for expected inflation. With regard to short-term interest rate only, this procedure may be warranted by the fact that, at very short horizons, actual inflation should not differ significantly from expected inflation.

A reason why the current approach is not necessarily the best is that, like every other metric, inflation has volatility. This can be estimated by considering a statistic-ally valid sample in case current projections do not foresee such extremes (there might, however, be shocks, as the following paragraph explains). With a distribution of values around a mean inflation, a Monte Carlo simulation can produce better estimates than the simplest approach.[6]

Watch out, however, for temporary shocks and spikes on current inflation (and inflation projections) which may cause current inflation to be a distorted measure of expectations, even at short horizons. For instance, this was the case in early 2001 when inflation was significantly affected by, among other things, the increase in oil prices. For longer time horizons the way to bet is that there may be even larger deviations between expected and current inflation. (More on inflation in Chapter 8.)

The other important element, particularly in connection to longer bond matur-ities, is the yield curve, discussed in section 7.6, and with it volatility in interest rate premium, which is the subject of section 7.7. Reference to the yield curve brings into perspective the issue of short-term and long-term maturities, which tend to correlate in a negative sense.

It has been a deliberate choice to focus in this chapter on the yield curve and its effects, while yields are discussed in detail in Chapter 9; as well as on volatility of interest rates within a maturity horizon, though maturities are the theme of Chapter 10. The reason is that:

- This chapter looks into the *dynamics* of interest rates
- While the subject matter of Chapters 9 and 10 is the *mechanics* of the two aforementioned issues.

As section 7.6 will show, quite often, with short rates down sharply, the yield curve dramatically steepens. For instance, in September 2001 the spread between 3-month Treasury bills and 30-year Treasury bonds was around 335 basis points. At that time, the 30-year Treasury and associated yield curve were used as a forecasting tool, and that configuration implied a sharp increase in economic development and earnings growth by the middle of 2002. But the steepening did not imply a pickup in inflation which, according to the experts, was likely to be falling through all 2002. The experts, incidentally, were nearly right.

What kind of protection should investors provide themselves with in such an environment that affects fixed income products? The principle is that *if* long-term interest rates are likely to rise, *then* the investor should expect negative total returns in the fixed-income market for all bonds bought under such expectations. Under this condition, *duration risk* should be avoided (see Chapter 10).

Investors will also be well advised to proceed with net asset value calculations, including intrinsic value computed with the currently prevailing real interest rate applicable over a given interest interval, for instance a year – or, better, on a quarterly basis – taking as a basis the level of principal invested at the start of the interval. This computation may be expressed in time units that differ from the nominal interval. The general algorithm expressing interest rate i is:

$$i_T = \frac{\text{Interest rate during a chosen time interval } T}{\text{Principal invested from the beginning of that interval}}$$

This approach also helps in providing investors and asset managers with another significant reference point, which is characterized by an inverse procedure. In many investments we wish to know how much we should invest at a given time to control a given amount at a specified date, but this approach involves the notion of *present value* (not to be confused with NAV), or discounted value – practically one looks from projected end results back to the starting point of an investment decision.

The experimental approach discussed in this section evidently requires a great deal of statistics, through which can be made extrapolations and inferences. Such statistics exist abundantly for dollars and sterling. The euro is a new currency, but since January 1999 statistics comprising a set of ten euro area retail interest rates have been published monthly in the 'Euro area statistics' section of the European Central Bank's (ECB's) Monthly Bulletin.

These euro statistics are produced according to a short-term approach, using already existing national interest rate statistics. However, while this ensures that some retail interest rate statistics were available from the start of Monetary Union, it also had some serious limitations. For instance, the underlying data is not harmonized and therefore such statistics should be used with caution:

■ Primarily to analyze time series development over time
■ Rather than making comparisons based on absolute level(s).

Moreover, because the term 'interest rate' is polyvalent, as we also saw in Chapter 6 with examples on loans, the tracking of historical information should have more than one dimension, and it should focus on both short-term and long-term rates. Critical variables for short-term rates are presented in Table 7.1, and for long-term rates in Table 7.2. It is also wise to regularly track money market rate and yield on bonds outstanding. As shown in Figure 7.2, the two do not coincide.

In connection to many of the interest rate variables shown in Tables 7.1 and 7.2, a *steady-state* approach has been developed by the ECB for retail interest rate statistics, referred to as '*MFI interest rate statistics*' (MFI stands for monetary financial institution). The aim is to produce a set of euro area interest rates on deposit and lending that provides a comprehensive, detailed, and harmonized statistical picture of the level of interest rates applied by MFIs and their changes over time.

Table 7.1 Short-term interest rates and the short-term market rate

■ Overnight money market rate
■ 3-month money market rate
■ Overdrafts to households
■ Short-term loans to non-financial corporations
■ Interest rates on certificates of deposit
■ Short-term savings deposits from households
■ Short-term time deposits from households
■ Overnight deposits from non-financial corporations

Table 7.2 Long-term interest rates and long-term market rates

■ 5-year government bond yields
■ 10-year government bond yields
■ Medium-term interbank loans
■ Long-term loans to non-financial corporations
■ Long-term loans for house purchase
■ Long-term loans for other mortgages
■ Long-term time deposits from households

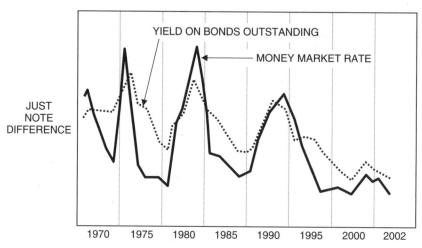

Figure 7.2 Trend lines on money market rate and yield on bonds outstanding in the German financial market, 1970–2002. (*Source:* Deutsche Bundesbank)

7.5 What's the purpose of rock-bottom interest rates?

As the careful reader will appreciate, interest rates underpin nearly all variables in Tables 7.1 and 7.2. But interest rates also may be nearly zero, and the best way to answer the question on whether an interest-free economy makes any sense is to look at Japan. Since the early to mid-1990s Japan has been in an extraordinary (but unhealthy) situation and willfully so, because the money practically has been free of cost. As a result, with its struggling economy, frail stockmarket, and cheap funds Japan became:

- A place to borrow,
- But not a place to invest.

With rock-bottom interest rates essentially offset by inflation in Japan, money has become a free commodity and, as such, it is streaming out of the country with speculators at the hub. The crash of Japanese interest rates, which has been engineered by the government, is shown in Figure 7.3. As a pattern, it is matched only by the fall of the dot.coms – with disastrous consequences for Japanese savers.

It was during the mid- to late 1990s that the Japanese interest rate regime got unstuck from that of other Group of Seven (G-7) countries. For instance, in the February–March 1997 timeframe in the United States, the Federal Reserve was preoccupied with how strong the dollar should be, but in Japan the headache was how weak the yen would get. Every few days a Japanese central banker would utter fretful remarks about the yen's decline.

One of the reasons why the yen weakened was that investors were pumping money out of Japan in search of higher yields. This was further fueling the bubble in the stock and bond markets in New York and Western European financial centers. Both speculators and investors were in the game of capitalizing on the gap in interest rates

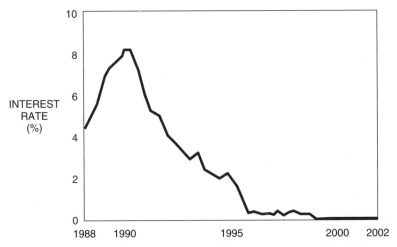

Figure 7.3 The overnight call rate of the Japanese yen, 1988–2002

between the yen on one side, and the dollar, sterling, Deutsche mark and other strong currencies in the other. Nor was 1997 an exceptional year.

■ Investments *from* Japan in dollar assets more than tripled in 1996 over 1995, to about $43 billion.

Many economists and financial analysts said at the time that those figures dwarfed the amount of yen borrowing, much of which cannot be traced when funds are raised in yen in Europe. Some analysts suggested that such covert borrowing could run as high as $40 billion to $60 billion a month, raising fears of a yen collapse as investors could react in a crisis by dumping yen. Such a crisis did not happen; what took place was that:

■ The Bank of Japan printed a lot more money than originally planned, and
■ The credit institutions that used to be the bedrock of the Japanese economy were damned.

This started in late 1994, while interest rates were rock-bottom. The first to go was Tokyo Kyowa and Anzen. Then in mid-1995 the Cosmo Credit Cooperative came down, a financial and political scandal, followed by the Hyogo Bank and Kizu Credit – leading the Japanese government (in 1996) to amend the Deposit Insurance Law and establish the Resolution and Collection Bank (read Bank of Bankrupt Banks) in 1997.

It was just in time, because in 1997 the Nippon Credit Bank failed, an internationally active bank with 15 trillion yen (US$140 billion) in assets, while the country continued being shaken by the earthquake of the *Jusen*, the housing loan organizations, like S&L and building societies. This crisis had started in 1997. Another bankruptcy in 1997 was that of the Hokkaido Takushoku Bank, a city bank with assets of 9.5 trillion yen. The Bank of Japan (read taxpayer) provided liquidity support, as with previous cases.

Indeed, 1997 was a bumper year for defaults, because Sanyo Securities also went bankrupt followed by Yamaichi Securities, Japan's fourth largest investment bank and broker, with assets of 22 trillion yen ($205 billion). This took place on 24 November 1997, and the Bank of Japan went to the rescue. Two days later, on 26 November, Tokyo City Bank went bust. It was *as if* near zero interest rates acted as a laxative on Japan's banking system.

Not to be left behind, 1998 started with a big bang. First, in February of that year the government established the principle of using public funds in a vain effort to solve the financial crisis. Then, a little later, the Long Term Capital Bank of Japan (LTCB) went bankrupt, with assets of 26 trillion yen ($243 billion). Two hundred billion here, two hundred billion there, and pretty soon we are talking big money.

In spite of clear signs that the policy of zero interest rates and massive salvage did not work, the Japanese government not only did not change its approach, but also established more bureaucracy – from the Financial Administration, to the Financial Crisis Management Committee, and Financial Reconstruction Committee (FRC). 'Committees cannot drive a company like committees cannot drive a car,' the original Henry Ford once said. Can committees lead a nation out of the long, dark tunnel into which it drove itself?

With hindsight, two reasons stand out to explain the fact that Japan's national debt in the decade from 1994 to 2004 went from less then 60% of Gross National Product (GNP) to more than 160 percent of GNP – overtaking in the process the highly indebted economies of Belgium, Italy, and Greece, where the national debt hovers around 100–130% of GNP. Still, the unworkable policy did not change, while:

■ Nearly zero interest rates (shown in Figure 7.4)
■ The continuing drain of the yen, and
■ Unsuccessful government efforts to jump-start the Japanese economy

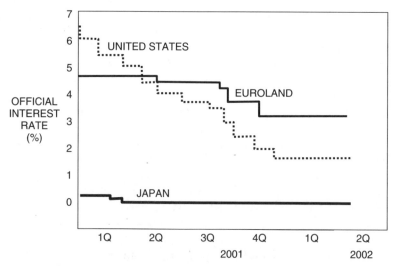

Figure 7.4 The zero cost of money did not help the Japanese economy recover. Official interest rates in the United States, Euroland and Japan in 2001 and 2002. (*Source:* Deutsche Bundesbank)

saw to it that the Bank continued flooding the markets with more liquidity. This had the effect of continuing to drive short-term interest rates further down (if this were possible), and by 2001 the central bank itself said that it planned to hold interest rates at zero until the country shook off what the government admitted was persistent deflation. Thereby, it announced contradictory aims.

Eventually, the market had the last word, as by September 2003 yields in Japanese government 10-year bonds (JGB) started to rise and this changed their relative attractiveness compared with US Treasuries. At the same time, because of the huge amount of exposure by speculators who borrowed yen, some experts thought that rising interest rates were going to shake the foundations of the global bond market.

What a difference a decade of mismanagement can make. After the Second World War, for 55 years Japan was a savers' paradise, JGBs were the world's biggest government bond market, largely dominated by domestic investors, and the rising sun was the sun of the financials. By contrast, in the mid- to late 1990s it was foreign speculators who called the tune – borrowing and selling yen to invest abroad.

Unwisely, the Bank of Japan helped the foreign speculators, by adopting the silly zero interest rate policy in 2001. Not to be left behind, many large Japanese investors/speculators, too, have been plowing money into overseas markets, mainly into US Treasury bonds.

This zero interest rates situation has been full of risks, over and above those which hit Japanese savers hard, indeed very hard. One of the major exposures has been of international dimensions. It came from the fact that *if* yields on the domestic Japanese market continue to rise from zero to something positive, *then* this tide may turn and add to volatility in the already shaky US bond market.

Another after-effect was supposed to be that of altering the P&L of the Japanese institutions' portfolio for the better. Jason Rogers, of Barclays, estimated that Japan's city banks had roughly 750 billion yen ($6.4 billion) unrealized losses on their JGB holdings, based on end-March 2003 figures; but they had unrealized gains on equity portfolios of 2300 billion yen on 21 August 2003.[7]

First, some analysts thought that zero interest rates confirmed by the Bank of Japan gave a big boost to Tokyo's stock market. Later, however, it was revealed that the 2003 pick-up in Japanese equities was mainly engineered by foreign investors borrowing nearly zero-cost yen. With this came the fear that rising interest rates could unravel Tokyo's stock market. With hindsight, this is what has happened, though the Tokyo equities lost their momentum.

In conclusion, if one draws up a balance sheet of nearly zero interest rates in Japan in the aftermath of so many years of experience, the liabilities side will be much heavier than that of the assets. The huge increase in national debt, huge capital outflows, lack of internal private investments, and above all the risk of global financial meltdown because of the pyramiding schemes that were built, mediate against zero interest. The assets side is meager, as there is not much to show in positive results.

It would have been much better to use the cheap money to give a serious clean-up to the banking sector, which since 1990 has continued weak and crowded with bad debt. Bringing back public confidence to the economy by getting the banks moving again as financial intermediaries is a far better policy than keeping rock-bottom interest rates for so long – which deprives savers of their income and only serves to fill the pockets of speculators.

7.6   The shape of interest rate curves

The *term structure* of interest rates is a subject that has attracted considerable attention in financial research. To estimate the term structure we need instruments whose prices depend on current interest rate levels. A good proxy is bonds. The reader should remember from Chapters 3 and 4, however, that a whole range of bonds is traded in the market, hence it is necessary to make choices.

One of the variables is credit risk associated to the issuer. As we have already seen, debtors range from sovereigns to multinationals, medium-sized, and smaller firms, whose likelihood of bankruptcy must be taken into account. To be attracted to lend money to riskier entities, investors ask to be compensated for default risk, and this is done through higher interest rates. The likelihood of bankruptcy means that:

■ Issuers with different creditworthiness have different term structures, and sometimes this different term structure has a market-wide bias.

For instance, for reasons that have been discussed, in the wave of Japanese bank bankruptcies in the 1990s, lenders instituted a *Japan premium*. Collectively, Japanese institutions had to pay higher interest to buy money in the interbank market.

■ Usually, however, the *spread* between what a given entity must pay over and above a benchmark is its own – and it has a good deal to do with its creditworthiness.

This spread between, for instance, default-free US Treasuries and other bonds, is essentially a *price discount* for higher credit rating (see also section 7.7). What it means is that there is compensation for the fact that the present value of a secured cash flow is lower than the present value of an uncertain cash flow due at the same date. Such uncertainty impacts on term structure level. For evident reasons:

■ The discount curve of a riskier issuer is below that of a risk-free debtor,
■ Credit risk (see Chapter 12) entails that both the spot and forward yield curves are higher.

There is no reason why the spread between term structures of two debtors cannot be calculated for different representations of time scales. Generally, however, it is expressed in terms of spot rates. Such spread-based term structure helps to integrate factors affecting a lender–borrower relationship:

■ Time to maturity risk premium, including creditworthiness.
■ Risk related to the likelihood of changes in an entity's default probability because of leveraged buyout (LBO).
■ Liquidity premium accounting for differences in liquidity of instruments, as well as global differences in liquidity.

Liquidity varies from issuer to issuer, from issue to issue, and from one market to the next.[8] Because of their large amount outstanding and greater debtor dependability, Group of Ten government bonds are much more liquid than corporates. Investors are paying a premium for such liquidity by accepting lower return of government bonds. Moreover, for the same vendor different bond issues may have different liquidity, depending on covenants, amount of issue, and other variables.

With this background we can look at the shape of an interest rate curve. This is a static picture because, as it should be appreciated, the shape of an interest rate curve changes daily in response to market forces. Figure 7.5 shows two examples both based on 10-year curves of implied forward overnight interest rates in Euroland.[9] Notice that:

- A few months down the line the steeper 30 June 1999 interest rate curve has been reshaped into a flatter curve.
- This flatter curve, however, has again steepened in February 2000, but at higher level of interest.
- A year later, in January/February 2001, the shape of the 10-year interest curve has changed, showing backwardation in its first year.

Backwardation is an interesting phenomenon that happens from time to time with commodities like oil and base metals – but also with money. In the latter case it means that money's future cost is negative. As shown in Figure 7.5(b), backwardation was the name of the game in January and February 2001. The interest on money, in this case the euro, becomes less than in earlier months *as if* money, as a commodity, was getting negative interest.

As this case study documents, the shape of an interest rate curve is dynamic, influenced by differences between the long-term, medium-term, and short-term rates. The gap between long and short rates, says Dr Alan Greenspan, is an *inflation premium* paid because lenders of long-term money expect the government deficit to continue to grow.

This brings into the picture what was stated in the Introduction about nominal and real interest rates. Investors demand the premium because of the expectation of inflation (see Chapter 9), which practically means that the money they have invested will be worth less and less. But there is another side to this argument. When the long-term interest rate curve flattens, as happened in October-to-December 1999 (Figure 7.5a), then in all likelihood inflationary trends are under firm control. As a result

- Investors get less return on bonds, and
- Low rates of interest turn investors to the stock market.[10]

Many events influence the slope of an interest rate curve, government borrowing as well as changes in the government's borrowing policy being one example; the term structure is another. For instance, on 31 July 2001, the US Treasury Department started to auction $8 billion to $16 billion worth of the bills weekly. As with all Treasuries, the new 4-week note required a minimum investment of $1000. Government officials said they expect the new securities to yield roughly the same as 3-month T-bills.

- The 3-month T-bills were at 3.52% at the end of July 2001.
- By contrast, the 30-year Treasury bond had a 5.55% yield that same day.

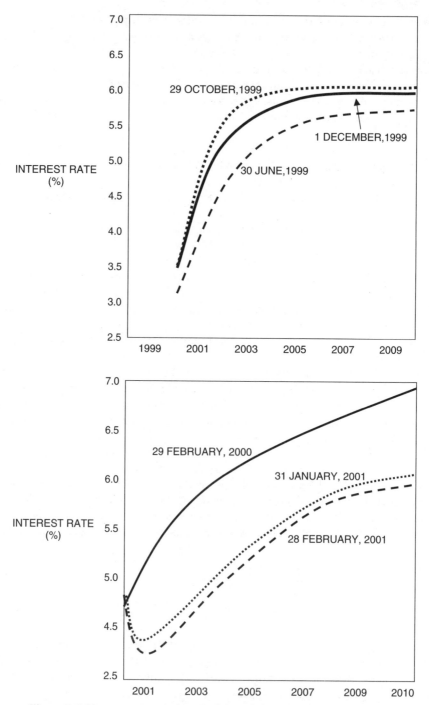

Figure 7.5 Ten-year curves of implied forward overnight interest rates in Euroland (*a*) in three different months of 1999 and (*b*) in 2000 and 2001 (percentages per year, daily data). (*Source:* ECB Monthly Bulletin, December 1999 and March 2001)

The difference in interest rate between 4-week bills and 30-year bonds by the credit-risk-free Treasury dramatizes the slope of the yield curve. Money market mutual funds, which invest in short-term corporate and government debt, were thought to be the biggest purchasers of the new security. Experts said that the 4-week bill aimed to allow the Treasury to manage more cheaply the wide fluctuations in its daily cash balance.

For comparative purposes, at that time the average money market fund paid 3.37%; the average 3-month certificate of deposit (CD) yield was 3.41%. Table 7.3 presents in a nutshell interest rates on CDs from 6 months to 5 years in July 2000 and July 2001, including the fairly significant difference in basis points, year-by-year. There is also a different type of comparison involving interest rates. Known as TED spread, this is the difference between the Libor rate and the interest rate on 3-month US Treasury bills. (Libor is an acronym for London Interbank Offered Rate. It is the interest rate at which one bank lends to another, and it is available at 8:00 am London time.)

A good way of looking into this issue is that when the market is still skeptical about where the banks are putting their depositors' money, the indicator of this skepticism becomes the TED spread, which expresses the premium over the yield on Treasury bills that eurodollar deposits yield.

When the TED spread grows wider, this is seen by the financial analysts as sign of a roaring banking system crisis. In the late 1980s, for instance, bank deposits yielded 20% more than 5-year Treasuries, and the carry was negative. Banks had to pay more for deposits than they earned on Treasuries, so they were buying non-Treasury securities to pick up yield.

Spreads were volatile. In 1998 the spread between deposit costs and Treasuries became as negative as it was in the late 1980s, a period when financials underperformed. Therefore, analysts believed that the Fed funds rate would have to decline to zero in real terms to improve banking system profitability. In retrospect, it did decline significantly, but stood well above zero.

At the same time, the only kind of loans that were growing were loans for securities purchases which accelerated from 40% year-to-year growth to 60%. A push towards commercial loans provided another income-earning vehicle, increasing the competition among credit institutions and swamping loans quality (see Chapter 12).

Furthermore, in the same timeframe the yield curve facing business was unsupportive of profits. The stock market was rather convinced profits could be sustained

Table 7.3 The cost of money with certificates of deposit

	27 July 2000	27 July 2001	Difference in bp
6-month	5.26	3.41	185
1-year	5.63	3.62	201
2½-year	5.79	4.05	174
5-year	6.15	4.70	145

Notice that the mode in distribution of basis points happens at 1 year.
Source: Statistics from *USA Today*, 27 July 2001

in the industrial sector, but the bond market was pricing-in profit risk. Quality spreads for corporates were at levels normally seen on deep slowdowns. Therefore, many analysts were of the opinion that the real problem with profits was deep-seated.

7.7   Modeling the volatility of interest rate premium

The last example in section 7.5 provided evidence on volatility of interest rates. Up to a point, the volatility of interest rate premiums may be empirically mapped through determinants of a structural model for valuing debt securities, particularly those of higher risk. For instance, a model developed by the Deutsche Bundesbank uses as proxies of crucial variables influencing interest rate behavior:

- Volatility of equity prices
- Interest rate level of risk-free investments, and
- The company's level of indebtedness.

Behind this approach is the Merton model, which looks at the payoff at maturity from holding a corporate bond, being subject to the risk of default, as equal to holding a long riskless asset *and* a short put option on the market value of the firm. With this approach, the strike price is equal to the nominal value of the bond. Say, for instance, that firm A issues a zero-coupon bond (see Chapter 4) with B nominal value.

- *If* the market value of firm A, VA, is greater than the nominal value of the bond at maturity, which means VA > B
- *Then* bondholder(s) will get back the amount B.

By contrast, if A's market value is lower than the nominal value B of the bond, then bondholder(s) will receive only amount VA which, while being the full market value of the company, is less than B (VA < B). Therefore, the repayment C to the bondholder(s) resembles the payoff from an option on the market value of the company, where the strike price is the nominal value of the bond. C is determined by the algorithm:

$$C = \min (VA, B)$$

A different way of looking at this transaction is that the bondholder(s) grant(s) the shareholder(s) a put option which the latter may exercise when the firm's market value is lower than the nominal value of the bond. Notice that a higher degree of the firm's indebtedness and a rise in the volatility of its market value,

- Raises the price of the put option, and
- Increases the interest rate spread of the bond relative to a risk-free asset.

In contrast to this, a higher riskless rate of interest lowers the value of the put option and could raise the spread. Moreover, a higher share price lowers the value of the put option, and by extension the interest rate minimum of non-investment grade bonds. This reveals another aspect of the approach: the Bundesbank model can be extended to junk bonds (see Chapter 4), using the volatility of equities and option pricing as proxies.

Let us see what this approach may mean in terms of volatilities of sub-investment grade debt in the real world. In May 2004, after nearly a year of high flying, junk bonds became the latest victim of rising interest rate expectations. The junk, or non-investment grade, end of the international debt instruments market has been hit as:

- Investors pulled back because of fears of rising interest rates, and
- This made bonds issued at current rates of interest less attractive to investors.

Because of this belated but clear investor reaction, from the end of April 2004 onward the junk bond market has proved a sensitive indicator of investor appetite for risk. For instance, the prices of emerging market issues have fallen in secondary trading, while owing to developing negative market sentiment and its own overindebtedness, Brazil cancelled an auction of domestic bonds.

Investors' fears were not appeased when in July 2004 the Bank of England raised interest rates by a quarter point to 4.5% – the fourth rise in eight months – despite a similar increase a month earlier. And the Swiss National Bank also raised interest rates by 25 basis points – an unexpected move.

At about the same time, Alan Greenspan said once again that America's interest rates could begin to rise in a 'measured' fashion. But the chairman of the Fed pledged that if inflation rose more sharply than predicted, the central bank would 'do what is required'. He also hinted that more aggressive increases might be needed to restrain price rises.

It was about time. A few weeks earlier, on 14 June 2004, the *Washington Post* carried a survey focusing on inflation of commodity prices in the Washington, DC, Maryland, and Northern Virginia area. The figures read:

- Cement up 10%, in a year
- Lumber up 20%, in six months
- Gasoline costs up 20%, in a year
- Steel up 21%, in a year
- Wire mesh up 53%, in six months
- Metal studs up 150%, in six months
- Plywood up 167%, in a year.

Given this shaping of market psychology, some analysts feared that the problems in emerging markets and junk bond sectors were starting to spread into investments in higher grade bonds. This brought an end to a two-to-three year period of exceptionally low US and euro interest rates, that

- Prompted a boom in bond investments of practically any grade, and
- Led to a surge in bond issues.

Already prior to the May 2004 sell-off of emerging markets debt, in April 2004 the prospect of a rate increase by the Fed led to an unloading of longer-term debt instruments on bond markets at large, pushing up the yield of 10-year US Treasuries from 3.89% to 4.15%. That 26 basis points was the biggest one-day increase since the Long Term Capital Management (LTCM) bankruptcy in September 1998.

For 2-year Treasuries, the yield shot up by 23 basis points from 1.62% to 1.85%. The average 30-year mortgage rate increased to 5.52% in the first days of April 2004, compared to 5.40% in the week before, and rose further the following week. Stock prices of mortgage lenders, home builders, and home improvement retailers were plunging.[11]

Based on these financial statistics, it is possible to develop an interest rate volatility model using volatility of equities and interest rate of risk-free investments as proxies. This would be quite sensitive to the changes described in the preceding paragraphs. Therefore, it will be in a position to provide regulators, bankers, and investors with information of immediate relevance.

Interest rate models are here to stay, and we will be hearing more of them in the future. In his speech on 29 August 2003, to the Federal Reserve Bank of Kansas, Dr Alan Greenspan called the combination of analysis and judgment by which the Fed operates *risk management*. He said when the Fed sets interest rates, it considers:

- The most probable forecast of the economy's growth, and
- Improbable outcomes with big consequences, such as deflation or financial collapse.

For example, in 2002/2003 the Fed cut rates more than conventional economic forecasts would have recommended because of the slight chance that low inflation could become 'pernicious' deflation, in which falling prices undermine heavily indebted consumers and businesses, also weakening the Fed's control.

'Some critics have argued that such an approach to policy is too undisciplined-judgmental, seemingly discretionary, and difficult to explain,' Greenspan said. 'These critics think the Fed should tie its actions solely to the prescriptions of a formal policy rule.'[12] While acknowledging the imprecision of his own approach, the Fed Chairman added that rules would inevitably fail, because of the complexity of underlying linkages that appear to be in a continual state of flux. (Notice that a similar statement is valid of models, which consist of rules.)

Greenspan's view was reinforced a day later, by a speech on 30 August 2003 by Vincent Reinhart, the Fed's director of monetary affairs and principal drafter of the statement that follows each Fed policy meeting. Reinhart acknowledged central banks' and market participants' need 'to speak more clearly and listen more directly to each other'. He gave three reasons the Fed and markets can disconnect. They might differ on:

- Type of economic outlook
- Dangers associated with a particular outlook, and
- Outlook on how interest rates should respond to such an outlook.

For example, markets expected the Fed to start raising rates as soon as the economy puts in a few quarters of good growth, as in previous recoveries. But in 2003 the Fed said it would be slower to raise rates this time, because it did not want inflation to go lower since this has its own perils. It took more than 6 months till, at the end of the first quarter of 2004, Fed executives raised the issue of upping US interest rates.

The fact that central bankers and regulators use models, the first as experimental tools in setting monetary policy and the second as assistants to their regulatory duties, is welcome. It will be proper, however, to keep in mind that every algorithmic and heuristic approach to real world situations has associated to it model risk.[13]

Notes

1 D.N. Chorafas, *Management Risk: The Bottleneck is at the Top of the Bottle*, Macmillan/Palgrave, London, 2004.
2 D.N. Chorafas, *Operational Risk Control with Basel II: Basic Principles and Capital Requirements*, Butterworth-Heinemann, Oxford and Boston, 2004.
3 D.N. Chorafas, *Economic Capital Allocation with Basel II: Cost and Benefit Analysis*, Butterworth-Heinemann, Oxford and Boston, 2004.
4 Merrill Lynch, *Global Research Highlights*, 18 June 2004.
5 Merrill Lynch, 'Fed rate hikes and your portfolio', 23 June 2004.
6 D.N. Chorafas, *Chaos Theory in the Financial Markets*, Probus, Chicago, 1994.
7 *Financial Times*, 23/24 August 2003.
8 D.N. Chorafas, *Understanding Volatility and Liquidity in Financial Markets*, Euromoney Books, London, 1998.
9 Statistics by the European Central Bank (ECB).
10 D.N. Chorafas, *The Management of Equity Investments*, Butterworth-Heinemann, Oxford, 2005.
11 EIR, 16 April 2004.
12 *Wall Street Journal*, 2 September 2003.
13 D.N. Chorafas, *Modelling the Survival of Financial and Industrial Enterprises: Advantages, Challenges, and Problems with the Internal Rating-Based (IRB) Method*, Palgrave/Macmillan, London, 2002.

8 Inflation indexing and impact of government deficits

8.1 Introduction

Inflation means higher prices, and higher prices are reducing the purchasing power of money and impoverishing the living standard. Basically, however, the aftermath of inflation is defined as a fall in the value of money, not as a rise in a price even if the commodity to which this rise pertains is core to the economy.

'What causes inflation?', Dr Arthur Burns, the former chairman of the Federal Reserve, asked his students in his seminars at Columbia University. 'Excess government spending causes inflation,' Burns said answering his own question (see sections 8.6 and 8.7 on this theme). Deficits create more money to chase the same amount of goods, and that is a precursor to inflation.

If inflation starts, and it worsens, it will move up the ladder of the economy faster and harder than most people imagine. And it will be prolonged as well as difficult to get it out of the system, as Dr Paul Volker's rigorous effort to curb the galloping US inflation in the early 1980s documents. For bondholders, inflation is both a curse and an opportunity.

- Investors with bonds in their portfolio lose out, as the nominal interest rate they receive may not even cover inflation, leaving them with a negative real interest rate.
- By contrast, investors buying bonds at inflation's peak in Western countries, where higher inflation is usually a spark, can look for rewarding interest rates in the longer term (see in Chapter 14 the discussion on interest rate bubbles).

Therefore, bond investors keep a close watch on inflation. In June 2004, the monthly survey of fund managers around the world by Merrill Lynch showed that they are becoming more concerned about the inflationary outlook. A record 87% of respondents thought that global inflation would be higher a year down the line – and though the majority of fund managers believed that inflation risks were modest, there was a sharp increase in the percentage of people who expected inflation to be a lot higher.[1]

No matter the deception by governments, and even some research institutes, that deficits do not matter – deficits *do* matter. In 2000, 4.1% of Euroland's GDP went to servicing public debt,[2] and this public debt steadily grew in the period 2000–2005, as the bigger of the EU countries continued with runaway budget deficits, in full disregard of the Stability Pact they had signed some years earlier.

One way or another, in the case of fixed income instruments as well as of industrial accounts, inflation is a factor that cannot be ignored. It is also a frequent phenomenon in a globalized economy. Investors buy securities and industrialists transact business in foreign countries, and in foreign currency terms, with the result that a merchant's books have to record transactions in a number of different currencies which, because of inflation, depreciate at widely different rates (see a bird's-eye view of foreign exchange risk in Chapter 3).

To deal adequately with the effects of inflation, investors must realize that the value of money changes over time. The dollar or pound of 2005 is quite different from the dollar or pound of 1945 at the end of the Second World War, as these were very different from their counterparts at the beginning of the 20th century. Inflation has eaten up their purchasing power.

Factors other than inflation also influence this most significant change. For instance, before 1914, when the British pound was on the gold standard, the value of money tended to remain fairly constant, though there were movements in the value of gold. But since 1914, when the country went off the gold standard, the value of the pound sterling has fluctuated widely, influencing the value of a bonds and equities portfolio in an investor's base currency which might have been different from the pound.

After having created it, governments try to counteract inflation in either of two ways: By price controls, which in the majority of cases are totally ineffectual, and by tightening interest rates. Interest rate changes, however, take up to two years to have their full effect on inflation, and therefore inflation continues to increase.

There are also forces working against each of these two moves. Price controls are anathema to liberal politicians, and an increase in interest rate may encounter political headwinds. For instance, the November 2004 US elections made it unlikely that the Fed would return interest rates to the 5% level believed to be necessary before late 2005, and inflation could keep rising till about 2007 in all likelihood.

Moreover, in a globalized economy, inflation acts in two dimensions: one is cross-country and cross-currency, making fixed income investments in different currencies less valuable than on the day the commitment was made. The other dimension is the arrow of time, as explained in the example of the pound before 1914, immediately after 1945, and in 2005. Over time, even minor inflation erodes the capital base. Both types of loss of value must be properly reflected in the investor's accounts.

8.2 Money is merchandise with great leveraging

It has been sometimes said that, like any other commodity, all money is merchandise, but for proper accounting purposes it is more convenient to make all merchandise money. The price of any one thing, including cash, can only be determined by a reference to some other commodity, which, by common consent or established law, is fixed as a standard – or, alternatively, is always adjusted to compensate for inflation.

President Ronald Reagan who, as a former actor, was a great communicator, expressed this beautifully when in one of his first televised addresses to the American people he took out of his pocket a couple of dimes and nickels, put them on the table and explained that this was what was worth a 1945 US dollar. As for what is called *the price of a currency*, if there were no paper money value it would have to be estimated by comparison to other commodities like gold or silver, as is the case with barter agreements.

Switzerland provides a good example of how far how fast inflation can erode the value of money, because it has traditionally been a low-inflation country. A stable economy, a strong currency, and modest increases in real wages have all contributed to keeping a lid on prices. But in the mid- to late 1980s the country faced a noticeable rise in the cost-of-living index.

For a number of reasons, in 1985 inflation was gaining speed over a period of months, showing no signs of any real slowdown. One of the reasons was the weakening of the Swiss franc against a basket of key currencies. The trade-weighted index published by the Swiss National Bank has shown that trend. While currencies like sterling and the dollar were weak against the Swiss franc, the Deutsche mark was at its highest since the early 1980s and, with the German Federal Republic as Switzerland's biggest single supplier, this was not without significance.

Moreover, the foreign exchange situation and an overall rise in world prices combined to make Swiss imports some 8.5% more expensive in 1989. For a country so dependent on foreign goods, this meant a not insignificant boost to wholesale and consumer prices, and therefore to inflation indices.

Marked inflationary impulses also rose from a high level of domestic and international interest rates. In October, the bank rate was raised to 6%. Then, at Christmas 1985, the National Bank decided to double to 2% the margin between average call-money rates and the Lombard rate, which applies for loans against securities and other collateral. This action pushed Lombard interest up to an unprecedented, for Switzerland, 10.5%.

Both short-range and longer-range inflation trends have to be assessed. To assess near-term inflation risk, analysts have developed quantitative ranking systems for gauging the degree of spare capacity in different economies. In one of these models, by Merrill Lynch, capacity rankings are based on inputs which use OECD estimates compared to current unemployment rate to gauge inflation pressures in the labor market. This model then uses OECD estimates of the output gap to create an index of an economy's spare capacity.

Output gap and economic slack correlate in a generic sense. A measure of *economic slack* across an economy is the output gap which consists of the difference between actual and potential GDP. 'Potential GDP' is a way of looking at spare capacity, since its usage would make up the actual GDP. Gross domestic product projections are made by assuming that the economy continues to grow at a rate defined by current trend. A rule of thumb is that:

- *If* the output gap is negative, there is spare capacity and
- Price pressures are absorbed by using such capacity rather than through inflation.

The OECD reckons that by mid-2004 in the US and Japan the negative gap has been more or less eliminated, while Europe still had a gap of about 2% of GDP. However, estimating spare capacity is an uncertain business, because there are many queries about potential rate of growth, as well as about what constitutes productive capacity. Is old plant to be counted in or out?

While, in spite of these uncertainties, the different models of measuring output gap and economic slack have their merits, failure to consider budget deficits contradicts the *Burns principle*. The way Dr Arthur Burns taught his students, with a 2004 budget deficit of 4.5% of GDP in the United States and 3.5% in Germany, France, and Italy, all four countries are prime candidates for an increase in inflation.

Let's face it, in early- to mid-2004 consumer prices escaped government control, as can be clearly seen in Figure 8.1 from US and Euroland statistics. Inflation numbers released in June 2004 indicate that while all Group of Seven (G-7) countries are concerned by rising prices, the United States, United Kingdom, and France top that list. Apart from government deficits, rising inflation has always been caused by:

- Excessive monetary expansion,
- Other strains on public finances, and
- The fact that monetary and fiscal policies become too lax.

The liquidity pumped into the market by central banks has to flow somewhere, and the 'somewhere' is in product prices. Lax monetary policies fuel bubbles in bonds, equities, and real estate – and these changes in prices are more visible than old-fashioned consumer-price inflation. Apart from budget deficits and fast growth in the money supply (see Chapter 1), four other reasons promoted greater visibility of inflation in 2004:

- In a time of globalization, most of the world's growth has been fueled by historically low interest rates.
- The world economy has been growing at its fastest pace for two decades, with low spare capacity as a reserve.

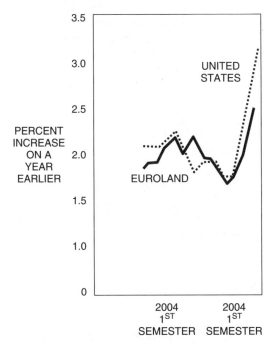

Figure 8.1 In 2004 consumer prices escaped government control. (*Source: The Economist*)

- Higher oil prices, seem to be here to stay even after the high demand by China abates.
- Governments look at the taxation of the poor through inflation as the best way to discharge their huge debts.

The China reference is significant in the context of this discussion because the country's imports contributed to the significant asset-price inflation in base metals. In fact, it is precisely the runaway prices of energy and metals that have been behind demands for interest rate hikes by economists.

Many economists said that both governments and central banks have underestimated the inflationary consequences of unusually low interest rates and of extremely high market liquidity. As for the argument that 'bond markets would not let inflation take off by raising the yields they are demanding' and this would automatically curb growth,

- Bond markets don't police inflation.
- This is the job of governments and central banks.

Increasingly, experts doubt the reasons given by authorities why the high inflation of the 1970s cannot return. Though it is argued that central banks have a better grip on money and hence inflation, and this may well be true, the problems of the 21st century are not the same as those of the 1970s. Practically, the only common ground between 'then' and 'now' is oil.

By June 2004, practically nobody could argue that inflation was not creeping up. The only question was 'how bad' the bad news was. Euroland's average rate of consumer-price inflation rose to 2.5% in the year to May 2004 – up from 1.6% in February 2004, and well above the 2% ceiling set by the European Central Bank (ECB).

In the United States too, the signs were not good. No matter what official statistics have been saying to appease inflation fears. During February and March 2004 consumer prices were up 4.3% annualized, even if 2.7% points of that rise came from a group of items which have a collective weight of just under 17% of all consumer wares.

- This special group grew at a rapid 16.1% annualized,
- While the remaining 83% of the share of consumer price index (CPI) advanced at a tame pace of 1.5% annualized.

The inflationary group has been hitting the consumers' pocket-book hard, because it consists of lodging away from home, gasoline, heating oil, alcohol, airline travel, women's and girls' apparel, education, and medical care. The problem lies in the fact that, by and large, these items represent *out-of-pocket* purchases, a term which covers:

- Non-durable goods, and
- Daily consumer goods and services.

Examples of daily consumer goods and services are food, beverages, tobacco, transport, fuel, postal services, hotels, restaurants, cafés, and hairdressing. These are expenses most visible to the consumer, and with this the effect of inflation becomes visible too.

8.3 Who pays for the shortfall in interest rates?

As a feature article in *The Economist* had it, by mid-2004 year-to-year America's nominal GDP has grown by 7% over 2003, while inflation has been around 3% and rising. From these statistics one would guess that short-term interest rates should be around 4% at least – which will make them positive in real terms, by just 1%.[3] *If* not, *then* there is an evident shortfall in interest rates hitting hard:

■ Savers, and
■ Investors in fixed rate debt instruments.

According to the Burns principle, governments create inflation. But governments also try to minimize the damage they have done, by pointing to 'core inflation' with food and energy stripped out. This fully disregards the fact that food and energy are everyday staples for all citizens. Leaving them out is cooking the books.

In more than one way, inflation is the *special tax of the poor*, and governments know it. 'We must tax the poor, they are the most numerous,' said André Tardieu, a French radical-socialist prime minister in the early 1930s. Governments have no excuse in not knowing that inflation is the most penalizing type of taxation of the:

■ Most weak member of a society,
■ Bondholders with low fixed interest rates, and
■ All creditors at large, including the banking sector.

The Federal Reserve in the United States, central banks in continental Europe, and the ECB, have been much more complacent with the rise in inflation than 10 years earlier, presumably to help the banks. The irony is that the inflation which followed penalized both credit institutions and bondholders. On the Fed's side, there is a significant difference between its interest rate policy in 1994 and in 2004:

■ In 1994, real interest rates were around zero.
■ By contrast, in 2004 real interest rates were negative.

Equity investors also suffered from these rock-bottom interest rate policies of 1% in the United States and 2% in Euroland. As with bond investments, there is *nominal dividend yield* and *real dividend yield*. Starting in the 1980s, and accelerating in the bubble years of the late 1990s, the nominal dividend yield has been minimal. If one subtracts the 3–4% inflation, the remaining real dividend yield is below zero.

Moreover, low US interest rates have resulted in large inflows of capital into emerging countries, as investors seek higher returns. Asian countries saw the most in funds inflows, and because most of them have tried to prevent their currencies from appreciating, their large purchases of US dollars caused an explosion of domestic liquidity – with all that means for each country's inflationary trend.

One of the inputs that could be used to document the Burns principle and its concern about the growing government budget deficit which it targets, is the staggering current account deficit of the United States. American businesses and consumers are spending much more than the US produces. Still another key input is that the measures which have been taken to stop a deflationary blowout (see section 8.5) have led to an explosion of debt and other financial claims.

Figure 8.2 shows a very interesting metric of inflation: the increase in debt per dollar of increase in gross domestic product (GDP) (statistics from the United States, annualized). As the reader will appreciate by looking at these statistics, the targeted highly inflationary indicator:

- Stood at somewhat less than $2 of debt to $1 of GDP in 1980
- Zoomed to about $5 in 1982/83, two years characterized by high inflation, and
- Topped $8 in 2004, a 800% increase in the 1980–2004 timeframe.

The message the reader should retain from this is that a great part of growth in the economy is offset by the accumulation of debt. According to the Fed, total debt in the US economy stood at $34 trillion. This represents slightly over $3 in liabilities for every dollar of an $11 trillion gross domestic product,[4] resulting in an economy that was leveraged three times over.

Such overall assessment of the balance of risks with regard to high gearing is bad news, as far as potential inflation is concerned. Moreover, at time of writing (in 2004) inflation expectations are associated with increased uncertainty surrounding oil prices, and a still questionable level of confidence in the strength of the recovery in economic activity. The only 'good news', so to speak, is the downturn in the unemployment rate at mid-2004, with the creation (to end June 2004) of nearly one million jobs. The fact this did not occur earlier reflected:

- The lagged effect of pickup in economic activity, and
- Huge outstanding contracts abroad by US firms, particularly in Asia.

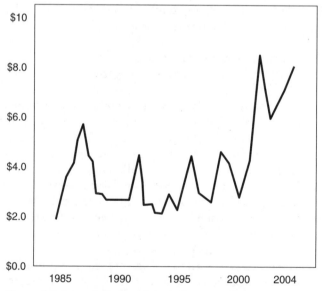

Figure 8.2 New dollars in debt for every dollar of increase in
GDP (annualized) in the United States over two decades,
1985–2004

A serious way of looking at these facts is that with short-term interest rates deliberately held low by central banks in the United States, Euroland, and Japan, but with inflationary pressures rising, bondholders face more than one dilemma. And there is also the risk of repetition of the 1994 scenario, where the bottom fell out of a highly leveraged bond market, though central bankers say that this time around this risk would be accounted for in the timing and size of interest rate hikes.

As it will be recalled from previous references to this issue, starting from a low interest base designed to give a helping hand to a banking industry wounded by the excesses of the mid- to late 1980s, the Fed increased interest rates on seven consecutive occasions in 1994 and January 1995. As soon as the market got the message of what was coming, not far from the end of the first quarter of 1994, yields on 10-year bonds rose sharply in almost all major countries.

In qualitative terms, this rise represented 200 basis points or more: from under 6% for the longer-term to nearly 8% in Germany and the United States, and from less then 6.5% to nearly 9% in the UK. These 200-plus basis points may not sound spectacular, but they translated into capital losses of 15–20% or more for bondholders.

- Worldwide, some $1.5 trillion has been wiped off the value of bond portfolios, and
- Around $600 billion, or 40% of this money, was in the United States alone.

The great bond bust of 1994, the worst bond-market loss in history, owes much to speculative buying on margin – that is, with borrowed money – as well as to the derivative financial instruments used to leverage speculative bets. In 1993, a year of declining interest rates almost everywhere, bonds looked like the place to be; speculators and investors loaded up with them. Cross-border orders, placed in different countries, played an important role in global leverage through fixed income products:

- Foreign purchases of British government bonds totaled $22 billion in 1993, four times the level of the previous year.
- In Germany, also in 1993, net foreign buying of government bonds doubled to nearly $100 billion.

The tidal wave of investment in bonds was driven by an almost universal 'conviction' that interest rates could only decline further. Bankers, investors, speculators and financial analysts who fell into this trap failed to detect the possibility that the Federal Reserve and other central banks will eventually upgrade short-term interest rates. Had they been more careful, they could have saved themselves big money.

Indeed, few people listened carefully to Fed Chairman Alan Greenspan in the winter of 1993; or, if they listened they did not recognize that he meant what he said. Yet, 'then' as 'now' there has been a rise in inflationary expectations.

In the aftermath of the 1994 bloodbath of overleveraged bond investors, the prices of debt instruments fell. Rising short-term rates made it less profitable and more dangerous to buy bonds with borrowed money. People and companies who had bought on margin or used derivatives, had to unload. This created a torrent. The rise of 40% in *The Economist*'s industrial commodity price could no more be shrugged off as just a ripple. Investors and speculators who waited too long to jump ship sank with it.

8.4   Convergence and divergence in inflationary patterns

Practically every country has its own inflation pattern. The period just prior to the introduction of the euro, as well as the few years after it, provides an excellent case study on the diversity of inflationary developments among the euro area countries, as captured by various dispersion indicators.

The first interesting observation is that inflation in the 11 Euroland countries declined significantly over the 1990s. Following the start of Stage Three of the European Monetary Union (EMU) in 1999, inflation dispersion continued to decline, and it reached a low level in the second half of 1999. Then, it picked up modestly until early 2001.

Since 2001, inflation dispersion in Euroland has remained broadly stable, before declining again during 2003 to levels close to those seen in the second half of 1999, then rising once again. Overall, however, Euroland has witnessed relatively persistent inflation differentials in the 2004 timeframe, either above or below the euro area average putting in question the targets and discipline provided by the EMU and the stability pact. This upset:

■ Bond investors, and
■ Those countries, like Holland, which abide by the Stability Pact.

The discipline which in 1998 characterized practically all countries that had decided to join the euro, did not repeat itself in the 2002–2004 years. As an example on inflation targets in 1998, Figure 8.3 presents, as a proxy, market projections on

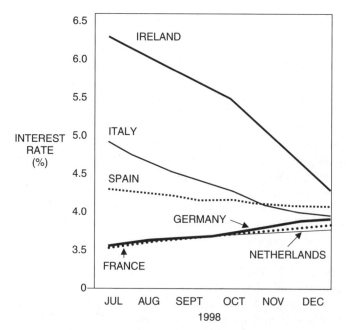

Figure 8.3 Market projections for three-month rates in six
EMU countries. (*Source:* Deutsche Bundesbank)

interest rate convergence in six Euroland countries: Germany, France, Italy, Spain, the Netherlands, and Ireland. The careful reader will appreciate how significantly Irish and Italian interest rates were projected to decline. They did so.

As far as inflationary discipline is concerned, in these early years of euro-enthusiasm, Euroland's single monetary policy implied a regime shift, the effects of which on price formation took some time to unfold. This is particularly the case in countries where inflation rates had been systematically above the common – but governments in 1938 appreciated the fact countries with above-average inflation rates suffer from:

- A certain loss in competitiveness, and
- Negative effects of inflation on real income.

After 2001, however, governments of countries participating in the euro adopted the rob-your-neighbor policy of the late 1920s, which led to the Great Depression. While inflation has fallen remarkably quickly in the first couple of years of the 21st century, since 2002 it started to rise as France, Germany, Italy, and Greece returned to deficit financing.

Post-mortem, many economists suggest that the strong general decline in inflation rates was largely the result of policy frameworks on behalf of the 11 Euroland governments, though some temporary factors also played an important role, such as:

- Cyclical developments
- A decline in food prices
- Some easing of energy prices, and
- Lagged effects of strong exchange rate appreciation against the euro.

Monetary, exchange rate, food and oil scenarios made a contribution to macroeconomic stabilization in the euro's 11 countries, by providing a credible frame of reference in regard to inflation expectations. On the other hand, fiscal performance continued to vary across Euroland, with fiscal deficits largely being of a structural nature.

To consolidate their fiscal front, the countries of Euroland needed to reform their public expenditure and revenue structures in a manner that is both sustainable and forward-looking, while keeping their debt level low. This is an important technical requirement, but it is also politically taxing, therefore governments don't give it priority on their agenda.

It should, of course, be taken into account that country differences in consumer habits play a substantial role in inflation convergence and divergence among sovereigns. These country differences concern, to a large measure, spending habits on clothing, food, energy, transport, newspapers, bars, cafés, restaurants, as well as travel, cultural and sport recreational services. That is why it is wise to watch the year-on-year rate of increase of the daily *out-of-pocket* expenditure index to get a perception on trends in inflation. In a grouping of countries, like Euroland, increase in the out-of-pocket index is not without historical precedent.

In the last analysis, however, interest rate spreads between individual euro-area countries are still mainly attributable to liquidity differences and, to a smaller extent, to different legislation regarding default risk. While all Euroland countries are, theoretically, on same or similar credit risk footing, the sovereigns themselves and some of their companies, do have different ratings of creditworthiness by independent agencies.

- Bonds issued by countries with a perceived higher default likelihood are riskier from the investor's viewpoint.
- Hence, borrowers have to pay their creditors a higher yield – a fact easily observable if one looks at Dutch and Belgian state bonds.

When this is the case, not only the average interest rate spread but also its dispersion widens. In this manner government bond yields in Europe are influenced by country-specific developments. Bond investors can capitalize on such differences to improve the yield of their holdings even if, always theoretically, a unique currency and fairly similar economic and financial factors characterize the 11 countries in Euroland, and this should not have offered opportunities for optimization.

8.5 An important BIS study on deflation

If inflation is unwanted beyond a certain low limit, so is *deflation* – in this case even in a benign dose. Deflation's pattern is shown in Figure 8.4, taking the slide of Japan's 10-year benchmark bond from 1.6% to 0.6% interest rate as an example (see also Chapter 7). Deflation is unwanted because it puts pressure on the financial system. As prices fall, the real value of debt increases, leading to difficulties in debt servicing. The producers/consumers also suffer.

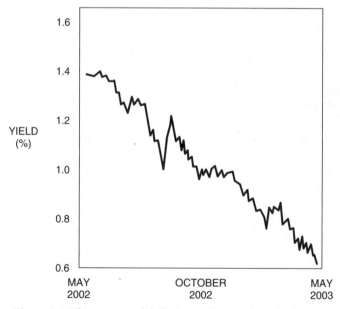

Figure 8.4 The pattern of deflation. An example with the cost
of money: Japan's 10-year benchmark bond

For countries like Japan, which since the Second World War have been accustomed to fast growth, a deflationary environment has been a new experience which is very challenging for the government, the productive sector of the economy, financial institutions, and the Japanese population as a whole. To this should be added the fact that we do not know enough about deflationary risks, particularly:

- How to deflect them
- How to handle them, and
- What the consequences are for credit markets.

As the 1990–2004 Japanese experience demonstrates, were deflation to come about, its aftermath would be very significant on the structure of the banking system and financial services industry at large. This is specifically a stress factor in countries where the prevailing culture in business and industry has been designed in an inflationary environment.

To get to know more about deflationary results and how to handle them, all governments, all central banks, all credit institutions, and all financial services companies, should be running scenarios for their future business plans based on a 0%, 1%, and beyond base rate of deflation. One aspect deserving particular attention is the fact that while they are losers in times of inflation, at times of deflation creditors and even bondholders with lower interest rates gain at the expense of debtors.

- *If* prices fall between the time a creditor lends money and is repaid,
- *Then* he or she gets back more purchasing power than was lent.

But between the time a merchant buys and sells goods, he will have to take a loss. At the same time, the government finds that the real burden of its public debt (see section 8.7) has gone up relative to tax collection and national income.[5] That's a basic reason why governments don't like deflation, and it is not the only one.

An equally potent reason for governments to watch deflationary pressures carefully, particularly from a macroeconomic viewpoint, is that around the zero line inflation and deflation follow a sinusoidal curve. The Bank for International Settlements (BIS) explains in an excellent way the reasons for and effects of this process. As the BIS 73rd Annual Report has it, when inflation is very low, deflation is arithmetically not far away. Furthermore, the *volatility of inflation* remains substantial, particularly when compared to a low level of inflation. To better appreciate this reference, it is wise to think of the Heisenberg principle: *Nothing walks on a straight line*. In real life terms, this is mapped in Figure 8.5 on the basis of BIS statistics.[6]

Associated to observed rates of inflation and deflation is a *measurement risk*. Since such observations are done through indices, the monitoring we do may understate or overstate the true rates of price increase and decrease, depending on:

- The indices, and
- Statistical methodologies being used.

For instance, as BIS notes, taking account of shifts in spending in response to changes in relative prices would have reduced CPI inflation, by means of using fixed weights, by almost half a percentage point in the United States in 2002. Similarly, Japanese deflation would appear more severe if measured by the private consumption deflator, rather than the CPI.

Still, in spite of measurement errors it is important to follow closely the switches between inflation and deflation when the two are observed around the base line (zero line). This sinusoidal curve is most clearly observable in the abscissa of Figure 8.5 in connection with the UK economy – an important reference because in the late 19th century Britain was already a well-settled industrial economy, while the United States was a developing economy with inflationary busts (though the big bust of the 1860s might have been an aftermath of the Civil War).

It is interesting to note in this connection that in the second half of the 19th century imperial Germany, too, was a developing economy – and together with the United States was the industrial challenger of Britain. In the mid-1860s Germany had a major deflation, at the −12% level, followed by an 8–18% inflation (probably due to the war with France).

On the heels of the events mentioned in the preceding paragraph came a one-year 10% deflation in Imperial Germany, then an inflation that lasted a couple of years, followed by a nearly 10% deflation in Imperial Germany. But by 1880 Germany, like the United States, settled in a pattern of less than 5% inflation and less than 3% deflation – always along a sinusoidal paragraph. The first dozen years of the 20th century saw no deflation and a rather contained inflation.

The BIS 73rd Annual Report notes that another interesting historical feature is that deflation in a variety of countries was rarely accompanied by an obvious deceleration in real gross domestic product. In fact, output typically kept growing. BIS names among reasons that might explain this event:

- Fairly flexible nominal wages
- Nature of the monetary regime
- Way in which price expectations were formed, and
- Historically modest debt levels.

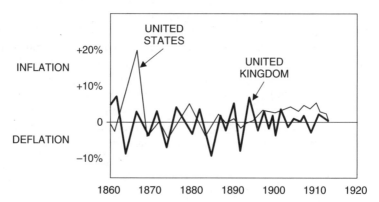

Figure 8.5 Putting inflation and deflation in historical perspective in the United States and United Kingdom, 1860–1913. (*Source:* Bank for International Settlements, with permission)

By contrast, the Great Depression of 1929–32 stands out as a notable exception, as there was a major collapse of output, an asset price crash, and generalized significant financial stress. In short, this was a period when many particularly unfavorable economic and policy developments interacted to produce the most severe economic contraction in a whole century.

These historical references are interesting and important inasmuch as, when viewed in the proper perspective, they can provide lessons for economists, businessmen, and policy-makers. As the Bank for International Settlements underlines in its Annual Report, under the current nearly globalized monetary system, policies aimed at delivering low and stable inflation:

- Work in a similar way to the implicit rules imposed by the gold standard in the years prior to 1914.
- But, at the same time, there exist evident differences between the two systems, which should be accounted for.

In both cases, the pre-1914 years and today, deviations from price stability cause a feedback response that effectively impact upon the behavior of prices. This takes the form of constraints in areas of monetary integration, like the Euroland. Indeed, it has been the aim of the Stability Pact signed by all 11 countries, which in the early years of the 21st century Germany (the Pact's promoter) and along with it France did not care to observe.

8.6   Debt financing by the public sector

Debt financing in the private and public sectors of the economy has a positive relationship with real economic activity and a negative one with interest rates. In the private sector, several factors, such as expansion of the industrial base, increasing demand by consumers and businesses, strong merger and acquisition (M&A) activity, and large movements in property prices, significantly affect debt developments.

By contrast with the first major recession of the 21st century, since 2001 debt financing has substantially decreased. Both economic slowdown and decline in M&As have had significant impact. On the other hand, while this has been an adjustment of private sector borrowers to an economy that got into hibernation, banks lost clients to the capital markets where firms may obtain better financing terms, as we have already seen in Chapter 6 and will discuss again in Chapter 11. Debt financing is done through:

- Loans granted by the banking sector
- Loans by non-monetary financial institutions (non-bank banks), and
- Debt securities issued by non-financial companies to the capital market.

Because bond investors purchase the debt instrument issued by the private and public sectors of the economy, these two are in competition with one another. This is how to interpret the news that (at time of writing) fiscal year 2004 is scheduled for a historically high deficit of $540 billion in the United States – the equivalent of more than $4000 per tax-paying household.

At a time when a slow economy slashes government revenues, the US Administration and Congress have increased spending for homeland security, agricultural subsidies, Medicare and Medicaid, and overseas military obligations. Compounding the problem have been two rounds of tax cuts that add an estimated $3 trillion of debt during the next 10 years.

There are precedents to such free spending policies. In the late 1960s President Lyndon Johnson refused to scale back the war on poverty at home, as costs for the conflict in Vietnam escalated. Johnson's pursuit of both butter and bullets led to great expenditures, and to what were then record-setting deficits. In turn, these created a decade of slow growth combined with high inflation – to so-called *stagflation*.

The years 2004 and 2005 may prove to be another milestone in deficit financing. Speaking to a Brookings Institution conference on Restoring Fiscal Sanity on 13 January 2004, former Treasury Secretary Robert Rubin emphasized that it is now necessary to highlight nonconventional effects of huge deficits. With this, Rubin warned that the use of traditional 'quantitative models' to predict whether or not there will be a major financial crisis, will not provide significant insight for policy-makers.

Figure 8.6 dramatizes the way US government deficits have spiraled out of control in the 2001–2004 timeframe. The Bush Administration's deficit goes well beyond the heights reached in the early 1990s, and it follows on the heels of rather modest government surpluses in the last four years of the Clinton Administration.

As Rubin aptly noted, virtually all mainstream economists believe there is a significant relationship between long-term deficits and interest rates. But conventional analysis of long-run deficits' effects is not telling the full story of their aftermath. Not only must governments borrow a large amount of capital from credit markets, crowding out private sector demands for capital, but they also prove unwilling to get rid of built-in destabilizers of the economy.

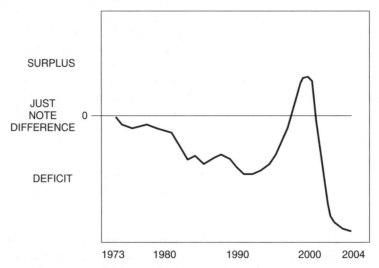

Figure 8.6 The pattern of US federal budget deficits over more that
three decades, 1973–2004

One of the larger destabilizers is the entitlement programs, such as statutory health insurance. Admittedly, providing for a reduction in expenses which are financed through deficits is no easy task. This will require not only more prudent screening of expenses, which is easier said than done, but also abolition of the one-off maternity payments, payments for over-the-counter pharmaceuticals, and so on.

Evidence that none of the measures so far taken in the United States and Europe is radical is provided by the fact that government deficits continue to accelerate. Particularly in an aging society, failure to bend the curve of growing social costs and health costs leads not only to steadily growing budget deficits but also to trouble further ahead, leaving open only one escape: state bankruptcy.

State bankruptcy hits bond investors particularly hard, but also the country's public at large. A fairly recent example of the luggage which comes with the government's bankruptcy is provided by Argentina, which saw 20% of its economy evaporate in 2001, and found it very difficult to:

- Mend fences with international creditors, and
- Slowly put itself back together, to help in its own recovery.

Walter Wriston, the former chairman of Citibank, once said that sovereigns don't default. This is not true. In 2003 the International Monetary Fund warned that some Asian and Latin American governments have loaded up with much more debt than a first glance might suggest. For instance, by the end of 2003 total public debt of Asian governments had risen to nearly 70% of their GDP, from less than 60% at the height of the Asian financial crisis in 1998. In Latin America, the debt ratio has climbed to 60% from about 40%, with Brazil being the largest sovereign debtor in the world. What has been particularly worrying economists at the IMF is that the world's poorer nations are on very shaky ground because:

- Their tax collection systems are weak and unreliable, and
- Their exposure to outside shocks is large to very large.

According to some experts in the general case, for the typical emerging-market economy, a probably sustainable government debt would be about one-third its current level, and even that is high. Moreover, accounting books and statistics are often cooked because governments can often push public debt off the books by setting up the loans through:

- Quasi-public corporations, or
- Private companies supported by government loan guarantees.

Notice that this is not only true of developing nations, but of all nations, including Western ones. And while it is said that domestic debt is less worrisome than foreign debt because a government taxes its citizen, time and again, it is often forgotten that domestic debt can also be more difficult to collect.

All of these reasons may have been in the mind of Robert Rubin when he said that if a crisis develops, there could be a sharp increase in defaults which is not projected through conventional analysis. Added to that is the risk that the international markets could lose confidence in a country's currency (Rubin was talking of the dollar) because of long-term current account deficits.

Should this happen, the international markets will become reluctant to engage in the rollover of very large amounts of government debt held abroad. This process can undermine business and consumer confidence, leading investors to demand still higher interest rates to compensate for:

- Credit risk
- Currency risk, and
- Interest rate risks.

The greatest warning by Robert Rubin in the 2004 Brookings Institution conference was the one he gave last, that all of aforementioned effects *could happen together*, thereby creating serious additional problems over and above the one conventional analysis can provide. '*Put them all together*, and you could have a very severe set of effects,' Rubin added.[7]

8.7 Government borrowing, money supply, and interest rates

The concept underpinning monetary base and money supply has been introduced in Chapter 1. According to statistics by the Federal Reserve, in the United States the volume of the money aggregate, M1, increased by an annualized 42.3% in 2001 (in part due to the liquidity injected by the Federal Reserve after 9/11) and it kept on growing at a rapid pace in the ensuing years. Also in 2001, the annualized growth rates of the broader money supply aggregate, M2, was 25.5%; and that of M3, 21.0%. These have been among the highest in 30 years.

Money supply has also been rising very fast in Japan, the UK, and Euroland, as governments have tried to jump-start the economy after the deflation of the stock market bubble, and found themselves obliged to inject more and more liquidity into the market. The trend curve of the M3 monetary base in the United States, up to 2003, is shown in Figure 8.7.

There is no limit to the expansion of the money supply by the banking sector, Dr Marriner Eccles, the chairman of the Federal Reserve in the 1930s and Second World War years, once said. Governments have taken good notice of this dictum in their debt financing policies, which are the subject of this section. They also more or less understand that getting rid of that debt might mean:

- Outright default or,
- The same thing in slow motion: inflation.

Despite all the noise about shrinking the budget deficit being crucial for a healthy bond market, there has been little connection between the steady increase in the deficit of the United States, France, Germany, and other countries during the past four years, and the direction of interest rates – because both the Fed in America and the ECB in Euroland deliberately kept short-term rates at a very low level. But the longer-term interest rate curve has steepened.

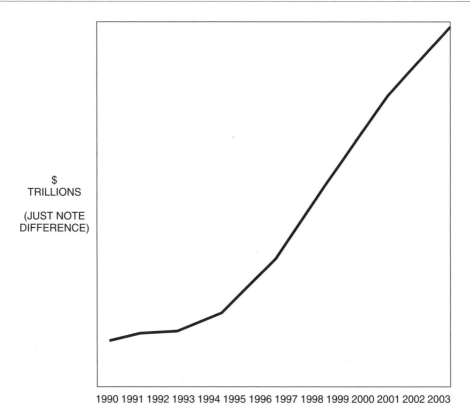

1990 1991 1992 1993 1994 1995 1996 1997 1998 1999 2000 2001 2002 2003

Figure 8.7 The exponential expansion of the US money supply: M3 statistics

Not only interest rate risk but also currency exchange risk has to be addressed. In 1978, the Swiss battled a surging Swiss franc by pushing short interest rates down to zero percent, and imposing a surcharge on foreign inflows. This surcharge made the effective interest rate of the Swiss franc negative for foreigners. At the same time, as another weapon to cope with a surging currency, the Swiss cranked up money growth.

In contrast, as Figure 8.8 shows, since the late 1970 the Federal Reserve has adopted a policy of steadily increasing the money supply, a process interrupted only for a few years in the early 1990s, then taking off at faster pace. By year 2000, the Fed adopted a second policy of ever-lower interest rates which has done wonders for the real estate market, allowing it to grow to levels well beyond economic reality and leading to a new bubble.

In this environment, speculators (and some investors) adopted the strategy of making large, leveraged real estate deals. There is a new metric for measuring profits made in real estate from leveraged positions, and it is known as *cash-on-cash*. Its algorithm is fairly simple:

$$\text{Cash-on-cash return} = \frac{\text{Actual home price appreciation in year 2}}{\text{Owners equity at end of year 1}}$$

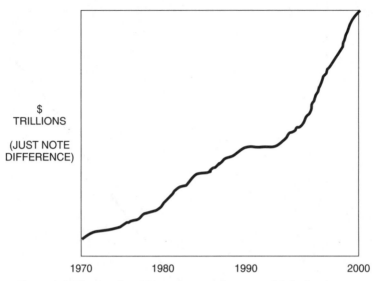

$
TRILLIONS

(JUST NOTE
DIFFERENCE)

        1970   1980   1990   2000

Figure 8.8 The trend in M3 money supply over a third of a century

In a holistic economic approach, there is significant difference if speculators (or investors) measure gain in actual home price appreciation or in cash-on-cash return. A study by Merrill Lynch which covered two decades, shows that:

- From 1982 to 1994, home ownership price appreciated about 75% and cash-on-cash 100%; which is no big difference.
- But from 1995 to 2003, home ownership price appreciated about 120% while cash-on-cash zoomed up 250%, more than double.[8]

There is no reason why not to use the same algorithm to judge returns on a portfolio composed of debt instruments. As long as the market is going along the investor's (or speculator's) prognostication, cash-on-cash will be ahead of the curve. But if these forecasts turn on their head, geared investors will feel the heat – and the most leveraged will go bankrupt. The same happens with home owners.

The use of quantitative measurement and of accounting procedures, which help to dramatize the effects of gearing, also helps in motivating those responsible to do something about it. A similar statement is valid about inflation. There are various models that attempt to quantify inflation's conventional effects; but as section 8.5 underlined, we also need algorithms and heuristics:

- Able to quantify non-conventional effects, and
- Convey the results in a comprehensive way to create a public reaction that would feed into the political process.

The Deutsche Bundesbank has developed a model which addresses the government debt ratio (read gearing) and its determinants. It starts linearly by considering that government debt at the end of a given period results from the debt level at the end of the previous period, and the deficit from the interest paid on the debt of the previous period. This model is briefly described in the Appendix to the present chapter.

The challenge is to extend this model to deal with non-conventional effects, as Robert Rubin has said. Also, to make feasible an experimentation on tail conditions, able to provide insight on the likely aftermath of outliers in continuing budget deficits, inflation pressures, and trends in interest rates.

8.8   Inflation-indexed securities

Since governments find it difficult to control their own budget, it is only proper that algorithms should exist which bring to the attention of the executive branch, as well as the parliament (or the Congress), the national debt ratio and its determinants. And because inflation, like death and taxes, cannot be avoided, the alternative of inflation-indexed securities comes into perspective (see also the discussion on natural or neutral interest rates and inflation-indexed securities in Chapter 9).

In the United States, a way to hedge against a possible resurgence of inflation, as far as national debt is concerned, is inflation-indexed Treasuries and inflation-adjusted Savings Bonds. They offer the safety of US government-backed assets, earnings are exempt from state and local taxes, and the investor gets some sort of inflation protection. These are an asset class which can be looked at as separate from bonds and stocks, and so bring diversification benefits in terms of inflation exposure.

A particular feature of these securities is that while the interest rate on inflation-indexed Treasuries remains the same for the life of the bond, every six months the principal is adjusted for inflation. Future interest payments are based on this adjusted principal. One way of looking at the adjustment of the principal is that inflation-adjusted savings bonds, or I-Bonds, come with two interest rates:

- A fixed return for the life of the bond, and
- A variable rate based on inflation that is credited every six months.

Treasury Inflation Protected Securities (TIPS) were first offered in 1997, and the following years saw falling inflation. Hence, they offered an insurance policy that investors really did not need. Nobody buys insurance for events they do not worry about and as a result TIPS had to trade rather cheaply to attract buying but, as we saw at the beginning of this chapter, the inflation environment has changed for the worse.

The US government seems committed to issuing approximately two new TIPS a year. By mid-1999 there were six of them: from 5-year to 10-year bonds. As the government keeps issuing TIPS, investment analysts are going to have more and more information to build an accurate inflation indexing curve. Apart from that, many investors look at inflation-sensitive Treasuries as an indication that the Fed:

- Is concerned with inflation rates beyond their current level, and
- It keeps a close eye on inflation expectations, since expectations can be self-fulfilling.

According to some experts, the Fed uses TIPS to gauge whether inflation expectations are changing. This can be done through the movement in the spread between the 10-year nominal Treasury bonds and TIPS.

Index-linked bonds with the amount repayable and interest rate linked to general price movements have been issued in several countries, beyond those chronically characterized by high inflation. For instance, since September 1998 France has been issuing government bonds which are inflation-indexed (OAT) with 10- to 30-year maturities. Interest rate on these bonds and the amount repayable are tied to the development of the French consumer price index.

The reader should notice that the interest rate paid on the aforementioned OAT does not fully correspond to the real interest rate, because the inflation adjustment takes place with a lag of three months, and tobacco is excluded from the inflation index. Nevertheless, a comparison to nominal interest rate of debt instruments with the same maturity permits the computation of implied inflation rates, known as *break-even* inflation rates – and the yield of these government bonds contains a liquidity premium, as the market for index-linked debt instruments is far less liquid than that for conventional government paper.

Different inflation-indexed schemes are followed with corporate debt instruments. In contrast to the above types of inflation-linked securities, an inflation-indexed corporate coupon bond tends to have relatively small dependence on actual inflation rates. The bond coupons are fixed at the assumed fixed inflation rate plus the guaranteed real rate.

- These fixed cash flows are discounted back as the current market real rate of return.
- Hence, the bond trades at a discount (or premium) when market real rates are above (or below) the guaranteed real rate.

When the price of this type of instrument is available, the current price and fixed future cash flows can be used to derive an implied real rate on the debt instrument. There are also available different types of derivative financial products claiming to provide inflation protection. An example is the 5-year Euro Note, by BNP Paribas, linked to Euroland inflation. Most evidently, this security carries both credit risk and market risk. BNP Paribas is rated AA− by S&P and Aa2 by Moody's. This particular debt instrument has been issued in 10 000 euro notes with 22 November 2002 the payment date and 22 November 2007 the maturity date.

The note's annual coupon payment consists of a fixed part of indicative 1.94% plus Euroland inflation, measured as annual percentage change of the underlying index. The coupon is paid annually and is floored at 0%, which means it cannot be negative even in a sharp deflationary environment.

Some analysts consider the aforementioned BNP Paribas notes as suitable for fixed income investors who expect an increasing inflation in Europe over the issue's timeframe. Similar to a bond investment, at maturity the note will be repaid at par by the issuer. The formula for calculation of the inflation is:

$$\text{Inflation} = \frac{\text{Index (September CPI current year)}}{\text{Index (September CPI previous year)}} - 1$$

The index is equal to the Harmonized Index of Consumer Prices (HICP) excluding tobacco, unrevised series. The publication by Eurostat is final. This and other offerings in the securities market aim at investors who look for a shelter from inflation, at the cost of assuming certain risks. In the general case, with inflation-indexed securities the real rate of return is the pivot reference. For other than derivative instruments, a simple formula helps to provide the nominal interest rate as a function of expected real interest rate, level of inflation, and risk premium:

$$i_n = (1 + i_r') \cdot (1 - f) \cdot (1 - r_p) - 1 \tag{1}$$

where:

i_n = nominal interest rate
i_r' = expected real interest rate
f = expected inflation
r_p = risk premium for uncertainty

Through this and similar algorithms, investors base their decisions on expected real rate of return adjusted for the aforementioned factors. A more precise model should consider the specific structure of the security, market psychology which influences future inflation trend, and possible surprises by regulatory authorities, including:

- Lower rates to keep alive the idea that the debt can be serviced, or
- Higher rates to dry up some of the low interest rate speculation and bolster pension funds, but also increase debt-service costs.

This very simple equation (1) can also serve in estimating cash flows associated with an investment. The nominal rate i is always greater than i_r' as f tends to be positive, and p is positive by definition. As an example, assuming:

i_r' = 5% per year
f = 2.5% per year
r_p = 1.0% per year

$$i_n = (1 + 0.05)(1 + 0.025) - (1 + 0.01) - 1 = 1.087 - 1 = 0.087$$

Given the aforementioned factors of inflation and uncertainty, for 5% real return the nominal rate must be 8.70% per year. Few investors, however, look into this issue of return on investment on debt through the perspective of inflation and uncertainty – or account for discounted cash flow by using the nominal interest rate.

Moreover, few investors integrate into their formula the consequences of credit risk, as should be the case (see Chapter 12). If there is credit risk in the investment, then equation (1) should become at least slightly more complex:

$$i_n = (1 + i_r') (1 - f) (1 - r_p) (1 + d_c) - 1 \tag{2}$$

where:

d_c = expected default risk of the counterparty

The best way to look at d_c is as likelihood of business failure over the period of the contract – essentially the maturity of the debt instrument, using tables published by S&P and Moody's which link default probability to rating for up to 10 years. In other terms, d_c can be calculated as a function of rating by independent agencies.[9] For instance, if the debt is issued by an A-rated company, the maturity is just one year, and all other variables are the same, then:

$$i_n = (1 + 0.05)\,(1 + 0.025)\,(1 + 0.01)\,(1 + 0.0311) - 1 = 0.0897 = 8.97\%$$

The impact of rating is not fully seen in this example because of the 1-year maturity and A grade. But credit risk counts for a great deal, and therefore Chapter 12 is devoted to this issue. Still, the notions outlined in this section help in appreciating risks and opportunities connected to inflation-linked bond markets, and the creditworthiness of issuers of debt instruments.

8.9   Choices necessary to overcome accounting insufficiency

The algorithm of the Deutsche Bundesbank, discussed in section 8.7 and explained in the Appendix, should be of interest not only to governments faced with increasing public debt, but also to industrial and financial entities with a policy of debt financing. Both sovereigns and credit institutions confront the problem of:

■ Debt at the end of period t, and
■ Budgetary impact from debt level at the end of previous period, t-1, and those preceding it.

Likewise, all investors should be interested in applying equation (2) in section 8.8, which includes credit risk. This algorithm is of interest not only in regard to new acquisitions of debt securities, but also in re-evaluation of portfolio positions which any serious investor, institutional as well as individual, should regularly do.

The able handling of reassessments must also confront the relative insufficiency of current accounting procedures, with *net present value* (NPV) estimates at the core (see also in Chapter 7 the discussion on net asset value, NAV). A classical accounting approach to overcome the effect of inflation which makes the figures in the book unreliable has been that of calculating expired expenditure as a percentage, not of the cost of assets but of the amount that will be required to replace the assets in due course. This has been seen as an improvement of the method of accruals where inflation eats up the assets' registered value.

Critics, however, comment that both accruals and percentages show ignorance of basic accounting principles which require that when paying in a currency or evaluating assets and liabilities, one must know what this currency is worth; that is, what is the assets' market value. One must also know what is their replacement value.

Gross replacement value (GRV) and net replacement value (NRV) are equivalent terms in calculating exposure. Gross replacement value is used when there is no netting contract, or when there is one that cannot be enforced because of a difference in jurisdictions. There is also another metric, known as *gross replacement cost* (GRC), which is slightly different from gross replacement value. Gross replacement value can be positive or negative.

■ If positive, it represents a loss in replacement and this has to be shown in financial analysis.
■ By contrast, a negative gross replacement value would indicate the entity makes a gain on this particular position (or transaction).

In the case of a financial institution, for example, net replacement value is essentially a netting replacement value, presupposing the existence of a master netting agreement. If the law of the land does not allow netting, then net replacement value cannot be used. The same is true if contracts operate across different jurisdictions, one of which does not allow netting.

In one of my meetings in the City of London, my interviewee made the point that net replacement value is a dangerous accounting concept, as it led to the downfall of LTCM. My inclination is to subscribe to the first half of the statement that netting, and therefore net present value, can be quite misleading. But I would not agree with the second comment. LTCM did not fail just because of NPV accounting, it bankrupted itself because of:

■ Overleveraging
■ Mismanagement
■ Scant risk control, and
■ An inordinate amount of greed.

As will be discussed in Chapter 15 in connection with risk management, a persistent problem is that huge derivatives losses at financial institutions and other entities are rarely announced though they are often dealt with by changes in leadership. This does not mean the new leadership will be better than the old, particularly in what matters most: effective risk control.

At the time of writing, experts think that changes in leadership are forthcoming at several firms, as the 2004 rise in long-term interest rates has generated huge losses in a number of derivatives portfolios. Indeed, since the second half of 2003 the Federal Reserve has been presented with difficult choices, each with its own risks, since there are constraints in monetary policy.

Under these conditions, the use of marking to market procedures for derivative instruments and other exposures taken by banks is the best avenue for transparency and market discipline. Statement of Financial Accounting Standard 133 by the US Financial Accounting Standards Board specifies that institutions should use fair value – defined as market value under conditions other than fire sale. Moreover, it is appropriate to include in fair estimates of value the impact of other factors, and most particularly:

■ Potential risk, as a function of what might happen to interest rates or currency rates, and
■ Peak exposure, which is replacement value in a worst-case scenario.

A sophisticated approach in projecting potential risk and peak exposure would require inclusion of all commitment in derivative and other financial instruments – with derivatives computed in credit equivalent risk. This requires demodulating derivatives amounts down to the level of core exposure, often called *toxic waste*, with the divisor chosen on the basis of historical precedence depending on prevailing financial conditions and market psychology.[10] Huge derivatives losses and government deficits correlate when taxpayer's money is used to salvage bankrupt credit institutions that are 'too big to fail'.

Appendix 8.A   The Deutsche Bundesbank algorithm

As stated in section 8.7, the Deutsche Bundesbank has developed a model that addresses the government debt ratio and its determinants. This algorithm starts by considering that B_t government debt at the end of period t, results from the debt level at the end of the previous period, B_{t-1}, and the deficit from the interest paid on the debt of the previous period, $B_{t-1} i$, where i is the average effective interest rate paid on government debt, less the primary balance S_t:

$$B_t = B_{t-1} + B_{t-1}i - S_t = B_{t-1} + D_t \tag{1}$$

where:

$$D_t = B_{t-1}i - S_t$$

If there is a primary surplus, part of the government's interest payment is financed from government revenue. In terms of GDP, equation (1) is supplemented by:

$$b_t = b_{t-1} \frac{1 + i}{1 + g} - s_t \tag{2}$$

where b_t and b_{t-1} are the share of GDP represented by government debt in period t, t − 1; s_t, the primary balance in relation to GDP in period t; and g the nominal GDP growth rate. The change in debt-to-GDP ratio is expressed by:

$$\Delta b_t = b_t - b_{t-1} \tag{3}$$

$$\Delta b_t = b_{t-1} \frac{i + g}{1 + g} - s_t \tag{4}$$

The Bundesbank algorithm accounts for the fact that the development of a debt ratio is negatively dependent on primary balance, and positively dependent on growth-adjusted interest payment on the previous period's debt ratio. A growth-adjusted interest rate

$$\frac{i + g}{1 + g} \tag{5}$$

contains the nominal interest rate effect: $\dfrac{i}{1 + g}$; real growth effect: $\dfrac{RG}{1 + g}$, where

RG = real GDP growth; and GDP deflator effect: $\dfrac{GD}{1 + g}$, where GD = GDP deflator.

Notes

1 Merrill Lynch, *Global Research Highlights*, 18 June 2004.
2 ECB Monthly Bulletin, June 2004.
3 *The Economist*, 19 June 2004.
4 EIR, 16 April 2004.
5 Paul A. Samuelson, *Economics: An Introductory Analysis*, McGraw-Hill, New York, 1951.
6 BIS 73rd Annual Report, Basel.
7 EIR, 30 January 2004.
8 Merrill Lynch, *Global Research Highlights*, 18 June 2004.
9 D.N. Chorafas, *Managing Credit Risk*, volume 1: *Analyzing, Rating and Pricing the Probability of Default*, Euromoney, London, 2000.
10 D.N. Chorafas, *Stress Testing: Risk Management Strategies for Extreme Events*, Euromoney, London, 2003.

9 Bond yields and benchmark government bonds

9.1 Introduction

The term *yield* was introduced to the reader in Chapter 3 and, since then, has been used on several occasions (particularly in Chapter 7); it has been left to this chapter, however, to fully define its computational methods, as well as to elaborate on the role of yield curves (which were also discussed in Chapter 7). Other issues covered in this chapter are presently prevailing approaches in estimating real interest rates from nominal rates, as well as ways and means to identify the benchmarks used to calculate spreads in basis points – for instance, corporates compared to credit-risk-free US Treasuries.

As the reader will recall, the yield curve is a dynamic mapping of values which describe, at a given point in time, the relationship between interest rates at different maturities. Its slope represents the difference between short-term and long-term interest rates – and, therefore, the income from a security as a function of its current market price.

We saw in the examples in Chapter 7 that historically the yield curve is steep. Other things being equal, this makes it profitable to invest in long-dated securities. However, as we also have seen, yield curves flatten and there is also backwardation. Moreover, because, as already stated, the concept of yield applies to all securities, it is necessary to distinguish between not only the debt instrument's nominal yield and real yield but, also, other yield types such as:

- *Dividend yield*, which is the current dividend as a percentage of market price of an equity.
- *Earnings yield*, a theoretical figure based on the last earnings per share, typically applied in conjunction to current market price.
- *Redemption yield*, normally used only in connection to fixed-interest securities.

Redemption yield is the interest payment over the remaining life of the debt instrument, plus or minus the difference between purchase price and redemption value. In this sense, redemption yield is earnings yield adjusted to take account of capital gain or loss to redemption. With fixed debt instruments, the nominal interest, or coupon, is unlikely to be the same as the actual yield.

In a simplistic form, a non-redeemable security such as a government bond, with a flat yield of 6% and par value of $1000, but a market price of $1050, provides an earnings yield of 5.7%. Actually, the formula is more complex, as we will subsequently see, because there are other factors also coming into the yield equation. Based on the bond's price and nominal interest rate,

- With bullet debt, we are interested to know yield-to-maturity, or *internal rate of return*.
- By contrast, with callable debt instruments which trade above par, we are after *yield-to-call*.

In the most general sense, the way to look at yield is that it will fluctuate with the price of the security, rising as bond prices fall and falling when bond prices rise. Investors also want to know yield spread (discussed in Chapter 7) and yield gap, as well as price value of a basis point and bond volatility.

An example of *yield gap* is the difference between the yield on ordinary shares and the yield on gilt-edged securities. If the latter exceeds the former, it is called the '*reverse yield gap*', which first appeared in 1959. The *price value* of a basis point is the change in the price of the bond if the yield changes by one basis point. This is a measure of price volatility in money terms (dollars, pounds, euro, and so on), as contrasted to price volatility as a *percentage* of initial price. The price value of a basis point is expressed as the absolute value of change in price.

Notice that for small changes in required yield, price volatility is the same, regardless of the direction of a change in yield. Hence, it does not make any difference if the investor increases or decreases the required yield by one basis point, when computing the price value of a basis point (more on this calculation in section 9.3).

Finally, with regard to the pricing of bonds, investors must appreciate that there can be a change in the relevance of factors explaining differentials among various issuers. For instance, before Stage Three of the European Monetary Unit (EMU), credit, inflation, and related exchange rate risk differentials were the main variables behind prevailing differences in yield. By contrast, in the monetary union of Euroland, apart from credit risk considerations, liquidity has become a major factor in defining investors' preferences for the various euro-denominated government bonds.

There is also the effect of financial market integration, which, in its narrow sense, considers the institutional conditions necessary for integration. By contrast, a definition of market integration in the broad sense also takes into account the willingness of investors to enter into crossborder transactions. Financial market integration does not happen automatically, just by removing foreign exchange risk.

9.2 Algorithms for computation of yield

Interest rates on any investment, including debt instruments, are not constant through time. The yield depends on several factors, including purchase price, nominal interest rate, time to maturity, carry cost of money, and of course security. All financial instruments have credit risk, though algorithms for yield calculation typically assume that there is no counterparty risk. This is the case of the algorithms presented in Appendix A and Appendix B to this chapter.

Prior to looking into computational procedures, let us start with some preliminaries. Investors usually purchase fixed income securities which have already been issued and trade in the secondary market. But they may also buy bonds on a *when-issued* or *to be announced* (TBAs) basis. Basically, TBAs are forward contracts targeting the

control of large positions with minimal cash outlay. Hence they are leveraged investments based, for instance, on generic pools of mortgages that will settle in some future
month. With TBAs:

- The coupon is specified, and
- Underlying mortgages must conform to certain criteria.

However, the actual mortgages constituting the pool are not determined until
settlement. Still, prior to settlement, investors actively trade TBAs, and they are
doing so without exchanging funds. Prices fluctuate as market conditions evolve.
This is not the type of instruments we will consider in this chapter.

The algorithms we will see on the computation of yields mainly concern debt
instruments traded in the secondary market, though they may also be applied with
other types of bonds. In the general case, investors use these algorithms for one of
three main reasons:

- To compute the yield of new bond investment(s), prior to commitment
- To know the internal rate of return of their holdings in debt instruments, and
- To be sensitive to changes in internal rate of return, so that they can reposition
  themselves, if need be, to market forces.

The concept behind the third bullet also includes simulation of likely financial
results through experimentation based on hypothetical change in fair values of debt
instruments held in a portfolio. This helps in making the investor and asset manager
sensitive to the volatility of interest rates. Steady sensitivity to market changes is
much more important if the portfolio positions are leveraged and/or are held not for
the long term but for the purpose of trading.

A modeling technique I have often used measures the change in fair values arising
from selected potential changes in interest rates. The market volatility being
employed reflects immediate parallel shifts in the yield curve of plus or minus 50 basis
points (bps), 100 bps, 150 bps, and 200 bps, over a 12-month time horizon (see also
the OTS model in Chapter 14).

- *Beginning fair values* represent the market principal plus accrued interest, prior to
  experimentation.
- *Ending fair values* comprise the market principal plus accrued interest after experimentation, at each of the aforementioned basis point thresholds.

Table 9.1 offers a matrix presentation which maps the outcome at these thresholds,
as well as main classes of portfolio contents. Alternatively, matrices can be presented
in graphic form, with numerical values available as back-up and greater detail,
through on-line database mining.[1] Notice that a similar matrix to the one in Table
9.1 can be made for yields.

Income derived from fixed interest instruments is measured in terms of coupon,
running yield, and yield to redemption. The nominal rate of interest or coupon gives

Table 9.1 Estimated fair value of a portfolio at a 12-month time horizon, under different interest rate scenarios

Issuer	Valuation of securities given an interest rate decrease of X basis points				Beginning fair value	Valuation of securities given an interest rate increase of X basis points			
	200 bp	150 bp	100 bp	50 bp		50 bp	100 bp	150 bp	200 bp
US government bonds									
UK government bonds									
Other sovereign bonds (by sovereign)									
State and municipal bonds (by class of entities)									
Corporate bonds with AAA and AA rating									
Corporate bonds with A and BBB rating									
Corporate bonds with BB rating									
Debt instruments by non-rated entities									
Total									

the interest earned annually as a percentage of the nominal value which accrues to the investor. This is relevant with regard to estimating the cash flow from a portfolio of fixed income securities and for taxation reasons. The running yield is the coupon as percentage:

- Of the issue, or
- Of the purchase price.

Running yield will be above (or below) the coupon, if bought price is below (or above) par. In this simple computation, maturity of the security (see Chapter 10) and redemption gains or losses are not taken into account. Redemption gains and losses are accounted for by computing yield to redemption, which also includes any gains or losses on redemption. Different formulas are used for calculation of yield. For private bond holders an approximate approach is provided by the simple formula:

$$\text{Yield} = \left(\text{coupon} \pm \frac{\text{Price gain or loss}}{\text{Remaining maturity (in years)}}\right) \times \frac{100}{\text{Purchase price}} \tag{1}$$

As an example of calculation of bond yield taking bond repayment into account, consider a 5.5% debt instrument of company 'X' bought at 89.5%, with term structure 15.4.2012. On the hypothesis this bond now sells at par, the annual yield will be the sum of two returns:

$$\frac{\text{Capital gain}}{\text{Number of years}} = \frac{10.5}{6.6} = 1.59 \tag{2}$$

$$\frac{\text{Coupon}}{\text{Paid price ratio}} = \frac{5.5}{0.895} = 6.15 \tag{3}$$

Sum of two returns   7.74

Notice that in this example the bond was bought below par. If it were bought above par, the factor in equation (1) would have been negative. While this approach is often used, it tends to confuse capital gain and yield proper. For the obtained result, the term *return* is more appropriate than yield.

As a return provided by the bond, yield must be computed to its maturity. Say that a 1-year bond has a 4% nominal value, but its market price stands at 92%. For an investment of $1000, at par value, the yield would have been $40, but dividing by 92 this gives an annual income of nearly $43.5 – or a yield of 4.35% when bought at stated discount below par. If the price the investor paid was 105%, then the yield for the same bond would have been 3.81%, with the investor getting $38.1 for each thousand dollars of investment.

Let us consider a 10-year bond, with every other reference remaining the same as in the foregoing example. A simple but approximate way to compute yield to maturity is to divide by 10, representing the years to maturity.

- The discount of 8%, for below par, or
- The higher cost of 5%, for above par.

This means, in the first case, that the yield will be 4.035%, while in the second case it will be 3.98%. In the one case as in the other, this simple approach spreads the effect of a discount or high cost linearly over the years to maturity. The algorithm is:

$$\frac{\text{Discount}}{\text{Years to maturity}} = \text{Pro rata basis points} \qquad (4)$$

Another algorithm for yield calculation starts with the instrument's current market price and yield-to-maturity (see Chapter 10) to obtain the internal rate of return. For callable bonds that trade above par, the yield-to-call is used for settlement purposes. For discounting reasons, the discount rate is related to the settlement price (purchase price), by an algorithm that takes into account:

- Purchase price
- Discount rate
- Maturity value, at par, and
- Number of days to maturity.

A more sophisticated approach will consider yield-to-maturity of a discount instrument in terms of its discount rate. Still another yield algorithm for callable bonds is that of the compound interest rate. The yield of fixed interest securities with annual interest payment and maturity of n years can be determined by the algorithm in Appendix A.

Behind the concern about a more accurate computation of yield lies the fact that the buyer of a debt instrument is practically paying *now*, but is purchasing money due in the *future*. Those further out funds are of two kinds:

- The regular coupon payment which represents the yield, and
- A lump sum at the end of the bond's life, which may be more than, equal to, or less than, purchase price – depending whether the bond was bought at a discount or at a premium.

Moreover, the amounts of interest accruing annually on different bonds differs. As a result, the annuity value factor cannot be used to determine the present value of all interest amounts. This can be done if interest payments are discounted individually. To determine the yield of bonds of this type, the present values of all disbursements, or redemption value and interest payments, and the purchase price are equated, using the algorithm in Appendix A.

9.3 Yield estimates, basis points, and yield curves

Yield estimates, and experimentation on different yields, require calculation of price value along a scale of a number of basis points. The price value of different thresholds of basis points is established by computing the difference between *initial price* and *actual market* price of yield changes by (chosen) basis points thresholds. This is under two hypotheses: (i) the yield is increased, and (ii) the yield is decreased. The computational procedure:

- Starts with the basis point thresholds and initial price at, say, 5% yield, and
- Provides the price at 5% plus yield by threshold, as well as price value at each basis point threshold.

In principle, when the price value of a basis point is smaller, the initial yield is higher. Also, the larger the price value of a basis point, the greater the convexity (see Chapter 10).

For small changes in required yield, for instance at the level of 10 basis points or so, the price value of 10 basis points is roughly that found by multiplying the price value of one basis point by 10. There is an approximate symmetry of price change for small 10 basis point changes in the yield, but this is not necessarily true for large changes. Inventors can compute the dollar price change, by dividing the price value of a basis point by the initial price.

$$\text{Percentage price change} = \frac{\text{Price value of a basis point}}{\text{Initial price}} \tag{1}$$

There is also an alternative method for computing the price volatility of a bond. This measures change in the yield for a specified price change. It is computed by first establishing the bond's yield if the bond's price is increased by a given amount, say $30 per $1000, or 3%. The yield value of the stated dollar price increase is the difference between:

- The initial yield, and
- The new yield.

In principle, the smaller the yield value of a dollar price change, the greater is the dollar price volatility. In this case, it takes a larger price movement to change the yield a specified number of basis points.

There is an interesting level of consistency between bond price volatility and the debt instrument's duration (discussed in Chapter 10). Other things being equal, the greater the maturity, the greater the price volatility. Also, the greater the maturity, the greater is the duration; and in principle, the lower the coupon rate, the greater is the duration.

The pattern of bond price volatility is a function of yield changes, expressed in the *yield curve*, whose concept has been introduced in Chapter 7. As a reminder, Figure 9.1 shows the implied forward yield curve in Euroland with 3-month changes: 31 March, 31 July and 30 September 1999.

As the careful reader will recall, the yield curve is one of the financial industry's most powerful predictors. In normal times, long-term bond yields are higher than short-term interest rates. This reflects the time value of money, which compensates investors for the higher risk of parting with their money for a longer period. But just before recessions or sharp slowdowns,

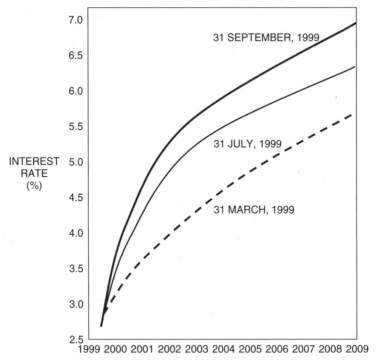

Figure 9.1 Change in overnight interest rates: implied forward yield curve in percentages per year (daily data)

■ Yield curves have often inverted (backwardation), and
■ Short-term rates can rise above long-term bond yields.

The shape of the bond yield curve impacts upon yield estimates. Pattern changes and future earnings growth correlate. When the yield curve is sloping strongly upward, which means that long-term interest rates are much higher than short-term rates, investors tend to expect faster economic growth – and also better corporate earnings, which is positive for equities.

Another way of making this statement is to say that the yield curve for debt instruments could be used as a predictor for equity investments, like the trend in price/earnings (P/E) ratios. When the P/E is high, investors seem to expect faster future earnings growth leading to a bull run. Also a good indicator for equities is whether earnings revert to the mean. Because earnings are more volatile than dividends, when earnings are temporarily high, the payout ratio – essentially dividends declared by the board – would be lower and vice versa.[2]

Investors should exploit this potential duality of service by the yield curve: as a tool for debt instruments, and a predictor for equities. Put at its most basic, however, the yield structure maps yield conditions in the capital market as a function of the residual maturity of debt securities – and it is established on the basis of a, usually limited, number of available yields on bonds by estimating a continuous function.

■ Typically, yield curves drawn up to 10 years (as the example in Figure 9.1) are fairly well documented.
■ By contrast, yield curves extending 30 years forward, like the one shown in Figure 9.2, are well done for the first 10 years then are extended in a straight line for the next 20 years – which does not make much sense.

Only listed government securities are used in the computation of yield curves, to assure that the financial paper on whose basis the curve if established is homogeneous. Analysts are particularly interested in studying the structure of yield curves because of their information content in regard to the capital market.

For instance, since the end of the 1980s the yield structure in the German capital market has nearly completed an entire cycle. Starting from a slightly inverse curve, the economic policy uncertainties in connection with reunification, at the beginning of the 1990s, led to an increase in long-term interest rates.

The inverse shape of the yield curve, observed at the beginning of the 1990s, revealed the impact of Deutsche Bundesbank's anti-inflationary policy. This has been reflected in rising money market rates, hence at the short-term end of the yield curve. Then, starting in February 1994, the German capital market was caught in the wake of the international upsurge in interest rates, and long-term interest rates have been distinctly above the short-term rates.

This, however, changed a couple of years down the line, influenced by US interest rates. As it will be recalled, in the first quarter of 1997 there were repeated warnings by Dr Alan Greenspan, as chairman of the Federal Reserve, that dollar rates might rise. This resulted in higher interest rates across the yield curve, but also a flatter yield curve – with an aftermath in Western Europe.

Finally, the yield curves of different currencies and currency exchange rates correlate. A flat yield curve is typically associated with stronger currencies while steep yield curves

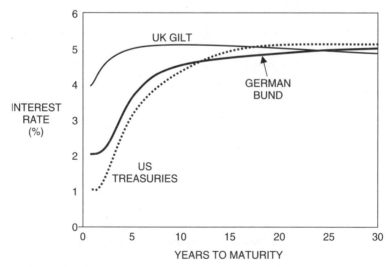

Figure 9.2 Thirty-year yield curve: common trend of three different government bonds at mid-November 2003

are associated with currency weakness. The major reason for this pattern is that the yield curve reflects the markets' expectations of central bank policies. Flatness indicates less implied risk in holding securities in the long term. Steepness reflects an added risk premium. This is another example of the services the yield curve provides.

9.4   Nominal, real, and natural interest rates, and inflation-indexing

The nominal interest rate is the one posted on the debt instrument. The reader is already aware of the fact that it would be a rare exception if the bond's price in the secondary market is at par and therefore the nominal rate and yield coincide; or that inflation is held at zero over the life of the bond, and the holder receives a real rate which is equal to the nominal. The *real interest rate* is the return the bondholders obtain on their investment, deflated by changes in the price index expected:

- From the period in which the funds are lent
- To the period in which the funds are repaid.

There is as well the *natural*, or neutral, interest rate defined as the real short-term rate with consistent return at its potential level, and a stable rate of inflation. Notice that in the short run, interest rates may deviate from the neutral rate as the economy experiences inflationary shocks representing a risk to price stability. Even if this is a

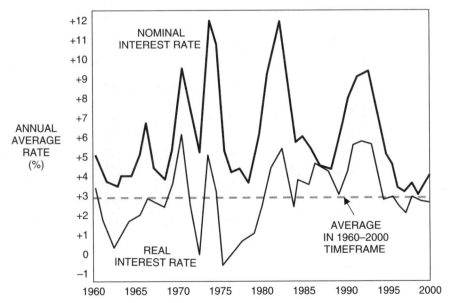

Figure 9.3 Nominal and real interest rates in the German capital market.
(*Source:* Deutsche Bundesbank)

non-trivial possibility, the natural real interest rate is considered to be a benchmark for monetary policy – or, at least in theory, an indicator of monetary policy stance by the central bank.

The downside of this benchmark is that, in practice, the natural interest rate is unobservable and can only be estimated on the basis of specific assumptions, as well as with a considerable degree of uncertainty. The investor can, however, profit from knowing certain issues related to developments in the natural real interest rate, including estimates and assumptions being made by policy-makers and market players. For instance, factors assumed to be instrumental in the decline of natural interest rates are the:

- Reduction of inflation risk premium, and
- Disappearance of exchange rate risk premiums, as happened in the EU following the introduction of the euro.

Nominal and real interest rates may coincide in the case of inflation-indexed securities discussed in Chapter 8, like TIPS, but this is only a small part of the total bond market. Much more representative is the divergence between the two metrics, as shown in Figure 9.4, based on a study done in late August 1998 on debt instruments of G-7, right after the bankruptcy of Russia.

It is not difficult to appreciate from Figure 9.4 that among the Western economies in this sample, investors in the dollar and the pound would have been well protected through inflation-indexed bonds. What attracts the issuer in offering such debt instruments is the lower nominal cost usually characterizing inflation-indexed debt instruments, reflecting the avoidance of paying an inflation uncertainty risk premium as the real rate is nearly guaranteed. Also, other things being equal, a longer maturity may be achievable using inflation-indexing.

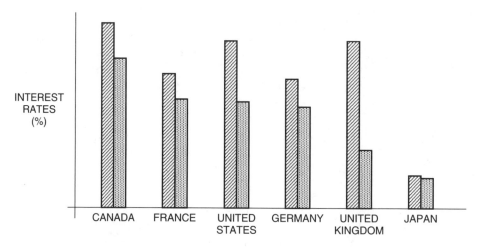

Figure 9.4 Six of the Group of Seven nominal and real interest rates in mid-1998, immediately after the bankruptcy of Russia

On the buyers' side, inflation-indexed debt instruments can assist investment managers to develop a longer-term saving and retirement income strategy, which is important for pensions, annuities, and other reasons. Alternatively, sophisticated investors may simultaneously enter into an inflation swap to convert a fixed rate bond into floating rate.

There are evidently negatives associated to an inflation swap. Apart from the cost, there is the question of the credit risk profile of the counterparty. On the other hand, indexed debt, too, creates a natural limitation on the type and range of issuers and issues. Credit risk premium demanded for lower credit quality may be significantly higher than for a conventional bond, with the result that a stated cost advantage of inflation-indexed financing is reduced, if not altogether eliminated.

Moreover, since inflation expectations cannot be measured directly, it is necessary to choose a method for computing them adopting, for example, an *ex post* approach. A measure of inflation expectations is constructed using the outlook for inflation over the relevant period. This, however, tends to yield a correct measure of the real interest rate only if the resulting real inflation turns out to be close to expectations.

There may also be computational problems. For instance, the most recent 10-year *ex post* real interest rate would require data for the inflation rate 10 years ahead, which is not available. In such case, an *ex ante* approach can be used, in which inflation expectations are estimated. Examples are:

- Explicitly forward-looking approaches based on statistical models that extrapolate inflation series into the future
- Econometric and structural models incorporating information regarding the whole issue of a debt instrument, and
- Direct measurement of inflation expectations, using survey data, with most surveys providing only qualitative responses which have to be converted into quantitative.

One of the advantages of a statistical filtering approach is that it makes possible time variations in the neutral real interest rate. The downside is that underlying hypotheses may not be very dependable. The value of estimates always reflects the dependability of the model. Critics also say that a statistical approach does not give a structural interpretation of movements in real interest rate.

Let us take a quick look into structural models. One type that has received increasing attention is a general equilibrium model constructed on the basis of explicit behavior of households and companies, with prices not necessarily sensitive to economic shocks. This approach permits the calculation of time-varying natural real interest rates and provides an explanation for the estimated changes. The trajectory of the neutral real interest rate is identified with the path of the actual real interest rate generated by the model.

Critics say that the underlying natural real interest rate in such an exercise may differ in notable respects from the theoretical definition of what constitutes a neutral rate. The pros answer that the natural real interest rate implicit in this approach is intended to provide a benchmark for the setting of short-term interest (indeed, the rate at very short horizons), and this is doable even if such a measure is volatile. Longer time horizons, however, are a different matter.

Surveys might offer an appreciation of longer-term interest rate trend, but the reader should notice that the horizon for inflationary expectations revealed through most surveys is too short for constructing long-term real interest rate projection. Therefore, as an alternative, some analysts take current inflation rate as a measure of inflation expectations, enriched with other references – like historical evidence by central bankers – which, up to a point, might help in foretelling inflation trends.

For example, when running a fiscal deficit a government not only draws resources away from the private sector, but also builds up an inflation momentum. In Chapter 8 we have looked in detail at this issue. In its way, a higher fiscal deficit will both increase the real interest rate and swamp private investment. Also, fiscal indiscipline introduces specific risk premiums into longer-term real interest rates on government bonds, which take two forms:

- A default risk premium to be introduced in the real yield on bonds issued by the deficit-ridden national government, and
- An additional source of uncertainty about the path of real interest rates over time, with the result that fiscal indiscipline invites even higher risk premiums.

All these factors pose challenges in pricing inflation-indexed bonds. Another problem is presented by the largely theoretical approach which consists of derivation of a real-estate zero-coupon curve. This is not too different from the construction of a nominal interest rate zero-coupon curve, provided there is a reasonably liquid market with a sufficient range of inflation-indexed securities, which have differing maturities. Such a condition does not occur frequently, therefore either of two solutions is used in practice:

- A term structure chosen to derive the real-rate yield curve with implied forward inflation rates, or
- Assumptions made about the shape of the real rate curve to approximate its zero-coupon equivalent.

The approach described by the first bullet has the advantage that it permits the valuation of options. The implied inflation term structure is computed by solving simultaneous equations of price as a function of the nominal discount factor through interpolation. The relatively small size of this market, however, presents another challenge by restricting investor participation.

According to expert opinion, lack of market size, at least in the early stage of development of this approach, leads to lack of liquidity in the securities under consideration. Still other problems have to do with transparency in accounting and with legal issues. There is a continuing debate about whether inflation-indexed securities constitute a separate asset class, even if inflation-indexed instruments have been in existence since the mid- to late 1980s (see Chapter 8).

On the other hand, disinflation, nominal exchange rate stability, and fiscal consolidation make a significant contribution to reducing distortions in the long-term real interest rate projections – also in releasing resources for private investment. The problem is that the approaches being taken are largely theoretical.

Theoretically, for example, the convergence process required the countries that formed the Euroland to introduce and pursue well-designed fiscal policies while a homogeneous monetary policy was established by the ECB. Through this, it was projected that the euro area would enjoy an environment of stable prices and more sustainable public finances. But, as we have already seen, France and Germany demonstrated in 2002–2005 that fiscal consolidation, while certainly needed, is only a chimera – fiscal indiscipline is the rule.

In conclusion, investors, bankers, and economists should keep in mind that real interest rates are determined mainly by real factors which have a nasty habit of being quite different from the theoretical. Yet, it is largely theoretical considerations that underpin the notion of a natural or neutral real interest rate. Real short-term interest rates that are consistent in the long run are a rare bird.

While the natural real interest rate is a concept potentially important for monetary policy-makers, it is not directly observable. It has to be estimated on the basis of specific assumptions, and the resulting estimates critically depend on these assumptions, as well as on a number of issues related to real life, which are not necessarily predictable. Natural real interest rates are, thus, sometimes more a myth than reality.

9.5   Fisher parity of nominal and real interest rates

Measuring real interest rates as well as their volatility, is a prerequisite to modeling them. As section 9.4 has documented, however, their calculation is associated with a number of problems, timing and intensity of inflation expected during the investment period, which cannot be observed directly, being an example. Certain basic financial principles may help in bringing this problem under control. For instance, real interest rates contain important information about investment conditions in:

- The capital market, and
- The economy's financing terms.

These two bullets interact and their interaction works both ways, as can be documented from an analysis of nominal and real interest rates over an extended timeframe. Unearthing such a relationship in the longer term is important because, as we have seen in Chapter 7, the central bank's monetary policy has a direct effect on interest rates only in the short term. Longer-term tracking can also be instrumental in identifying trends.

Should we use nominal or real interest rates in this analysis of historical time series? According to the opinion of many economists, the use of nominal rather than real interest rates can lead to wrong estimates, particularly when the research targets the longer timeframe. On the other hand, what is really offered through debt instruments is nominal interest rates, the real interest rates being computed in the aftermath of inflationary, as well as inflation expectations.

It is easy to understand how these two requirements contradict one another. A way to go around such a contradiction is to have an algorithm that links nominal and real interest rates in a way that permits study and research. This is done through the *Fisher parity* formula outlined in Appendix C.

Named after Irving Fisher, who in 1930 formulated a hypothesis about the adjustment of the nominal interest rate to inflation rate, the algorithm in Appendix C rests on the hypothesis that,

- A 1% increase in the expected rate of inflation leads to a 1% increase in the nominal interest rate.

This hypothesis tends to apply in the long term. While in the short term there is a marked connection between nominal interest rate and the inflation rate, this is not necessarily a one-to-one relationship and the Fisher algorithm does not work well.

Moreover, the Fisher parity is based on certain restrictive assumptions. For example, tax considerations are omitted, even if, in practice their role is not negligible. Also, it is assumed that investors are indifferent as to whether their investment is nominal or real, as long as the yield differential is in line with expected inflation (see Chapter 8).

If an inflation risk premium is included and it fluctuates over time, this will relax the connection between nominal and real rates over the short term. By contrast, in the longer term, nominal interest rates and the rate of inflation tend to move in parallel. As a result, from a statistical viewpoint, the Fisher parity can give commendable results.

While these restrictions reduce the domain of applicability of the Fisher model, it is most important to have on hand a dependable theory that permits one to follow nominal and real interest rates in a fairly dependable manner. As Figure 9.3 has shown, nominal and real rates can deviate substantially: in the early- to mid-1960s and through the 1970s fixed income debt instruments in the German capital market provided their holders with a negative return. This briefly repeated itself in 1996/1997, at a time when values in the equities rose.

There are also other considerations related to the existence of debt instruments to bring to the reader's attention. One of them is that while official statistics permit investors and analysts to do a documented study of interest rates and yields, such statistics are not truly neutral, in the sense that usually they tend to underestimate inflation, for evident reasons. Alternatively, the consumer price index represents an acceptable approximation of overall price level.

Though such bias always exists, inflation-indexed bonds like the two examples given in Chapter 8, one from the United States the other from France, could serve as inflation's proxies. In an economy without that type of debt instruments, it is necessary to have, along with nominal interest rates, information about inflation expectations in order to calculate the future real interest rate relevant in terms of macroeconomic developments.

By contrast, for short-term interest rates it may be enough to extrapolate the current inflation rate into the future. Many investors deduct the most recently measured rate of inflation from the interest rate of debt instruments, when computing real rate in the short term. However, when applied to long-term interest rates, this procedure is misleading since it is implicitly assumed that in the years ahead inflation will develop exactly as it did in the past months, which in unrealistic.

For greater accuracy in longer-term calculations, some banks use the autoregressive integrated moving average (ARIMA) method. With this approach, the development of a non-stationary variable is reproduced using its lagged values and past forecasting errors. This enables one to study periods for which dependable inflation statistics are not available.

When reasonably accurate statistics are available on capital market rates(s) and consumer price index, then these should be used. Behind this choice is the fact that the yield on debt securities outstanding corresponds to the opportunity costs of a financial investment, even if the actual financing costs are generally higher. Bank rates relevant to financing tend to run parallel to capital market rates.

It should be noted that not all banks use the same mathematical tools, and different models reach different conclusions about the level and properties of inflation – and therefore of real interest rates. Also, economic theory relates more closely to yield of productive capital rather than to real monetary interest rate. At the positive end, however, these two types of real interest rates are related through arbitrage.

Another issue to bring to the reader's attention in connection with the evaluation of yield obtainable through debt instruments is the *interest parity* theory. At its foundation is the principle of one price for fixed-interest financial paper. This is considered to be homogeneous, which is a weak hypothesis, but distinction is made between:

- Covered interest parity, and
- Uncovered interest parity.

These two are based on different assumptions, targeted to capture different segments of capital markets. According to the covered interest parity theory, the return on domestic issues corresponds to the return on foreign paper with a hedged exchange rate risk. The interest rate differentials between two economies under study are offset by the swap rate of exchange rate between the two currencies.

By contrast, the uncovered interest parity provides no hedging against exchange rate risk. Therefore, expected exchange rate movements, and not the swap rates, are compared with national interest rate differentials. Experts suggest the wisdom of dividing uncovered interest parity computational procedures into two parts:

- One resembling covered interest parity, and
- The other involving speculative components, requiring the forward rate to be about equal to expected exchange rate.

Prior to closing this section, it is appropriate to bring to the reader's attention that loans, too, are characterized by a distinction between nominal and effective interest rates. The International Securities Markets Association (ISMA) has developed an algorithm which distinguishes between:

- Annualized agreed rate (AAR)
- Narrowly defined effective rate (NDER), and
- Annual percentage rate of charge (APRC).

The annualized agreed rate is individually agreed between the bank and the customer; then it is converted to an annual interest rate. This is a simplified version of the narrowly defined effective rate, which equalizes the present value of all commitments other than charges, future or existing, agreed by the reporting agents and borrowers. The AAR algorithm is presented in Appendix D.

Finally, to complete the brief description of these three alternatives, the annual percentage rate of change contains, in addition to what has been stated so far, any other related costs. For instance, costs for credit rating, investment and other research, administration, preparation of documents, guarantees, credit insurance, and so on.

9.6   US Treasuries as benchmarks, futures, and forwards trading

Practically every country, at least among the Group of Ten, has its own benchmark which it uses to compute the spread between corporate debt instruments. Typically, such a benchmark is a 10-year government security of that sovereign, taken as being free of credit risk. Globalization, however, and US financial dominance after the Second World War, have seen to it that 10-year US Treasuries are generally appreciated as a good benchmark. A global reference has distinct advantages – but there is a downside as well, as we will see in this section.

As the careful reader will recall from previous discussions, debt instruments issued by governments can be both short-term and long-term obligations, made available to the general public. The terms and provisions of debt in a bond have always been found in a separate document, the *indenture* (explained in Chapter 3); but there are also differences related to the terms used.

For instance, a US Government Note has usually meant obligations with shorter maturity than US Government Bonds, and a limited number of holders, whose terms and provisions are set forth in the document itself. Generally, all US government securities can be classified as:

- *Bills*, a term used to designate obligations with a maturity up to 120 days
- *Certificates of Indebtedness*, ranging in maturity from 120 days to 1 year
- *Notes*, whose maturity ranges from 1 to 5 years, and
- *Bonds* issued for over 5 years, formerly up to 30 years but now up to 10 years.

It is precisely this 10-year US Government Bond that is used as a benchmark. The same is true for the government bonds of other countries. The United States, United Kingdom, and German 10-year yield curves, we have seen in Figure 9.2, are based on this type of bonds.

US Government bonds are traded in $1/32$ of the percentage point. It is interesting to notice that the yield value of a $1/32$ for the 30-year bonds have been lower than for the 5-year bond. The principle is that the lower the yield value of a price change, the greater the dollar price volatility.

Corporate bonds and debt instruments, by contrast, as well as municipal bonds are traded in $1/8$ of a percentage point. Investors in these markets frequently compute the yield value of an $1/8$, though more recently the decimal rate is also used; for instance 5.625% rather $5\frac{5}{8}$.

As it can be seen from the foregoing taxonomy, the US government has spread out the maturities of its regular new issues over a wide range to attract many types of investors, both in the United States and internationally. This helps in reducing borrowing costs. In terms of amount outstanding, the US government bond market is both:

- The largest sovereign bond market, and
- The most liquid one, worldwide.

US Treasury securities are generally held by investors anywhere in the globalized market, with the 91-day Treasury bill, 10-year Treasury bond, and formerly available 30-year Treasury bond yields being key global interest rates. The Treasury bill is issued at discount, pays no coupon and matures at par. The Treasury bonds are coupon securities issued approximately at par, pay a coupon in two equal amounts every six months, and mature at par.

The discussion about nominal interest rates and real interest rates evidently applies with government bonds, unless these are inflation-indexed (see Chapter 8). Beyond that, however, come other factors affecting a global benchmark because private savings and investment decisions depend on:

- Households' preferences regarding consumption in different periods
- The technology and productive opportunities available to different firms
- Special effects, which may come from the introduction of a new common currency, like the euro.

The model of currencies, bonds, their risks and their yields is made a little more complex by the fact that the public sector's net saving affects the determination of the real interest rate. All these factors are interdependent – and at the same time they are also different from one country to the next.

Given these complexities, it is not easy to judge the prospects for real economic growth only by observing the level of real interest rates. It is proper to first analyze the factors that influence the level of real interest rates, and then assess their implication(s) for growth, and their feedback (if any) to inflation.

In spite of this, it makes sense to have a government bond as a global, generally acceptable sovereign security, particularly when that country's monetary policies focus on the maintenance of price stability. Short of this, there is uncertainty associated with the incorporation of higher risk premiums in real rates, particularly so when investors require appropriate compensation for intrinsic inflation which does not yet show up in statistics.

Invariably, high fiscal deficits and debt levels eventually depress the real interest rate, as the public sector demands a larger share of the available funds for its expenses. In addition, fiscal indiscipline brings the sustainability of the public finances into question, generating fears of a government default – and thereby waiving the credit risk-free feature of a government bond. By contrast, well-designed and properly maintained monetary and fiscal policies allow the capital market to allocate resources more efficiently over time. In turn, this:

- Raises the productive potential of the economy, and
- Improves growth, as well as employment prospects.

A bond issued by a government that can be used as a global benchmark is also important because of the growing amount of *futures trading* in debt instruments. The increase of global futures trading on long-term government securities has opened new possibilities for portfolio managers of fixed income instruments. Among the reasons for growth experienced by this market have been:

- Increased interest rate volatility, underscoring the need for controlling risk by means of hedging, and
- The fact that as volume has risen, investors gained confidence in the breadth of the market, and got a better appreciation of assumed risks.

Bond futures provide investors with the opportunity to trade in government securities, in a market ancillary to the traditional over-the-counter (OTC) market. Though an investor's transactions may make one or the other market more active, *cash* and *futures* have different aspects for market players, even if their prices are linked. Bond futures are traded on an exchange and have standardized specifications regarding:

- Underlying security
- Face amount per contract
- Delivery price, and
- Delivery date(s).

Other important characteristics are: delivery mechanism, deliverable grade, price quotation, minimum price fluctuation, maximum daily price fluctuation, expiration cycle, and last day of trading. As the reader will appreciate, these are not exactly the same variables as those that characterize the cash market.

Bond futures are traded in different exchanges. For instance, US Treasury Bonds are listed at the Chicago Board of Trade (CBOT), and London International Financial Futures Exchange (LIFFE). Also at the Singapore International Monetary Exchange (SIMEX), and the Sydney Futures Exchange. US Treasury 5-Year Notes are traded at CBOT and at the FINEX in New York. The UK Long Gilt is traded at London's LIFFE; while Japanese Government Bonds are listed both at the Tokyo Stock Exchange (TSE) and at the LIFFE.

By contrast, bond forward agreements, as well as forwards on other commodities are executed over the counter. Forwards in the US government bond market usually extend less than six months, though on occasion, they may be longer. Standard US government bond transactions with next-day settlement could be seen as forward contracts, where the forward settlement date is one business day after trade date.

9.7 The Federal Open Market Committee, Fed funds rate, and discount rate

Chapter 7 stated that in a free economy the central bank sets short-term rates, but long-term rates are established by the market. The setting of short-term interest rate targets more than one goal – a major one among them being the regulation of the economy, whether calming its overheating by raising interest rates, or stimulating it by cutting them.

In the early 1990s and in the 2000 to 2003 timeframe, for example, the Federal Reserve delivered successive adrenaline to a faltering US economy through short-term interest rates cutting. Fed executives also hinted that the Board stood ready to provide more, in rate cuts. The pattern of these years is shown in Figure 9.5.

The US central bank's policy-making body on interest rates is the Federal Open Market Committee (FOMC), which consists of 12 voting members: all seven Fed governors, plus five of the 12 presidents from the Federal Reserve district banks. The FOMC holds regular meetings every 6 weeks at which it sets the short-term Fed funds rate, the most important interest rate controlled by the Federal Reserve.

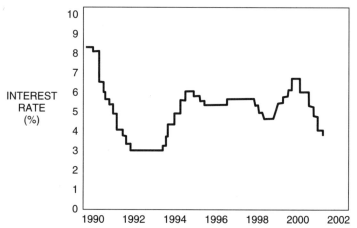

Figure 9.5 The Federal Reserve target rate decreased significantly
on two occasions within a dozen years

- The short-term Fed funds rate is the rate correspondent banks charge each other for overnight loans.
- Controlling the Fed funds rate is key to the Federal Reserve's power over the US economy, because it provides control over credit conditions.

The open market operations of the Fed, which consist of buying and selling US Treasury bonds, cause an increase or decrease in the Fed funds rate. Such operations are conducted through the New York Federal Reserve. As reasons for cutting the Fed funds rate, the central bank often cites a continuing decline in capital spending, continuing weak corporate profitability, fall in consumption and housing expenditures, and other principal concerns about the economic outlook.

Using its familiar formula to signal how it sees the economy in the next few months, the Fed sometimes says that risks are still being weighted 'toward conditions that may generate economic weakness in the foreseeable future', or that some of key economic indicators remain flat. When the Fed says so, this is a hint that, without evidence the economy is improving, or at least stabilizing, the central bank could cut rates again at its next FOMC meeting.

Alternatively, the Fed may address concerns about inflationary risks. It does so if measures of inflation have accelerated, as monitored by the consumer prices index and by the gross domestic product (GDP) implicit price deflator. But the central bank may also suggest it saw little real need to fear a price surge. In principle:

- *If* labor and product markets are easing,
- *Then* inflation is expected to remain contained.

Since 1994, the Federal Reserve has made public its decision about changes to Fed funds rate. Since 1987, however, several years before this greater openness in interest rate decisions and intentions occurred, the very announcement of a change in discount rate has been watched carefully by all concerned – since this has been the principal means the Fed has used to communicate its interest rate policy.

Whether it raises, cuts or keeps interest rates steady, the Fed's action impacts upon both the stock market and the bond market. A rate cut usually, though not always, sends the Dow Jones Industrial Average, as well as the Nasdaq Composite, higher. It also reduces the yield on bonds by a percent (depending on their maturity), thereby increasing their price.

It should be recalled that by buying or selling government bonds in open market operations the Fed manages both the monetary base and interest rates in the economy. Debates in academic and economic policy circles have ranged for years about whether it is still possible to measure the monetary base accurately, given the complexity of a modern economy. This led to the policy of:

- Targeting specific interest rates,
- Rather than tinkering with monetary base numbers.

There is a timelag between interest rate decisions and their effect on the market, and sometimes response is not at targeted level. By October 2003, in an effort to jump-start the US economy, the Fed had brought short-term interest rates at their lowest level for almost half a century. The Bank of Japan had done so much earlier, and the European Central Bank has not been much behind. In real terms, after adjusting for inflation, the average interest rate in the G7 economies became negative for the first time since the 1970s, when inflation soared.

By January 2004, most experts were asking the question: Have rates now hit the bottom? The answer was not given by the central banks, but by financial markets, which started to bet that the next moves in interest rates would be upwards. For example, in early 2004 the futures market was implicitly forecasting that American interest rates would rise from 1% to 1.5% by June 2004 and to 2.3% or even 2.5% by December 2004. Euroland rates, too, were expected to rise from 2% to 2.8% or 3% by the end of 2004, and the market predicted that the Bank of England would increase them too.

As some economists pointed out, however, the flaw in these interest rate prognostications is that 'this' economic cycle is not typical (if a typical economic cycle ever existed). Thanks to a post-bubble hangover, America's recovery was the slowest in modern times, with annual GDP growth averaging 2.7% compared with 4.7% during the first two years of the previous eight recoveries. Beyond this,

- Global outsourcing,
- Greater productivity, and
- Other reasons

saw to it that employment was not picking up.

Thesis and antithesis, as expressed in the preceding paragraphs, invaded the ranks of Fed watchers, who wanted to see if the central bank knew something they did not. There have been two 'somethings' open to speculation:

- How much the hydra of inflation was raising its many heads, and
- Whether the Fed governors thought that the 2.7% of GDP was sustainable.

A tough test for any central bank is to use monetary policy to kill runaway inflation. The Federal Reserve faced this challenge in the early 1980s, as the US inflation rate was hovering around 14%. Then, as now, two decades later, consumer debt was growing faster than consumer incomes, approaching a historic peak – up to that time. The prospect of continuing inflation seemed more certain than any political promises to stop it.

Dr Paul Volcker, the then chairman of the Fed, had made up his mind to kill inflation, and in this he had the support of President Reagan and his Administration: 'We've lost that euphoria that we had fifteen years ago, that we knew all the answers to managing the economy,' Volcker conceded, as he made rounds of public speeches and testimony before congressional committees, defining the problem in two parts:

- The tangible effects of inflationary pressures on the economy, and
- The psychological momentum of inflationary expectations.[3]

Both issues briefly described in these bullets are present in every inflationary financial landscape (see Chapter 8). *If* people believe that rising prices are inevitable, *then* they would be inevitable because of hedging forward. For instance, labor unions demand escalator contracts to protect their members' real wages from inflation's erosion, producers postpone new capital investment; creditors ask for higher interest rates; retailers anticipate next month's cost of replenishment and labor costs, by raising *this* month's prices.

At the times when these events were taking place the Fed was not targeting interest rates. Instead, the FOMC set annual target ranges for the rate of money growth it expected to allow. For instance, for M1, the most basic money supply aggregate, the Fed had a target growth rate of 1.5–4.5%, but the money supply had been growing at an annual rate of more than 10%. The question most investors, bankers, and analysts asked was how far the central bank was willing to push up rates.

According to different accounts, in 1979, when the galloping inflation posed the challenge of a policy change, both the Fed's Board of Governors and the FOMC were divided and drifting, because of indecision and weak leadership by William G. Miller. (Miller had preceded Volcker as Fed chairman.) Lack of leadership had produced months of contention and much confusion.

Moreover, in 1979 there was political pressure by the Carter Administration to do nothing and wait, as a sharp rise in interest rates would unsettle economic factors with an evident aftermath on the approaching presidential elections. Some board members, however, took a proactive stand to save the economy at the 11th hour.

'It is not an easy thing to vote against the president's wishes,' Henry Wallick, a member of the Federal Reserve Board of Governors said, 'but what are we appointed for? Why are we given these long terms in office? Presumably, it is that not only the present, but the past and the future have some weight in our decisions. In the end, it may be helpful to remind the president that it is not only his present concerns that matter.'[4]

Appendix 9.A   Yield of fixed interest bonds, with annual interest payment and maturity in n years

$$P = \frac{p}{q} + \frac{p}{q^2} + \cdots + \frac{p}{q^n} + \frac{R}{q^n} \tag{1}$$

$$P = p \cdot \left(\frac{1}{q} + \frac{1}{q^2} + \cdots + \frac{1}{q^n} \right) + \frac{R}{q^n} \tag{2}$$

where:

P = purchase price, in %, including accrued interest
R = redemption price, in %
p = coupon rate, in %
n = maturity in years
$\frac{1}{q}$ = conversion factor in compound discounting

It is:

$$\frac{1}{q} = \frac{1}{1 + \dfrac{y'}{100}} \tag{3}$$

where:

y' = yield in %

The expressions p/q, p/q^2 ... give the discounted interest payments, or cash value of interest payments. A different, simplified way of writing equation (2) is:

$$P = p \cdot \frac{q^n - 1}{q^n \cdot (q - 1)} + \frac{R}{q^n}$$

$$P = p \cdot A_n + \frac{R}{q_n} \tag{4}$$

where:

$$A_n = \frac{q^n - 1}{q^n \cdot (q - 1)}$$

A = annuity value factor

For maturities of 3–4 years or less, equation (3) can be resolved to yield y', but this is not possible for larger maturities. Therefore, in these cases the yield is determined iteratively for all securities in the portfolio, according to this algorithm. An estimated yield value is initially assumed and inserted into equation (3).

Because the value determined for the right-hand side of equation (4) will still deviate from actual value, the estimated value of the yield is changed slightly and reinserted into the model. Such gradual approximation to the actual value of the yield is continued until both sides of the equation match to a certain predetermined degree of accuracy.

With equation (4) the yield y' is computed iteratively by gradual approximation. Where interest is accumulated, only the present value of the redemption has to be equated with the purchase price. The equation for computation of the yield in this case is simplified to:

$$P = \frac{R}{\left(1 + \dfrac{y'}{100}\right)^n} \tag{5}$$

where:

P = purchase price
R = redemption value (equal to 100 plus accrued interest and compound interest)
y' = yield in percent
n = maturity in years

Appendix 9.B Yield of fixed interest bonds: an alternative computational procedure based on cash flow

Again, based on a credit risk-free assumption, the price of an investment can be computed as a function of its cash flow, yield, and maturity. A straightforward algorithm is:

$$P = \sum_{j=1}^{n} \frac{c_i}{(1 + y)^j} \tag{1}$$

where:

P = purchase price
c_i = cash flow in year j
y = yield in percent
j = year of estimate
n = maturity in years

The simpler equation for calculating current yield from bonds is:

$$y_c = \frac{c}{P} \cdot 100 \tag{2}$$

where:

P = purchase price
y_c = current yield
c = bond coupon

Equation (2) is too elementary because it ignores gain or loss arising from holding the bond, does not consider time value of money, and does not take account of maturity. Yet, leveraged investors do care about time value of money, and so do traders and market makers.

An improved algorithm, known as simple yield to maturity, corrects the maturity shortcoming:

$$y_s = \frac{c}{P} + \frac{100 - P}{nP} \tag{3}$$

where:

P = purchase price
y_s = simple yield to maturity
c = bond coupon
n = maturity in years

Still Equation (3) does not account for time value of money, or for gain and loss from holding the bond.

A more complex algorithm which maps the pattern of a bond's coupon payments, its gain or loss over the remaining of life of the bond, time value of money, and annual yield to maturity is the internal rate of return of gross redemption yield, y_g. The gross redemption yield or annual yield to maturity is computed by solving the algorithm:

$$P = \frac{c}{(1 + y_g)} \frac{c}{(1 + y_g)^2} + \cdots + \frac{c}{(1 + y_g)^n} \frac{R}{(1 + y_g)^n} \tag{4}$$

where:

P = purchase price
R = redemption payment (usually at par)
y_g = gross redemption yield (annual year to maturity)
c = bond coupon
n = maturity in years

Algorithm (4) can be rewritten:

$$P = \sum_{j=1}^{n} \frac{c}{(1 + y_g)^j} + \frac{R}{(1 + y_g)^n} \tag{5}$$

Both equation (4) and (5) presuppose annual coupon payment. If coupon payments are biannual, then (5) is modified to:

$$P = \sum_{j=1}^{n} \frac{c/2}{(1 + \frac{1}{2}y_g)^j} + \frac{R}{(1 + \frac{1}{2}y_g)^n} \tag{6}$$

Because algorithms (4), (5), and (6) have two variables, P and y_g, they cannot be restructured to solve for y_g alone. Instead, as also noted in Appendix A, their solution requires iteration by estimating the value of y_g and calculating P through successive numerical steps.

Essentially y_g is used to discount a bond's cash flow to the next coupon payment, subsequently discounting the value back to date of computation – which practically makes y_g the *internal rate of return*.

Appendix 9.C   Fisher parity algorithm linking nominal and real interest rates

The Fisher parity algorithm is expressed in the form:

$$i_r = i_n - f^e \tag{1}$$

where:

i_r = real interest rate
i_n = nominal interest rate, with same maturity
f^e = expected inflation rate for the period in reference

More precisely, as far as this parity equation is concerned, it is:

$$(1 + i_n) = (1 + i_n)(1 + f^e) \tag{2}$$

Solving for the nominal interest rate i_n yields:

$$i_n = f^e + i_r f^e \tag{3}$$

For small values of i_r and f^e, the second term in the right side of the equation is approximately equal to zero, thereby simplifying the Fisher parity algorithm.

Appendix 9.D   The ISMA algorithm for narrowly defined effective rate

$$i_a' = \left(1 + \frac{i_a}{m}\right)^m - 1$$

where:

i_a' = annualized agreed interest rate
i_a = agreed interest rate
m = number of interest capitalization periods per year

Appendix 9.E   Brief list of symbols frequently used in Chapters 7, 8, and 9

P	= purchase price
i	= interest rate
i_a	= agreed interest rate
i_a'	= annualized agreed interest rate[5]
i_n	= nominal interest rate
i_r	= real interest rate
i_T	= interest rate over chosen time interval T
t, t − 1	= time periods
n	= years, maturity in years
m	= number of interest capitalization periods per year
p	= coupon rate in %
y	= yield in %
j	= year of estimate
c	= cash flow
c_j	= cash flow in year j
f	= expected inflation
d_c	= expected default of counterparty
r_p	= risk premium for uncertainty

Notes

1 D.N. Chorafas, *The Real-time Enterprise*, Auerbach, New York, 2005.
2 D.N. Chorafas, *The Management of Equity Investments*, Butterworth-Heinemann, London, 2005.
3 William Greider, *Secrets of the Temple*, Touchstone/Simon and Schuster, New York, 1987.
4 William Greider, *Secrets of the Temple: How the Federal Reserve Runs the Country*, Touchstone/Simon and Schuster, New York, 1987. The quotation relates to the inflation of the late 1970s and the Carter presidency.
5 The '"' is not a sign of derivation, but a sign used in the present case to limit the number of postscripts.

10 Maturity and duration

10.1 Introduction

The secret to bond buying is not only in the yield. Though yield is a crucial factor, the *maturity* of the debt instrument also plays a crucial role in investors' risk and return, as well as to other critical conditions attached to the security. A bond is issued with a fixed date when it will mature, and the issuing entity must repay the security's principal amount, usually at par value.

- Maturities of debt instruments issued by corporates can range from one year to 30 years or more.
- Other things being equal, the longer the maturity, the higher the yield because the investor has to wait longer for his or her principal to be repaid.

As we have already seen, however, not all bonds are repaid at maturity. Many corporate debt securities are structured to allow the issuer to pay off the debt prior to the stated maturity date or they are perpetual. They can pay prior to due day through optical call, with early redemption provisions. Securities are typically called after interest rates decline, because their issuer may capitalize by going to the market with bonds at lower interest rates.

Investors who hold their bonds until maturity, will obtain the yield-to-maturity if they reinvest their capital at the yield-to-maturity rate. However, if bonds are called, the difference between *yield-to-maturity* and *yield-to-call* comes into play. Investors who get early repayment may have to reinvest their capital at a lower interest rate. Hence, two most important yield measures to consider in evaluating bond investments are:

- Yield-to-call, and
- Yield-to-maturity.

Both help to a significant degree to decide whether the bond's yield allows profitable returns. Yield-to-maturity considers the interest rate on the face of the bond and the debt instrument's price. Also the likely capital gain or loss if the bond is held to maturity.

By contrast, the yield to call cannot be computed in a deterministic way, because the call of the security is stochastic – at the discretion of the issuer. But it can be modeled through Monte Carlo simulation,[1] based on hypotheses about the likelihood of a call by the issuer in reference to:

- A downward trend in interest rates, and
- The history of the issuer, as well as of the issuer's industry, in calling back debt instruments.

A rational way to protect oneself from callable bonds is not to buy them in the first place. An investor who has bought them, for whatever reason, should use a time distribution on the investments, which helps in exercising damage control in connection to callable debt instruments.

Known as *laddering*, this timeframe of maturity distribution for fixed income instruments is important also for another reason having to do with the aftermath of globalization of risk and return. Global investing is a sound investment strategy *if*, and only if, investors are fully aware of the risks they take, including yield-to-maturity and yield-to-call in different jurisdictions. Laddering increases investors' flexibility by seeing to it that debt securities mature at different intervals, permitting investors to:

■ Keep an even cash flow, and
■ Reduce their overall exposure to adverse moves by issuers.

Appropriate laddering sees to it that when interest rates rise proceeds from maturing issues can be reinvested at higher yields. Another advantage that can be gained by enlarging the bandwidth of the maturity spectrum, as well as balancing the positions, is that the distribution of maturities not only between years but also within the year gives better control of the investment. Since most corporate bonds pay interest annually or semiannually, an investor needs separate issues with sequentially staggered monthly payment dates to create a personalized plan that provides monthly income.

Beyond the yearly and monthly distribution, a laddering strategy should benefit from interest rate projections. If a bond holding must be sold prior to the maturity date, a change in interest rates between the time the bond was purchased and the time it was sold will negatively affect the return on the bond, where interest rates are rising. To the contrary, a major rise in inflation may exceed the interest paid by the bond till it matures.

■ An increase in interest rates following the bond purchase would cause a capital loss if the bond were sold before maturity.
■ Inflation would result in a total return that is less than the computed real yield-to-maturity, at time of purchase.

Yield-to-call assumes that the investor will hold a bond to the assumed call date and that the issuer will call the bond on that date. As already mentioned, as interest rates in the market decline, the likelihood that the bond will be called also increases. Moreover, a capital loss could occur if the bond were called at a price lower than the original purchase price, due to the premium paid in buying the bond.

As we will see in this chapter, a more analytical measure than maturity is *duration*. It is a metric of a bond's price sensitivity to interest rate changes, commonly defined as the weighted average of the maturities of the bond's coupon and principal repayment cash flows. Investment experts consider duration as being better than maturity in making fixed income instrument decisions. Maturity and duration are compared in section 10.5.

This chapter aims to provide the reader with insight into the notion of duration. It has been a deliberate choice to ignore many of the complexities associated with duration and convexity (see section 10.6) as well as to avoid incorporating elements of uncertainty in connection to cash flows or the bond's call and put provisions. Furthermore, as with Chapter 9, the equations requiring more than an elementary mathematical background have been concentrated in the Appendices.

The reader should always be very careful with uncertainties associated to financial instruments because they lead to complexities that can have a significant impact on measurements being used. In turn, they have practical implications in investment management, all the way to risk control. Interest rate risk involves both credit and market exposure, as we will see respectively in Chapters 12 and 14, while Chapter 15 will provide an integrative approach to risk management.

10.2 Duration defined

There is no standard about investor choices as far as the maturity of a bond is concerned. Its choice depends on several factors regarding the issuer, the security itself and the market. A well-known AAA- or AA-rated company feels free to issue longer life debt instruments. By contrast, a BB company is usually constrained to short maturities, because longer ones would not attract investors given the likelihood of default. Within a broader perspective, the chosen maturity is often a function of:

■ Capital market conditions, and of
■ The established financial record of the issuing corporation.

For example, under similar market sentiment, a highly rated company is able to sell its unsecured debentures with a maturity of 30 years or more, whereas a less recognized firm sells its bonds with a much shorter maturity date, as well as higher interest coupons. Many people think that such differences reflect mainly the opportunistic character of corporate financing, but there is enough rationality to substantiate them.

In other cases, maturities may be short owing to the high rate of interest prevailing in the market, because of an anticipated temporary need of funds. Conversely, they may be longer to take advantage of favorable financial terms, particularly when interest rates are low and relatively permanent capital is desired. This has been the case in the 2001–2003 timeframe, when companies with market clout capitalized on the lowest interest rates for 46 years.

From the point of view of the investor, however, it is ordinarily the security of the issue, its yields, and the laddering strategy followed in portfolio construction which become all the more important as the maturity is lengthened. Long maturities have embedded risk that the general credit position of a company may not be forecast for long periods (see also the discussion on credit rating in Chapter 12).

Investors' appetite for maturity of bond investments changes over time. In 2004, some surveys have shown that managed bond portfolios were at historically short maturity levels in relation to their benchmarks – indicating that bond managers were unusually bearish toward long-term bonds. A contrary opinion to this, however, has been that bond managers' fears were overdone. Some analysts thought that the long bond would rally sooner than most investors expected it to, fueled by:

- The high degree of leverage built into the US economy, and
- Changes in the interest rate curve due to the Federal Reserve's tightening.

Because of these reasons, in mid-2004 some analysts projected that the volatility index (VIX) would rise and long-term interest rates might fall during the rest of 2004 – with the outcome that the more bearish investors are about the outlook for the S&P 500, and the more they think that volatility will increase, the more they should expect from the financial sector:

- Poor absolute returns, and
- Superior relative returns.

A different way of looking at the concepts outlined in the preceding paragraphs is that investing in bonds is a transaction which, like every other transaction, has its maturity – which provide it with a *time dimension*. It seems logical that, from an investment viewpoint:

- The longer the maturity of the transaction, the greater the opportunity for the instrument's price and yield to move.
- Hence, the more rigorous must be the attention which we pay to the risk and return assumed with such transaction, and this brings into perspective the concept of duration.

The Introduction briefly stated that duration is a better measure than maturity, but it did not say why. Starting with the fundamentals, the *duration* of a fixed interest rate instrument is commonly defined as the weighted average of maturities of the bond's coupon and principal repayment cash flows. The weights are the fractions of the bond's price represented by cash flows in each time period.

Estimates derived from the *Macaulay's* algorithm for duration (see section 10.4) rest on the so-called standard (or simple) duration approach. This is an acceptable approximation of a portfolio's exposure to changes in economic value – particularly so for relatively non-complex institutions (more on this later).

The downside is that these estimates focus on *repricing risk*, which is just one form of interest rate risk exposures. As a result, they may not reflect interest rate risk arising from other sources; for example, from changes in the relationship among interest rates within a time bracket, which is *basis risk*. Moreover, given that such approaches use an average duration for each time bracket, the estimates may not account for differences in actual sensitivity of positions that can arise from differences in:

- Coupon rates,
- Timing of payments, and
- The risk of options.

Duration of a whole portfolio of debt instruments is that of its individual positions weighted by the share of market value which each position represents. For each debt instrument, its duration provides an estimate of how much a bond's price will change as yields change. This computation can be used to approximate, in percent, the debt instrument's price. Duration will:

- Increase for a given decline in yield, and
- Decline for a given increase in yield.

The relation brought forward by these two bullets documents the statement made in the preceding paragraphs that duration is also a measure of cash flows integrating into itself three metrics:

- The coupon
- Maturity, and
- Bond's yield.

Duration is higher, the lower the coupon, longer the maturity and lower the yield of the bond. For bullet bonds (straight, non-callable, see Chapter 5) the price increase for a given decline in yield is greater than the price decrease for the same increase in yield. This asymmetry in returns happens because of convexity. *Convexity* is a metric of how duration changes as yields change (see section 10.6).

Duration's behavior is different for callable bonds. With calls by the debt instrument's issuer, and prepayments, duration decreases given that calls and prepayments shorten maturity. As the reader will recall from Chapter 4, callable bonds can have several negative effects on the value of the investor's portfolio, of which this is an example.

10.3   Modified duration and price sensitivity

As a mathematical concept, duration is designed to measure the *price-sensitivity* of debt securities to small parallel changes in interest rates. In computing the weighted average maturity of all payments of a security, coupons plus principal, the weights represent the discounted present values of the payments.

There is also another basic concept, known as *modified duration,* which consists of duration divided by a factor of one plus the market interest rate, r. Duration value is equal to current market value multiplied by annual modified duration.

Both duration and modified duration provide a linkage between the movement in a bond's price and its yield to maturity. For this reason, a different way of looking at duration is as the *time-weighted maturity* of a bond. This is a more sophisticated approach than a linear maturity formula. The algorithm for modified duration is:

Approximate percent change in price =
$$100 \cdot \text{Duration} \cdot \text{Percent point change in yield} \qquad (1)$$

Modified duration is an elasticity which reflects the percent change in economic value of an instrument for a given percentage change in $1 + r$, where, as stated, r is the market interest rate. As with simple duration, modified duration assumes a linear relationship between:

- Percent change in value, and
- Percent changes in interest rates.

Behind equation (1) lies the fact that duration is an estimate of percent change in price of a debt instrument for a 100 basis point (1% point) change in yield. Because of the relative advantages which it presents in sustaining a risk and return framework with fixed interest instruments, since the development of Macaulay's algorithm in the 1930s (see section 10.4), duration has become:

- A major determinant of a bond's interest sensitivity, and
- The way of judging a relationship between yield and price.

The weighted average maturity of all payment flows from a bond is a better metric than one that rests on a simple linear function. (More on this in the comparison between maturity and duration in section 10.5.) Analysts who use duration extensively say that they like it because it incorporates both:

- The maturity effect, and
- The coupon effect

into a single numerical measure of a bond's price sensitivity. Also it can be used to compare different instruments or portfolios of fixed interest rate instruments in terms of price sensitivity. In principle, a high duration bond's price is more sensitive to interest rate changes than is the price of a low duration bond. Duration and modified duration are also one of the main methods used in connection to futures and options, particularly interest rates futures. Alternatives are:

- The basis points approach, and
- Regression analysis of statistical data streams.

According to the Basel Committee on Banking Supervision,[2] duration-based weights can be used in combination with a maturity-and-repricing schedule to provide an approximation of the change in the bank's economic value that accounts for a particular change in market interest rates. A relatively simple procedure is based on the premise that:

- An *average duration* is assumed for the positions that fall into each time band, and
- The average duration is multiplied by an assumed change in interest rates to construct a weight for each time band.

Different interest rate changes are sometimes used for different time bands, reflecting changes in volatility of interest rates along the yield curve. Weighted gaps are aggregated across time brackets to produce an estimate of change in economic value of the bank, resulting from changes in interest rates – whether these are real or hypothetical. Alternatively, an institution can estimate the effect of changing interest rates by calculating the precise duration of each:

- Asset
- Liability, and
- Off-balance sheet position.

Subsequently the net position for the bank based on these measures can be derived. Experts believe that this provides a more accurate result than applying an estimated average duration weight to all positions in a given bracket, because it increases the algorithmic sensitivity to factors affecting duration, and to their changes over time.

An advantage of the duration algorithm in comparison to alternatives is that it explicitly uses known information about maturity, coupon, and price characteristics of bonds under study. The downside is that this approach requires that the analyst either:

- Assumes what certain relationships will be in the future, which is subjective, or
- Finds a more objective way to estimate such relationships and the way they may change.

By contrast, regression analysis uses historical information to compute hedge ratios. On the surface, this looks more objective. However, apart from the fact that the past is not a prognosticator of the future, a historical data approach critically depends on the implicit assumption that the estimated credit market relationships:

- Are stable, and
- Will continue being stable in the future.

If this is not the case, then duration can be a better rounded procedure. Two economists, Edwards and Ma, suggest that a sound strategy is to estimate hedge ratios based on both duration and regression analysis, then compare to see whether they yield comparable hedge ratios.[3] If they don't, the analyst or investor should understand *why*, and he or she will be well advised to revisit the assumptions and hypotheses being made. This is, incidentally, a *golden rule* in all scientific work, including physics and engineering.[4]

10.4 Macaulay's duration algorithm

In 1938, Frederick Macaulay, who then worked for the US National Bureau of Economic Research, developed the duration algorithm that bears his name.[5] Its output can be used as a proxy for value over the length of time a bond investment is outstanding, as we saw in section 10.2.

- By defining *duration* as weighted average term-to-maturity of the bond's cash flows,
- Macaulay's algorithm helps to evaluate the price sensitivity of a bond to small changes in interest rate.

The algorithm also assists decisions in connection to other financial products like options pricing, where the calculation of duration contributes to estimating *theta*.[6] With bond investments, Macaulay's algorithm assists in evaluation of and experimentation with, weighted average time to maturity, as a consequence of assumptions regarding the term structure. For instance, that the term structure is flat and will only move in parallel shifts.[7] For an *option-free* bond with semiannual payments,

- The cash flow for periods *1* to $n - 1$ is one-half the annual coupon interest.
- In period *n*, the cash flow is the semi-annual coupon interest plus maturity value.

The structure of Macaulay's formula reveals that the magnitude of the effect of an interest rate change on, say, a bond's price, will depend on both the bond's maturity and its coupon level. For a given change in interest rates, the change in bond prices will be greater:

- The longer the maturity of the bond, and
- The lower the coupon rate on the bond.

Such relationships exist because more distant cash flows are increasingly affected by the compounding effects implicit in the bond's pricing formula. By incorporating these cause-and-effect relationships, Macaulay's duration becomes a useful measure of the debt instrument's price sensitivity to interest rate changes, giving a value in terms of periods.

Macaulay's algorithm is presented in Appendix 10.A. The reader should remember that Macaulay's algorithm measures duration in periods, not in years. However, the result which it provides can be converted to duration in years through equation (2), dividing by the number of payments made per year:

$$\text{Macaulay duration (in years)} = \frac{\text{Macaulay duration (in periods)}}{k} \tag{2}$$

where:

k = the number of payments per year

Appendix 10.A provides two formulas for calculation of duration. In the first, duration of a fixed income instrument is a function of: coupon payment in period *n*; number of payment periods; principal payment at maturity *m*; maturity of the debt instrument; yield to maturity; and date of last payment.

With the second equation, the duration of a fixed income instrument is a function of the transaction price of the bond; interest or principal repayment at period *t*; current annual yield to maturity, divided by the number of payment periods in the year; and number of payment periods.

As shown in Appendix 10.B, a different way of approaching Macaulay's duration is through the present value, PV, of the bond's cash flow. This is expressed in periods, with duration being a function of: present value of cash flow in period *i*, and total present value of the debt instrument's cash flow – as well as the period when cash flow is expected to be received and the number of years to maturity.

As we saw in section 10.3, still another formula is that of *modified duration*, whose algorithm is given in Appendix 10.C. Being a function of the original Macaulay's duration, and yield to maturity, modified duration is a measurement that finds several practical applications.

By measuring the percentage change in its price relative to price change in the bond's maturity, the modified duration provides a percent measure of price volatility. It also relates the percentage change in bond price to absolute change in yield to maturity. Accounting for bonds paying interest on a monthly basis, the modified duration algorithm becomes:

$$\text{Modified duration} = \frac{\text{Macaulay duration}}{(1 + \text{yield}/1200)} \tag{3}$$

Furthermore, to estimate the price sensitivity of option-free instruments for which cash flows are independent of interest rates, such as Treasuries and straight corporate bonds, the *effective duration* formula shown in Appendix 10.C is used. Effective duration is the percentage change in the price of the relevant instrument for a basis point change in yield, and it is an important algorithm for experimentation reasons.

With effective duration, price/yield is the partial derivative of price in respect to yield. (For an application of effective duration in conjunction with basis points, see section 10.5.) Using the algorithm in Appendix 10.C, for a bullet bond with price 105% and modified duration 2.5 years, if yield goes up by 1%, the price would fall roughly by:

$$\frac{105.0 \cdot 2.5}{100} = 2.62 \text{ points}$$

Certain important properties have nevertheless to be observed. This algorithm is only valid for option-free securities with deterministic cash flows. By contrast, it can give misleading results for interest rate contingent claims, and it is inaccurate for more exotic instruments such as collateralized mortgage obligations (CMO), adjustable rate mortgages (ARM), and so on.

An advantage of the duration approach is that it explicitly employs known information regarding coupon, maturity, and market price of the bond. But it also has shortcomings, like the estimation of annual yield (which itself can be approached through different methods), and the fact that different algorithms now compete for Macaulay's inheritance.

The careful reader will recall from section 10.2 that the alternative approach is regression analysis, which uses historical data to calculate hedge ratios. Its major shortcoming lies in the assumption that historical market relationships will prevail in the future. This is evidently a weak argument, because of the prevailing volatility in credit markets.

10.5   Results obtained with duration versus maturity

The computation of critical factors influencing debt investments looks simpler with straight bonds where the age-old concept of *maturity* has guided the hand of financial analysts. But this is no longer the case once the instruments get more complex. As briefly explained in the Introduction, a bond's maturity measures:

- The time of receipt of final principal payment, and
- Therefore, the length of time the investor is exposed to market risk and credit risk.

The credit risk is the default or severe downgrading of the counterparty's standing. The market risk comes from the fact that interest rates may increase, therefore devaluing the remaining cash flows as well as the price of the bond.

In this perspective, maturity is an inadequate measure of the sensitivity of a bond's price to changes in interest rates, even of simpler types of bonds. The reason is that its linear approach ignores the effects of coupon payments, and prepayments of principal. Say, as an example, that an investor has two bonds, both maturing in 10 years.

- The one is zero-coupon and pays $10 000 at maturity.
- The other pays a coupon of $500 annually and $5000 at maturity.

While the cash flow looks the same over the stated horizon, the zero-coupon investor must wait 10 years to receive any money. By contrast, the other bondholder gets nearly half the bond's cash flow prior to maturity. On average, the investor receives the cash in 5.5 years:

$$\frac{1 + 2 + 3 + \cdots + 10}{10}$$

This average (as nearly all averages) is an inadequate metric of the effective life of the bond, as it falls short of reflecting the fact that payment at the end of the period is ten times bigger than the intervening coupon payments.

- A weighted average may be a better approach, which would give as an answer 7.75 years.
- However, this method, too, is inadequate because it leaves out of the equation the time value of money.

This is, most likely, what led Frederick Macaulay – back in 1938 – to develop an algorithm that corrects such shortcomings, as a better alternative than maturity regarding the measurement of the effective life of the bond and its return. Yet, it took nearly 35 years till financial analysts and sophisticated investors started to use Macaulay's approach to the calculation of a bond's interest rate risk.

In the preceding sections, we have already seen some of the many uses for Macaulay's duration algorithm. The list is longer than the results shown so far, as it includes several other issues that are fairly important in modern finance. For instance,

- Duration of risky and complex loans
- Duration of mortgage-backed securities
- Duration of embedded options
- Duration of floating rate loans
- Duration of demand deposits and savings deposits, and
- A certain level of assistance in bond pricing.

Hedging connected to investments is another applications example. In order to determine the number of futures contracts for a hedge, it is necessary to obtain an a priori estimate of a hedge ratio. As explained in section 10.1, depending on the type of hedge, different methods are used to estimate this ratio. With interest rate futures the methods are:

- Duration, and
- Basis points.

The two can work in synergy through *effective duration*, which helps in computing percentage change in actual price with respect to changes in yield. Say, for instance, that we wish to generate two different sets of cash flows, and their corresponding prices – experimenting with scenarios that are up 50 basis points (bp) and down 50 bp. The algorithm is:

$$\frac{\text{price (down 50 bp)} - \text{price (up 50 bp)}}{\text{price of base case}} \tag{4}$$

This and similar formulae help to measure price sensitivity of any fixed-income security with or without embedded options. As an example, for a fixed income security with price 93% and effective duration 2.7, if interest rates go up 1%, the price would drop roughly by:

$$\frac{93.0 \cdot 2.7}{100} = 2.51 \text{ points}$$

Algorithmic solutions permit handling of interest rate contingent claims as well as straight bonds. The suggested approach is longer than modified duration for deep discount mortgage-based securities (MBS), and CMO companion bonds. But it is shorter than modified duration for high premium MBS and ARM. It also produces realistic negative duration, and bearish CMO residuals.

Duration is also extensively used with bond pricing, since its provides a useful measure of the bond's sensitivity to interest rate changes, and it incorporates both maturity and coupon into a single numerical measure of a bond's behavior. Among other applications, this can be used to compare the price sensitivity:

- Of different portfolios among themselves, and
- Of different bonds within the same portfolio.

As has been already explained, in the general case but only in the general case, bonds with short maturities and high coupons have *low* duration. By contrast, bonds with long maturities and low coupons have *high* duration. This can be best appreciated if one recalls that weights, in the weighted average, are present values of each cash flow expressed as a percentage of the present value of all the bond's cash flows – and, therefore, they are underpinning the bond's price. Moreover, Macaulay's algorithm is linked to the price volatility of a bond, and a modified form of it can help in accounting for the transaction price (purchase price) of a bond. This is presented in Appendix 10.D.

The duration algorithm, which accounts for purchase price of the debt instrument, is a function of interest payment in period *t*; number of payment periods in the year; annual yield of the bond, both in absolute value and divided by the number of payments in the year; and transaction price of the bond. Among themselves, these are the ingredients which help in making a factual and documented pricing of fixed income instruments.

In conclusion, Macaulay's algorithm is so useful because it defines a proxy that incorporates the weighted average of maturities of a bond's coupon and principal repayment cash flow. It should be remembered that the weights are fractions of the bond's price represented, in each timeframe, by the cash flow – and that in modern finance *cash flow* is king.

Unlike maturity, duration is a measure of the sensitivity of a debt security's price to changes in yield. Because a low duration bond will show a lesser change in price for a given change in yield than a high duration bond, floating rate debt instruments usually have very small interest rate sensitivity: hence, low duration.

Macaulay's duration algorithm is also a useful tool in the calculation of *intrinsic value* of an investment, since it is largely based on the *discounted cash flow* of the coupon stream. That is the amount by which the bond's price is changing for a unit change (one basis point) in interest rates. This is the sense of the reference made to *theta*.

10.6 Practical applications of duration and convexity

In sections 10.2 to 10.5, duration has been examined along the lines of a calculation based on the timing of future cash flows. As the careful reader will recall, duration has been considered as the life in years of a notional zero-coupon bond whose fair value would change by the same amount as the real bond in response to a change in market interest rates. Hence the similitude to theta.

The usefulness of information about the duration of a bond, or a portfolio, might be enhanced by also disclosing the convexity. *Convexity* is the extent to which duration itself changes as prices change – capturing the curvature of the price movement – and it arises for several reasons. Prior to looking into these reasons, however, it is proper to define convexity – as well as concavity, its opposite.

Concavity and convexity can be defined in different ways. The simplest is a geo-metric approach. In Figure 10.1, the polygon OABCD constitutes a *convex* set of points: given any two points in this polygon, the segment joining them is also in the polygon, which is not the case with concavity. An extreme of a convex set is any point, in that set, which does not lie on a segment joining some other two points. For instance O, A, B, C, D are extreme points.

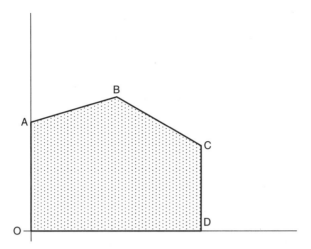

Figure 10.1 Example of a convex polygon

The geometric definition of convexity also applies to point sets in a three-dimensional space: A solid cylinder is a convex set, but a hollow cylinder is not. If a space of higher dimensions is involved, the geometric interpretation becomes less obvious, and we need to turn to an algorithmic definition of convexity.

For an analytical expression of this same statement on convexity, let z be a function x_1, x_2, $(z = f(x_1, x_2))$. This is a two-variable function which is convex if, for any pair of distinct points E, F on its graph, line segment EF lies either on or above the surface defined by the function in reference. It is *strictly convex*, if line segment EF lies entirely above the surface.

Inversely, the function $z = f(x_1, x_2)$ is concave if, for any pair of distinct points E, F the segment EF lies either on or below the surface. And it is strictly concave if it lies entirely below the surface. Moreover,

- If $f(x)$ is a convex function, then $-f(x)$ is a concave function.
- If functions $f_1(x)$ and $f_2(x)$ are both convex, then $f_1(x) + f_2(x)$ is also convex.

The same principle applies with concave functions. As the reader will appreciate, the foregoing definitions use no derivation, and therefore pose no requirements of differentiability. However, *if* $f(x)$ is differentiable, *then* convexity and concavity can be defined as its first derivative, as shown in Appendix 10.E.

Many bond issues have positive convexity. With positive convexity, the price increase for a given decline in yields is in excess of the price decrease for the same rise in yields. This means that positive convexity works in the bondholder's favor, and investors can capitalize on it.

Negative convexity arises when long maturity cash flows have less weight when yields decrease, and more weight when yields increase. With negative convexity, duration increases as yields rise and decreases as yields fall. This is important to the investor inasmuch as many mortgage-backed securities (MBS), callable corporate bonds, and preferred shares have negative convexity,[8] which is hurting investors.

The way it has been presented in Appendix 10.E, convexity and concavity will be *strict* if the weak irregularities in the above two functions are replaced by strict irregularities. This is in conformity to the analytical definition of geometric properties, which specifies a convex curve as one that lies above all its tangent lines, while a concave curve lies below them.

In the financial world, the counterpart of the foregoing definitions is that as yield to maturity changes, a bond's duration also changes, making modified duration a predictor of price change for very small changes in yield to maturity. For instance, if yield to maturity is 5% and modified duration 3.60%, this implies that a 100 basis point change in yield to maturity will result in a 3.60% change in bond price.

By contrast, as yield to maturity increases to 6.5% modified duration falls to 3.40%, implying smaller price changes for subsequent changes in yield to maturity. These two examples show that the price response of a bond to changes in yield to maturity is a function not only of the bond's modified duration, but also its convexity. Respectively:

- Modified duration measures the sensitivity of bond prices to changes in yield to maturity, and
- Convexity measures the sensitivity of duration to changes in yield to maturity.

In a way, this is duration's theta which, as discussed, measures the change in an option's premium with respect to time of maturity. Theta is the metric of time-decay, on a day passage of time. The longer an option's time to expiration, the more valuable it is.

Experts consider a positive convexity as being desirable for the straight bond, because it indicates that prices are rising faster than they fall. Convexity tests should be based on both historical and hypothetical scenarios, to provide insight on likely changes, and help in repositioning a portfolio against market forces.

According to Buttner and Rajadhyaksha, duration management of a bank's investment portfolio is a difficult task, given that most banks short convexity in an attempt to earn excess returns. Market fluctuations impact the duration gap, causing portfolio managers to buy or sell securities purely to manage volatility and affect earnings returns. For example, as interest rates drop many portfolio managers:

- Buy Treasuries, agency debt, and other assets, or
- Do fixed interest rate/flexible interest rate swaps.[9]

Take as an example a bond that has 20 cash flows. If yield to maturity increases, the present value of the 20th cash flow will decrease the most, that of the 19th cash flow will decrease by a smaller amount, and so on. The most recent cash flow will be affected the least. The reason duration will decrease is that the more distant cash flows are assigned less and less weight.

Take as another example a debt instrument designed to have only two cash flows, one after the first year and the other after the tenth year. If yield to maturity increases, the present value of the first cash flow will change by a significantly smaller amount than the change in the present value of the second cash flow. In fact:

- The weight assigned to the time receipt of the first cash flow will decline only slightly.
- But the weight assigned to the time to receipt of the second cash flow will decline significantly, leading to a more important change in duration of the bond.

There are several interesting applications which can be done on the basis of these principles. An important one concerns risk-adjusted duration and yield spread. Risk-adjusted duration is a risk metric in which effective duration is augmented for:

- Negative convexity
- Interest rate volatility
- Incremental prepayment risk
- Spread risk
- Currency risk
- Hedging, and
- Gearing of the portfolio.

In this list, spread risk estimates reflect percentage change in the portfolio's market value because of changing yield spreads. These map the risk premium demanded by investors for holding securities of a lesser quality than credit-risk-free US Treasuries.

Notice that yield spreads are volatile. They narrow and widen in response to a number of factors, including liquidity, changes in credit quality, market volatility, supply and demand, perceived future conditions, and investor sentiment. All of them affect the investment domain in which the algorithms are applied.

Other applications of duration and convexity enable fixed income portfolio managers to operate according to their convictions about likely changes in interest rates.

- If an investor expects interest rates to fall, he or she should increase the duration of their portfolio in order to leverage the price appreciation that will occur *if* this takes place.
- By contrast, if the investor expects an increase in interest rates, he or she should reduce duration to protect the portfolio from price losses, when such increase takes place.

Among other interesting applications of duration and convexity is that of hedging exposure to liabilities. For instance, the portfolio manager can hedge a liability stream by means of a portfolio of equal duration and convexity. Such a strategy may work as long as its present value equals the present value of the liabilities at the outset.

- *If* the present value of liabilities exceeds the present value of assets available for hedging,
- *Then*, the duration of the portfolio must exceed the duration of the liabilities.

The opposite statement is valid if the value of the portfolio's value exceeds the value of liabilities. Duration must be adjusted to relate the *dollar* change in price to changes in yield to maturity, in order to hedge a portfolio of liabilities with a different value.

Moreover, a debt instrument could be hedged from interest rate shifts by working backwards, setting its duration equal to the investor's holding period. In this case,

- *If* interest rates rise,
- *Then*, the capital loss will be offset by the gain from reinvesting the cash flows at higher yields.

When interest rates fall, the reduction in income resulting from reinvestment of cash flows at lower rates could be offset by the capital gain. Investors should, however, be aware that these are theoretical considerations. In practice, gains and losses are asymmetric, and this should be taken into full account in any study and experimentation.

Appendix 10.A   Macaulay's algorithm for calculating duration of a fixed rate instrument[10]

$$D = \frac{\displaystyle\sum_{n=1}^{m} \frac{nC_n}{(1+i)^n} + \frac{mA_m}{(1+i)^m}}{\displaystyle\sum_{n=1}^{M} \frac{C_n}{(1+i)^n} + \frac{A_m}{(1+i)^m}}$$

where:

D = duration of a fixed income instrument
C = coupon payment in period n
n = number of payment periods
A = principal payment at maturity m
m = maturity of the debt instrument
M = date of last payment

Or alternatively:

$$D = \frac{1}{P} \sum_{t=1}^{n} \frac{t \cdot L_t}{(1+y)^t}$$

where:

D = duration of a fixed income instrument
P = transaction price of the instrument
L_t = interest or principal repayment at period t
y = current annual yield to maturity, divided by the number of payment periods in the year
n = number of payment periods

The reader should remember that Macaulay's algorithm measures duration in periods, not in years. The result can be converted into years through equation (1), in section 10.3.

Appendix 10.B Present value approach to computation of duration

Expressed in periods, the duration is:

$$D = \frac{PVC_1 + PVC_2 + PVC_3 + \cdots + PVC_{n-1} + PVC_n}{\text{Present value of total cash flow (PVTC)}}$$

$$= \frac{\sum\limits_{i=1}^{n} PVC_i}{PVTC}$$

where:

PVC$_i$ = present value of cash flow in period i, discounted at prevailing period yield
PVTC = total present value of bond's cash flow
i = period when cash flow is expected to be received ($i = 1, \ldots, n$)
n = number of years to maturity

The calculation is done with number of periods to maturity taken as number of years times k (rounded down to the nearest whole number), where k is the number of periods (or payments) per year.

For instance, $k = 2$ for semiannual payment bonds, and $k = 12$ for monthly payment bonds.

Appendix 10.C Modified duration and effective duration

The formula for modified duration is:

$$D_m = \frac{D}{(1 + y)}$$

where:

D_m = modified duration
D = original Macaulay's duration
y = yield to maturity

The formula for effective duration is:

$$\text{Effective duration} = \frac{(-1)}{\text{price}} \cdot \frac{\partial \text{ price}}{\partial \text{ yield}}$$

With effective duration, the price/yield ratio is equal to the partial derivative of price in respect to yield.

Appendix 10.D A duration algorithm accounting for purchase price of the bond

$$D = \frac{1}{P} \sum_{t=1}^{n} \frac{t \cdot x_t}{(1 + y)^i}$$

and $y = \dfrac{Y}{n}$

where:

> D = duration
> x_t = interest payment of a bond in period t^{11}
> Y = annual yield of the bond
> y = current annual yield of the bond, divided by the number of payments in the year
> P = purchase price of the bond
> n = number of years to maturity

For instance, a 2-year bond with a coupon of $x_t = 6\%$ paid every semester, purchased at $P = 96$ and having an annual yield to maturity of 9%, will have a duration D_s by semester equal to:

$$D_s = \frac{1}{96} \left(\frac{1 \cdot 3}{(1 + 0.045)^1} + \frac{2 \cdot 3}{(1 + 0.045)^2} + \frac{3 \cdot 3}{(1 + 0.045)^3} + \frac{4 \cdot 4}{(1 + 0.045)^4} \right.$$

$$\left. + \frac{4 \cdot 100}{(1 + 0.045)^4} \right)$$

But the annual duration D_a will be:

$$D_a = \frac{D_s}{2}$$

Appendix 10.E Concavity and convexity

In principle, a function $f(x)$ can be concave or convex. It is convex if, for any given point y_1 and any other point y_2 in the domain, it is:

$$f(y_1) \geq f(y_2) + f'(y_2)(y_1 - y_2)$$

where $f'(y_2)$ is the first derivative of $f(y_2)$. It is concave if:

$$f(y_1) \leq f(y_2) + f'(y_2)(y_1 - y_2)$$

Convexity and concavity will be *strict* if the weak irregularities in the above two functions are replaced by strict irregularities.

This is in conformity to the analytical definition of geometric properties which specifies a convex curve as one that lies above all its tangent lines, while a concave curve lies below them, as discussed in section 10.5.

Notes

1 D.N. Chorafas, *Chaos Theory in the Financial Markets*, Probus, Chicago, 1994.
2 Basel Committee, Principles for the Management and Supervision of Interest Rate Risk, BIS, Basel, July 2004.
3 F.R. Edwards and C.W. Ma, *Futures & Options*, McGraw-Hill, New York, 1992.
4 D.N. Chorafas, *Modelling the Survival of Financial and Industrial Enterprises: Advantages, Challenges, and Problems with the Internal Rating-Based (IRB) Method*, Palgrave/Macmillan, London, 2002.
5 Frederick Macaulay, 'Some theoretical problems suggested by the movements of interest rates, bond yields and stock prices in the United States Since 1865', National Bureau of Economic Research, 1938.
6 D.N. Chorafas, *Advanced Financial Analysis*, Euromoney Books, London, 1994.
7 Karl Ahlander, *Aspects of Modern Treasury Management*, Institute of International Business, Stockholm, 1990.
8 Martin J. Mauro, *Primer of Duration and Convexity*, Merrill Lynch, New York, 2004.
9 Michael Buttner and Ajay Rajadhyaksha, 'Constructing optimal benchmarks for bank investment portfolios', in Leo M. Tilman (ed.), *Asset/Liability*, Euromoney, Institutional Investor, London and New York, 2003.
10 Notice that the definition of symbols and their meaning in Appendix 9.E is not applicable to this chapter.
11 Can be either coupon interest or principal repayment.

Part 4
Bonds, bond markets, credit rating, and risk control

11 Bonds, money markets, capital markets, and financial organizations

11.1 Introduction

No market is ever a *zero-sum game* – the term referring to a process, method, condition, or investment in which the gains and losses of the different players sum up to zero, for every possible choice of strategies. *If* they were zero sum, *then* what some of the players lose the others gain. This is not the way markets work. Whether we talk of equities or of debt instruments, all players might gain and all players might lose, depending on which way the market goes.

'Zero sum' is a term which comes from game theory. Suppose there are only two players, X and Y which, between them, control 'an amount equal to 100'. Whatever increase in capital the one of them achieves, through trading and/or investments, the other one loses – in an amount exactly equal to the gains of the other. The importance of this type of game is that the players are *in pure conflict*.

No pure conflict is found in investments. The way the markets work is much more complex than game theory supposes, though there are lots of games played in money markets and capital markets (see sections 11.3 and 11.4). There is also complementarity between players in the market, as well as instrument linkages, as shown in Figure 11.1.

Bonds are traded both in the capital market and in the money market (more on this later), and because they constitute an important asset rotation tool, they have to be handled in full regard to fixed income allocation strategies. Bonds are also an equity rotation tool. For instance, after a temporary peak in bond yields in early May 2004, the first two of the three top performing sectors in the S&P 500 have been utilities and the financials. Both are rate-sensitive. Consumer staples came in third position.

Moreover, the behavior of debt instruments in the market, and associated volatility of their key variables, influences other factors which impact on market response and prices. For instance, interest rates and yields play a crucial role in connection to credit risk, so much so that there is a problem for the central bank in easing pre-emptively because it produces lower interest rates right when the credit cycle deteriorates. Often, the result is:

- Limited lending, as banks continue to tighten their landing practices, or
- Underpricing of credit risk; as happens with auto loans and consumer electronics loans offered at 0% financing.

Where are debt instruments being traded? Many people, including experts, believe that dealing on bonds takes place in the capital market. This is only half true. In real

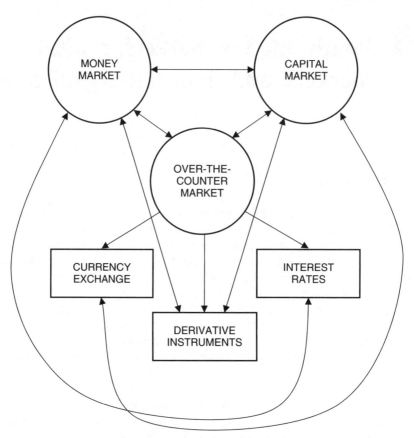

Figure 11.1 Financial markets that work in unison and complement each
other in trading debt instruments

life some debt instruments are traded in the money market (see section 11.3) and
others in the capital market (see section 11.4). Typically,

■ Short-term debt instruments are traded in the money market, and
■ Debt instruments of longer-term maturities, over one year, are handled in the capital market.

A snapshot of new debt issuance, published on 21 May 2004 by Merrill Lynch,
is shown in Table 11.1. The short term dominates – which means money market
deals. There is as well a gray area between the money market and capital market
for bond trading, as shown in Figure 11.2. For instance, floating rate notes are
traded in the money market even if their maturity is over one year, presumably
because:

■ Of their impact on interest rates, and
■ Their use for inflation indexing reasons.

Table 11.1 A 2004 example of new issuance of debt loaded at short-term maturity

Announcement date	Maturity	Issuer
Treasury financing		
May 20	3 and 6-month	
May 24	1-month	
May 24	2-year note	
May 27	3 and 6-month	
June 1	CMB 6/15	
June 7	CMB 6/15	
June 7	5-year note	
June 7	10-year note (R)	
Agency financing		
May 20	1-month	Freddie Mac
May 20	3-month	Freddie Mac
May 20	6-month	Freddie Mac
May 24	3-month	Fannie Mae
May 24	6-month	Fannie Mae
May 27	1-month	Freddie Mac
May 27	3-month	Freddie Mac
May 27	6-month	Freddie Mac
May 27	12-month	Freddie Mac
May 27	5-year	Freddie Mac

Source: Extracted from a table in *The Market Economist*, Merrill Lynch, 21 May 2004

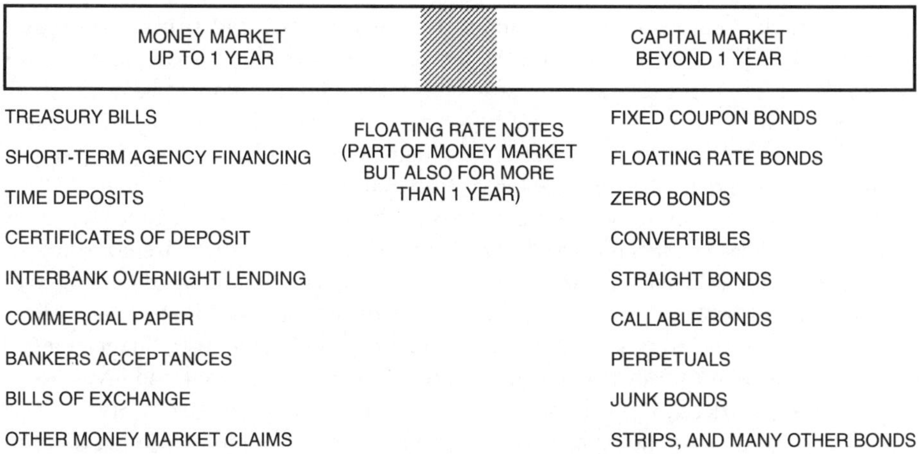

MONEY MARKET UP TO 1 YEAR		CAPITAL MARKET BEYOND 1 YEAR
TREASURY BILLS	FLOATING RATE NOTES (PART OF MONEY MARKET BUT ALSO FOR MORE THAN 1 YEAR)	FIXED COUPON BONDS
SHORT-TERM AGENCY FINANCING		FLOATING RATE BONDS
TIME DEPOSITS		ZERO BONDS
CERTIFICATES OF DEPOSIT		CONVERTIBLES
INTERBANK OVERNIGHT LENDING		STRAIGHT BONDS
COMMERCIAL PAPER		CALLABLE BONDS
BANKERS ACCEPTANCES		PERPETUALS
BILLS OF EXCHANGE		JUNK BONDS
OTHER MONEY MARKET CLAIMS		STRIPS, AND MANY OTHER BONDS

Figure 11.2 Bonds are traded in both the money market and in the capital market, with maturity a basic, but not exclusive criterion

Indexed inflation notes are money market instruments, as this market is more flexible and adaptable to rapid yield changes than its capital market counterpart. Indeed, the capital market is generally considered to be *the* market for equities an, to a significant extent, debt, but as we have seen debt is also traded in the money market.

It is also interesting to note that trading in some of the money market debt instruments predates those dealt with in capital markets, and by far. Bills of exchange, which include trade bills and commercial bills, first appeared as 'new financial instruments' in medieval times. Historical records show they were traded at the Foire de Lyon in the 13th century by Italian bankers like Bardi who preceded the Medicis as Europe's top bankers.

At about the same time can be found the origin of bankers acceptances, which are written documents issued by a borrower to the bank, with promise to repay the money lent. In a way emulating the history of bonds (see Chapter 3), bills were originally assignable, but not really negotiable because the bearer did not have the right to recourse against previous holders – until negotiability became generalized in the early 17th century.

Basically, the money markets' origins find themselves in mercantilism and merchant banking. Traders in goods developed into dealers in bills of exchange, and at the same time they became active in what was at the time the sense of international trade. The mark of an expert exchange dealer was to find new ways around and through the bill markets, especially in time of war. It is interesting to note that following Harvey's discovery of the circulation of the blood in 1621, John Law and many others argued that credit is the blood of society.[1]

11.2 Growth of the bond market

Business, Dimosthenes said, is built on confidence. This is true of any transaction, and most particularly of debt investments where the investor bets on borrowers' ability and willingness to face up to their contractual obligations. This is true with all loans, but in classical lending by commercial banks the credit institution is expected to exercise due diligence in screening the loan in respect to the borrower's creditworthiness. By contrast, the average investor who buys a bond does not have the ability to do so and must rather concentrate his or her efforts on diversifying by spreading risk between different issuers, preferably guided by the grade given to the issue and the issuer by independent rating agencies (see Chapter 12).

Generally speaking, in the Western countries the market for debt instruments is liquid. This, however, does not mean that all bonds are liquid; some of them are not so easy to buy and sell. Much depends on the issue and on the issuer. Commercial banks, investment banks, and brokers trade in bonds, on their own behalf and that of their clients; they do so both in the primary and in the secondary market. Moreover, financial institutions issue their own debt instruments and at the same time they are bond investors.

In emerging markets, bond issues have been led by commercialization of government debt and, at least in regard to government securities, bond trading develops earlier than equity trading. In Group of Ten countries there have been several bond market boosters. The debt of the American, British, German, French and other governments has contributed greatly in opening up the high quality bond market, albeit at lower yield than that of corporates. In the early 1960s, a big booster with global financial impact has been the *eurodollar* market of deposits and issues.

■ Amounts outstanding indicate the inventory of debt securities at the end of a given period.
■ All securities must be valued, in principle, at nominal (face) value, though national differences exist in the valuation of deep-discounted debt instruments.

As has already been discussed, companies borrow money by issuing and selling debt instruments, including bonds and medium-term notes. The primary difference between the two is that medium-term notes can be offered continuously, through a process of self-registration, therefore without the costly and time-consuming procedures required for a formal underwriting of bonds.

Medium- to longer-term bonds are generally issued by companies designated as *investment grade* by the recognized independent rating agencies. This means ratings from AAA to BBB. The ease of self-registration procedures provides companies with a cost-effective way of offering securities on a regular basis increasing their ability to tailor:

■ Maturity dates,
■ Interest payment frequency, and
■ Other terms which may suit investor needs, and their own.

Short-term debt instruments generally have an original maturity of one year or less, even if they are issued under longer-term facilities. All other issues, including those with optional or indefinite maturity dates, are classified as being long-term. Redemptions comprise all repurchases by the issuer against cash, whether at maturity or earlier – while net issues are issues minus redemptions during a given period.

The reader is also aware of the fact that companies are currently obtaining an increasing amount of their funding through corporate bonds. This is more pronounced in markets like Germany and Italy, where the corporate bond market has long been ovsershadowed by bank lending, as companies traditionally depended on their house bank for funding.

In Germany, at the end of 2003, the corporate bond market had reached more than 6% of gross domestic product (GDP). Still this is considerably lower than in the United States or France, where bonds have long played a significant role in corporate financing, with the outstanding volume of bonds and money market instruments equivalent to around 25% of GDP.

As US and French statistics show, healthy money markets and capital markets for corporates have many after-effects. One of the most interesting is that bondholders, who used to be an afterthought in a corporation's investor relations while shareholders stole the spotlight, have now become subject to attention from senior management. Indeed, as far as investor relations are concerned bondholders play a crucial role, particularly for debt-burdened companies.

For instance, to stay alive companies which find themselves in financial difficulties have to persuade creditors to swap high-interest junk bonds for stock, or less-valuable paper. That means their management is stepping up efforts to hand-hold bond investors, soliciting their goodwill through meetings and public relations efforts.

But not all public relations campaigns and financial plans they are intended to support, work. Even the threat of imminent demise does not always carry the day with investors. In September 1990, as it was sinking deeper into trouble largely because of failed real estate loans, the Bank of New England tried to engineer a $700 million swap with bondholders. Creditors backed away, thinking the move was too late. They were right. Regulators seized the bank a few months later, on 6 January 1991.

This example also speaks volumes about the volatility in bond prices which may come from market forces, or in the aftermath of event risk. Of particular concern to equity and debt investors is the fact that there are few sources which provide pragmatic volatility estimates and these are not so frequently updated. Therefore, financial analysts tend to:

- Develop their own algorithms, or
- Adapt existing ones to new needs.

An example from the stock market is the use of two measures of volatility: standard deviation of S&P Composite daily price changes; and average spread between the daily high and low prices for the S&P composite. Differences in spread are also a good indicator of the volatility of debt instruments.

- As we have seen in Chapter 7, there are tools for modeling the volatility of interest rate premiums, and
- A good metric for debt instruments is the spread between the bonds of a given company and the benchmark US 10-year Treasuries (see Chapter 9).

Finally, the fact that bond offerings by governments, companies, and other issuing entities are increasingly done in the globalized debt market, brings into perspective the critical role of cross-border regulation. In the liberalized world marketplace, the central bankers' task, and that of other regulatory agencies, is double edged.

- They must ask whether the economy under their jurisdiction is overheating, with inflationary consequences, and
- They must watch out that bond markets are not overshooting to the point of threatening a systemic risk.

Behind this second bullet point lies the fact that in the 21st century the bond markets' over-reaction is the equivalent of a banking panic. Central banks and bank supervisors are not only very careful within their jurisdiction, about:

- Market liquidity
- Interest rates, and
- Response to debt instrument offerings

they also watch careful what happens in the jurisdiction of other major sovereigns. As the May 2004 monthly bulletin by the European Central Bank (ECB) had it:

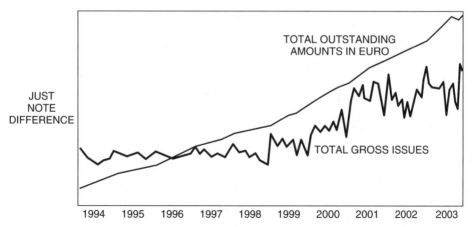

Figure 11.3 Ten years of total outstanding amounts and gross issues of securities other than shares issued by euro area residents. (Presentation aimed at underlying trend, based on ECB statistics)

In the United States, ten-year government bond yields increased sharply, by around 70 basis points, between the end of March and 5 May [2004]. Most of the increase occurred in early April, following more favorable than expected US labor market developments. In the euro area [yields] increased by 25 basis points between end-March and 5 May and ended the period at 4.3% ... The increase in long-term government bond yields in April [2004] seemed to a large extent to be a reflection of developments in the United States.

This direct quotation describes in a very pragmatic way the impact of globalization on bond markets. Within regional markets, as well, total gross issues and total outstanding amounts are rising. As Figure 11.3 shows, based on statistics by the ECB, the total outstanding amount in euro is rising faster than total gross issues, which demonstrates that the size of each debt issue is also significantly increasing.

11.3 Importance of the money market

Reference has been made in the Introduction that the money market has preceded the capital market by several centuries. Today, one way of looking at the money market is as the short-term counterpart of the capital market where long-term financial contracts are traded. Nevertheless, as we have seen with floating rate notes, a clear dividing line between the short- and long-term areas cannot be drawn using economic criteria because, in the last analysis:

- Short-term and long-term are determined subjectively by jurisdiction, and
- Much depends on the planning horizon of economic agents, and on the way they structure and trade their instruments.

In principle, deposits, advances, and short-term loans are issues which interest the money market. The common practice is that statistics concerning maturities of one year or less belong to the money market. This definition, however, is elastic, since some reserve banks, Banque de France and Banca d'Italia being examples, put the short term at 6 months.

In a broad sense, the money market denotes all available facilities for borrowing and lending money within the timeframe in reference. In certain cases, this tends to include also longer-term borrowing or lending. Increasingly, however, economists and bankers refer to the market for long-term funds as the capital market, restricting the term money market to the market for short-term money. In this latter case, the money market consists of two sectors:

- The *direct*, or customers' loan market, characterized by the close and personal connection between borrowing customers and their bank, and
- The *indirect*, or open money market, with objective relations between borrower and lender, where the loan is usually negotiated through intermediaries and the lender and borrower do not meet.

With this distinction, the indirect money market is *impersonal* and it is not necessarily formally organized. This means that, for the most part, there is no well-established meeting place, like an exchange, at which intermediaries come together. An example of buying and selling securities in a formal meeting place would be the stock exchange.

The way it works with all open markets, there is a group of borrowers in the money market providing demand for funds, and competing among themselves for financial resources. There is also a group of lenders providing supply of money, competing in the placement of their funds. Moreover, there is a group of intermediaries, who act as brokers, providing facilities for bringing together the bids and offers of borrowers and lenders:

- The money market provides an outlet for demand and offer of funds, and
- Negotiations are carried on in the offices of brokers, dealers, and bankers or through the use of on-line facilities.

Through money market transactions, funds are made mobile. Both borrowers and lenders, therefore debtors and creditors, obtain access to the money market which may operate on a local, regional, national or global scale. The more financial transactions get internationalized, the less the money market has geographical boundaries – unless different jurisdictions impose artificial ones, largely related to their currency.

Market transactions are used by market participants, such as commercial and investment banks, insurance firms, manufacturing companies, service enterprises, public authorities, or institutional investors, for liquidity management. An important distinction is between:

- Money market transactions, which are central bank money, such as credit balances with the central bank, and
- Those involving transactions based on bank deposits, which enable non-bank entities to synchronize their payment flows.

But to face some of their clients' currency needs, and to comply with their minimum reserve requirements, credit institutions additionally need central bank money.

Moreover, through the money market, too, individual banks enable themselves to adjust their reserve positions:

■ They sell paper in the market as circumstances arise, which require banks to add to their cash, and
■ They purchase paper arising in the money market, because of its quality and also because it provides a means of diversifying loan portfolios.

As these examples demonstrate, the money market is not a single simple market but *a family* of closely related markets; and each of them has its individuality. Bankers' acceptances, bills of exchange, and commercial paper markets provide specialized financing facilities to both foreign and domestic trade.

Over the years, different forms of securitized lending and borrowing in the money market have emerged besides the pure transactions in funds, which predominate – for instance, paper which is bearer or order bonds, short-term government paper like Treasury bills, commercial paper, and certificates of deposit (CDs). Notice that today the term 'commercial paper' covers a wide range of transactions, while at originally it had to have a commercial type of transaction in the background.

■ Generally, money market commercial paper is issued in the form of a discount, and
■ Its yield is representative of money market rates for similar maturities, if its credit rating and liquidity are sufficiently high.

Floating-rate notes have a comparable yield and risk profile to those of money market paper. A similar reference can be made to money market fund certificates. In principle, these are issued for an unlimited period of time, but they are a type of indirect money market fund investment.

Securities are often used as collateral for money market lending and borrowing. The main transactions of this type are sale and repurchase agreements (repos), whereby liquid funds are provided against the temporary transfer of securities. (Repos are discussed in Chapter 6.)

In a fairly broad sense, money market paper can be seen as a securitization of potential central bank money. This is the case if the reserve bank undertakes to purchase such securities. Or, if it is required to meet all liabilities arising from financing paper issued on its initiative.

For instance, the Deutsche Bundesbank operates in this way because section 21 of its Constitutional Act (the Act) provides the legal basis for specified money market paper, with a commitment to purchase it. This gives the holders the option of converting such securities into central bank balances, at any time.

The Act entitles the Bundesbank to buy and sell specified debt instruments in the open at prevailing market prices in order to regulate the money market. Formerly a major role in this connection was played by financing paper created by public sector borrowing, such as Treasury bills and Treasury discount paper. Furthermore, section 42 of the Bundesbank Act provides the option of issuing short-term debt instruments for the purpose of managing the money market, independently of the issue of financing paper.

The Bundesbank is liable to the German federal government for meeting all obligations arising from such issues. However, since the move to flexible money market management in the mid-1980s, the Bundesbank has almost exclusively used the instrument of securities repurchase agreements to meet its operational objectives in the money market. The liquidity and interest rates of these open market operations, which are reversible at short notice, guarantee that the central bank can rapidly bring to bear the desired money market conditions.

The issue of a transnational currency adds to the functions and reach of the money market. Take the euro as an example. Typically, the Eurosystem's money market management operations are aimed at enabling euroland's credit institutions to fulfill their minimum reserves requirements consistently, thus maintaining the level of the overnight rate as measured in terms of the weighted average Eonia rate (Eonia stands for euro overnight index average.) This is supposed to be done as close as possible to that targeted by the Governing Council of the ECB. The requirement is:

- Predicting fluctuations in credit institutions' demand for central bank balances, and
- Offsetting them in a timely manner through appropriate open market operations.

One of the crucial variables the ECB and the central banker of each euro country are watching is the volume of monthly refinancing operations with a 3-month maturity – as well as the volume of other operations which may also play a role in the refinancing of the banking system. Also monitored are the banking system's liquidity needs and whether these are covered by the Eurosystem's move to add to the volume of weekly main refinancing operations (MROs) with a 2-week maturity.

An example is the use of *split tenders*, which involve carrying out a reduced volume 2-week operation, and an additional 1-week operation instead of a 2-week main refinancing operation. On the other hand, a drawdown in the Eurosystem's net foreign reserves boosts liquidity needs, and there are other factors affected by valuation changes – such as the substantial build-up during 2003 of the Eurosystem's holdings of euro-denominated securities not connected with monetary policy.

As these examples demonstrate, money market operations add up to a fairly complex system, which requires fine tuning. The different segments that comprise the open money market are closely interrelated so that conditions in one of them affect the others. The broad competition that exists for money market funds tends to set, at any one time, a pattern of rates between different classes of paper and securities, as well as between them and loans by banks. In other cases, the most interesting aspect of competition is between the money market and the capital market.

11.4   Importance of the capital market

The capital market as we know it today was invented in the mid- to late 19th century in the United States (more on this later). *If*, however, the trading of equities – which was for more than a century its main objective – is taken as reference, *then* its origin dates back to the very beginning of the 17th century, and the place is Amsterdam.

Share certificates were first issued, and traded, in Amsterdam in 1602, in connection with the Dutch East India Company.[2] For any practical purpose, shareholdings have existed since that time though asset management by equity investors was very simple, with the investor more or less acting as a mini-merchant banker by advancing funds to a trading company.

This being said, the sophisticated and polyvalent capital market, the way we know it today, was born in New York propelled by capital needs credit institutions could not satisfy alone. Its time had come because of the largest project that far in American history: the building of coast-to-coast railroad networks which required vast sums of money. These projects started a few years after the end of the Civil War in 1865.

With the growth of the modern capital market nearly fourteen decades ago, came investment banking houses which made it relatively easy for industrialists and for magnets of the transport industry to tap a wide pool of American and European capital. It comes as no surprise that the largest US industrial and transport enterprises, who were the main beneficiaries of the early years of the capital market, accumulated through it huge financial resources in the years between the 1870s and the First World War.

Notice that to a substantial extent, capital market financing has been a self-feeding cycle. Railroads transported ore to the furnaces, and the mills produced steel for the rails. The construction of railroads and rapid urban growth gave work to unskilled immigrants, and the new working force:

- Provided labor for growing industrial enterprises, and
- Increased the demand for their products, thereby improving their bottom line.

To finance their growth, these enterprises issued common stock. It needs no explaining that the outstanding common stock is usually the nucleus of control of an entity, carrying with it a range of benefits as well as of responsibilities and risks – which are ordinarily associated with ownership. Equity traded in the capital market is the first security to be issued by a corporation and the last to be extinguished.

Common stockholders are owners of a company; their equity is usually voting stock. Theoretically at least, stockholders have the right to elect the board of directors, except under special circumstances. Also theoretically, stockholders are in a position to control the policies of the entity so long as it remains solvent. They are entitled to any income remaining after prior claims of creditors and other investors have been met. If the company is dissolved, they are entitled to all that remains, if anything, after everyone else has been satisfied.

By contrast, preferred stock creates a form of ownership which is limited, and not final or residual. *Preferred stockholders* have a position intermediate between that of common stockholders and bondholders. Sometimes preferred stock carries a vote; more often it does not. It typically has a set rate of dividends that must be paid, before any dividends can be allocated on the common stock. Preferred stock also has priority over common stock in the case of liquidation.

Buyers and sellers of securities traded in the capital market come together to accomplish something that none of them could achieve alone. This is a simple concept, but one that has been forgotten by many in the boom years of the market, when speculators called the tune and investors who trusted their capital to equities, and debt instruments traded in the market, have seen their savings evaporate. The principle behind the growth of capital markets has been that:

- Scale,
- Scope, and
- Structure

all depend on what an organization is trying to do – and on how well it can do it. Industrial and other organizations are the means to ends, not ends in themselves. They exist to serve the needs of the economy, as well as of people who are both inside them and outside them, part of the larger social structure of an economy.

The downside of capital markets is that they can be manipulated, and they often are. This is done in several ways – from spreading of rumors, which if persistent can lead to great euphoria and higher equity prices or alternatively to panics, to fake equity analysts valuations and outright insider trading. Insider trading still happens in various forms, at the expense of other capital markets participants, even if in most Group of Ten countries this has finally been outlawed.

The events which took place in the go-go late 1990s and the 28 April 2003 settlement with the Securities and Exchange Commission of ten well-known Wall Street firms provide the documentation that the capital market can be manipulated by the few against the interests of the many.[3] This works against Dimosthenes' dictum about business confidence.

There are many examples of how the few game the capital market system and take its investors to the cleaners. Extracurricular activities is one of them. Bill Gross, an influential bond-fund manager, worries that US firms are generating an unusually large share of their profits from *financial bets* that depend on interest rates remaining low.[4] Other companies sell options to their own stock – which is a kind of insider trading.

If the capital market works in ethical and unbiased way, trading in a properly regulated exchange helps to define in a fair manner a company's value to investors. However, when discussing the market value of quoted companies, it is necessary to recognize the absence of uniform definition of the term *capitalization*:

- Some experts consider it as being the sum of the value of the stocks and bonds outstanding, while
- Others look at it as equal to fair valuation of the company's equity, without fire sale or fictitious values.

According to the second bullet, however, capitalization is the computation, appraisal, or estimation of present value using as proxy the market price of shares multiplied by outstanding shares of the entity. While originally the word might have been primarily used in the sense of a rather subjective valuation, the aforementioned quantitative expression now usually accompanies the more classical qualitative connotation.

Prior to 1912, in the United States, stock certificates carried a nominal value per share: the *par value*. If a company was capitalized at, say, $100 000, this probably meant that 1000 shares at $100 par were available for distribution. Moreover, in many shares the corporation or its officers were not permitted to sell the stock for less than the par figure. Under these conditions there was a tendency for the par value to be the equivalent of the actual worth of the stock at the time of beginning corporate activity, unless the equity sold at a premium.

Evidently, this potential equality of par value with market value, defined by buyers and sellers in the exchange, would exist only momentarily. Because business is dynamic in character, market values are changing constantly in response to gains and losses accruing to the enterprise, consequently increasing or decreasing the value of common stock as a result of:

- Market action, and
- Accounting results.

One of these accounting results is the *book value* of common stock. It tells its worth as shown by accounting records, usually calculated through the accruals method. Basically, this is a simple formula: assets less liabilities and other claims preceding the common stock, divided by the number of shares outstanding equals the book value per share. Book value, however is by no means *fair value*, reflecting the real worth of the enterprise to its owners. Quite often it is nothing more than an irrelevant figure.

At any given time, an entity may have a fair value in excess of book value; or, alternatively, much less than what the books say. And it is not unlikely that management action may see to it that such a condition is reversed at another date. The best proxy of fair value is *market value*, because it tells what the market thinks of a company's worth – but as we have seen, this, too, can be manipulated through news, rumors, and in other ways. We will return to the issue of market value and of accruals accounting in section 11.5 in connection with the allocation of money among fixed income instruments.

11.5   Capital allocation in fixed income instruments

One of the issues on the front burner which has to do with markets and investments is that of criteria applied in screening debt instruments – everything from new issues to positions already inventoried in the portfolio will be regularly reviewed and reevaluated. We may concentrate into a half-dozen bullet points what has been said in the preceding discussion on the choice of bonds about investors who know how to manage their money. They look after:

- Issuer and creditworthiness of issuer
- Nominal interest, real interest, and yield
- Maturity and duration
- Currency and foreign exchange risk
- Liquidity of the instrument in the market, and
- Risk and return within the chosen investment horizon.

The risk and return evaluation which interests us in this section, concerns a portfolio of debt instruments, and key variables associated to it like yield, duration, laddering, creditworthiness and other factors characterizing the portfolio's structure and return. The background to this discussion (as well as to the themes in subsequent sections of this chapter) is *good management*, which is instrumental in distinguishing:

- Successful investors, as well as asset managers and credit institutions
- From those foolish investors who insist on buying the Brooklyn Bridge, no matter how many times they hear it's already been sold.

What are the topmost objectives of a bond investor? Way up the list of basics are *capital preservation* and *income* (in that order); the latter is counted on the basis of real interest rate and yield, rather than nominal rate which may be unrealistic because of inflation. The next critical factor is laddering of maturities in a way that:

- Provides a balance within the chosen time horizon, and
- Satisfies the individual investors' goals in terms of portfolio management.

For capital preservation purposes recommended a concentration in high-quality instruments is recommended. Notice that even for AA corporates, maturities should be no longer than five years. By contrast, for Group of Ten sovereigns maturities can be longer, *if* the bonds are bought at periods of high interest rates – therefore, of high yield. Also for capital preservation purposes, the so-called *aggressive growth* debt instruments, which are largely junk bonds, should be avoided no matter what the salesman (who wants to place them) tells the investor.

- *If* an investment plan targets growth,
- *Then* one should put one's money in equities, not in bonds.

Moreover, because from time to time volatility and risk characteristics vary (and they may even vary so widely), the specific investments chosen are important. Some types of debt instruments, particularly those involving derivative products, are not appropriate for all levels of risk tolerance. (More on this in Chapter 15.) In a recent report to investors, one of the brokers had this to say on fixed income allocation: 'We shifted 3% out of cash and 2% out of both corporates and preferreds, and added 3% to MBS, and 2% to both short-term bullet agencies and Treasuries.'

Not every reader of this document probably appreciated that these are switches investors may do, but not necessarily along the lines of the foregoing reference. Shifting 'out of cash' means getting more invested and slightly less liquid, with 'how much' depending on the initial cash position. On the other hand, increasing exposure to MBS means higher risk – which, in the above advice, is counterbalanced by US government agencies and by Treasuries. Such counterbalance is not symmetric.

The choice of bonds may be influenced by interest rate trends. Inflation-adjusted government bonds are a case in point. In early June 2004, as interest rates were rising, experts cautioned about the TIPS market (see Chapter 8). Their argument has been that relatively controlled inflation accompanied with rising nominal yields suggests that real yields are on the rise. In a rising real yield environment, TIPS would be expected to underperform the price movement of nominal bonds.

Moreover, the investor's tax status should evidently be given due consideration in fixed income choices and capital allocation. As an example, the same broker's advice has been: 'We recommended longer maturities in the municipal market than the taxable market because muni[cipal] yields are not likely to rise as much.' (This advice is directed to American investors, because interest from municipal bonds is not taxed in the United States.)

Also, to follow one's fortunes and misfortunes with investments in an analytical and factual way, it is necessary to have and use a first class accounting system. Chapter 8 has already brought the reader's attention to present-day accounting insufficiency.

The following paragraphs further emphasize the crucial role accounting plays in sound investment management.

To start with, one of the strengths of a portfolio consisting of liquid bond investments is that they have a market-sensitive price. This permits marking to market. However, as the careful reader will recall, historical accounting ordinarily fails to record either possible or actual appreciation and depreciation values. This leaves much to be desired in terms of managerial information because the market is dealing constantly in terms of the future outlook, not of the past.

Critics of current managerial accounting insufficiency also say that while sometimes market values are based on analytics, quite often they are biased by market psychology and the prevailing trend, which is not reflected in present value reports. There are two answers to this comment to be brought to the reader's attention.

First, *if* fair value is taken as market value other than under fire sale conditions, *then* market psychology is reflected into this fair value – since investors' psychology impacts upon the market price. Second, while it is true that market value is *no exact value*, for the simple reason that many of the criteria used to 'make the market' are subjective, market prices are the best indicator of what a portfolio of debt instruments is worth at a given point in time.

In a free economy the outstanding characteristic of a market is its realistic adjustment of prices in response to changing conditions. It is not at all surprising that the market may not accept the value of an entity as expressed in its books. For a successful corporation the market value of its stock and of its bonds is often in excess of the book figures, but it is below the books for a company that is not worth its salt.

One lesson that the late 1990s and early 21st century years taught has been the powerful effect on corporate behavior of short-term moves in share prices. Although company executives now feel under less market pressure since the discrediting of Wall Street analysts who pushed them to have ever-shorter time-horizons, they still bear the market's call.

Where these notions lead us is to the dual role of the capital market: as an intermediator with deeper pockets than any single entity operating in it and as a mechanism which – based on common interactive action – is able to produce a proxy of fair value which, because of lack of a better estimate, is taken as the real thing.

To investors, this proxy is so much more valuable if there is *accountability* in the money market and in the capital market. It is a fundamental principle of free societies that both private company executives and public authorities need to be accountable to the general public, from which their mandate and independence ultimately derive. Accountability can be best understood as the legal and institutional obligation for ethical behavior, all the way to explaining one's decisions clearly and thoroughly to the stakeholders.

11.6 The biggest assets of a bank: a management perspective

Whether debt instruments are traded in the money market or in the capital market, at the bottom line they are somebody's liabilities for which a counterparty pays good money, and handles them as their own assets. Counterparties use other assets, like cash, to finance these acquisitions, and they often employ intermediaries – which brings the role of money and banking into the perspective.

Money is several things at the same time. It is *raw material* for the banking industry, since without it banks cannot act as financial intermediaries. It is a means for *transacting business*, as well as *a means of exchange*, providing a time-honored substitute to barter agreements. Money is also *a unit of measurement* between reference points; and it constitutes the *basis of accounting*.

At the same time, money is *a store of value*, its intrinsic value coming from the fact that it is limited in supply. Regulating the supply of money is the responsibility of central bankers (see Chapter 1). The fact that each country practically has its own central bank, gives a further role to money and makes it a sensitive aspect of sovereignty.

In case of a common monetary unit, like the euro, used by a group of sovereigns, not only is there a central bank of central banks to manage the common currency – which is the role of the ECB – but also the central bankers of the different euro countries must work closely together and coordinate their activities. Such coordination has implications both for money markets and for capital markets. The reader should pay attention to the following quotation by the European Central Bank:[5]

> The Treaty establishing the European Community (EC Treaty) and the Statute of the European System of Central Banks and of the European Central Bank . . . , confer several tasks on the European System of Central Banks (ESCB). These tasks have to be carried out by the European Central Bank (ECB) and the national central banks (NCBs) of all Member States of the European Union (EU).
>
> Under the acronym 'ESCB' referred to in the EC Treaty, two realities coexist. On the one hand, 'ESCB' refers to the ECB and the NCBs of all the EU Member States. On the other hand, and by the effect of other provisions, 'ESCB' also refers to the ECB and the central banks of only those EU Member States that have adopted the euro.

There is a duality of roles, but not necessarily a complementarity. This might one day pose problems because central banks regulate both the monetary base and velocity of circulation of money; therefore, the money supply of the country under their jurisdiction (see Chapter 1). Moreover, in collaboration with an accounting standards board, central banks must also look after reliable financial reporting by commercial banks. And either alone or in coordination with a financial supervisory authority, which comes under the Ministry of Finance, they are responsible for the examination and regulation of the banking industry.

To the contrary, it is not part of the functions and responsibilities of central banks to look after the interests of bond investors. For any practical purpose, it is the responsibility of the clients of the banking system – and therefore of the market – who should ask critical questions related to the nature and dependability of banking services, such as what exactly is the bank's business:

- Taking money?
- Giving loans?
- Paying bills?
- Providing investment advice?

Figure 11.4 presents ten successive layers of critical queries which require factual, documented, and forward-looking answers. These queries range from the role of money to strategic planning (see section 11.7), with banking services in the middle. Banking is a service industry, but who pays for the services? Who assures their quality? Who takes care of operational risk, including fraud?[6] And how much should the client be billed?

As service entities, banks must organize, deliver, control, and price their services like industrial products. They should also select the right customers to whom to offer them, because customers have their profiles, preferences, strengths and weaknesses – and products should sell at a profit.

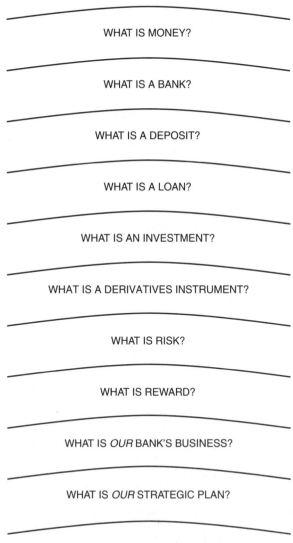

WHAT IS MONEY?

WHAT IS A BANK?

WHAT IS A DEPOSIT?

WHAT IS A LOAN?

WHAT IS AN INVESTMENT?

WHAT IS A DERIVATIVES INSTRUMENT?

WHAT IS RISK?

WHAT IS REWARD?

WHAT IS *OUR* BANK'S BUSINESS?

WHAT IS *OUR* STRATEGIC PLAN?

Figure 11.4 Functional layers change slowly but the characteristics of each layer change rapidly in function of risk and return

Service organizations, the products which they offer, the market's response to them, and the products' pricing bring up another critical question. Which are a bank's, indeed any organization's biggest assets? It may sound unorthodox, but the biggest assets of any company, not only of a bank, are *not* in the balance sheet. They are:

1 Its customers
2 Its employees, and
3 Its technology.

'The bank is information technology in motion,' Walter Wriston, the former CEO of Citibank, once said. But people – the customers and the employees – are much more important than technology. This is every organization's first principle of sound management (more on this in section 11.7).

Companies are made up of people and people make the difference, not only at top management but at every level: profitable banks have often seen their chief executive officer (CEO) at the frontline of setting goals, and of seeing that these are met. CEOs must also be keenly interested in the drive for efficiency. Paul Kennedy says: 'Without clear directives from above, the arteries of the bureaucracy harden, preferring conservatism to change, and stifling innovation.'[7]

Table 11.2 gives a snapshot of responsibilities and performance indicators of CEOs, as these tend to be phrased among leaders in the banking industry. The chief executive's job description is cast in a few lines: its elements must be very few, very brief, and very clear.

In unprofitable banks, the CEO leaves the responsibility for efficiency to others – or, more precisely, to nobody. It is not often written in these terms in textbooks and

Table 11.2 Job description of chief executive officer

Responsibilities	Indicators	Objectives
Assure long-term survival	■ Establish strategy ■ Focus on market goals ■ Select strategic products ■ Assure low cost production	
Handle major client relations	■ Meet with CEOs of client companies ■ Meet with ministers of finance, in all countries the bank operates ■ Assure client relations are properly handled by associates	Yearly goals (5 to 10)
Effective management of corporate resources	■ Clean balance sheet ■ Control of risk exposure ■ High tech literacy ■ Market development ■ Return on investment	

in reference books on management and banking, but the two top CEO responsibilities are to assure:

- Customer profitability, and
- Rigorous internal controls.[8]

Both must be properly designed into a credit institution's system of governance. When they are, they give the bank a unique competitive edge. It is also appropriate to appreciate that the person who commands the enterprise is not a mere technician. He is the animator, promoter, planner, and organizer – who values above all the qualities of hard work, creative imagination, unbiased judgment, and ethical behavior.

Based on a study I made in the mid-1990s as a consultant to the board of a major money center bank, Figure 11.5 presents the percentage population of the credit institution's clients with corresponding percentage share of the bank's profits and losses (P&L). Notice that the top 2% of the clients, who contributed about half of the

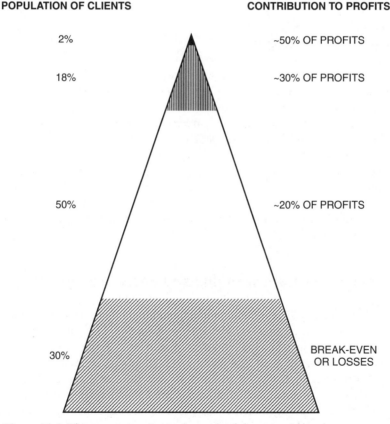

POPULATION OF CLIENTS

2%

18%

50%

30%

CONTRIBUTION TO PROFITS

~50% OF PROFITS

~30% OF PROFITS

~20% OF PROFITS

BREAK-EVEN
OR LOSSES

Figure 11.5 The counterparties at the peak of the pyramid made greater use of new financial instruments. It is here that the profits, but also the greater risks are found

Table 11.3 Criteria for greater efficiency in corporate banking, outlined by Hewlett-Packard

	Average	Worldclass	Achieved by HP in 1 year
Banks per $1 billion of revenue	17	3	10
Bank accounts per $1 billion of revenue	127	7.5	30
Average no. of accounts per bank	7.5	2.5	3

bank's profits, used to a very substantial measure new financial instruments – with all this implies for astute risk management.

Another fact of which the reader should take notice is that the competition for top clients (not necessarily for all clients), intensifies. This is making research, development, and innovation (R,D&I) in the financial industry one of the foremost top management responsibilities. Innovation in financial products requires two of a company's major assets:

■ Well-trained people, and
■ Mastery of high technology.

Superiority in R,D&I is necessary not only to acquire new top clients, but also for defensive reasons. Industrial and merchandising companies today have a policy of radically reducing the number of banks they deal with, as well as the number of accounts. At an international conference in Monte Carlo in June 2003, organized by Trema, Hewlett-Packard presented the statistics shown in Table 11.3.

Last but not least, a sound business principle is that a financial institution must be extremely careful about what it is doing with its clients. *Reputation* takes a lifetime to build and it can be destroyed in one hour. Whether we talk of money market or capital market operation – or of selling to the clients the debt of a bankrupt company, as has happened in Italy with Parmalat[9] – short-term profits should never blind management to reputational risk.

11.7 Need for forward planning and decisive action

Section 11.2 has focused on the bond market, section 11.3 on the money market, and section 11.4 on the capital market. The theme of section 11.5 has been capital allocation in fixed income instruments, and that of section 11.6 the broader management perspective – including the most important assets of a bank or, more precisely, of any enterprise. With planning being one of the basic functions of management, it has been left to this section to present to the reader the need for forward planning.

Managers cannot determine whether their subordinates are accomplishing what they have hoped for, unless they have projected a future course of action. Only bad news come 'accidentally' to an organization, and even that has sometimes been fed by wrong plans, or plans that are poorly executed. 'The plan is nothing,' President Eisenhower once said 'Planning is everything'. Planning the process, is most important to every organization, particularly when top management ensures that it is flexible:

■ Flexible
■ Based on choice among alternatives
■ Supported by an experimental approach
■ Enriched with detail, and
■ Kept under steady update.

A credit institution's business plan should always reflect the evolution taking place in banking, be able to feed the organization's strengths, and be ready to deal with its weaknesses. Any person, any business, any nation, needs to know its strengths.

■ What do we do *well*?
■ Where are the leaders?
■ Which are the fields where we perform?

Strengths are always specific, and they are typically *unique*. We get paid for our strengths, for what we do well, for the job in which we are masters – not for our weaknesses. This is true of any endeavor, investments being a case in point.

Do we know our strengths? Are we developing them over time? Are we taking advantage of them? Is our entity's history and culture, as well the skills, training and experience of its people, fit for handling wealth constraints? Time constraints? The differences between the two from the viewpoint of client handling, as well as associated requirements for financial services, are explained in a nutshell in Figure 11.6. For example:

■ Personal banking addresses itself to a client base which is money-rich but time-poor.
■ By contrast, the time-rich but money-poor characteristics of the client base are those of the retail banking clientele.

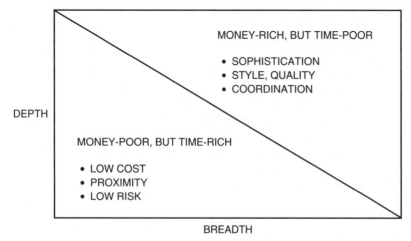

Figure 11.6 Opportunities and constraints connected to wealth and time in the client base

Both could be the basis of a lucrative business if properly planned and organized, as well as manned with skill. In the 1980s and 1990s, Citibank presented an excellent case of a retail banking strategy which made it a force to be reckoned with in many countries around the world. On the other hand, personal banking and wealth management can also be a very profitable business, in which Swiss banks are organized to excel.

The choice of globalization, of which we spoke in Chapter 2, should be part of our master plan's evaluation, even if we decide to keep out of it. *If* we adopt globalization, *then* we should follow Walter Wriston's dictum which says that 'national borders are no longer defensible against the invasion of:

- Knowledge,
- Ideas, and
- Financial business.'

'The eurocurrency markets', Wriston says, 'were fathered by controls, raised by technology, and grew as refugees from national attempts to allocate credit and capital which have little or no relation with finance and economics.'

Despite what they may say publicly, governments hate the global market because they cannot control it. But, to be ahead of the curve in their plans and actions, companies have to do research on markets, products, human resources, and technological developments; use feedback from operations to update goals and streamline procedures; as well as find inconsistencies among the component plans: product, market, financial, human capital, technological – and correct them.

Not only effective planning requires the elaboration of alternative strategic plans, based on different major options, and experiment in them; it is also necessary to do worst-case scenarios, and create a news alert for management – particularly in connection to risk control. Globalization has prerequisites that did not exist in local or national markets, whose limits are easier to grasp. 'Like the ocean, global financial markets are never at rest. Like women, they are never entirely predictable,' said Sir George Bolton.

The answer to the challenges of globalization, financial innovation, and technology cannot be found in protectionism, stumbling backwards to old frontiers. 'Protectionist measures redistribute income – from the average citizen to those doing better than average. And they harm efficiency in the process,' suggests Alan S. Blinder, an economist and former vice chairman of the Federal Reserve.

Neither is protectionism a solution to the competition by non-banks. For instance, insurance companies, which provide policies for houses and can also finance them; supermarkets and department stores, which have an enormous client database; vendor's acceptance corporations, making their profits from the sales margin of products they sell; brokers, who anyway deal in financial instruments. Given the magnitude of this competition, surviving banks will be those who are:

- Low-cost producers and distributors of services
- Innovators of new financial products
- Sharp marketers of their services, and
- Steady investors in human capital as well as in high-technology solutions.

In Germany, Citibank Privatkunden boasts a cost-income ratio (overhead) of just 44%. This is a little more than half that of other German banks' retail operations. Astute management planning and control assures that in its 300 German branches, Citibank Privatkunden staff spend 50% of their time with customers.

In Japan, Shinsei, the reborn Long-Term Credit Bank of Japan (LTCB), which collapsed in 1998, has a clean balance sheet – an exception among Japanese credit institutions. LTCB used to be a huge bureaucracy, which under political patronage provided low-margin corporate loans. After default, the government seized the bank, absorbed its $37 billion in bad loans, and sold it to New York's Ripplewood Holdings. As president of reborn Shinsei bank, Masamoto Yashiro,

- Cleaned up the bank's balance sheet,
- Made it a low-profile industrial lender,
- Rolled out a menu of financial products, and
- Overhauled its archaic information technology.

But when it started calling in loans to deadbeat Japanese borrowers, such as Sogo, the department store chain which a short while later went bankrupt, relations with the government grew tense. However, the clean balance sheet policy paid dividends. Shinsei had $501 million in profits on 31 March 2002, while other big Japanese banks had lost billions.

As these examples document, the best answer to the challenge of survival is rigorous planning and forceful, decisive management action. Planning must look forward by a number of years. What will our bank be doing in the next 10 years? The next 15 years? What is going to be our customers' profile 10–15 years from now? The customer needs and requirements? The database characterizing needed to satisfy in an able manner our customers' and our management's information requests? Other critical planning questions are:

- Which are the products and services we should research, develop and further?
- What resources are necessary to get ahead of the competition and stay ahead?

Products die and new products can take years to develop and take hold of the market. Figure 11.7 gives examples from the manufacturing industry. I had two professors of finance and management at UCLA, Dr Neil Jacoby and Dr Louis Sorel, who never accepted as an answer in case study analysis that a company went bankrupt because of financial problems. They instilled in their students the belief that the top reasons for business failure are:

- Lack of products with market appeal, and
- Management's ineptness, featherbedding, or plain lack of conscience regarding its responsibilities to shareholders, bondholders, employees, and society at large.

Able management requires foresight and insight, but also willingness and ability to take risks. There are, however, limits, and these are best described by the advice given in the late 1960s by George Moore, then CEO of First National City Bank, to Walter

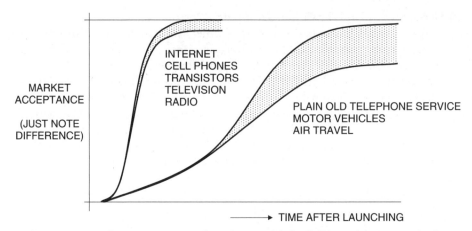

Figure 11.7 Product acceptance and market growth for killer applications and other successful products

Wriston, whom he had chosen as his successor: 'Be brave to scare Chase. But not so brave to scare me.'

Another piece of advice by Moore to Wriston concerned business challenges and ways and means for coping with them: 'If we do not have troubles, we would not have any priced people around to solve them.' Along the same line of reference, one of my professors at UCLA taught his students that: In life we don't really have problems, we have opportunities – and a person or a company without problems becomes decadent, because it does not have the challenge to move ahead. This is the best advice to be given to any investor.

Notes

1 Charles P. Kindleberger, *A Financial History of Western Europe*, Allen & Unwin, London, 1984.
2 D.N. Chorafas, *The Management of Equity Investments*, Butterworth-Heinemann, Oxford, 2005.
3 D.N. Chorafas, *Management Risk: The Bottleneck is at the Top of the Bottle*, Macmillan/Palgrave, London, 2004.
4 *The Economist*, 15 November 2003.
5 ECB, Monthly Bulletin, June 2004.
6 D.N. Chorafas, *Operational Risk Control with Basle I: Basic Principles and Capital Requirements*, Butterworth-Heinemann, Oxford and Boston, 2004.
7 Paul Kennedy, *The Rise and Fall of the Great Powers*, Random House, New York, 1987.
8 D.N. Chorafas, *Implementing and Auditing the Internal Control System*, Macmillan, London, 2001.
9 D.N. Chorafas, *The Management of Equity Investments*, Butterworth-Heinemann, Oxford, 2005.

12 Credit quality and independent rating agencies

12.1 Introduction

Every entity is exposed to credit-related losses in the event of non-performance by counterparties. Therefore, it is absolutely necessary to monitor creditworthiness of counterparties and their default likelihood. The term *counterparty* denotes an entity or person to whom the bank has an on-balance sheet and/or off-balance sheet credit or market exposure, or other type of exposure like a legal one. An exposure may take the form of a loan, of a derivatives transaction, or other commitment.

With reregulation of financial markets which has come with globalization, and the new supervisory rules and guidelines like Basel II, investors will have to substitute generalized crisis risk for the specific risks of individual transactions – from investments to other commitments. In the coming years the right investment approach will probably defy past neat labels of 'growth' and 'value', taking the form of *expected losses* (EL) and *unexpected losses* (UL)[1] due to failure on the part of any customer, correspondent bank, or other counterparty to fulfill assumed obligations towards our company or ourselves.

This chapter focuses on credit quality, credit risk, and credit rating. The credit exposure resulting from all types of financial transactions is the worth of contracts with a recognized positive fair value. By contrast, a negative fair value indicates the impact of market risk (more on this in Chapter 14). Few people truly appreciate that:

- *Credit* is a financial term with a moral lineage, which goes beyond its meaning debt.
- Credit is trust given or received, typically in expectation of future payment for property transferred, fulfillment of promises given, or other reasons.

As its name implies, a credit rating tells a story about a counterparty's or instrument's creditworthiness. A high credit rating allows comfortable access to money markets and capital markets, as well as diversification of funding. The evaluation of creditworthiness is very important to both investors and issuers, given the magnitude of new financial paper brought to the market every year.

Banks have been classically doing credit evaluation of their borrowers, but in the majority of cases the rating scale they have been using has been coarse-grain, with only a few thresholds. This is no more satisfactory. By contrast, independent rating agencies have had two advantages over internal ratings of credit institutions. The rating scale they developed and use:

- Is fine-grain, with up to 21 thresholds, and
- It is applied world-wide, which fits well the credit rating requirements of a globalized economy.

As far as credit quality of issuers and of debt instruments is concerned, investors rely on ratings assigned to corporate, sovereign, and other debt by independent rating organizations, like Moody's Investors Service (Moody's), Standard & Poor's (S&P), and Fitch Ratings[A]. These services analyze and rate bonds according to the issuer's ability and willingness to pay interest and repay the principal. An example of rating used by Moody's and S&P for investment grade bonds is given in Table 12.1.

Table 12.1 has ten investment grade thresholds. A nearly equal number of thresholds (they vary by rating agency) are non-investment grade. They range from BB+ in S&P, or Ba1 in Moody's, to C and D, the latter indicating default.

Not only companies, and therefore counterparties, are rated for their creditworthiness in regard to new loans and as issuers of debt instruments, but also the instruments themselves and specific credit conditions characterizing them. Ratings impact on credit decisions, trading decisions, and investment decisions. Credit decisions are all decisions on:

- New loans
- New securitizations
- New participating interests
- Loan increases and extensions
- Revisions of participating interests
- Restructurings
- Overdrafts
- Definition of borrower-specific limits, and
- Changes in risk-relevant circumstances.

Because counterparty risk is alive and well, borrowers and potential borrowers must be re-rated at least once a year to capture their current risk situation. Also,

Table 12.1 Investment grade bonds rated by independent agency

	S&P	Moody's
Best quality	AAA	Aaa
High quality	AA+, AA, AA−	Aa1, Aa2, Aa3
Upper medium quality	A+, A, A−	A1, A2, A3
Medium quality	BBB+, BBB, BBB−	Baa1, Baa2, Baa3

ratings must be subject to internal stress tests. Moreover, internal and external auditors should audit the quality of ratings, and adequacy of their use.

While banks rate their loans clients, correspondent banks, and trading partners, they are themselves rated by the independent rating agencies in terms of their corporate governance and finances. Globalization means this is becoming increasingly important. As far as credit risk is concerned, the best advice to companies is to get a grip on its fundamentals and to get moving in doing something constructive about it. Credit risk is everyone's concern. Poor credit rating will not cease to exist because it is ignored.

12.2 Independent credit rating agencies

Independent credit rating agencies first saw the light of day as statistical organizations in the late 19th century. In the United States they are regulated by the Securities & Exchange Commission (SEC). Their size varies significantly, and it takes years to develop a credit-rating franchise. It is not that easy to get a SEC designation to operate a nationally recognized statistical rating organization (NRSRO, a term coined in 1975) in the United States; it is also fairly difficult to develop the necessary skills, particularly so if the rating agency wants to develop global dimensions.

Since the beginning, the objective of rating by independent agencies has been to provide an unbiased opinion on creditworthiness. This is *not* an advice, or a recommendation. Fundamentally, rating agencies aim to inform; it is not part of their mission to protect anybody.

- Up to a point, the protection of investors is the job of bank supervisors, by means of assuring credit institutions under their authority are financially sound.
- By contrast, the parties responsible for malfeasance are the attorney-general, police, and judiciary – and there has been plenty of criminal action in the early years of the 21st century.

The growing role of rating agencies is easily explained by the fact that in a globalized market economy there is always the possibility of financial and industrial companies going bankrupt – but at the same time investors should know of their credit status. Creditworthiness is a crucial variable in nearly all business decisions.

If the supervisory authorities have a policy of too much tight reign to avoid bankruptcies, this will kill entrepreneurial activity. In this case, prevailing laws and regulations will be counterproductive. In the banking industry, in particular, regulators can only set a minimum capital standard.[2] They cannot and they should not target 100% security. Legislators and regulators must define what kind of security they want. The regulators mission is to:

- Provide conditions for orderly market behavior
- Create market transparency, and
- Avoid systemic risk, which will tear apart the financial fabric.

Notice that as far as debt instruments are concerned, the regulators don't aim at stockholder protection beyond that of guaranteeing an orderly market. Taking care of individual investors is not part of their charter. Information on credit status is the mission of independent rating agencies which, as we saw, address the default probability of bonds and issuers, including banks, funds, other companies and sovereigns; and also securitizations and structured financial transactions.

The role of regulators, rating agencies, and financial analysts versus investors is shown concisely in Figure 12.1. While, as we will see in section 12.6, there are general principles for credit rating, every sector of the economy also has its own criteria which impact on the default probability of companies operating in it. Other things being equal, shareholders and bondholders who know the probability of default assigned by rating agencies have better protection than those who don't.

For instance, in the insurance industry the credit risk of the insurer is judged by its solvency – that is, the company's ability to pay the claims arising from policies it has underwritten. The insurer's rating corresponds to bond rating, but the predominant factor is that of criteria proper to the insurance industry, distinguishing between regulatory capital and economic capital: The capital demanded by regulators typically stands at 4–5% of assets in life insurance, and 15% of revenue in non-life insurance.

To calculate economic capital an insurance company has to set its risk tolerance, which impacts on the economic activity it undertakes. It also has to account for the so-called *rating agency factor*, which gives a perception of the insurer's creditworthiness from the outside. This is also a function of risk tolerance.

Banking and insurance are classical examples of creditworthiness. There are other industry sectors which are novel in the credit rating business. A case in point is the

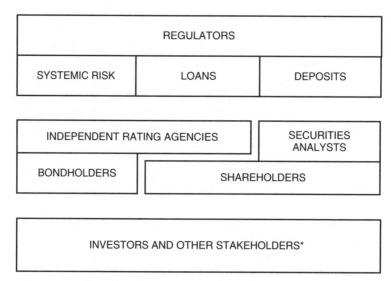

Figure 12.1 The role of regulators, rating agencies, and analysts *vs.* the investors (*for instance, in insurance, the policyholders)

securitization of ship insurance by appealing to capital markets (see Chapter 11). In the future, shipowners will be increasingly faced with a two-tier market:

- Big operators who will most likely securitize their risks
- Small to medium companies will continue through brokers.

Moreover, as the market evolves marine insurance companies may act as aggregators of risk and securitize their products. Some experts say that involving the capital markets is not necessarily good for shipowners – but *if* securitization is done, *then* credit rating is a 'must'.

In ship insurance, as in every financial domain, successful securitization requires first class professionals, and plenty of statistics (see also Chapter 6 on securitization). One of the troubles ship insurance may face with securitization of risk is that sometimes the statistics are depressing. For instance, Hull and Machinery (H&M) insurance:

- Makes money 3 years out of 10, and
- Loses money 7 years out of 10.

Munich Re says H&M Insurance loses big money: 22% per year on average. When such statistics become public knowledge, there will be no rush of investors to put money in a process where profits are a chimera, and creditworthiness might be weak. This is a good example of the transparency that should characterize ratings. Transparency in credit rating includes not only grade decisions but also their rationale,

- Explaining the criteria and definitions used to arrive at a rating decision, and
- Communicating the analyst's views about trends and outlook.

Market dynamics mean that investors don't always take notice of risks involved in low credit rating. Often, though not necessarily always, continuing equity doldrums, as in the 2000–2004 period, lead to a corporate bond market rally prompting a shift towards riskier assets. This is evidenced by tightening of *credit spreads* – the premium of corporate bonds over government bonds (see Chapter 3).

With investors rushing to buy debt instruments, concerns about equity markets and their relationship to credit spreads are forgotten – particularly so if there is an imbalance of supply and demand for new issues. In mid-2004, for instance, corporate issuance was running at a level of 40% below the levels of mid-2003, as companies have focused on:

- Reducing debt, and
- Cutting down capital expenditure.

Because credit rating is based on both quantitative analysis and judgmental factors, it is part of rating agencies' responsibilities to identify the assumptions underlying their analysis, and document the results of their review in arriving at opinions about credit grades. Part and parcel of such documentation are the reasons why they may stop covering a company. Furthermore, it is useful to obtain a self-assessment of rating agencies' performance.

It is appropriate to add that factual and documented credit rating by independent agencies is the cornerstone to the new capital adequacy framework (Basel II) by the Basel Committee on Banking Supervision. Many institutions, particularly big banks, say that they have their own credit rating system and don't need the independent agencies. This however forgets:

- The advantages presented by a global credit rating system
- The fact that in a globalized economy the probability of default should also be universally defined, and
- That transparent universal credit rating is indispensable for investors in appreciating whether the pattern of default is improving or deteriorating.

Banks typically keep their credit information close to their chest. By contrast, rating agencies make it public. This speaks volumes about the contribution of independent agencies to the control of credit risk in a globalized economy. And let us not forget that if investors are not able to know about an entity's and issue's creditworthiness, then they should not put any money in it.

12.3   Main players in credit rating in the global market

Of an estimated 140 independent credit rating agencies in the global market, only four stand out: Standard & Poor's, Moody's Investors Service, Fitch Ratings, A.M. Best and Dominion Bond Rating Service. Each has built a reputation by providing widely quoted ratings. Moody's and S&P are by far the largest rating firms; Fitch is the third largest. A.M. Best operates principally in the United States and focuses almost exclusively on the insurance sector.

The relative standing of the four companies in market share is shown in Table 11.2. Notice, however, that these figures are approximate and they can change significantly by industry sector, for instance in the case of insurance companies. Typically, many entities and issues are rated by more than one agency.

The eldest on record, Poor's Publishing, was established in 1860. In 1941 it merged with Standard Statistics to form Standard & Poor's, now a division of McGraw-Hill. Time-wise, the second on record is A.M. Best. It was incorporated in 1899, as

Table 12.2 Approximate market share of the four main independent rating agencies

	Global share	Insurance industry share
Standard & Poor's	40	30
Moody's	40	17
Fitch	14	7
A.M. Best	4	44
Other	2	2

Source: Statistics from Sigma, No. 4, 2003

specializing in information (and later in rating) for the insurance industry. Moody's Investors Service was first established in 1900, ceased to exist during the US market crash of 1907, and restarted operations in 1909.

Statistics has been a major aspect of the work of these firms as, at their beginning, they started as publishers of financial data. Other independent rating agencies came much later. IBCA was incorporated in 1978. In 1997 it merged with Fitch. Fitch Ratings is controlled by Fimalac, a French-capital holding. Other companies in the same holding are Duff & Phelps, Core Rating, specializing on corporate governance, and Thomson Bank Watch.

For reasons explained in section 2, during the last two decades of the 20th century, independent rating agencies have assumed increasing importance in rating companies and debt. The new capital adequacy framework by the Basel Committee specifies that independent rating of creditworthiness is very important in capital allocation for credit risk. In fact many banks are now revamping their own credit rating system on the range of the thresholds featured by independent agencies.

By contrast, the US Congress raised concerns about credit rating agencies after the bankruptcy of Enron in December 2001, saying the agencies only reduced investment-grade ratings on the Houston energy-trading company's debt a few days before Enron went out of existence. As a result of these concerns, a corporate-reform bill adopted in July 2002 ordered the US Securities and Exchange Commission to issue a report on rating agencies, focusing on areas such as:

- Possible conflicts of interest, and
- Monopolistic barriers to entry by competitors.

Similar concerns exist in the European Union. Mid-2004, investors, bond issuers, and banks approached the Committee of European Securities Regulators (CESR), which is assessing the need for legislation on the credit rating industry, expressing concerns about:

- Transparency,
- Conflicts of interest, and
- Treatment of non-public information within the industry.

The basis of their arguments has been that credit agencies should put in place policies and procedures to manage inherent conflicts of interest in their individual business models. The European Banking Federation (FBE) said that agencies should disclose whether ratings are solicited or unsolicited, as unsolicited ratings are based solely on publicly available information. This argument, however, forgets that unsolicited ratings have a greater independence of opinion[B].

But while bond market participants have been calling for changes in the way credit rating agencies operate, they also strongly opposed demands to introduce a legal framework to govern the industry – which is an even more pressing need. 'Legislation is not the appropriate route in this regard,' said the FBE. 'Self-regulation through an international code of conduct would establish a well-functioning balance between the different interests of rating agencies, investors and issuers.'[3] This thesis is weak, because regulation of the so far unregulated bond market is definitely necessary – and credit rating is part of it.

For their part, credit agencies including Standard & Poor's, Fitch Ratings, and Moody's Investors Service, are opposed to regulatory interference. They, too, prefer a system of self-regulation. The agencies are pointing out that they have already met many of the new demands from investors and issuers. Critics, however, say that the basic issue of facilitating the entry of new credit rating agencies into the market is still unanswered.

According to other market observers, one of the basic problems for would-be rating agencies is that the designation of a nationally recognized statistical rating organization has not been formally defined, so that everybody really knows:

- What it means to be such an outfit,
- What it takes to become one, and
- Which may be the formal appeals process for firms working on credit rating that are denied recognition.

At a day-long meeting at the SEC mid-November 2002, regulators acknowledged that designations of nationally recognized statistical rating organizations seem to limit the number of credit-rating agencies, and may be a barrier for entry by newcomers. Mid-November 2002, the Securities and Exchange Commission began hearings on the part played by credit rating agencies in capital markets and their role in the meltdown of the energy trading sector. Other issues, too, did not escape scrutiny.

Institutional investors and corporate-bond issuers, participating at the aforementioned SEC meeting, endorsed changes that would raise the number of rating agencies, and could shed more light on how credit analysts develop ratings. 'We would definitely advocate more NRSROs,' said Deborah Cunningham, of Pittsburgh-based Federated Investors. But in the opinion of Frank Fernandez, of Securities Industry Association, building a credit-rating business takes time, talent, and money, and it is not clear whether investors want a panoply of ratings rather than reliance on a few proven providers.[4]

For their part, rating agencies have been busy in restructuring their credit evaluation process, and in refining their method. Part and parcel of this effort is the need to address new types of credit risk, including hidden ones. The measures being taken include:

- Seeking additional disclosure, and
- Revising the way analysis of a business is incorporated in the consolidated rating of a parent.

At root, the rating methodologies of the main credit rating firms share many common features (see section 12.6). Each uses qualitative and quantitative information, employs both proprietary and public data, has a capital adequacy model, and assigns ratings through a committee process. The accuracy of these ratings is often judged through:

- Their ability to predict defaults, and
- Their contribution in documenting a pattern of credit spreads.

Credit spreads are correlated with ratings[C], a process reflecting the fact that debt ratings are useful predictors of default. In fact, it is precisely for this reason that regulators have increasingly incorporated reference to credit ratings in their rules regarding an entity's financial staying power.

The ability to prognosticate financial failure is assisted by the fact that, in the evaluation of debt and of creditworthiness, ratings are instrumental in defining a contractual *rating trigger*. This is a special cancellation clause that allows one party to take protective action if the credit rating of its counterparty falls below a predetermined threshold. Use of the trigger acts as feedback to the rating process.

Notice, however, that this is not a novelty that has come with rating. *Financial triggers* are fairly common in the corporate world. They are essentially credit-protection devices. Also present are product-related triggers, such as those embedded in insurance policies in association with financial ratings.

Experts say that while rating triggers are quite helpful as alarms on creditworthiness, they can also backfire. For instance, investors who believe they are protected by a rating trigger in a contract, might discover that its presence has caused insolvency or a default that harms all creditors including themselves.

Because of this concern, Moody's investigated the use of rating triggers by US insurance companies, and European companies in general. What it found is that although insurers use rating triggers extensively, the triggers pose few immediate risks – and, thereafter, the concerns of some of the experts do not seem to be documented.

This and other studies, however, have brought home the fact that not only independent rating agencies but also banks in their credit rating efforts must be very careful in factoring in the volatility of income streams – particularly those that are unregulated – as well as some companies' propensity for expanding far too fast. Since Enron's bankruptcy, regulators have uncovered deceptive trades, designed to inflate volumes and profits.

A good deal of doubt has been placed on some companies supposedly using marking to market accounting, but in reality employing creative accounting practices that credit up-front the value of a future contract. The *prepays* engineered by Enron with the complicity of major banks provide an example.[5]

All players in credit rating – whether independent agencies or the banks themselves – should be on their guard about possible deceptive practices and the ability of some companies to steadily invent new creative accounting gimmicks. Both quantitative and qualitative evaluations are necessary, which take into account the entity, its instruments, risk management policies, modeling procedures, financial reporting practices, compliance with regulatory disclosure requirements, observance of established accounting standards, and quality of corporate governance.

12.4 Credit assessment, credit monitoring, and asymmetry of information

A credit rating system is not just grades and thresholds. As the Basel Committee aptly suggests, it comprises all methods, processes, and controls, including data collection, data mining, and other information technology supports vital to the assessment of credit risk, and to the dynamic upkeep of grades. As it should be recalled, these grades are individual, pertaining to every rated entity or issue. Therefore, Basel says that to qualify an internal rating-based (IRB) solution must have two distinct dimensions along a dual frame of reference:

■ Both individually, and by class
■ Both in a quantitative, and in a qualitative sense.

Basel says that to qualify, an internal ratings-based solution must address risk of borrower default and transaction-specific factors influencing creditworthiness. As we will see in Chapter 15, accuracy and precision in credit rating can be significantly improved by working in parallel on financial and business data.

Typically, though not always, financial data is objective. Objectiveness presupposes that the entity's reporting practices are trustworthy. By contrast, business information is largely subjective, based on the opinion of credit analysts or examiners, senior management meetings, and non-quantifiable other factors.

One of the problems with analytics, and data streams at large, is the existence of an asymmetry of information, particularly in the domain of debtors and potential lenders. Regardless of whether the relationship involves bank lending or bonds sold in the capital market to investors, the lender bears a default risk but does not participate in the profits.

■ Debtors are sometimes tempted to provide misleading information on risks and profitability,
■ Actually many of them are carrying more high-risk projects than they admit to their bank or to the rating agency.

The problem lenders face is that if they have incomplete information, this can lead to adverse selection of counterparties. There is also moral hazard, should the creditors not be able to monitor the use of credit granted, and funds are diverted by borrowers to projects and uses other than those stated – without the bank or the investor knowing it. This is integral part of exposure assumed with the democratization of lending (see Chapter 1).

Similar problems connected to asymmetry of information also face independent rating agencies, as well as certified public accountants (CPAs, chartered accountants) in their external auditing functions. While the majority of these entities do a commendable job, they can only have access to the information the rated (or audited) company provides.[6]

Another interesting lesson from real life is that asymmetric information tends to decrease in inverse proportion to the size of the firm. Major listed public companies, particularly those of settled industries considered as 'blue chips', have stricter internal requirements for published financial data, which make it possible to look into the state of their finances with somewhat greater accuracy.

At the same time, however, the cost of credit assessment is largely independent of the firm's size, which means such cost has a greater impact, in relative terms, on smaller companies. Furthermore, the legal form of financial disclosure, and associated penalties for misinformation or lack of them, place limits on the scope and depth of credit rating – and therefore on capital market-based financing.

Correct and careful credit assessment of a company's or debt instrument's creditworthiness is important because its absence can lead to adverse selection problems by investors. Furthermore, steady monitoring must assure that a given rating continues to be the actual case. Just like bank lending, lending by the capital market through purchase of bonds presupposes the availability of sufficient information for credit assessment as well as continuous monitoring. In a sense, this is a process underpinning *market discipline*, which should be based on:

- Reliable financial reporting, and
- Greater transparency than so far available.

Credit rating can never be based on rumors. When reliable information prerequisites exist, tapping the capital is a rewarding option for those companies that have a good reputation as borrowers. But they must renew this reputation through reliable financial reports and by means of greater transparency.

When the outlined stipulations are in place, long-term credit rating is meaningful, and AA really means high quality, through one to three notches below AAA (depending on whether the rating is AA+, AA, or AA−). Table 12.3 shows the rating scales used by the main independent agencies. Notice the distinction between investment grade and speculative grade ratings.

Table 12.3 Long-term debt rating by Moody's, S&P and Fitch IBCA

S&P and other agencies	Moody's	Credit message
Investment grade		
AAA	Aaa	Very high quality
AA+	Aa1	
AA	Aa2	High quality
AA−	Aa3	
A+	A1	
A	A2	Good payment ability
A−	A3	
BBB+	Baa1	
BBB	Baa2	Adequate payment ability
BBB−	Baa3	
Speculative grade (non-investment)		
BB+	Ba1	
BB	Ba2	Uncertainty in payment ability
BB−	Ba3	
B+	B1	
B	B2	Higher risk investing
B−	B3	
CCC+	Caa1	
CCC	Caa2	Vulnerability to default
CCC−	Caa3	
CC		
C	Ca-C	Bankruptcy likelihood or other major shortcoming
	Da[a]	

[a]Fitch Ratings further distinguishes between DDD, DD, and D.

It is advisable to keep in perspective that when an independent agency rates a company AA+, this does not mean that the entity in reference could not be AAA or AA. But, as shown in Figure 2, the likelihood of AAA is very low; and the same is true of the possibility of AA.

A similar principle exists in rating students in a school, say in a scale from 0 to 4, with 4 being the best. The grade for a good student may revolve around 3.0 as a median, but might go up to nearly 4.0 or down to 2.5 reflecting a certain uncertainty in evaluating the student's performance. In the same way, the grade of an excellent student reaches 4 as an upper limit but starts at 3.5, or so, as a lower limit.

In Figure 12.2, the triangles defining the AA− to AAA range overlap. This is intentional, to reflect the uncertainty inherent in grading – particularly at the lower level of the possibility function, which is the ordinate of the diagram. In essence, the graph in this figure maps the *fuzzy sets* reflecting grades of creditworthiness.

- The overlap reflects the uncertainty that exists in all grading, and
- This quantitative presentation incorporates subjective judgment, such as, for instance, more than, about equal, or less than.

It is appropriate to notice that, contrary to appearances, this graph helps to 'defuzz' what is essentially a rather subjective appreciation – which is a problem inherent in all grading, evidently including that of creditworthiness of entities and instruments. There is no way to assign a crisp score, but there are ways to defuzz the fuzzy characteristics of at least particularly subjective judgments, as this example documents.

Defuzzing is done by evaluators of creditworthiness who use as a background for their opinion an assigned score. If an entity's rating, for example, is AA+, one

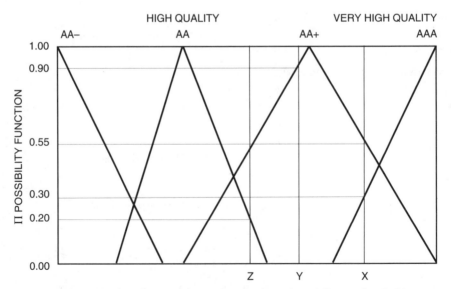

Figure 12.2 Defuzzifying creditworthiness along four different thresholds

evaluator – indicated as X in Figure 12.2 – may say that the company in reference is, in his or her opinion, 'better than AA+ but not quite AAA'. In this example, such a statement would mean that it is 30% AAA and 55% AA+. (In possibility theory the sum of likelihoods may be less than, equal to, or more than 1.)

For evaluator Y, this same entity is nearly AA+; while for Z, it stands between AA+ and AA. These three opinions as to the entity's creditworthiness differ, but not by so much as they all revolve around AA+. In other cases the differences in opinions might be much larger. This is only normal. After all, difference of opinion is what makes the market.

12.5 The process of bond rating

As we have seen in Table 12.3, the rating of bonds bifurcates into two main classes: *investment grade*, which includes ratings from AAA to BBB; and *non-investment grade*, in which are lumped all other grades, from BB to C and D. Instruments rated AAA, the best quality, carry a very low degree of investment risk and are generally referred to as gilt-edged. Characteristically,

■ Interest payments are protected by a stable margin, and
■ The investor's principal is generally secure.

Bonds rated AA are judged to be of high quality and together with the AAA they constitute what are generally known as high-grade bonds. AA+, AA, and AA− debt instruments are rated lower than the best bonds because margins of protection may be somewhat less than with AAA securities.

Fixed income instruments rated A have many favorable investment attributes, being considered as upper-to-medium grade obligations. The security they provide to principal and interest is considered adequate, but certain elements may be present which suggest the possibility of impairment some time in the future. Therefore, investors must be careful and vigilant.

The lower grade of investment level bonds is rated BBB with BBB− the last threshold. These are considered as medium-grade obligations: they are neither highly protected, nor poorly secured in terms of principal and interest payments. Even BBB− appears adequate for the present, but certain elements are viewed as unreliable over a greater length of time, and there is always the risk of downgrading to junk status (see Chapter 4).

Still, as a mid-2003 Merrill Lynch report had it, in the United States around 45% of the investment grade fixed income market is BBB−, or one step away from falling into junk status. In the medium-term, the broker says, corporations are more likely to be managed for cash and for the debtholder than for the equity-holder. Hybrid securities that offer an attractive coupon and equity participation may also be an area that would benefit in a 'lower for longer rate' environment.[7]

This loading near the bottom of the investment grade scale is a recent phenomenon. The distribution of new offerings in debt instruments in the United States has significantly changed since the late 1980s. Table 12.4 shows 15 years of evolution in a share of the market by four different grades of creditworthiness: AAA, AA, A, BBB.

Table 12.4 The change in creditworthiness in rated bond issues in the United States, 1988–2002

	1988	1991	1994	1997	2000	2001	2002
AAA	17	10	5	5	3	4	4
AA	30	17	16	15	13	14	14
A	31	48	47	47	51	41	37
BBB	22	25	32	32	33	41	45

Source: Statistics by Merrill Lynch

From the start of the period under consideration till 2000, statistics document that the most frequently issued bonds had A rating, but

- In 2001 the A and BBB frequencies were at par, and
- In 2002 the A ratings had been overtaken by BBB.

A threshold below BBB−, of course, are bonds that are rated BB+, and are judged as having speculative elements in their creditworthiness. Their future cannot be considered well assured: the protection of principal and interest payments may well be below moderate, with uncertainty of position characterizing their class – which is essentially that of junk bonds.

Creditworthiness is even worse with bonds rated B. They generally lack characteristics of a desirable investment, and the investor has no assurance of payments and interest. The maintenance of other terms of the contract, like covenants, is also questionable. This is particularly true over longer periods of time.

Investors should not take lightly the likelihood of bond defaults, which rise significantly during adverse economic and financial conditions. As shown in Figure 12.3, both in the United States and in the rest of the world this has happened twice during the past 20 years: in the early 1990s and in the 2000–2003 timeframe.

Defaults and insolvencies shown in these statistics include inability to meet interest payments and capital repayments. The percentages in the ordinate indicate number of issuers affected in proportion to all issuers with a credit rating. This percentage is, of course, higher in lower rating thresholds, particularly junk bond levels.

Below the BB− level is B rating, followed by CCC rating. These are bonds of very poor standing. Their issuers may be not far from default, and they may also present other dangers to principal and interest. Even worse are bonds rated C, the lowest rated class of fixed income instruments. Only speculators would buy B or worse-rated debt, in the hope of the issuer's turnaround followed by the instrument's significant appreciation. This sometimes happens with sovereign debt.

Credit ratings may be upgraded, as a company's fundamentals improve, but the risk of downgrading is typically higher than the probability of upgrading. Based on European statistics from the 1990 to 2003 timeframe, in a percent basis, the number of upgrades compared to the number of downgrades, tends to vary between:

- 20% under conditions of deteriorating credit quality, and
- Nearly 60% when the economy is strong and credit quality generally improves.[8]

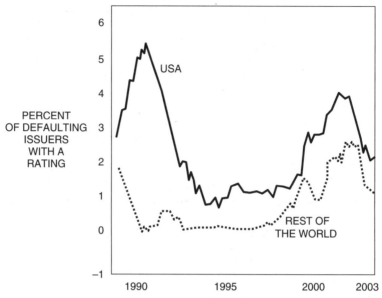

Figure 12.3 Defaults and insolvency by bond issuers (monthly average over 12 months). (*Source:* Statistics by Deutsche Bundesbank, Monthly Report, December 2003)

In a way fairly similar to European statistics, in the United States, too, there are noticeable fluctuations in the ratio of downgrades to upgrades. Usually the number of downgrades in periods of economic slowdown tends to be higher, while at the top of the economic cycle, upgrades tend to rise but they rarely if ever exceed downgrades.

Internationally, too, credit downgrading is more likely than upgrading, across nearly all rating categories. This reflects a selection process which sees to it that many otherwise sound companies that issue bonds after they are given a good rating by the agencies find obstacles in their way and run into troubled waters.

The cost of downgrading can be significant both to the bondholder and to the entity itself. Apart from the growing risk of default which may hit the principal (see section 12.7), bondholders end by earning less than the actual interest rate of the bond following downgrade of the issuer. Usually, after a downgrade:

- The cost of the lesser entity's debt instruments falls, and
- There is a corresponding rise in the yield of the fixed interest rate bond.

Take Ericsson as an example of the cost of the issuing entity's downgrade. In late July 2002, following significant financial losses, Ericsson's credit rating was cut to junk status, in a move that threatened the Swedish telecommunications equipment maker's plans for a heavily discounted SKR 30 billion (US$3.2 billion) rights issue. Ericsson said the financial impact of that decision would lead to an increase in the company's financing costs by about SKR 101 million ($10.2 million) a year, which is the cost of a one-notch downgrade from BBB− to BB+.

Companies whose securitized debt is at the brink of junk status sometimes add covenants that stipulate a statutory compensating higher yield. This is a good example of compensation demanded by investors to buy such bonds. Ratings are not made just for curiosity or scientific reasons related to thresholds in creditworthiness:

- Credit ratings are practical instruments, and
- If they are not always 'correct', they are better than having no compass at all in one's investments.

Also significant in terms of information regarding creditworthiness of debt instruments are statistics regarding the rating of new bond issues. Such statistics vary from one country to the next, but the way to bet is that all issuers try to obtain a higher rating than their debt justifies. For instance, they target A or better, by sugar-coating their offer to the market. By means of:

- Offering some collateral,
- Having a guarantor, or
- Retaining the worst tranche of the security.

There are also an amount of bonds, usually less than 10% of total issues, which are unrated. This does not necessarily mean that they are poor quality. Some issuers don't like to pay for credit rating, but without a dependable source evaluating the creditworthiness of issuer and issue, the investor is in uncharted waters.

Many companies are capitalizing on the investor's fear of the unknown in an effort to promote their debt instruments even if the rating is low. Sometimes, this bears fruits. For instance, since the mid-1980s when junk bonds were aggressively pushed in the capital market, the pace of their sales has increased. In early 2004, in the Euro area, the volume of non-investment grade bonds amounted to around 50 billion euro, which is 500% more than at the beginning of monetary union on 1 January 2002.

Particularly in Europe, the telecommunications sector has initially been the dominant force in non-investment-grade securities. At the end of 1999, it roughly held a 50% share of the European market for junk bonds. Subsequently, however, consolidation in the technology sector and the increasing involvement of companies from other industrial sectors has seen to it that by the beginning of 2004 the telecoms share in junk bond issues fell to about 7%.

12.6   A frame of reference for loans quality and creditworthiness

The discussion in sections 12.2 to 12.5 has primarily focused on rating agencies and their thresholds in creditworthiness, but banks also have a system for evaluating credit risk, which uses scores for loans quality. The following is a practical example of 14 rules for establishing and using an internal grading system at the level of a credit institution.

Rule number 1 in bank loans has been to *look for guarantees*, particularly by the state or other sources with a stronger financial position than the borrower. If such guarantees are not explicit, rule number 2 says *ask for collateral*, but accurately evaluate its worth. In this connection, the use of fuzzy engineering along the lines of the example shown in section 12.4 and Figure 12.2 is recommended.

In an economy that is highly dynamic, it is wrong to look at collateral in a static way, for instance evaluating it one-tantum and applying a *haircut*. Not only do the prices of securities given by the borrower change all the time, but also changing is the financial condition of entities whose equity is reflected in the collateral. Therefore:

- The calculation of collateral's value, and its update, should account for both these variables, and
- This value should be based on marking to market analysis of financial and business data regarding the borrower.

On these two premises, rule number 3 is to carefully study the counterparty's *balance sheet* (B/S), including footnotes. Ideally, this should be done over a period of 20 years of financial statements, with 10 years a minimum. The P&L (*income statement*) should be examined over the same timeframe.

Because many borrowers use the money to gamble in derivative financial instruments, B/S and P&L analysis are no longer enough. A self-respecting lender should *analyze the total recognized gains and losses* (STRGL) of the borrower. This is what regulators now require credit institutions to report – and the majority of inputs in this financial statement are marked to market (see Statement of Financial Accounting Standards 136 in the United States). This is rule number 4 in the panoply of credit analysis by the lender.

Because intrinsic value is so important in judging a company's worth, rule number 5 is to carefully *evaluate the borrower's cash flow* – followed by number 6, *perform the acid test*, as well as examine medium range assets and liabilities. Among other things the acid test provides a linkage between short-term and longer-term lending rates.

Both credit institutions and rating agencies have a classification of creditworthiness associated to short-term debt ratings. The best grade is known as prime rate[9] and it expresses the ability of issuers to service punctually senior debt obligations, which have an original maturity of less than one year. Among such obligations are:

- Commercial paper
- Bank deposits
- Bankers' acceptances (see Chapter 11), and
- Obligations to deliver foreign exchange.

A simple algorithm shown in Appendix 12.A provides the relation between prime rate, higher-up rates, and acid tests. Moreover, other things being equal, a leveraged company has higher risk of going under. Therefore, rule number 7 advises *calculate the leverage of equity*. The equity to loans ratio has become a very important criterion, as proxy for equity should be taking the company's market capitalization, while liabilities are carried at book value. This is essentially a *solvency* ratio.

- A company is solvent when its *assets*, priced at fair value, exceed its liabilities.
- The best way of marking to market a company's assets is its *capitalization* which is equal to the price of its shares multiplied by the outstanding common stock.

Liquidity should not be confused with solvency, though there are cases where it is difficult to distinguish illiquidity from insolvency. There is also the fact that illiquidity can lead to insolvency, or to the need to put on the block certain assets at a fire sales price. All this should be taken into account in loan management.

Another important rule, number 8, is that of studying the counterparty's history of past loans, and the way the entity has faced up to its obligations – including delays, restructurings, and defaults. Loans are not, of course, the only frame of reference, and rule No. 9 advises to *analyze the market's reaction to company offerings* – bonds, preferred stock, common stock, as well as how well the underwriters have done.

This leads to another market-oriented variable, and the No. 10 rule: *examine the company's market appeal*, including products and share of market. Has the company an established policy in product innovation, and steady upgrade of current product line? What's the long range strategic plan (see Chapter 11)? Where will the money come from to pay the interest and repay the loan?

Two more rules, numbers 11 and 12, look into the way the company is managed. The first of the two advises study of the level of *productivity* and, most particularly, its *overhead*. In well-managed companies the overhead is low. The second, prompts examination of the policy of *employee relations* – and current practices associated to it. Strikes can kill a company, as Alitalia and so many other flag airlines have found out the hard way.

Last, but not least, rule number 13 says that loans officers and the loans committee must *make sure they understand the quality of the borrower's management* – past, current, and upcoming. This can be done through personal meetings with the CEO, CFO, Chief Technology Officer (CTO), and other senior executives, as well as by means of thorough evaluation based on objective criteria like:

- Research program
- Loss reserves
- Risk control
- Solvency margin.

As was discussed at the beginning of this chapter, one of the basic questions in choosing a methodology for credit rating is whether to base oneself on financial information alone or on both quantitative and qualitative information – the latter being subjective and management-oriented. Much can be learned from the way independent rating agencies proceed in their credit evaluation. Table 12.5 presents an example on critical factors used by S&P and Moody's in judging the creditworthiness of insurance companies.

Because the factors to be taken into account are so many, the use of models focusing on estimating the probability of default can help. On the other hand, qualitative analysis can take into account factors that a model cannot – for instance,

Table 12.5 Rating criteria for insurance companies

By Standard & Poor

1 Industry risk
2 Management and corporate strategy
3 Business review
4 Results from underwriting
5 Investment policy and results
6 Interest rate risk management
7 Capitalization
8 Liquidity
9 Capital and capital requirements

By Moody's

1 Competitive situation
2 Regulatory trends
3 Adequacy of equity capital
4 Investment risk
5 Profitability
6 Liquidity
7 Group interrelationships
8 Products and distribution channels
9 Quality of management and organization

circumstances and assessments, which are not easily quantified. In every analysis of creditworthiness, qualitative and quantitative approaches should be made to complement one another.

12.7 Risk-adjusted return on capital

Time and again, the procedure that has been outlined in section 12.6 in regard to evaluation of quality of loans has proved to be an effective management tool. Its objective is that of enabling the user to be in charge of credit risk. Risk-adjusted return on capital (RAROC) can be found at the roots of risk-based pricing of loans – a reason why its practical applications have become a standard throughout the banking industry.

Developed by Bankers Trust in the early to mid-1980s, risk-adjusted return on capital is a good example on an early and successful effort to quantify the creditworthiness of a counterparty, and account for it in loan-pricing decisions. Typically, when a borrower (sovereign, company or individual) goes to a bank for a loan, a binary decision is made: 'Go/No go' or, more precisely, 'Qualify/Not quantify'. By contrast, risk-adjusted approaches are not binary:

- They stratify the borrowers population, and
- Put a premium on pre-established risk threshold.

RAROC targets credit risk through sequential evaluation of the applicant's financial condition. Between 'qualify' and 'not qualify', are one or more 'may be' decision alternatives. If the result of an examination leads to uncertainty, hence 'may be', a new test takes places – and if the borrower qualifies in *that* test, then that borrower will have to pay a higher premium to cover the extra risk. A bird's-eye view of this method is shown in Figure 12.4.

Over time, RAROC became an increasingly sophisticated computer-based assistant to loans decisions, increasingly used in screening and evaluation of requests for funding. The methodology used is sequential sampling for quality control reasons, which dates from the days of the Manhattan Project in the Second World War.

The reason why the scope and frequency of use of this strategic tool have grown over time is found in the fact that it constitutes an objective methodology which makes feasible evaluation of credit risk not just by accepting or refusing a loan – but also by providing a platform for pricing decisions.

Well-managed banks monitor RAROC on a daily basis on their business portfolio and, when necessary, they evaluate some of their more active accounts as frequently as every 15 minutes. Few people who know about RAROC appreciate, however, that a whole cultural and technological infrastructure is necessary to support it.

- The cultural change must be promoted by management, and
- The technological infrastructure must be steadily kept up.

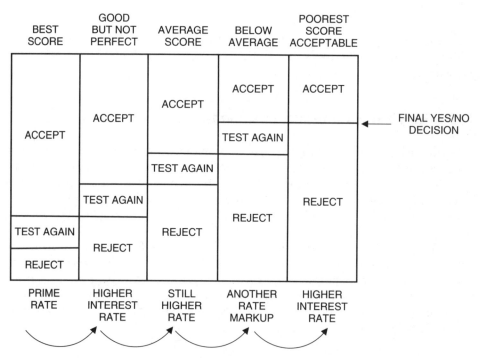

Figure 12.4 A sequential sampling plan avoids inflexible Yes/No decisions by taking a greater risk covered by higher interest rate

For instance, in 1994, some ten years after RAROC's introduction, Bankers Trust thoroughly reorganized its Corporate Risk Management System to monitor risk in general, and RAROC in particular, in *real time* across a broad spectrum of business activities. This solution promoted the bank's ability to implement risk-based pricing on a global scale, with a high degree of timeliness across a variety of product lines. Risk-based pricing has been applied for any counterparty, at any time, anywhere in the world. In the background to this have been:

■ A management policy to steadily improve return for risk being taken, and
■ An efficient restructuring of business operations, based on the bank's own Global Assets Application Architecture (GAAA).

GAAA promoted a model-based real-time risk assessment which aimed to quantify the likelihood of default. The aim has been to enable responsible loans officers to decide in a factual way whether a particular risk is worth running. Both central and distributed risk control operations contributed to this outcome.

■ Within a business line, *local risk management* followed up on exposure at loan officer and trading desk level.
■ Centrally, *global risk management* was charged with developing the proper policy for exposure control, as well as with setting business line limits.

Behind this bifurcation of responsibilities has been the fact that calculated risks covered by premiums – the RAROC way – permit the expansion of lending and securities trading activities. In turn, factual management control permits the further build-up and marketing of a credit institution's financial services. Such policy, however, requires:

■ Continuously enhancing the quality of the bank's screening and pricing processes
■ Developing not only new financial products but also methods to manage their exposure, and
■ Having access to reliable databases that are mined in real time through knowledge artifacts – the only way to be ahead of the curve in possible alerts.[10]

As these points document, not just one factor but many contribute to successful risk control. The reality test is helping management to decide where to draw the line in terms of exposure. An able answer requires that one both quantifies and qualifies the risks taken with *any* counterparty, *any* instrument, *any* market, at *any* time. In information system terms such solution a highlights the need for:

■ Having available online the total committed position of the bank, expanded out to fine detail
■ Sustaining the ability to experiment regarding the after-effects of volatility, liquidity, and maturity, and
■ Interactively performing risk and return evaluations, with no geographic limitations and no time-zone constraints.

Banks are able to take advantage of such methodology if they are already at the frontier of risk measurement, have transaction-tracking capabilities, develop algorithms for calculation of portfolio exposure, and are able to deploy sophisticated performance evaluation. Moreover, top management's policy should see to it that each of the bank's business lines, and foreign subsidiaries, monitors and manages its risk positions, while through real-time processing and reporting it enables central operations to keep overall control.

To perform such a mission in an able manner, the credit institution must also have a comprehensive *common language* for discussing risk – a language that is continually refined with formal definitions underlying the calculation of exposure. This is particularly important in a globalized economy, where professionals of different backgrounds and cultures interact, and the way to bet is that risk and return does not mean the same thing to all of them.

The message the reader should retain from all this is that while the mathematics of RAROC date back to sampling procedures, operating characteristics (OC) curves[11] and statistical tables developed, as has already been stated, in connection with the Second World War atomic bomb project, a bank must also do a lot of *value-added* work in order to reach commendable results.

Value-differentiation in the implementation of RAROC is so important because only an accurate, timely, and steady risk assessment helps to size up dangers so that responsible officers can decide on a documented basis if a particular risk is worth running.

Appendix 12.A   An algorithm linking prime rate, higher up rates, and the acid test

The ratio of current assets (CA) over current liabilities (CL) has been known as the *acid test*. *If* this ratio is negative, *then* the company is insolvent. But positive values don't necessarily mean financial health. The x_i are thresholds by type of company and industry.[12]

$$\text{If } \frac{CA}{CL} \geq x_1, \text{ use } y_1, \text{ the prime rate}$$

$$\text{If } x_1 \geq \frac{CA}{CL} \geq x_2, \text{ use a short-term interest rate equal to } y_1 + e_1$$

where:

CA	= current assets
CL	= current liabilities
CA/CL	= critical ratio, known as acid test
x_1	= CA/CL ratio justifying prime rate
y_1	= prime rate
e_1	= premium to cover insurance for CA/CL less than x_1

This process testing successive thresholds of $x_1, x_2 \ldots x_n$ interest rates can be repeated many times over in a stratified manner. This process can be mapped into an operating characteristics (OC) curve, which helps to distinguish levels of confidence: α (Type I error, producer's risk), and β (Type II error, consumer's risk).

One example of a now-popular process using OC curves is RAROC (see Section 12.7).

Notes

1 D.N. Chorafas, *Economic Capital Allocation with Basel II: Cost and Benefit Analysis*, Butterworth-Heinemann, Oxford and Boston, 2004.
2 D.N. Chorafas, *Economic Capital Allocation with Basel II: Cost and Benefit Analysis*, Butterworth-Heinemann, Oxford and Boston, 2004.
3 *Financial Times*, 7 September 2004.
4 *Wall Street Journal*, 18 November 2002.
5 D.N. Chorafas, *Management Risk: The Bottleneck is at the Top of the Bottle*, Macmillan/Palgrave, London, 2004.
6 In the United States the dependability of financial information has been improved by the Sarbanes–Oxley Act of 2002 which makes the CEO and chief financial officer (CFO) responsible, in a penal sense, for the accuracy of financial statements given to regulators, auditors, and the public. The European Union, too, is contemplating a (watered down) version of Sarbanes–Oxley.
7 Merrill Lynch, *Global Market Strategy*, 25 June 2003.
8 Deutsche Bundesbahn, *Monthly Report*, December 2003.
9 D.N. Chorafas, *Managing Credit Risk*, Volume 1 – *Analyzing, Rating and Pricing the Probability of Default*, Euromoney, London, 2000.
10 D.N. Chorafas, *The Real-time Enterprise*, Auerbach, New York, 2005.
11 D.N. Chorafas, *How to Understand and Use Mathematics for Derivatives*, Volume 2 – *Advanced Modelling Methods*, Euromoney Books, London, 1995.
12 In the United States, Dun and Bradstreet has been publishing industry tables with thresholds at the level of quartiles for several decades.

[A] Until recently, these have been the Nationally Recognized Statistical Rating Organization (NRSRO), by the Securities and Exchange Commission (SEC) which currently has a weak form of supervision over rating agencies. A.M Best and Dominion Bond are recent additions to these three companies. Many other rating agencies that are not NRSRO also exist.
[B] Unsolicited ratings are an interesting case. S&P says that less than 1 percent of its ratings are unsolicited. Moody's note that it discontinued unsolicited ratings 5 years ago (*The Economist*, March 26 2005), however many other independent rating agencies do them.
[C] More precisely, with *point-in-time* ratings rather than through the classical *cycle ratings* of independent rating agencies.

13 Case studies on credit quality

13.1 Introduction

In the late 1970s, which means a generation or so ago, any list of the most important US banks would have included Bankers Trust, Chemical Banking, Manufacturers Hanover, Continental Illinois, First Chicago, Republic of Texas, Seattle First, and many other institutions. All are gone now, merged into other banks, and in some cases the acquirers too have been absorbed by other credit institutions.

Many big US banks ran into problems in the 1970s when they made large loans to Latin American countries, particularly Mexico, Brazil, and Argentina, that had to be restructured in the 1980s. Also many lost a lot of money in commercial real estate and in the oil business at the end of that same decade and in the 1980s. By 1990, a lot of credit institutions were in deep financial difficulty, which resulted in a wave of mergers. The winners have been banks that have maintained their strength – in significant part because they had a solid consumer base.

The case study on the bankruptcy of a financial institution, that of Penn Square presented in section 13.3, is a lesson on how financial staying power disappears when management is no longer in control. Not only credit institutions fade away but also the financial centers of gravity change. Two of the largest US banks, Wachovia and Bank of America, are now based in Charlotte, North Carolina, which was not previously viewed as a major financial center, and institutions based there were simply known as 'regionals'.

Whether we talk of a financial institution or of any other organization, like the industrial and transport organizations whose case studies are included in this chapter, if a company's credit quality deteriorates and its credit rating changes (see Chapter 12), holders of its bonds suffer heavy losses – or at least experience a decrease in the value of their investment. The opposite happens if the entity's creditworthiness improves.

There are different ways to compute the price impact of a rating change. The most popular is to multiply the change in yield between initial and new rating by the modified duration of the bond (see Chapter 10), which expresses the percentage change in price associated with a 100 basis point move in interest rates (see Chapter 7). Usually, this approach employs either:

- The average yield-to-maturity, or
- A call option with adjusted spread, by bond rating class.

Caouette, Altman, and Narayanan mention three other methods for calculating migration in credit rating on a bond's value.[1] One is that of estimating the possible rating change for the forward zero-coupon curve for bonds in the new rating category, whether this is higher or lower than the one at which the debt instrument has been purchased by the investor.

Marking to market by observing price changes of a statistically significant sample of bonds of different rating classes is another approach which helps in analyzing price impact of the issuer's change in rating. One could also use information on rate impact when the independent rating agency first placed the issue (or entity behind it) in its watch list, and made this event known.

Still another alternative is to unbundle observed market spreads of bonds in different credit rating categories. This can help to isolate and identify the impact of expected drift (or surge) in rating, particularly when combined with the corresponding historical aftermath of changes in rating, which has been observed with issuers and/or their debt instruments.

Because some of the methods being used rest on prognostication, it is proper to bring to the reader's attention that unless the information and models employed in the comparison are displayed, the downgrade, upgrade, or default evaluation tools cannot really be compared because results are unverifiable. Notice, as well, that the current regulatory line of Basel II, which is allowing greater use of models for capital adequacy purposes, is that models must be convincing. They must:

- Cover a timeframe that includes different economic cycles, and
- Be transparent in regard to the statistics they are using, prognostications they make, and their algorithms or heuristics.

Moreover, investors should always keep in mind a method's shortcomings. A report published by the Bank of England found that both equity-based and ratings-based approaches to credit risk modeling have serious limitations. In particular, it noted that a 'major problem with credit risk models is that it is extremely difficult to assess the accuracy of the risk measurements they supply'.[2]

While these references are not made to diminish the interest investors, analysts, and bankers should have in the development and use of models, they do suggest that modeling is not everything. Considerable insight can be gained through qualitative approaches displayed by means of real-life case studies, which is the objective of this chapter.

13.2 Large financial institutions and their assets

The prospect of bank failures is one of the key topics discussed at central bank meetings because, among other reasons, of the 'too big to fail' label, which really means too big to be allowed to go bankrupt. Therefore, either explicitly or implicitly taxpayers' money is used by the reserve bank and the government to bail out any big bank which belongs to this 'too big' category and becomes insolvent.

There is a general market feeling that, deposit insurance aside, depositors and creditors of the largest credit institutions are more likely to be protected by government intervention in the event of financial troubles than their counterparts in small banks.

Continental Illinois in the United States, in the 1980s, and Credit Lyonnais in France, in the 1990s, provide examples. By contrast, Penn Square, the case study in section 3, was left to its own devices.

One of the problems during the past couple of decades is that, as the banking industry continues to consolidate, assets held by banks 'too big too fail' expand, and this raises the taxpayers' bill. Opponents to the policy of salvaging bankrupt credit institutions, which makes a mockery of free markets, advocate letting some banks fail if they deserve to do so – even at the risk of some short-term turbulence.

According to the view of free market advocates, this is the only means of eliminating the general perception that large banks will receive special treatment if they become troubled. Bank bailouts have many hazards, and the ongoing discussion is in which case the risks are greater: in the failure side, or in the salvage. Central bankers fear widespread bank failures will trigger a crisis that will destroy the global financial fabric. Opponents to bailouts through government money point out that they constitute a moral hazard because they are:

■ Increasing the risk appetite of bank management, and
■ Reducing its professionality in keeping exposure under control.

The common thread which runs through bank failures is that of superleveraging. High risk appetite is satisfied through high gearing by means of debt; overexposure to derivative financial instruments; huge loans concentrated to one industry, like real estate or oil exploration; and other types of speculation. This financial irresponsibility is leading to disaster.

Size and risk appetite tend to correlate. Mergers and acquisitions (M&A) have a significant role to play in a market economy (other than filling the coffers of investment banks), but as one of my professors at UCLA taught his students: 'Growth for growth's sake is the philosophy of the cancer cell.' Which is the size of an institution that might be considered optimal? There is no answer to this query. But there is an answer to the question on whether two fragile credit institutions could create a strong one by merging. The answer is that they don't.

In December 2003, *Business Week* published an eye-opening critique of suitors to Germany's Commerzbank, the country's third largest but a wounded credit institution about which merger talks are 'on-again, off-again'. In the background was the fact that on 12 November Commerzbank had announced it had written off the value of its holdings in a string of companies. The bill of this write-off was $2.7 billion and the bank planned to issue 53.3 million new shares to buttress its core capital.

Chairman Klaus-Peter Müller's explanation has been that Commerzbank was cleaning up its $460 billion balance sheet so it would be in a position to return to profitability. But is was clear to analysts that Commerzbank, which reported a net loss of $2.6 billion for the three months ended 30 September 2003, was likely to lose $2.3 billion for the year and, was putting itself on the auction block. Within that perspective, here is what *Business Week* had to say about five of the suitors:[3]

■ HypoVereinsbank: large but troubled Munich bank which is keen to expand.
■ Citigroup, already has a successful German operation; it would also like to expand.

- Credit Suisse, declared earlier in 2003 that it wants to buy a German bank.
- Royal Bank of Scotland, wants to build its credit card and personal loan business in Germany.
- BNP-Paribas, says it is interested in a German acquisition to give it a wider Euroland base.[4]

This wave of merger is what has happened in the United States since the 1980s. In the process it wiped out some of the better-known brand names in American banking, and it created mammoth organizations which, by any standard, are 'too big to fail'. On top of this comes the issue of rapid inflation in asset prices.

In 1985, Citicorp was the biggest bank in America, with $174 billion in assets. At that time, the top 10 US banks had just $775 billion in combined assets. In 2004 Citicorp has $1.26 trillion in assets, nearly a 725% increase, and the top 10 banks have a combined $4.7 trillion in assets, an increase of 606%.

Through its merger with Travelers insurance, Citi seems to have grown faster than its peers in the original 1985 top 10. This is, however, the wrong conclusion for the reason that of all individual credit institutions in that list only Citicorp, reborn as Citigroup, and Chemical Banking, renamed JP Morgan Chase, have survived as independent entities. Here is the 1985 top 10 list, in order of importance:

- Citigroup
- BankAmerica
- Chase Manhattan
- Manufacturers Hanover
- JP Morgan
- Chemical Banking
- Security Pacific
- Bankers Trust
- First Interstate
- First Chicago

BankAmerica bought Seattle First, Continental Illinois, and Security Pacific, but then itself was bought by the Nation's Bank (former North Carolina National Bank) which adopted the Bank of America trademark. In 2004, in a drive to create a still bigger institution, Bank of America bought Fleet Boston, which was the result of other mergers, mainly in New England.

From the banks in the 1985 top 10, Chemical Banking bought Manufacturers Hanover, then Chase Manhattan, but retained the Chase brand – and subsequently Chase bought JP Morgan to become JP Morgan Chase. Bankers Trust was bought by Deutsche Bank, and the label disappeared. First Interstate and First Chicago were bought by Bank One (which is not in the 1985 list), but in 2004 Bank One fell to JP Morgan Chase.

This same process of concentration in the financial industry has occurred on a global scale, where many of the banks which topped the list in 1985 have disappeared into others. More than anywhere else this is true in Japan, where already huge credit institutions, but not far from bankruptcy, have been merged into even larger but not-that-stable financial giants.

The Mitsubishi Bank took over Bank of Tokyo to form Tokyo–Mitsubishi; Sumitomo and Mitsui formed SumitomoMitsui Financial; Dai-Ichi Kangyo Bank, Fuji Bank, and Industrial Bank of Japan merged into Mizuho, the largest of the Japanese giants; and the labels of other Japanese city banks went up in smoke through more mergers, like the UFJ Holdings Group.

As a list published by *Forbes* in 2003 brought to its reader's attention that financial giants (some of which have feet of clay) dominate the corporate world on a global scale. In 2003, of the top 50 companies in the world, ranked by assets, all but three have been banks, insurance companies or other financial entities. The three that are not – General Electric, General Motors, and Ford – are non-bank banks, greatly depending on their large financial arms which account for significant percentages of their assets.

Notice that also included in this *Forbes* list are Fannie Mae, in third position, and Freddie Mac in thirteenth. Both are highly troubled financial institutions, overexposed in securitized mortgages and other derivatives. This is also true of a significant number of other banks and non-banks in the *Forbes* top 50 list. One way to appreciate the shock wave if any one of these giants were to fall down is to take the Penn Square failure and multiply is by 1000 or more.

13.3   Bank failures: the case of Penn Square

In 1982 the failure of the relatively small bank, Penn Square of Oklahoma City, which had about $190 million in uninsured deposits, caused large losses at credit institutions across the United States. Notable has been the loss of up to $240 million for Continental Illinois, which went bankrupt. That year was not the best for the US banking industry:

- Penn Square was the twenty-first US bank to close in 1982, and
- The majority of failed banks were absorbed by healthier credit institutions in government-arranged transactions.

Penn Square is an interesting case study on both the positive and negative side of leveraging. As the result of highly aggressive lending practices, this credit institution grew from a $30 million consumer-oriented bank, when it was taken over by Bill P. Jennings in 1976, into a $470 million entity when it crashed, six years down the line.

Even $470 million, however, is small in terms of deposits. Yet, Penn Square was highly aggressive in lending to the oil and gas industry. It also sold more than $2 billion of its loans to other banks across the country. This is one of the best examples on the potentially disastrous results of loan gearing and debt trading – which is today done through credit derivatives[5] and credit swaps.

As will be recalled, 1982 was a year of high inflation, in the aftermath of two oil shocks of the 1970s, and of stagnation. With the energy business in a recession, it became questionable whether many of these Penn Square loans to independent oil and gas developers could be repaid.

- Federal officials said, at the time, the bank's weakness was due to a large volume of problem loans.
- Banking sources raised questions as to whether some of the collateral that the bank had said was behind some of the loans was actually there.

As a result of its relationship with Penn Square, Continental Illinois of Chicago, the sixth largest US banking corporation in the early 1980s, announced that it would show a loss – but in the first installment of its announcement it declined to say how large the loss from its activities with Penn Square might be. The $240 million tag, which spoke volumes about the Chicago bank's exposure, was put on by financial analysts a little later on.

Continental was reported to have invested about $1.2 billion in energy-related loans developed by Penn Square. In addition, banking sources suggested that Continental had made direct loans to the Oklahoma bank, which amounts to a double exposure and reflects negatively on the credit institution's professionality:

- Buying Penn Square's oil and gas loans, and
- Making new loans to the same counterparty so that it could make even more loans to oil and gas enterprises.

With red ink running like a torrent, the Oklahoma bank was up for sale. While many credit institutions had engaged in transactions with Penn Square that were not too different from those of Continental, because they were not certain how large its total liabilities and losses were, none was willing to acquire it. Therefore, for the third time in its history, the FDIC established a special bank, Deposit Insurance National Bank (which opened on 7 July 1982, in Penn Square's offices) to facilitate the refunding of deposits.

Deposit insurance, however, covers up to $100 000 in deposits, not hundreds of millions in bank-to-bank loans. Continental Illinois was not alone in its troubled relationship with Penn Square. In terms of losses it was followed by Seafirst of Seattle, the biggest banking organization in Washington state, which had invested about $400 million in loans developed by Penn Square.

Among other big US banks that were involved with Penn Square were Chase Manhattan, Northern Trust, and Michigan National Bank. Chase Manhattan Bank was reported to have invested about $250 million in energy loans generated by Penn Square. Moreover, mid-May 1982, Chase Manhattan had already lost an estimated $270 million as a result of its dealings with Drysdale Government Securities, an obscure firm that was shunned by most other large banks.

Northern Trust (now Wells Fargo, after its acquisition of nearly bankrupt Wells Fargo) was at the time the fourth-largest bank in Chicago. In 1982 it reported that it had invested about $125 million in a similar pattern of unwise Penn Square loans, which had been identified as the problem behind the red ink.

The Michigan National Bank was reported to have invested nearly $200 million in loans generated by Penn Square. In addition to the large out-of-state banks, about 30 credit institutions in the State of Oklahoma itself were reported to have invested in loans generated by Penn Square, and their wounds had to bleed.

The way it was reported at the time, there had been disagreements among the federal bank regulators – the FDIC, Comptroller of the Currency (OCC), which regulates federally chartered banks, and Federal Reserve Board – over how to handle the Penn Square problem. These disagreements are a good example of the dilemma facing regulators on whether to allow good money to run after bad.

The Fed and the OCC seem to have opposed closing the bank, but William M. Isaacs, the FDIC chairman, prevailed. Sources at Wall Street added that the Federal Reserve was concerned about the uninsured depositors – which were primarily other depository institutions such as commercial banks, savings and loan associations and credit unions – and the effect the bankruptcy of Penn Square would have on them. As subsequent events proved, this concern was real. But the question remains: should taxpayers' money be used to save dreadfully mismanaged banks from failure?

13.4   Commercial paper turning to ashes: the case of Penn Central

The classical form of financial crisis starts when the sudden failure of a major bank, or group of banks, leads traders and investors to refuse to deal with other institutions thought to have similar vulnerabilities. The same is true about dealing with other banks engaged in markets disrupted by the failure of a major credit institution or industrial organization. This is particularly true *if*:

■ The failed firm is a member of one of the settlement and payment systems, and
■ Its failure may cause disruptions to other firms in the system, or a broader systemic stress.

What has been stated about banks is also valid of debt instruments issued by overleveraged entities that find it difficult to stay alive. An often cited example is the failure of Penn Central Railroad in 1970, which precipitated a crisis of confidence in the US commercial paper market. This made it more difficult for other commercial paper issuers to roll over their maturing debt.

Among well-managed financial institutions, many view firms with large commercial paper outstandings as potential sources of systemic risk. Underlying this negative reaction is the speed with which commercial paper funding can evaporate. There is a fashion in everything. US securities firms, for instance, reduced their reliance on the commercial paper market in the wake of the Drexel and Salomon affairs.

In a similar way, a liquidity crisis in a large financial firm could grow into a solvency crisis if uncertainty about the severity of outstanding problems, and other conditions relating to the entity, leads counterparties to cut off funding channels. Or, to refuse to enter into transactions which the company needs to manage its exposure.

■ In theory, creditors should be willing to lend to an illiquid, but solvent, institution.
■ In practice, the lending may not occur because creditors cannot determine rapidly enough the true extent of difficulties.

There are cases where even temporary illiquidity can be interpreted as a sign of coming insolvency, and creditors run for cover. Alternatively, creditors may not be able to agree among themselves as to how to deal with the problem. As the Penn Central case helps demonstrate, the perception of problems plays an important role in the propagation of financial disturbance in a wider market sense.

A brief historical perspective helps in appreciating this statement. Following the merger of the Pennsylvania Railroad and New York Central Railroad, the resulting Penn Central Transportation Company was America's largest railroad and sixth largest non-financial corporation. Among its real estate assets were the Waldorf Astoria Hotel, the Commodore Hotel, the PanAm Building, and 15 other valuable properties in mid-town Manhattan.

Visible real estate and other assets saw to it that Penn Central was thought to be well capitalized, a sure bet for corporate loans. Yet, it failed. Its bankruptcy today provides a good example of how a booming new financial product, such as the services to which *commercial paper* was put in the mid- to late 1960s, can go all wrong.

For starters, commercial paper is the corporate IOU, a product typically maturing in 90 days, hence of short enough timespan to help weather interest rate risk. But unlike secured loans and mortgages, it is an *unsecured debt*. What made the commercial paper market ideal for the inflationary time of the late 1960s was precisely its:

- Short-time horizon, and
- Low interest cost.

Further than that, commercial paper was a product with controllable expenditures and enough secrecy, because it was exempt from registration and disclosure requirements imposed by federal security laws. The use of commercial paper as short-term financial paper was also a travesty of the original commercial paper concept – that its issuance had to be linked to a commercial transaction, making that transaction a sort of virtual collateral.

Because with the transaction-independent form of commercial paper money was lent for days or months rather than for years, in spite of the lack of regulation which represented a departure from classical banking practices, financial intermediaries and other investors came to believe that commercial paper entailed no more risk then Treasury Bills. Reliance was also placed on the fact that the US National Credit Office (NCO) was in a way:

- Overseeing quality issues, and
- Controlling risk related to the commercial paper market.

Scant attention seems to have been paid at the time, by bankers, analysts, and investors, to the fact that NCO was no regulatory body but merely a minor outfit of Dun and Bradstreet. True enough, the National Credit Office had been in business since 1920, but it operated with only a skeleton staff.

- To monitor 600 companies it employed no more than four analysts, and
- Its research seems to have lacked depth, due not only to its reduced level of staffing but also to elementary research policies.

To make matters worse, the NCO's commercial paper department seems to have been of scant importance to its owner's corporate operations. As a result, no new policies and procedures were adopted by Dun and Bradstreet when the commercial paper market boomed. Yet, this NCO office was a core piece in the $40 billion commercial paper business by the late 1960s.

In a way predating the junk bond market of the 1980s, the lack of appropriate information and of thoroughly studied regulatory controls meant that as the 1960s came to a close the commercial paper market became less creditworthy than it was earlier on in the decade. This reflected badly on companies overexposed in that market. By late 1969, $200 million worth of Penn Central commercial paper was outstanding, raising critical questions:

- How would the transportation company redeem it?
- Would it issue new paper of the same sort?
- What would happen if this paper found no buyers?

Far from being idle questions, these are issues critical to the wallet of banks and of investors – but nobody seems to have come up with the right answers. Today exactly the same questions apply to credit derivatives and credit swaps – while once more no evident answers appear to exist.

- *If* we forget the failures of the past
- *Then* the way to bet is that we are going to repeat them all over again.

Therefore, the lesson the reader should retain from the commercial paper case study with Penn Central, is that whether we talk of commercial paper or of other short-term instruments, few issuing companies have within their means the ability to redeem the maturing of the instruments which:

- They have developed, and
- Sold for cash to the market.

This is a mistake in appreciation of financial staying power, made not only by individual investors but also by banks and the banking industry as a whole. In a way reminiscent of the commercial paper crises faced by Penn Central in 1969/1970 timeframe, many of the outstanding off-balance sheet products today are illiquid, or at least that is what some financial experts suggest in private conversations.

What keeps the system going is the issuance of new products, but the risk is that a pyramiding effect might develop. Finding willing counterparties is an integral part of the derivatives market just like back-up credit was an indivisible characteristic of the commercial paper market. How big should such back-up credit be to act as a counterweight?

In 1969 Penn Central had a backup line of credit of about $100 million, less than half the over $200 million Sword of Damocles. Notice that, on all evidence, NCO approved this arrangement because it assumed that the issuing company also had readily sellable assets. Yet,

- In 1969/70 the bond market had already started being inhospitable, and
- Penn Central could not sell a railroad or even a hotel at the spur of the moment, even if it tried to do so in a fire-sale.

Counting their potential losses, banks were not willing to advance more funds unless the US government was ready to bail out Penn Central. Nobody can criticize this decision. And though the Nixon Administration reluctantly agreed to come to the rescue, the House Banking and Currency Committee challenged the legality of the proposed guarantee.

On Sunday 21 June 1970 Penn Central filed for protection under the Federal Bankruptcy Act. The failure of such a big corporation created widespread uneasiness. The timing, too, was peculiar – to say the least. The Penn Central default came when the amount of maturing commercial paper was seasonally high, because of mid-year statement dates. The rest is history.

After the crash of Penn Central the Federal Reserve intervened decisively. One of the measures was suspending the interest rate ceilings above which banks have not been able to bid for new deposits. This started the whole movement of deregulation, beefed-up the money market and, two decades later, it also brought the crash of the savings and loans (S&L), with a gaping hole of over $800 billion.

13.5   The bankruptcy of Asia Pulp & Paper

Many lessons can be derived from the commercial paper failure at Penn Central. One of them is that rating agencies, like NCO, are not always awake. Another, that early signals of an impeding failure should not only be properly captured, but also exploited all the way in real time – so that countermeasures can take effect. Different algorithms permit the automation of this process. Examples are:

- The proxy of market capitalization divided by book value liabilities, and
- The *acid test*, which is the ratio of current assets over current liabilities.

Lack of vigilance can cost dearly. Many investors lost a small fortune in the Penn Central crash. As one of these investors, the treasurer of a US college had it, when he indicated his concern over results of the acid test, the Penn Central representative reassured him that there was no need for concern since total assets exceeded $6.5 billion. Was that enough?

This was a one-sided evidence. Even if these $6.5 billion was not an overvaluation, the crucial question was not total assets but *current assets*: how do they compare to *current liabilities*? This is not a query often asked by investors. If it were, I have no doubt that many companies would find themselves overexposed and the same is true of their bankers and investors.

- Agreeing to be a player with a new financial instrument that provides both hedging and profits is one thing.
- Overexposing oneself to unknown factors embedded in an obscure balance sheet is totally another, and it is not an acceptable practice.

Investors and asset managers who are not rigorous with evaluation procedures wake up with nightmares. Here is a case study on credit risk with globalization. This is a first-class lesson on the problems of corporate finance in emerging markets, as well as on the companies that ride the wave till their bankruptcy hits the stakeholders – among them:

- Fee-hungry Western investment banks
- Investors greedy for yield, or diversification, but blind to credit risk
- Lax national regulators, and
- A company management with global ambitions but little regard for prudential governance.

For many years, Asia Pulp & Paper (APP) has been one of the darlings of investors, particularly because big name banks promoted it as a sound investment. To the eyes of bankers, institutional investors, and people who trusted their assets to it, APP combined in one setting an emerging countries gem and an emerging industry wonder (in the country where it sprang). Beyond that, it was endowed with vast raw materials resources.

The list of 'blessings' was long, but in February 2001, after a 20% plunge in global paper prices over the previous three months, Asia Pulp & Paper defaulted on its bank loans and on its bonds. The default triggered what became a $13.4 billion debacle – one of the biggest investment catastrophes in the history of Asian companies and which caught Western investors by surprise.

The failure of APP downgraded the quality of investment advice provided by many analysts and other counselors who were proved wrong in their judgment. As a horde of assets went up in smoke, hundreds of institutional investors and creditors were left holding paper worth pennies. On 3 July 2000, NYSE moved to delist APP's American depository receipts (ADRs), whose value had plunged from over $16.69 in 1997 to 12 cents.

As creditors, auditors, and lawyers worked on this case, disturbing questions started to emerge. APP had won the confidence of investors by securing the support of leading financial firms, including JP Morgan, Merrill Lynch, Morgan Stanley, CSFB, and Goldman Sachs. These institutions had collectively underwritten billions in APP bonds and equities. Moreover,

- Arthur Andersen had audited the books of APP since 1994, and
- APP securities had passed the regulators' scrutiny both in Washington and in Singapore.

Yet nobody outside the Asian company's top management (and even this is not certain), really got the full picture of how shaky the finances were. This included an astonishing variety of debt offerings issued by APP's offshore subsidiaries. Reportedly, there were also some murky deals and loans galore that went sour. (More on APP in section 13.6.)

What happened with APP in July 2000 repeated itself in December 2003 with Italy's Parmalat – the hedge fund with a dairy product line on the side.[6] Both are excellent case studies in murky finances and non-transparent statements which have much more to do with ineffective management which, to cover its shortcomings, has adopted the policy of:

- Cooking the books, and
- Taking investors to the cleaners.

In both cases, Parmalat and APP, as well as in many others, not only billions of dollars have disappeared because of mismanagement and murky accounts, but more billions seem simply to have slipped away. The huge amount of money Morgan Stanley, JP Morgan, Merrill Lynch, Goldman Sachs, and CSFF raised for APP, from investors, in the six years since its creation in April 1995, seems to have left some $3 billion to $4 billion unaccounted for, according to financial analysts.[7]

One of the things which surprised many knowledgeable people is that some of America's biggest asset management firms, including Fidelity, New York Life Insurance, Putnam Investments, Massachusetts Mutual, and John Hancock Financial Services, bought APP securities. The same lack of prudence with other people's money has meant that some of them, and others too, are now going for the so-called alternative investments which they consider just as 'sound' as Asia Pulp & Paper in old days – and we have seen the results.

13.6   Banks can be light-hearted in evaluating credit risk

Many banks are simply not careful enough with their bets. Some of the risk and return evaluations which I have seen, connected to major banking loans, read like something a junior account executive puts together during the first quarter-hour of a brainstorming session with the borrower's top brass. Credit institutions thus become prisoners to poorly documented lending decision which abound in their portfolio:

- Though they have nothing to do with the democratization of credit, and
- Are not covered in the worst case through taxpayers' money in the aftermath of socialization of risk.

The APP debacle, which was the theme of section 13.5, is a case in point. The company's debt reached $13.4 billion, gathering steam over the years in a low frequency/high intensity event. This is similar to those which characterize many deals, particularly leveraged propositions in the financial industry. Low management standards and scanty supervision allow exposure to geared counterparties to gain speed, until:

- It spikes, and
- It bursts.

Debt became a monster because different Western and Asian banks helped APP and
Eka Tjipta Widjaja, its founder, to overleverage. The first credit institutions to give
APP a hand were Hong Kong and Shanghai Banking Corporation (HSBC) and the
Indosuez Bank. Each contributed a $100 million debt issue in early 1996 – a relatively
small start.

Afraid to miss the bandwagon, other institutions upped the ante. That same year,
Yamaichi Securities, of Tokyo, and Peregrine Investments, of Hong Kong, issued debt
instruments of $350 million and $200 million respectively, while UBS-Asia topped
them all with $600 million. The rush to throw good money down the drain gained
momentum.

Morgan Stanley was not left behind. Its underwritings on two different occasions
in June 1997 were $600 million each time. By then, bad investments were coming in
multiples. Merrill Lynch doubled the bet, also on two different occasions, both in
December 1997; the one with $1.25 billion and the other with $1.44 billion.

Most evidently, Goldman Sachs could not let its competitors take the icing off the
cake. In 1997 the investment bank, a newcomer to the APP deals, contributed an
underwriting of 'only' $245 billion; but it made up for it right after, in spite of the
Asian crisis – with two underwritings of $500 million each. By year 2000, the rush
to have good money run after bad ended with two last shots: Morgan Stanley did an
underwriting of $403 million, and JP Morgan of $100 million.

Small game that $100 million – except that by that time there were only a few
months left between this new injection of cash, and APP's bankruptcy. All these
assets, underwritten by the best-known investment firms and lavishly contributed to
by small-brained investors, have gone up in smoke. This throwaway capital seems to
have been channeled through dozens of companies incorporated by APP in tax
havens like the Cayman Islands, Cook Islands, Mauritius, and other offshores.

The lesson to retain from this debacle is no different from the one we will hear
in a few years' time about funds of funds where institutional investors and private
individuals pour money through alternative investments.[8] Greedy people ands assets
mismanagers are ready to bet their shirt for 'greater profits', forgetting altogether
about the security of their assets. Investors seem to never learn that:

- The more complex is the money network and the less transparent are the deals,
- The less able one is to track what is happening to one's capital, or to understand
  its eventual disappearance.

As history repeats itself time and again, it is precisely this same type of people and
companies who are now not only ready but also happy to throw their money into
highly leveraged derivatives deals. Neither were derivatives alien to the Asia Pulp &
Paper drama. Indeed, what seems to have saved some of the investors from losing
money in this abyss is that APP had lost part of its wealth in different derivatives
investments and in various real estate gambles in the Asian region. As this became
known, some investors kept their money in their wallets. Others did not, yet:

- The fact APP had derivatives losses was known since 1994 and 1995.
- Ironically, this was before the money safari started, and billions of investors dollars
  were condemned to oblivion.

There were also private placements galore, exempt from registration under Rule 144A of the US Securities Act. As a result, some of the larger deals of APP financing were never filed with the Securities and Exchange Commission. The parties who gambled with other people's money had failed to bring the investors' attention to the fact their deals concerned an entity which, to a large part, escaped prudential supervision.

Whether subscribing to public offerings or making private placements, banks and institutional investors went for these deals without clear knowledge – or at least appreciation – they were high-risk; they simply answered the call of big name underwriters. Those who saved their fortune were the prudent ones who did research APP's chances to become a viable entity, took notice of its derivatives losses, and were turned away by:

- The company's opaque structure, and
- Its record of payment disputes with suppliers.

In a way very similar to alternative investments, those who cared to inform themselves about what was happening with APP had plenty of opportunity to find reasons why they should shy away from it. According to Standard & Poor's, APP's interest coverage averaged only 1.5 in the 1996–98 timeframe. This is contrary to norms regarding the ratio of debt issuers of good standing, and it is one reason why in 1997 the notes of Asia Pulp & Paper received only B+ rating – a level below junk bonds.

Back in 1995 when APP was Asia's rising star, and the value of the company's stock past $12, its interest payments were $448 million. By 1999, the last year Asia Pulp & Paper reported full year results, annual interest payments had zoomed to about $660 million. Yet, even in 2000 'investors' were happy to throw the problem company yet another $503 million of good money.

The most ludicrous story about how some investors behave without due consideration of credit risk is that in 1998 the rating agencies reduced APP's grade to CCC. This is the nearest thing to plain default. Yet in that year the company's underwriters were able to get into its coffers a cool $1 billion in real money. Much of it came from investors who cared very little about the company's loss of creditworthiness.

Like old soldiers who never die, imprudent investments also go on. Years down the line, increasing divisions among creditors held up a $6.7 billion restructuring agreement which began being negotiated when APP defaulted on $13.9 billion in debts years ago. Several creditors had reached agreement, in principle, on two key sticking points in a contentious debt work-out. However, a new stumbling block came up: how many creditors it would take to declare APP in default again – which tells of the creditors' concern about the prospects of a second APP default.

13.7 A case of creditworthiness: investing in oil companies and their oil reserves

A financial report to investors (shareholders and bondholders) issued by one of the major brokers in mid-2003 had this to say about the prospects of one of the key industrial sectors: 'In equities, we recommend low beta, higher quality companies with strong brand names that pay dividends over the higher beta, low quality companies that have excessive valuations. Globally, we recommend that investors focus on *energy* which we believe could be the next great growth sector . . .'

Energy was the keyword in this investment advice. Energy was also the investment of choice of another of the leading investment banks, which recommended to its clients to go for oil and gas entities. The way a third bank phrased its thoughts in a late 2003 report on recommended investment strategy was that:

- The fastest growing energy source over the next two decades is expected to be natural gas, increasing by 2.8% a year and nearly double to 176 trillion cubic feet annually by 2025.
- At the same time world oil demand is expected to jump 50% from 2003 levels of 78.6 million barrels per day to 119 million barrels per day by 2025 – and companies with large oil reserves were particularly recommended.

To back up this statement regarding investors' focus on oil reserves, it was also noted that China overtook Japan in 2003 as the world's second biggest oil consumer after the United States, creating a faster than expected increase in the world's oil demand. And as for the immediate future, it was stated that Chinese demand for oil in 2004 was expected to average 6.07 million barrels per day, a rise of 10.6%, following 11% growth in 2003.

The stage was thus set for oil companies to prosper, but not for those whose oil reserves were wanting. Royal Dutch/Shell is a century-old company with 115 000 employees around the globe. It is not a start-up enterprise that tries (or at least should try) to impress the market with inflated numbers about its earnings and its reserves of the precious material. Yet, about a quarter of the oil and gas reserves reported in Shell's books, seem to have existed only in the imagination of its CEO and members of the board.

Misinforming a company's shareholders and the public should not be taken lightly, because each barrel of estimated reserves represents an imputed future income stream for the entity owning it. Such a potential income stream evidently:

- Influences the current equity value of an oil concern, and
- Serves as collateral for credits from financial institutions.

In January 2004 Shell's chairman, Sir Philip Watts, had to quit after the company's admission that it had vastly overestimated its oil and gas reserves. Walter van de Vijver, chief of exploration for Shell, also lost his job. This was not the end of the saga of misinformation, nor of the boardroom musical chairs. Two more times, at the end of March and in April 2004 Shell again had to correct its statement about reserves – again downward. With the third 'correction' Shell's chief finance officer, Judy Boynton, gave up her CFO responsibilities.

At the time of this third correction, on 19 April, an American law firm, Davis Polk and Wardwell, published excerpts from an internal 463-page report concerning the background to Shell's false reserve estimates. The company's new leadership had commissioned that study in January 2004. Many of the revelations cited in the report came from e-mails between Shell's head of oil research and the company's CEO. For instance, it has been reported that in November 2003, van de Vijver sent an e-mail to chairman Watts, saying: 'I am becoming sick and tired about lying about the extent of our reserves issues and the downward revisions that need to be done because of far too aggressive/optimistic bookings.'[9]

- Cooking the books through creative accounting is an old trick by now.
- Cooking up engineering data identifying oil and gas reserves is a new game in town.

Other documents have revealed that the manufacturing of fake reserves dated back to early 2002, with Shell's senior executive being aware that the company's estimates about its oil reserves were far too high. According to the aforementioned report, Shell's top brass was playing for time, or for some miracle to happen at the company's exploration sites in Angola and elsewhere.

Seen from a different viewpoint, however, Shell's faked numbers may just be a prelude to other, similar revelations by energy companies, as finding new oil reserves becomes increasingly difficult. In Shell's case, the faked oil and gas reserves amounted to 4.5 billion barrels according to the figures in the public domain. Even if this misinformation only concerns oil reserves, and not production, and one takes $38 per barrel, the price at time of writing, as the basis for calculating Shell's errors – then in accounting terms we talk of an over $170 billion 'mistake'.

Curiously enough, in mid-May 2004 the capitalization of Shell, that is the total market value of Shell shares which imploded at the beginning of 2004, was 140 billion euro ($182 billion). In other words, Shell's capitalization was 20% lower than the fraudulent amount of the company's oil and gas reserves. Both bond and equity investors should take notice. The regulators, too, have shown interest in this scam.

At the end of July 2004, Royal Dutch/Shell agreed to pay about $150 million in fines to American and British regulators, following investigations into its downward revision of reserve estimates. FSA's penalty was £17 million ($30 million). That by SEC was four times higher, at $120 million.

In terms of P&L this $150 million might have been a drop in the ocean, as Shell announced profits of nearly $3.8 billion in the second quarter of 2004, up 16% from the same quarter a year earlier. But the company's reputation for accuracy in financial reporting was dented, which cost more than a few million. And there have been other oil company woes.

'What is $2 billion nowadays?', asked an article in *The Economist*.[10] It answered its own question by making reference to a report from Hermitage Capital, an investment fund, accusing Gazprom, Russia's state-run gas monopoly and the world's biggest gas producer, of losing $2.1 billion in 2003 due to inefficiency and suspect accounting.

Hermitage Capital's complaints caused barely a ripple in Russia's markets, but this does not mean that investments in other Russian oil companies were free of worries. In fact, even after the August 1998 bankruptcy, investors in Russian bonds have not been rewarded nearly enough for the risks they have taken.

Evidence of creative accounting and other data-massaging practices has been brought home after the problems at some of the issuers like Yukos, the oil company, and Sodniznesbank. It looks *as if* Russian borrowers stuffed masses of questionable bonds into the portfolios of investors who had almost no idea that they should be compensated for buying debt instruments of high risk.

Until the middle of 2003, as foreign and domestic investors were piling into foreign-currency Russian bonds, issuance surged from $629 million in 2001 to $8.7 billion in 2003. And in just the first five months of 2004 Russian companies issued another $3.4 billion. Furthermore, more domestic corporate bonds were issued in the first four months of 2004 than in the whole previous year.

The irrational note in this rapid acceleration of Russian debt instruments which are thrown onto the market is that both local and global investors fell over one another in their eagerness to buy anything that showed a glare of return. Prices rose spectacularly. The yield on a one-year bond issued by Gazprom, which in spite of what the previous paragraphs stated is considered a blue-chip issuer in Russia, fell like a stone. Investors seem to have forgotten that Gazprom does not have an investment-grade rating. As a result of this oversight investors sent Gazprom's bond yield:

- From 10% in September 2003,
- To 6% in late March 2004 without accounting for the credit risk being taken.

Yield on Uralsvyazinform bonds, a Russian telecom company with a single-B rating from S&P's, fell from over 13% at the start of December 2003, to under 8% at the beginning of April 2004. Only investors with questionable professional competence and a colossal risk appetite should have gone for a B issue – and, even so, never at below a very healthy spread over comparable US securities.

Neither were investors spared the downgrades. Yukos, which once was Russia's biggest oil company, saw its creditworthiness downgraded to CCC by S&P after Mikhail Khodorkovsky, its CEO, was arrested in October 2003 and the firm was charged with tax evasion. This sharp fall from grace took place in April 2004 – a little too late.

About a month later, on 26 May, a Moscow court declared that Yukos must pay the $3.5 billion the tax authorities said it owed them, and more claims were said to be on their way with default not far from being in sight. Investors living on hope expected the Russian government would find some accommodation for Yukos, but on 9 July 2004 the deadline for paying past taxes was not extended and, for all practical purpose, the 'oil giant' was bankrupt.

When I was young, there was a saying that the state lottery is the taxation of the stupid. If this is the case with lottery, think about how to characterize investors who bet on B- and CCC-rated bonds.

Notes

1 John B. Caouette, Edward I. Altman, and Paul Narayanan, *Managerial Credit Risk*, Wiley, New York, 1998.
2 *International Finance Review*, 16 June 2001.
3 *Business Week*, 1 December 2003.
4 From that time till mid-2004, when these lines were written, none of these hypotheses materialized. The worst case of all would have been that of HypoVereinsbank buying Commerzbank. The Munich-based bank itself has been a wounded institution following its many acquisitions – and most particularly of Bank Austria.

5 D.N. Chorafas, *Credit Derivatives and the Management of Risk*, New York Institute of Finance, New York, 2000.
6 D.N. Chorafas, *The Management of Equity Investments*, Butterworth-Heinemann, Oxford, 2005.
7 Business Week, August 13, 2001.
8 D.N. Chorafas, *Alternative Investments and the Mismanagement of Risk*, Macmillan/Palgrave, London, 2003.
9 EIR, 7 May 2004.
10 *The Economist*, 12 June 2004.

14 Market risk with bonds

14.1   Introduction

In the preceding chapters several practical examples have documented that an investment in bonds is exposed to market risk. This arises from changes in interest rates and, in the case of debt instruments denominated in other than the investor's currency, from changes in foreign exchange rates. Market risk exists with all commodities – from the price of oil to that of base metals and precious metals to equities and debt instruments.

Interest rate risk could be hedged, but this requires good knowledge of derivative financial instruments and first class risk control (see Chapter 15) which are beyond the reach of the typical investor – as well as of many institutions. Yet, several of them offer what they call 'risk management services', and very often get burned.

For instance, a retail bank may act as principal in interest rate hedging transactions with its loan customers. Then, for each interest rate hedge entered into with a commercial borrower, the lender would proceed with a complementary transaction with a correspondent bank. By doing so, the lender would:

- Retain no interest rate risk on the loan,
- But will have credit risk in the event that either or both the commercial borrower or correspondent bank defaulted, on its respective obligations.

For their part, borrowers may use, in connection to interest rate risk hedging, a combination of financial instruments including medium-term and short-term financings, variable-rate debt instruments, and interest rate swaps. Provided this is done for hedging commercial transactions and *not* for gambling, such strategy permits the company to manage the interest rate mix of its debt portfolio and related market risk exposure relating to borrowing.

For instance, borrowers may enter into interest rate swaps in which they agree to exchange various combinations of fixed and/or variable interest rates based on established notional amounts. The objective of maintaining this mix of fixed and floating rate debt is to be in charge of the overall value of cash flows attributable to the debt instruments.

A similar statement is valid in connection to foreign exchange risk. Companies enter into various currency deals, principally forward exchange contracts and purchased options, and cap agreements, aiming to achieve better protection from volatility in currency rates.

For instance, companies that conduct their business on a multinational basis in a variety of foreign currencies use a risk management policy aimed to preserve the economic value of cash flows in non-functional currencies. They may hedge all significant booked and firmly committed cash flows identified as creating foreign currency exposure on a rolling 12-month basis.

An industrial company may hedge foreign exchange risk in certain sales and purchase contracts by embedding terms that affect the ultimate amount of the cash flows under the contract. Regulatory requirements must be observed. US companies, for example, tend to hedge all types of foreign currency risk to preserve the economic cash flows not only in accordance with corporate risk management policies but also in observance of financial reporting under SFAS 133 of the Financial Accounting Standard Board (FASB).

The examples used in the preceding paragraphs are primarily those of hedging through derivative financial instruments. The use of derivatives and the control of risk associated to them is not the subject of this book – and moreover the text is primarily oriented to the investor, not the issuer.

Investors, too, face interest rate risk and possibly currency exchange challenges. There are also risks other than the two principal ones just described. A portfolio of mortgage-backed securities is exposed to prepayment risk, which connects to interest rate risk in the sense that prepaid capital must be reinvested, sometime at a lower interest rate than that of the original investment.

Prepayment risk can be experimented with through Monte Carlo simulation. Among necessary tests, is the use of prepayment patterns to project MBS cash flows and their dependability. These should incorporate uncertainty about future refinancing rates, to value the homeowners' prepayment options.

Underlying these examples is the search for a protection from exposure resulting from identified market risks. Both investors and industrial companies aim to provide themselves with the flexibility to deal with longer-term forecasts as well as changing market conditions, always watchful that:

■ The cost of hedging is not excessive relative to the level of risk involved, and
■ Hedging strategies do not create more exposure than the one they aim to cover.

The reader should keep in mind that market risk is not one but a whole family of exposures primarily concerned with price volatility and liquidity prevailing in the market. Market factors creating a hazard may be due to unexpected changes in interest rates, fluctuations in exchange rates, exceptionally adverse economic conditions, aftershocks from major defaults, and a number of other reasons. Market risk can be magnified by derivative instruments because of their gearing, even if these instruments theoretically aim to provide a means of control over market risk.

14.2 A broader view of market risk

Implicitly, the Introduction to this chapter defined interest rate risk as the potential impact from changes in market interest rates affecting the fair value of assets and liabilities on an investor's portfolio or, in the case of a firm, having an impact on its balance sheet and profit and loss statement. A similar statement has been made about currency exchange risk. Both interest rate risk and currency risk affect the annual results an asset manager would show to the client.

Interest rate risk and forex risk are not the only market risks that can hit an industrial firm, bank, insurance company, pension fund, or asset management entity. As the Introduction explained, organizations have cash flow obligations to meet, and part of the investments they make as a 'war chest' are exposed to market volatility.

- Bonds are subject to interest rate risk and currency risk
- The value of stocks fluctuates as a result of equity price risk, and
- Both debt instruments and stock are exposed to other risk factors against which they must always be ready to position themselves.

A portfolio of investments, and most particularly leveraged portfolios, can face trying times. Three of the major factors in the stock market's quick swings and downside trend, after the end of March 2000, have been the role of hedge funds that go short, day traders who buy and sell on-line through snap investment decisions, and the media. When a company makes an announcement today, such as warning that its profits will be lower than expected, this is disseminated almost instantly on television, by websites, and through financial networks.

- Day traders and other players react, buying and selling shares on fast disseminated rumor(s), thus quickly driving prices up or down.
- Often, the price swings are an overreaction, but even so they add significantly to market volatility, and also create a market psychology which amplifies trends.

Similarly, by going short, at the rate of about one-third of their investments, hedge funds push the market down, and this process becomes a self-feeding cycle of negative psychology which decimates not only stocks but also debt instruments and, at times, whole capital markets. I have chosen as an example the case of Germany's Neuer Markt, a technology companies exchange, and Sweden's OM, which is a blue ribbon company exchange.

First, a brief historical background. Neuer Markt has been the relatively recent German answer to the NASDAQ. It prospered at a rather fast pace in the go-go late 1990s, but with the 2000/2001 downturn in technology stock fortune, the young (1997-born) Neuer Markt has sunk like a stone. Its current valuation is a faint image of its high water mark.

One might say that's life with equities. But there have also been a series of scandals, including alleged insider trading by executives of Neuer Markt listed companies. These undermined investor trust in the viability of start-ups. 'The whole market has been tainted,' said Cyril P. McGuire, executive chairman of Trintech Group, a Dublin maker of software for electronic-payment systems that is listed on Frankfurt's Neuer Markt and New York's NASDAQ.[1]

Nearly half of the firms in the Nemax 50 index have fallen by roughly 95% from their peaks. The German index itself has shed more than comparable technology company markets in London or Paris, which were its peers. And the Neuer Markt has been falling further behind NASDAQ, which in the second quarter of 2001 regained some lost ground, while Nemax 50 continued to weaken.

This uninterrupted fall of the German technology index has put intense pressure on Deutsche Börse, where blue chip companies are listed – and which is also Neuer Markt's parent. The listing scandals did not help. As part of a plan to restore credibility, the Deutsche Börse planned to require all listed companies, including DAX Index firms, to adhere to tougher reporting standards – something that should have been done from the start, rather than trying to bend SEC's regulations for German companies listing at NYSE.

Belatedly, Deutsche Börse and Neuer Markt companies have been asked to give detailed information about stock options, research and development expenditures, and their investments. If they fail to meet the new standards, they will be removed from the Neuer Markt; and the same will happen if their shares or market capitalization fall below a certain level. Notice that all this talk about penalties is expressed in future terms, while the damage has been (and continues to be) done. Critics say that those responsible for the Neuer Market have forgotten the old adages that:

- It is better to lose your eye than your name, and
- Confidence takes a whole life to build up and a day or two to destroy.

The lack of confidence is fathering market risk for all of the players, not only the wrong-doers – and, as has already been explained, the market is no zero-sum game. All its players might gain and all its players might lose, depending on how the chips are falling, and the chips will be falling 'this' way or 'that' way depending on counterparty risk, market risk, business confidence, and prevailing psychology.

Exchanges, too, are subject to the market's evaluation and approval. As a hedge fund can lead itself to bankruptcy by running out of cash, a stock exchange can drive itself against the wall through imprudence. OM, the Swedish exchange operator and trading-system developer, had a sky-high share price and even made a bid to buy the London Stock Exchange (LSE) to the tune of £800 million ($1.45 billion). Since then, however, it has seen its market capitalization dive. Analysts point out several reasons for this debacle. They say that:

- Weak corporate earnings,
- Falling stock prices, and
- Lower share volume in trading

painted a poor short-term picture for OM, which derives most of its revenues, in some form or another, from market turnover. Indeed, OM's Transaction Unit consists of the bourses it owns and operates, the most important of which is the Stockholm Stock Exchange. It also includes the OM Fixed Income Exchange and UK Power Exchange in London.

- The Transaction Unit saw a 28% fall in sales in the first half of 2001, amid lower trading volumes and equity derivatives fee cuts.
- By contrast, OM's Technology division, which develops trading systems, saw sales rise 73% in the first half of 2001 – but this was not enough to offset heavy losses in transactions.

In other terms, the market did not think that the Technology division could develop the level of sales necessary to counterweight the drop in OM's trading-related business.

The company's Transaction Unit was also hit by fee cuts of around 40% in February 2001 for equity derivatives, due to tougher competition from Deutsche Börse and other exchanges. In the aftermath, OM recorded a pre-tax loss of 36 million krona ($3.5 million) for the first half of 2001, compared with a pre-tax profit of 473 million krona in the first half of 2000.

By traditional standards, this should not have been enough to justify the huge drop in OM's stock price. But the mid-2001 market has not been traditional by any standard. It was a highly nervous one which got scared of its own excesses. Hedge funds, special alternative investment vehicles (SAIVs), and the banks behind them should take notice. The same meltdown can hit the leveraged products which they sell; and this can happen nearly overnight for the same reasons.

While the classical example in connection to the severe 2000–2001 downturn, in market psychology and market values, is the crash of the technology sector, which not only hurt investors deeply but also led to more leveraging of financials, the careful reader will notice that market risk is by no means limited to just one sector. Both as a concept and as a process it can also hit the exchanges, like OM and Neuer Markt, not just the companies listed in them.

14.3   Interest rate bubbles and bond market meltdown

In a meeting held in New York in 1997 on the management of market risk associated to debt instruments, one of the lecturers used the 1994 bond market meltdown to demonstrate how monetary policy-makers sometimes fail to see the after-effect of successive interest rate hikes – seven in tandem in 1994, as shown in Figure 14.1. The lecturer first outlined the damage this market risk did overall to bondholders' assets. Then, he explained the measures he took as an asset manager, citing the Chinese proverb: 'Policies are ordained on high, below there are countermeasures.'

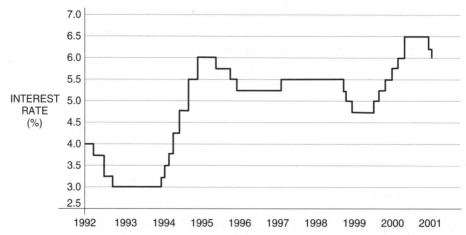

Figure 14.1 Interest rates on Federal funds over a 10-year timeframe, 1992–2001

Subsequently, the lecturer went on to say that the 1994 bondmarket meltdown could be repeated. He emphasized that, years ago, an economy-friendly interest rate policy should have placed:

- High interest rates on very risky speculative financing, such as derivatives, and
- Lower rates on lending for medium- to long-term investments in infrastructure and production.

This was not done. By mid-1997, according to the same thesis, the world's financial system had become so inflated that to raise interest rates on the bubble could only service to blow out the bubble. Notice that at that particular time, mid-1997, the meltdown of Asia's 'tigers' had started and, in consequence, one of the bubbles was already exploding.

At that same conference, however, another of the lecturers expressed serious doubts about a two-tier interest rate system, saying that it does not make sense because financial markets do not work that way: 'What some economists have suggested is emulating the higher interest rate through special taxation at the source applicable to leveraged deals,' still another lecturer said, adding that 'today exactly the opposite happens: it is the dividends which are doubly taxed.'

The sense of the meeting was that whether we talk of bonds or equities, it is not easy to be in charge of market risk, neither is it really feasible to regulate cross-border and most particularly cross-current money flows. The minority opinion was that this might be necessary, because since April 1995, when the Bank of Japan took emergency measures supported by a worried Clinton Administration and the Federal Reserve, the financial markets lived in the fear that a Japanese collapse would bring down with it the entire globalized financial system.

During the conference, the most discussed scenario of a possible meltdown started with the fact that the Japanese government and private banks and insurance firms held, at that time, over $500 billion in US Treasury securities. Were Japanese banks or the government forced to liquidate even a sizeable part of that amount, it would precipitate a crisis globally, beyond anything seen in the 1930s.

It did not happen that way, and though this worst-case scenario and variations of it have been repeated several times since – including a Japanese–Chinese dumping of US Treasuries discussed in early 2004, the worst case has not taken place. What did happen, however, was the bond market bubble of 2003 and 2004.

In the three years from March 2000 to March 2003, crashing stock market bubbles eliminated $16 trillion of financial asset value worldwide. To calm the markets, the central banks responded by injecting more liquidity, but this has not been successful in boosting the stock markets or the economies, while liquidity pumping created some new financial asset bubbles.

In his *Richebächer Letter* of July 2003, former Dresdner Bank chief economist Kurt Richebächer wrote: 'During the late 1990s, Mr Greenspan was keen to foster the stock market bubble. . . . Now, he is keen to foster the three new bubbles that he has kindled in fighting the burst of the stock market bubble:

- The house price bubble,
- The mortgage refinancing bubble, and
- The bond bubble . . .'

Greenspan, Richebächer further stated, signaled to the marketplace his determination to accommodate unlimited leveraged bond purchases, adding that endless liquidity is available for the taking by the speculative financial community. The direct result has been a credit and bond explosion of bubble proportions, that paralleled the excesses of the equity bubble in the late 1990s. In the opinion of the same commentator,

- The influence of the bond bubble of 2003 has been pervading the whole economy and financial system, and
- Its bursting may have apocalyptic consequences at global scale, as practically every institution is exposed to it.

According to other experts, the consequences may not be apocalyptic but they will surely be severe, outpacing those of the 1992–93 bond speculation bubble which exploded in 1994. To calm the fear of financial markets about a repeated market risk scenario, the Fed let it be known that 'what happened in 1994 will not be repeated in 2004'. Many experts, however, doubt that it is possible to engineer a soft landing, particularly if inflation flares up.

According to expert opinion, to better appreciate the amount of embedded risk in successive interest rate increases, it is appropriate to recall that the Federal Reserve pushed down short-term interest rates from 6.0% to 1.0% within 30 months, thereby creating all the conditions for supergearing the bubble in the bond market. Commercial banks could:

- Borrow short-term funds from the Fed at rock-bottom interest rates, and
- Invest the borrowed money into non-investment grade bonds offering much higher interest, a process known as *carry trade*.

The Fed's successive rate cuts to a level not seen for 46 years evidently pushed up the market price of bonds. Because debt instruments are constantly traded on the market, their price is determined by discounting all remaining future income streams, by a comparison of the bond's fixed interest rate to the monetary short-term interest rate.

Under these conditions, the long low interest rates policy over 30 months automatically pushed up the market prices of all outstanding bonds. The Fed signaling further rate ensured that the bond bubble continued to grow. Notice that both speculators and private investors contributed to the bubble of the first years of the 21st century. Among the latter, millions of households were lured to sharply increase their mortgage debt by:

- Rising home prices, and
- New lows in mortgage rates.

Moreover, the refinancing of old mortgages often included a cash-out component which helped to prevent private household consumption in the US from collapsing. This served policy-makers because at least one sector of the economy, the overindebted consumers, was still kicking while the business sectors went into hibernation.

The case of Japan gives a glimpse of the aftermath, in trying to gain insight into possible consequences of rising interest rates. At the end of June 2003, Japanese government bonds (JGB) suffered their biggest slump in two years. A few days later, on 3 July, a bond auction by the Japanese Finance Ministry drew just half as many bids as the previous month's sale, leading on the same day to the biggest JGB plunge since September 1999. Also the German and the British government bond auctions on 2 July drew the lowest demand in several years.

Japanese 10-year bond yields reached a record low of 0.435% on 12 June 2003, but by 3 July had shot up to 1.125% – a difference of 690 basis points. On 4 July the JGB crash continued, driving 10-year yields at one point to 1.40%. To appreciate the impact of these statistics, it should be recalled that Japan has the largest government bond market in the world, with $4.7 trillion in outstanding debt, compared to $3.3 trillion US government bonds.

The contagion effect did not take a long time to show itself at the other side of the Pacific. Contributors to interest rate uncertainty and to the selling of US Treasuries by investors have been the 2003 announcements by the government on its record-high budget deficits. In February 2003, the Office of Management and Budget (OMB) was still forecasting deficits of $304 billion for fiscal year 2003 and $307 billion for FY 2003. But by late August, of that same year the OMB was forecasting budget deficits of $455 billion and $475 billion.

Experts predicted that the real figure might be in the $500 billion to $600 billion range, and they were wrong only in the sense that it landed higher than that. It is not difficult to understand that something is wrong with an economy that experiences such huge budget deficits – a sense of the market worsened by the fact that the US current account deficit continues to deteriorate.

14.4   Measuring exposure to interest rate risk

Every investor should be measuring and monitoring interest rate risk. Asset managers and banks having complex debt instruments in their portfolio and, using sophisticated risk profiles, should employ more rigorous interest rate risk measurement systems than those based on simple maturity schedules. There are two basic prerequisites to the effective management of interest rate risks, and of market risk at large:

■ A sound methodology (see the Basel Committee's method in Appendix 14.A), and
■ Analytical thinking assisted by appropriate tools.

The two bullets correlate because, to a large extent, analytical thinking is a method of work that is objective and detached from factors that bias one's thoughts and opinions. At the core is the will to challenge the 'obvious' and to experiment. For instance, simulation models involving projected future interest rate paths can provide assessments of potential effects of changes in interest rates on:

■ Earnings
■ Economic value, and
■ Assumed exposure.

Historical trends can be of assistance in formulating hypotheses and estimating coming changes. Quite pertinent are forward interest rate estimates, like the example in Figure 14.2, which reflects a mid-2003 prognostication of forward European interest rates.

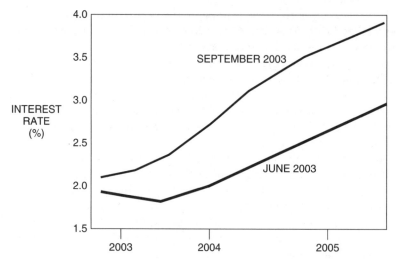

Figure 14.2 Two-year forward European interest rate estimates

Interest rate risk resulting from changes in the *yield curve* (see Chapters 7 and 9) should be given due attention, because repricing mismatches can expose the investor or bank. Yield curve risk arises when unanticipated shifts in the slope and shape of the yield curve have adverse effects on the overall financial position.

Well-managed financial institutions as well as astute investors and portfolio managers who do their homework, employ parallel yield curve shocks up and down. Also, they use stress tests that steepen and flatten the yield curve (see section 14.9) – with parallel computation of capital at risk over both short-term and long-term horizons.

Nevertheless, even if the position is hedged against parallel movements in the yield curve, the underlying economic value of a long position in 30-year government bonds hedged by a short position in 10-year government bonds could decline sharply if the yield curve steepens. Historical data on gains and losses can produce values that assist in simulation of future events.

In terms of interest rate risk profiles, an increasingly important source of interest rate risk comes from the options embedded in many financial assets, and most particularly outstanding liabilities and derivative instruments in the portfolio. Financial products with embedded options should be managed most carefully, their use being important also in non-trading activities of credit institutions, including instruments like:

- Bonds and notes with call or put provisions,
- Loans giving borrowers the right to prepay balances, and
- Different types of non-maturity deposit products, offering depositors the right to withdraw funds at any time without penalties.

A commercial bank's main concern in interest rate risk management in connection to the aforementioned instruments is practically the same as that of its regulators: that somewhere down the line, asymmetrical payoff characteristics of financial products with optionality features can present significant challenges to the credit institution, because they are generally exercised:

- To the advantage of the holder, and
- Disadvantage of the seller.

Furthermore, a growing number of both explicit and embedded options may involve significant leverage which magnify the influence of option positions on the financial institution, increasing its risks. Different timetables should be examined in a forward-looking study, and alternative scenarios should be tested, in fulfillment of the spirit of the old proverb that 'the difference between a statesman and the Messiah is the timetable'.

One commonly used method to present the potential impact of market movements is to show the effect of a one basis point, or 0.01%, change in interest rates on the fair values of assets and liabilities. This is analyzed by time brackets within which the entity has sorted its debt instrument commitments.

Generally known as sensitivity analysis, such a presentation tends to be easily understandable by management. The quantitative estimates are also used as inputs to the value at risk (VAR)[2] model used by a financial institution to monitor its overall market risk, of which interest rate risk is a part. Reference to VAR (and its weaknesses) has been made in Chapter 1. Many banks have developed improved models which aim to assure that the estimates senior management receives:

- Show the potential net impact of change in interest rates on the fair values of both assets and liabilities subject, to fixed interest rates, and
- Provide, on request, a detailed estimate on gains and losses of position in the portfolio by category, currency, and time bracket.

Both primary and derivative instruments in trading and non-trading activities, as well as off-balance sheet commitments must be included in these estimates. It is also wise to distinguish between trading and non-trading portfolios. Some banks make this distinction follow an internal classification, which usually differs from the accounting classification of trading and non-trading assets and liabilities.

For instance, trading usually includes all assets and liabilities that are kept in the trading book and which receive a value-at-risk treatment for capital adequacy purposes. By contrast, under non-trading are classified all other assets and liabilities that are kept on the banking book, including derivatives designated as hedging instruments for hedge accounting reasons.

14.5 Reporting to regulators: an example from the Office of Thrift Supervision

Many regulators require interest rate tests to be made on assumed market risk by the institutions under their jurisdiction, with results reported to them on a daily basis. Following the severe financial problems which hit the American thrifts (or savings and loans (S&L), equivalent to the UK building societies) because of mismatch risk, the Office of Thrift Supervision (OTS) requires that all S&Ls make:

- Sensitivity measurements
- Worst-case scenarios
- Capital before-shock calculations, and
- Capital after-shock calculations.

This thorough experimental approach, which must be done by each S&L, with daily results reported to OTS, takes current commitments and market interest rates as inputs. Then, it computes possible exposure by changing the current interest rate 100, 200, 300, and 400 basis points up and down.

The benchmark adverse condition is the 200 basis points shock level, with 400 bps being the stress test. This is one of the best examples I have found of using technology to strengthen an institution's internal control. Timothy Stier, an S&L director, explained that the OTS has also developed a lot of other models which assist the S&L's senior management in handling interest rate risk, and other risks.

The choice of the OTS advanced applications as reference to the measures regulators take to keep market risk in control is intentional because today accountability for internal control is at board level, a statement equally true in several European countries. 'Pursuant to the first sentence of Paragraph 1 of Article 39 of the Austrian Banking Act (Bankwesengesetz, BWG) it is the executive board's responsibility to establish, keep up and revise the internal control. This responsibility is seen as part of their duty of diligence', wrote Dr Martin Ohms of the Austrian National Bank.[3]

Senior management, Timothy Stier suggested, should see to it that all material positions and cash flows, including off-balance sheet positions, are incorporated into the interest rate measurement system. Where applicable, this data must include information on coupon rates and cash flows of associated instruments and contracts.

What about reporting on exposure to derivative financial instruments? In the United States, few thrifts have come into the derivatives market. This is the case with 76 out of 1119 S&Ls. 'Once in a while we find a thrift who bought a reverse floater, but the majority of the savings and loans keep out of this market,' Stier said. Still, the reporting rule is generally applicable, which is right, because it leaves no loopholes.

Regulators insist that management pays special attention to those positions with uncertain maturities. Examples include savings and time deposits which provide depositors with the option to make withdrawals at any time. To increase sensitivity to factors of timing, management should ensure that basic assumptions used to measure interest rate risk exposure are re-evaluated at least annually – and more often when necessary. Moreover,

- Hypotheses made in assessing interest rate sensitivity of complex instruments should be explained properly, and
- Any adjustments to underlying data should be documented, while the nature and reason(s) for the adjustments must always be explicit.

The OTS sees the aforementioned rules as basic policy steps, necessary for rigorous interest rate risk management. Whether we talk of a commercial bank, a thrift, an asset manager, or an individual investor, interest rate risk significantly increases the vulnerability of the entity's financial condition to market liquidity and volatility, while leveraging brings many unknowns into the picture.[4]

Savings and loans, as well as commercial banks, have experience with deposits and loans – but senior management does not always appreciate that while interest rate risk is a part of financial intermediation, an excessive amount of it poses a significant threat to an institution's earnings and to its capital.

- Changes in interest rates affect a bank's earnings by altering interest-sensitive income and expenses.
- They also impact on the underlying value of the bank's assets, liabilities, and off-balance sheet instruments.

Future cash flows change when interest rates change. As has been underlined in section 14.4, the interest rate risk confronting banks comes from several sources:

- Repricing
- Yield curve
- Basis risk, and
- Options risk.

All these are factors affecting the level of exposure and, therefore, must be addressed steadily in a rigorous manner, and not from time to time or only from a limited angle.

As the careful reader will appreciate in this and the following sections, both the guidelines and the models developed by OTS are, in their basics, quality control measures – with particular emphasis on quality of management. As such they are complemented by the statistical quality control principles and charts,[5] as well as by approaches based on behavioral science.

14.6 Risk points and exposure patterns

A *risk point* represents the amount of gain or loss that would result from a given movement in interest rates. In some cases this is a fixed movement – for instance, 1%. In others, a changing estimate, or pattern, of likely movements is used, and it is regularly adjusted in the light of recent historical data which may provide new insight to the study of assumed exposure.

One of the alternative approaches to study and research is to put the threshold of sensitivity as low as 1 basis point in interest rate change, followed by 5, 10, 20, and 25 basis points. When interest rates are volatile such basis point differences can give rise to unexpected changes in cash flows and earnings spread between assets, liabilities, and derivatives of similar maturities or repricing frequencies (more on this in section 14.7).

Several banks have an overall risk point limit which is often sub-allocated to different trading desks and portfolio positions. Others find that this is not necessarily the best approach because the planning and control of risk point limits is not an exact science.

Instead, top management wants to know the change in value in inventoried positions, if and when interest rates change by 'x' basis points – or by a given fraction of 1%.

Because interest rates are volatile, this concern is perfectly justified. Even when the central bank stays put, interest rates vary intraday, daily, weekly and monthly, often upsetting the most carefully laid out plans – unless an entity exercises utmost vigilance over its portfolio positions. Macroscopically speaking, the pattern of interest rate volatility is shown in Figure 14.3 over a 60-year timeframe.

The reader will recall that the experimental method which has been implemented and applies to the US thrifts, within the framework of OTS policy studied in section 14.5, takes current interest rates and changes them 100, 200, 300, and 400 basis points up and down with *adverse condition* being the plus or minus 200 basis points change. For the US banking industry, the Office of the Comptroller of the Currency (OCC) has developed models which assist in handling interest rate risk with prudential financial reporting distinguishing between:

- Trading, and
- Risk management.

I am not privy to the assumptions made by OCC regarding the impact of interest rate volatility on earning and cash flow, but do have a good example of basis points changes. The 1988 Annual Report of Cisco, the telecom equipment company, elaborates a hypothetical change in fair value in the financial instruments in its portfolio at 25 July 1998. Management says that:

- These instruments are not leveraged and are held for purposes other than trading
- But they still have shown significant sensitivity to changes in interest rates.

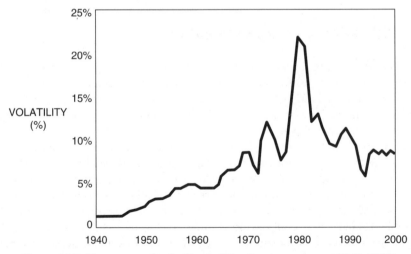

Figure 14.3 Sixty years of volatility in US prime interest rate, 1940–2000

Cisco's method is, to my judgment, an excellent paradigm for financial institutions as well. The modeling technique that has been used measures change in fair value arising from selected potential changes in interest rates. The market changes entering this simulation reflect immediate parallel shifts in the yield curve of plus or minus 50 bp, 100 bp, and 150 bp over a 12-month time horizon.

- *Beginning fair values* represent the market principal plus accrued interest, dividends, and certain interest rate-sensitive securities considered cash and equivalents for financial reporting purposes.
- *Ending fair values* comprise the market principal plus accrued interest, dividends, and reinvestment income at a 12-month time horizon.

In its 1998 Annual Report, Cisco observes that a 50 bp move in the Federal funds rate has occurred in 9 of the past 10 years (1988–1998); a 100 bp move has occurred in 6 of the past 10 years; and a 150 bp move has occurred in 4 of the past 10 years, with the last reference being on 30 September 1998. In other words:

- Volatilities of 50, 100, and 150 bp are fairly frequent and senior management must be always ready to face their aftermath.
- The 200 bp volatility, which, as we have seen, is an OTS benchmark, is not as frequent but neither is it an outlier.
- By contrast, the 300 and 400 bp volatilities (both plus and minus) used by the OTS model can be seen as outliers, and therefore benchmarks for stress testing.

Variation in assumed market risk and its impact on a company's or a portfolio's liquidity, solvency, even earnings, is an important objective of interest rate risk analysis. Unexpected losses threaten the financial stability of the entity, undermining its capital adequacy, and affecting market confidence. Loss of market confidence can damage a company much more deeply than money being lost.

Interest rate risk and the health of the economy correlate both between themselves and with currency exchange rates. The East Asia crisis of 1997 provides an example. For years the central banks of Asia's 'tiger' economies had followed a rather rigid currency exchange policy fixed to the US dollar. This led to:

- A significant appreciation of regional currencies
- Relatively high domestic interest rates
- Diminution in export competitiveness
- Large current account deficits, and
- Excessive borrowing in foreign currencies by companies and sovereigns.

Domestic entities wrongly thought they were insulated from currency exchange risk by fixed forex rates put in place by their governments, because these were sustained over a number of years. The fact that domestic interest rates were high made it attractive for borrowers, including credit institutions, to get foreign financing – particularly so, since foreign investors willingly contributed to each country's liquidity, without exercising due diligence in respect to credit risk and market risk.

Economic growth, easy borrowing conditions, better interest rates abroad than at home, and a theoretically fixed exchange rate, encouraged overleveraging. And there is no evidence to suggest that anybody exercised steady prudential risk control, let alone making stress tests and worst-case scenarios (see section 14.9). For the most part,

- These capital inflows were not hedged, and
- Their contribution to money supply was not appropriately studied by local central banks.

Moreover, a substantial portion of such inflows were short-term lending, by investors and speculators who kept an eye on ways and means to pull their money out very fast. All this made the local economies of East Asia extremely fragile, and it took one big stumble in Thailand to bring down the whole house of cards, with the effects felt as far as South Korea, which had been widely considered to be East Asia's dynamo.

14.7   Broadening interest rate exposure and mismatch risk

Interest rate risk constitutes a large part of trading exposure taken by credit institutions. This is clearly demonstrated by banks that compute VAR estimates separately for each risk type and for the whole portfolio, using simulation. Table 14.1 provides an example from a money center bank, published in its quarterly report of 2003. In the second quarter of 2003, the average 1-day, 99% VAR was $64.3 million. This represented:

- A 31% increase quarter-on-quarter
- Or, 39% increase year-on-year.

Such an increase was primarily attributable to higher interest rate and mortgage interest rate trading positions. Other exposures, like foreign exchange, decreased, while equity exposure remained relatively stable. These statistics are revealing on the consequences of interest rate exposure.

Interest rate and any other market risk due to volatility, and other reasons, should always be subjected to simulation and to experimentation. Among well-managed credit institutions and industrial companies with debt instrument exposure, significant interest rate shocks come as no surprise, because the attention paid to interest rate changes prior to real life shocks permits them to be ahead of the curve.

Experimentation permits senior managers to broaden their minds. It is no secret that in the banking industry it is net interest income that has traditionally received the most attention. While this continues being an important element of profitability, what has changed is the pattern of risk associated with interest income.

While banks have expanded into activities that generate fee-based and other non-interest income, for instance from trading activities, they have also acquired a new and significant interest income exposure.

Table 14.1 Trading exposures (1-day, 99% VAR) at a major money
center bank

	VAR by risk type		
	30 June '03	31 Mar '03	31 Dec '02
Interest rate	87.2	56.9	54.7
Foreign exchange	10.9	15.3	18.7
Equity	19.0	17.6	16.5
Commodity	0.6	0.8	0.5
Subtotal	117.7	90.6	90.4
Diversification benefit[1]	(42.1)	(36.1)	(31.1)
Total	75.6	54.5	59.3
	Total VAR		
	Q2 2003	Q1 2003	Q4 2002
Period end	75.6	54.5	59.3
Average	64.3	49.2	46.4
Maximum	107.9	76.3	59.3
Minimum	47.5	39.4	36.8

[1]Crédit Suisse Group, Quarterly Report, Q3 2003

- Not only loan servicing but also various asset securitization programs can be highly sensitive to market interest rates.
- More deadly can be interest rate exposure from interest rate derivatives, which have a long life – sometimes up to 30 years.

In connection to the second bullet, growing exposure to interest rate derivatives has led both the management of commercial banks and supervisors to take a broader view of the potential effects of changes in market interest rates, and to factor these effects into their risk and return equation under different interest rate environments. Variation in market interest rates can affect the economic value of a bank's:

- Assets
- Liabilities, and
- Derivatives positions

in a most important manner. As sections 14.4 and 14.5 briefly brought to the reader's attention, the savings and loans debacle of the late 1980s in the United States originated in their role as financial intermediaries and had to do with the painful *mismatch risk* that arises from the differences in:

- Maturity of fixed rate loans, and
- The drive for new deposits to be attracted at a high interest rate, to sustain the bank's cash flow.

Such cash flow underpins the bank's assets, liabilities, and off-balance-sheet positions. Interest rate mismatches are quite frequent in banking, and they can expose an institution's income and underlying economic value. Therefore they have to be identified and corrected well before crisis hits. A bank that funded long-term fixed rate mortgages with short-term deposits could face a decline in both

- The future income arising from the position, and
- Its underlying value if interest rates increase.

A relatively simple but effective enough way for measuring a bank's interest rate risk exposure is through a maturity and repricing schedule. This distributes interest-sensitive assets, liabilities and derivatives positions into a number of predefined time brackets according to:

- Their maturity, if fixed rate, or
- Time remaining to their next repricing, if floating rate.

Assets and liabilities lacking definitive repricing intervals, like sight deposits, or actual maturities that could vary from contractual maturities like mortgages with an option for early repayment, are usually assigned to repricing time bands. This is rather subjective, done according to the judgment of bank officers. *Gap analysis* is based on this procedure using simple maturity/repricing schedules to generate indicators of:

- Interest rate risk sensitivity of earnings, and
- Projected changes in economic value due to changing interest rates.

Gap analysis has been one of the first methods employed to measure a bank's interest rate risk exposure. Another method, which we have studied in Chapter 10, is duration. The reader will recall that *duration* measures changes in economic value resulting from a percentage change of interest rates, under the assumption that:

- Changes in value are proportional to changes in the level of interest rates, and
- The timing of payments is fixed, which is a simplification referred to as simple duration.

Chapter 10 has presented as alternatives modified duration and effective duration. Effective duration not only relaxes the simple duration's linear assumption, as well as the notion that timing of payments is fixed, but it is better able to provide exposure patterns – because it addresses the percentage change in the price of the relevant instrument for a *basis point* change in yield. Basis point risk arises from imperfect correlation in the adjustment of the rates earned and paid on different instruments with otherwise similar repricing characteristics.

14.8   Hedging interest rate risk in a commercial bank

The preceding sections have explained that interest rate risk is inherent to most businesses, and it is arising from a variety of factors: fixed rate bonds and loans whose servicing becomes too expensive when interest rates fall, mismatch between loans and deposits, differences in the timing between contractual maturity or repricing of assets, the nature of outstanding liabilities, obligations derived from derivative financial instruments and other reasons.

Net interest income can also be affected by changes in market interest rates. One of the reasons not often talked about is that of banks that provide servicing and loan administration functions for mortgage loan pools in return for a fee. When interest rates fall, the servicing bank experiences a decline in its fee structure as the underlying mortgages repay.

Moreover, as far as a credit institution's bottom line is concerned, a good deal of difference is made by the pattern of the interest rate spread. Chapter 6 has made reference to positive and negative interest rates. Based on my experience as a consultant to the boards of financial institutions, Figure 14.4 emphasizes five main allocation channels of the margin which exists between the two. Rare is the case of a credit institution that proactively assigns part of the margin between positive and negative interest *as if* it were buying reinsurance against interest rate risk.

This is an expensive oversight because even floating rate assets and liabilities are exposed to basis risk. The reason is the difference in repricing characteristics of relevant pairs of floating rate indices, such as the savings rate and 6-months Libor. Furthermore, a growing range of financial products have embedded options that affect their effective duration and pricing.

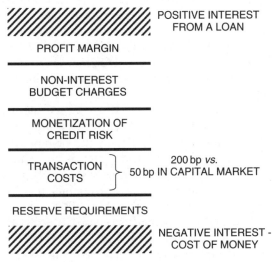

Figure 14.4 The difference between cost of money and interest from a loan is by no means net profit

Some experts suggest that, for better risk management, it is wise to segregate interest rate risk into two broad classes: trading and non-trading. Interest rate risks arising from non-trading business activities should:

- Be captured at the point of business origination, and
- Be subject to a transfer pricing mechanism.

Within this overall process, tier-1 banks ensure that for client business that has no contractual maturity date, or directly market-linked customer rate, like savings accounts or current accounts, the interest rate risk is transferred from business areas to the treasury. This is usually done by pooled transactions. Typically such products contain embedded options in respect of withdrawal, pre-payment, and rate setting; therefore, they cannot be economically hedged by single back-to-back transactions.

The inherent interest rate risk in these products is managed through replicating portfolios of revolving fixed-rate transactions of predefined maturities, which approximate the cash flow pattern of specific positions. At the same time, in addition to interest rate risk resulting from client business, interest rate risk also arises in connection to non-business balance sheet items, like equity investments. Hedging the associated exposure is a decision that implicitly creates non-trading interest rate exposures.

In all these activities particular attention must be paid to identifying outliers in terms of interest rate risk profiles, which are not typical of *our* bank, or of the part of *our* business that is being monitored. Sensitivity tests are recommended, such as measuring the potential impact of a 1, 5, 10, and 20 basis point(s) parallel rise in interest rates on the market value of each balance sheet item – a process that has already been discussed.

So much for quantitative approaches. There are also qualitative factors to be taken into account, particularly connected to political events that impact on interest rates and exchange rates. These should provide input for scenario analysis. Let's take the 2003–2004 American political environment as an example. From the perspective of 2003, for political rather than for economic reasons, analysts were of the opinion that the chances of an interest rate increase by the Federal Reserve before the November 2004 presidential election were very low. However, new data pointing to a pick-up in inflation (see Chapter 8) changed that perspective – with the likely consequence being a sell-off on the bond markets.

Remembering the bonds earthquake of 1994, several speculators started to reposition themselves against the market. The movement in moving out of fixed interest rate positions started on 2 April 2004, pushing up the yield of 10-year US Treasuries by 26 basis points. This was the biggest one-day increase since the bankruptcy of the LTCM hedge fund ransacked the global financial system in September 1998.

It is interesting to look with hindsight at the repositioning that has been going on by hedge funds and overleveraged investors. On 14 June 2004, the Bank for International Settlements (BIS) reported that during the first quarter of 2004 derivatives turnover rose to $272 trillion in notional principal amounts. This represents an unprecedented rise of 31% compared to the last quarter of 2003.[6] Why the risk?

Most of the first-quarter 2004 growth in the derivatives market came from an explosion of trading during the second half of March, with fixed income derivatives at the epicenter. This might well have been a pre-emptying of highly geared bond portfolios, as speculators tried to avoid the bloodbath which they suffered in 1994 when the Fed raised interest rate seven times in a row.

There have also been inflationary fears fed by widespread concern about the growing dual deficit: Federal budget and current account. As will be recalled from Chapter 8, Dr Arthur Burns said that it is government deficits which create inflation. In 2002–2003 measures taken to overcome deflationary pressures led to a rapid growth of debt at federal corporate and consumer levels, with a corresponding increase of IOUs.

- As long as these IOUs are treated as having value, the financial system is more or less solvent.
- But *if* the confidence in them fades, the fiction around them fails, and the financial system comes under severe stress.

Let's face it: ours is a debt-propelled economy and its growth is driven by the accumulation of debt. According to the Federal Reserve, total debt in the US economy stood at $34 trillion at the end of 2003. This means more than $3 in debt for every dollar of the $11 trillion gross domestic product (GDP) of the United States. More worrisome is the fact that since the Russian meltdown and LTCM crisis, in August/September 1998, the Federal debt has increased by $12 trillion, or 54% of its previous level.

Hedging interest rate risk in a comprehensive manner should never ignore these facts about the torrent of red ink. If it does, the hedges will be lopsided. Neither should it be forgotten that with debt growing almost twice as fast as the real economy, and the different governments around the globe being afraid to take rigorous corrective measures, inflationary pressures are unavoidable.

Consider the American example: more than $4.6 in *new* debt for every $1 increase in GDP, with the real economy having lost its ability to close the debt gap – a fact as dramatic as it can be in the United States, Western Europe, and Japan. The evidence of this growing amount of debt is found in the record levels of bonds sold in Group of Ten countries. In the United States alone about some $7 trillion in new bonds were issued in 2003. In the aftermath,

- The previous record of $5.4 trillion in 2002 expanded by a large margin, and
- The value of bonds outstanding has been pushed to nearly $221 trillion.

The fastest growing debt obligations in the United States have been mortgage-type securities, which accounted for $3.2 trillion of the new bonds issued, a new record; and a 39% increase in 2003 from 2002 numbers. Moreover, mortgage originations increased to $3.8 trillion in 2003. The good news is that about two-thirds of the increase in mortgages were refinancings to take advantage of lower interest rates. The ongoing mid- to late 2004 and 2005 increase in interest rates will curtail that activity.

14.9 Stress testing for interest rate and forex risk, according to the Basel Committee

The shock on portfolio positions provided through a stress test should be significant enough to capture the effects of underlying exposure beyond the confines of normal operations.[7] In connection with interest rate risk, the Basel Committee advises that the stress test addresses embedded options and convexity (see Chapter 10) within the framework of assets and liabilities characterizing a financial institution.

Tests for outliers should evidently be done in a way that is practical to implement, but also cost-effective. The methodology to be chosen must accommodate the analytical examination of all trading book and banking book positions. For exposure reasons, the stress test should include all interest rate instruments, whether these are assets or liabilities in the balance sheet.

Compared to the more detailed thresholds for interest rate tests, which we have seen in the preceding sections, the Basel Committee has retained a one-level 200 basis point shock – but it also advises inclusion of exposures revealed through scenarios incorporating duration characteristics, maturity bands, basis point risk, gap analysis, yield curve twists, inversions, and other relevant tests necessary for overall management of interest rate risk.

One of the taxing tasks when stress testing interest rate risk is how to deal with positions where behavioral maturity differs. This may come from the fact that, on the asset side of the balance sheet, positions may include mortgages and mortgage-related securities subject to prepayment with minor or no penalty. This is a problem that has been addressed since the late 1980s by means of option-adjusted spread (OAS), treated through Monte Carlo simulation.

Speaking from personal experience, I believe that more rigorous tests are necessary to focus on interest rate volatility and its aftermath, threshold-by-threshold. At each of these thresholds, both market risk and counterparty risk should be tested – including a worst-case drill for big bank failure. Because the assets of *our* bank are liabilities of other financial institutions and industrial entities and vice versa, a worst-case scenario should consider:

- How likely is a big-bank meltdown, and
- What is the course central banks might adopt, by G-10 country?

Different alternatives must be evaluated: doing nothing at all and letting the bank fail (Barings); closing the gap through taxpayers' money (Crédit Lyonnais); taking temporary hold of the bank, then closing it down (Bank of New England); taking hold, restructuring it, and selling it (Continental Illinois Bank); obliging the shareholders/investors to put up the capital (LTCM); converting loans and other liabilities into equity, after canceling current equity.

In connection with foreign exchange risk, both stand-alone and in conjunction to interest rate risk, the stress testing methodology to be adopted should provide relevant shocks for all main currencies, as well as for testing selected non-G-10 currency exposures. For exposures in G-10 currencies the Basel Committee advises employing either:

- An upward and downward 200 basis point parallel rate test, or
- Observed interest rate changes at 1st and 99th percentile using a 1-year (240 working days) holding period and a minimum 5 years of observations.[8]

For exposures in G-10 currencies, Basel advises either: a parallel rate shock substantially consistent with 1st and 99th percentile of observed interest rate changes under the above conditions, similarly using a 1-year holding period and a minimum 5 years of observations.

As these regulatory requirements document, for both interest rate and forex stress tests banks must have adequate information and first-class systems support for measuring, monitoring, and controlling their exposures. Reports must be provided on a real-time basis to the bank's board, senior management, and individual business line managers concerned by these tests.[9] Assumptions made in connection to stress tests must be in line with:

- The bank's compliance with policies and limits
- The behavioral pattern of prepayment activities, and
- Changes in parameters occurring, or expected to occur, during the period covered by the study.

In terms of methodology, the Basel Committee advises the inclusion of all assets and liabilities belonging to the banking book and trading book, as well as all off-balance sheet items which are sensitive to changes in interest rates – evidently including all interest rate derivatives. These should be slotted into a maturity bucket, with on-balance sheet items treated at book value, while the off-balance sheet are marked to market.

Derivatives should be converted into positions in the relevant underlying. Quantitative information to be considered is the principal amount of the underlying, or notional underlying amount. Futures and forward contracts, including forward rate agreements (FRAs), should be handled as a combination of long and short positions.

- Options must be tested according to the delta equivalent of the underlying, and
- Swaps, including interest rate swaps, treated as two notional positions with relevant maturities.

Basel advises a computational process consisting of five procedural levels. The first is to offset longs and shorts in each time bracket, resulting in a single short or long position in that bracket. The second is to weight resulting short and long positions by a factor which reflects the sensitivity of each position in the different time brackets, to an assumed change in interest rates.

The third procedural level is to sum the resulting weighted positions, offsetting long and shorts, leading to the net short or long weighted position of the banking book in a given currency. The fourth is to compute the weighted position of the whole banking book by summing the net short and long weighted positions calculated for different currencies. The fifth and final computational level is to relate the weighted position of the whole banking book to capital.

These procedural levels imply that stress tests should not just address interest rate and currency exchange risks each taken as stand-alone, but also the two of them in conjunction. This has become necessary because many banks are exposed to interest rate risk in more than one currency.

An excellent example on stress testing for interest rate and forex risk is provided by the Basel Committee. To assist the monitoring by supervisors of interest rate risk exposure, across credit institutions, the Committee recommends that banks should provide results of their internal measurement systems, expressed in terms of the change in economic value relative to capital, using a standardized interest rate stress test. This must reflect a fairly uncommon and stressful rate environment, able to capture the effects of:

- Embedded options, and
- Convexity (see Chapter 10) within the bank's assets, liabilities, and off-balance sheet exposure.

Moreover, the interest rate shock should be straightforward and practical to implement, as well as able to accommodate diverse approaches. Its underlying methodology should provide relevant output for both G-10 and material non-G-10 currency exposures.[10]

The non-G-10 currencies test is important to international banks because they are exposed to interest rate risk in more than one currency. For this reason, the Basel Committee says, they should carry out a similar analysis for each currency accounting for 5% or more of either their banking book assets or liabilities, using an interest rate shock calculated according to the preceding outline.

Apart from the rigorous approach that should characterize the interest rate and foreign exchange stress tests, it should be appreciated that these will be so much more effective when the board clearly identifies the persons responsible for managing interest rate risk. To avoid potential conflicts of interest the board and CEO should also assure that there is adequate separation of duties in key elements of the risk control process. No executive should have authority over both frontdesk and backoffice, even less so the risk control responsibilities.

Appendix 14.A   The Basel Committee's approach to control of interest rate risk and optionality

Let us start with the premise that interest rate risk is a market exposure that affects a credit institution's financial condition. Risks associated to interest rates are classical parts of both loans book and investments book. But at the same time, interest rate volatility:

- Is an important source of a bank's profitability, and
- Protecting the bottom line poses a significant threat to a bank's earnings and capital base.

Volatility in interest rates affects a bank's earnings by changing its net interest income, the level of other interest-sensitive income, and operating expenses, as well as the underlying value of the bank's assets, liabilities, and off-balance sheet (OBS) instruments. Therefore, the Basel Committee recommends that interest rate risk is monitored on a consolidated, comprehensive basis, to include all forms of interest rate exposure – both qualitative and quantitative aspects.

Companies should take notice that rigorous interest rate risk management practices require appropriate board, CEO, and senior management policies as well as oversight. Other 'musts' are sound risk management policies and practices; steady risk measurement, monitoring, and control functions; as well as comprehensive internal controls and independent audits.[11]

The qualitative characteristics of interest rate risk management include a number of issues, such as: whether the bank has an independent risk control unit responsible for the design and administration of risk measurement, monitoring, and control functions; the existence of an internal measurement system appropriate to the nature, scope, and complexities of the bank; as well as internal policies, procedures, systems and controls focusing on interest rate risk.

Moreover, high quality interest rate risk measurement systems necessarily use assumptions – and such assumptions must be pragmatic and well documented. Experimentation on interest rate risk must be supported by databases and data streams whose contents are reliable and accurately processed. Another crucial factor is whether the institution has adequate skill to conduct rigorous interest rate risk management.

The way the Basel Committee sees it, the quantitative dependability of interest rate risk control will depend on accurate processing of price sensitivity of various financial products; vulnerability of capital and earnings under differing interest rate changes (more on this later); and monitoring of various other aspects of interest rate risk, including:

- Mismatch and repricing risk
- Yield curve risk
- Basis risk, and
- Optionality risk.

As we have seen in the body of this chapter, a most often encountered form of interest rate risk is the result of timing differences in maturity for fixed rate loans, *mismatch risk*, and *repricing* for floating rate loans, of a credit institution's assets and liabilities, and off-balance sheet positions. Mismatches are an integral part of banking, but they can also expose an institution's income and underlying economic value to major fluctuations as interest rates are volatile.

The Basel Committee emphasizes that *optionality* is an increasingly important source of interest rate risk. It arises from options embedded in many bank assets, liabilities, and derivatives portfolios. Its control is complex, due to the fact that they may not only be stand-alone instruments, like exchange-traded options or over-the-counter (OTC) contracts, but:

- They may also be embedded within other instruments, and
- In the case of embedding, the effect of interest rate changes on exposure is not transparent.

Instruments with embedded options include different types of bonds with call or put provisions; loans that give borrowers the right to prepay balances; and non-maturity deposit instruments giving depositors the right to withdraw funds at any time without penalties. Furthermore, an increasing array of options can involve significant leverage which magnifies the influence of changes in interest rates on option positions.

The Basel Committee emphasizes that all these instruments have an asymmetrical payoff, with the result that optionality features can pose significant risk, particularly to those who sell them. The reason for this risk and return asymmetry is that options held are generally exercised to the advantage of the holder.

Because of the magnitude of the impact each type of interest rate risk may have on the bank's profitability and survivability, the Basel Committee says that the board of directors should be informed regularly of the interest rate risk exposure of the institution, as well as regularly assess the monitoring and controlling of such risk against established guidance, limits, and levels of risk acceptable to the bank. Moreover, senior management must assure that the structure of the bank's interest rate risk control is effectively managed.

The Basel Committee advises that banks should clearly define the individuals and committees responsible for controlling interest rate risk, assuring that there is adequate separation of duties in key elements of the risk management process to avoid potential conflicts of interest. Another basic requirement is that senior management identifies interest rate risk(s) inherent in new instruments before being introduced to the market. Major hedging or risk management initiatives should be approved in advance by the board, and complex embedded interest rate risk issues thoroughly analyzed to make the effects of interest rate changes not only transparent but also comprehensible.

Notes

1 *Business Week*, 30 July 2001.
2 D.N. Chorafas, *The 1996 Market Risk Amendment: Understanding the Marking-to-Model and Value-at-Risk*, McGraw-Hill, Burr Ridge, IL, 1998.
3 D.N. Chorafas, *Implementing and Auditing the Internal Control System*, Macmillan, London, 2001.
4 D.N. Chorafas, *Understanding Volatility and Liquidity in Financial Markets*, Euromoney Books, London, 1998.
5 D.N. Chorafas, *Reliable Financial Reporting and Internal Control: A Global Implementation Guide*, John Wiley, New York, 2000.
6 EIR, 25 June 2004.
7 D.N. Chorafas, *Stress Testing: Risk Management Strategies for Extreme Events*, Euromoney, London, 2003.
8 Basel Committee, *Principles for the Management and Supervision of Interest Rate Risk*, Basel, September 2003.
9 *Business Week*, 30 July 2001.
10 D.N. Chorafas, *The 1996 Market Risk Amendment: Understanding the Marking-to-Model and Value-at-Risk*, McGraw-Hill, Burr Ridge, IL, 1998.
11 D.N. Chorafas, *Implementing and Auditing the Internal Control System*, Macmillan, London, 2001.

15 The control of risk under Basel II

15.1   Introduction

'It is not difficult to finish, what is difficult is to start,' said Talleyrand, the French diplomat who served as foreign minister to the Directorate, Napoleon, and three French kings, and as prime minister to one of those kings. This book started with the democratization of credit, socialization of risk, and the effect of globalization on investments in debt securities; it is finishing with the control of exposure.

Risk is one of the most frequently used words in the preceding 14 chapters, as well as one of the few taken as being known by the reader. The time has come, however, to return to the fundamentals, define risk and uncertainty, look at their impact on financial transactions, and examine what the Basel Committee on Banking Supervision – and most particularly Basel II – says about risk control.

Etymologically, risk is the chance of injury, damage, or loss; a hazard. Though accurate, this definition has to be somewhat adjusted for financial and other transactions, as well as for policies, where risk is assumed willfully and executed under cover of some authority. An adjustment would require that financial exposure is examined both:

- *Quantitatively*, as a hazard in the sense of the word as used in insurance, and
- *Qualitatively*, as a deliberate decision of assuming exposure through leveraging, trading in uncharted waters, being careless about the aftermath of loans and investments, or by targeting higher returns through other ways and means.

In banking, risk is expressed quantitatively as the probability or degree of loss. Such probability is not just mathematics. It is a function of:

- *Type of loss that is covered*: default, interest rate, exchange rate, type of accident
- *Nature of, and counterparty, to a transaction*: person, company, commercial or financial operation.

Experts think that in a globalized economy the classical way of computing loans loss provisioning may become unstable, because of greater market risk uncertainty and reduced knowledge of the counterparty – which amplify credit risk. Greater emphasis also needs to be placed on derivatives exposure, particularly over-the-counter (OTC) deals which are written off-balance sheet (OBS). Within this environment of amplified exposure, risk management has as an objective to:

- Identify fundamental risk factors
- Determine linkages and establish metrics

- Take measurements, test, reach conclusions
- Elaborate dynamic correction capabilities, and
- Track the execution of orders regarding the control of exposure.

Policies established by the board of directors should see to it that risk control has wide powers, because nearly all types of financial transaction involve a certain degree of uncertainty. As Figure 15.1 suggests, uncertainty and risk correlate – the former being at the root of the latter. To overcome uncertainty and measure risk, we must make assumptions about the most likely course of events and their effect on the positions which we have taken, or we are taking. The challenge with assumptions is that:

- They are usually subjective, and
- Their aftermath cannot be easily measured *a priori*.

This is particularly true as we are living in a period of significant transition in the role of financial instruments and business transactions for reasons stated in Chapter 1 and Chapter 2. This statement has also to be appreciated under another perspective: the fact that the global financial system evolves:

- From one dominated by banks
- To one with deep and liquid capital markets featuring many and diverse players.

These players make up the market and with them credit risk becomes market-tied. Moreover, the morphing of credit risk into market risk, and vice versa, increases price volatility, which becomes further driven by transborder financial flows. If risk control principles are to be observed, the end result can be costly in capital adequacy terms. Hence the attention Basel II pays to regulatory capital and the way to compute it.[1]

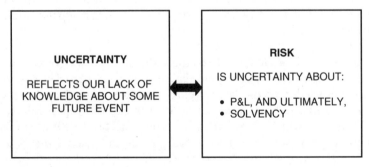

Figure 15.1 Uncertainty and risk correlate in every financial transaction

15.2 Risk management defined

The careful reader will recall from previous discussion on this issue that risk management is a combination of judgment and analytics. Every investor must have a policy for risk management, which establishes a guideline, sets limits, and puts in place a system of alarms. As Chapter 7 emphasized, the setting of risk management's goals must account for:

- *Probable* evolution of credit risk and market risk by instrument and counterparty, and
- *Improbable* outcome due to unexpected risks, credit deterioration, market volatility, liquidity squeeze, event risk, and other reasons.

Independence of opinion is most crucial to the control of both probable and improbable exposure. Risk managers have different opinions than traders, loan officers, and investment advisors due to differences in outlook concerning: risk appetite, types of risks being taken, time horizon of these risks, resulting core exposure (toxic waste), and sustainability of returns. Also in regard to:

- Available economic capital to face assumed risks, and
- Skills on hand to face adversity as it develops – the famed troubleshooters.

Troubleshooters are experts in dynamic risk control. The dangers to which we are exposed continue to evolve because financial markets are living organisms. New instruments and globalization (see Chapter 2) increase volatility. Market dynamics impacts every portfolio, even if the individual investor, bank, or other entity were to hold the inventory of assets and liabilities fixed.

By establishing rules for capital adequacy, financial analysts with a sharp pencil and regulators are watchful of differences between market value of assets and percentage discounted value of all future cash flows. The resulting *economic value* of an entity is the true measure of its longer-run financial staying power, even if this is not reported on classical financial statements. Financial staying power is also key to the management of liabilities.

Because judgment and analytics are the two major ingredients in risk control, the availability of first-class information technology plays a crucial role in timely and effective management of exposure. A real-time response on the status of liabilities and assets, based on scenario analysis and other experimental tools – and reflected in the entity's virtual balance sheet – makes possible dynamic utilization of capital at risk based on accurate and detailed financial results.[2]

The term *virtual balance sheet* identifies a balance sheet assembled on-line, on request. Its contents are global, and tier-1 financial institutions see to it that it integrates all their assets and liabilities, doing so in less than 30 minutes from request to reporting. In counterpart to this fast response, management accepts less accuracy, with deviations at the 3–4% level which is typical with engineering calculations. The virtual balance sheet is part of the company's internal accounting management information system (IAMIS). Here are some of the capabilities which it should provide:

- *Location,* of a major exposure as it develops
- *Orientation* of trend of this exposure, so that its impact may be grasped correctly
- *Identification* of component parts of this exposure, and desk(s) which contributed to it
- *Experimentation* and simulation of results along alternatives strategies in repositioning.

Real-time solutions present distinct competitive advantages, including the rapid visualization by management of risk and return. Figure 15.2 presents a radar chart which permits senior executives to have intraday information on exposure on-balance sheet and off-balance sheet, as well as by major client, instrument, market, and credit limit. Private investors may choose a spreadsheet presentation, but there should always be a compass pointing to assumed risk – and its component parts.

As Chapter 14 brought to the reader's attention, in every organization stress tests must supplement the capital-at-risk approach, permitting their users to look at exposure in cases where market conditions change abruptly or are disrupted.[3] Stress tests are particularly useful in calculating more accurately the impact of large market moves: value-at-risk (VAR) measures are a better fit for small movements than for big swings or for outliers.

Information based on the results of stress tests and worst-case scenarios should be compared with information on the virtual balance sheet which, as the previous paragraphs have explained, presents senior management with reliable (if approximate) *current* positions. With these two elements available interactively in real-time, every responsible executive has a factual and documented basis for exercising management control.

Interactive experimentation by means of modeling sees to it that, in terms of overall effectiveness, it is *as if* the company's books are closed instantaneously under different scenarios that are expected to happen sometime in the future, with

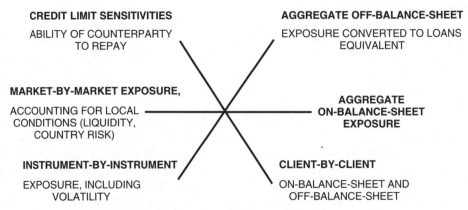

Figure 15.2 Radar chart for off-balance-sheet risk management

a certain likelihood – from 'normal' conditions to extreme events. To reach these results, however, senior management and the organization as a whole must address several important issues.

First and foremost, it must establish a policy which makes risk control the cornerstone to both strategic planning and daily execution. Underpinning this policy should be the board's, CEO's, and senior executives' appreciation that risk management is indivisible from the management of change. This policy should also be a straightforward exercise to determine the:

■ Functions, and
■ Actions of risk control.

Second, management must establish metrics that permit their users to measure whether objectives are being attained, describe the nature and magnitude of exposure(s) being taken and their reasons, and present reliable information on limits and tolerances associated to exposure(s). This information is necessary not only to inform, but also to perform modeling and experimentation. Moreover, because quite often a few major risks and their evolution dominate exposure, the third rule in risk management is to:

■ Consider each major risk individually
■ Set a margin or limit on every major risks
■ Test correlations among major risks, and
■ Establish correlation between major and secondary risks.

As the roles and duties of risk management, and of senior management, presented in this section document, the process of being in charge of exposure has many aspects – from sharpening and steadily testing the adequacy of internal controls, to measuring, analyzing and monitoring all risks, identifying those which are major, and reporting on each one of them daily and intraday.

Intelligence gathering is a major element in the control of risk. For the lender, as well as for the investor, it is vital to have on hand intelligence on risk factors and their development. It should moreover be possible to analyze and consolidate these risk factors, as well as apply ingenuity in bringing exposure under firm control.

High technology can be used in instrumental ways for intelligence purposes. For instance, to help in gaining insight in risk evaluation, developing effective support systems, and make possible experimentation on the evolution of identified risks – whether the goal is trading, loans, portfolio management, or financial planning. In turn, the steady process of such assessment requires first-class organization.

At the same time, the money spent on risk control must be commensurate with the risks being controlled and their materiality. Therefore, the policy I have been advising to the boards of banks I have been associated with as consultant has been along the line of the omega curve in Figure 15.3. This presents three different risk control solutions, depending on:

■ The company's risk appetite
■ Its financial staying power, and
■ The market to which the financial institution addresses itself.

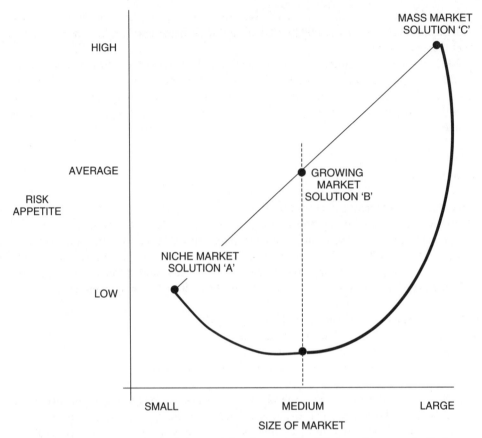

Figure 15.3 Omega curve and the need for three totally different risk control solutions

Still, no matter if the chosen solution is big or small, it is necessary that senior management steadily reviews obtained results and prompts further development of the risk monitoring system. The board and CEO should pay steady attention to effective ways and means for management control, as well as get involved in the test phase of new system versions.

It is evident that it is a basic responsibility of senior management to take corrective action immediately a deviation occurs by counterparty, trader, loans officer, underwriter, investment advisor, or any other player in the system under the company's responsibility and jurisdiction. This is not always done; often a bad situation is left to run its course, till things get beyond repair.

15.3 Basel II requirements for financial analysis and business analysis

Reference to the Basel Committee on Banking Supervision, and its contribution to capital adequacy of credit institutions, has been made in Chapter 5. At the end of June 2004, central bank governors and heads of supervision of the Group of Ten endorsed the publication of the new framework, which regulates international convergence of:

- Capital measurement, and
- Capital standards.

This framework targets risk-sensitive minimum capital requirements for banking organizations, through solutions which range from more basic, the Standardized approach, to more sophisticated, the Advanced Internal Ratings Based (A-IRB) approach. The Basel Committee makes the point that:

- Improvements in internal processes
- More advanced risk handling techniques, and
- The increasing use of securitization

have significantly changed monitoring and management of exposure among credit institutions. They have also enlarged the bandwidth of supervisory activities by involving much more than balance sheet items. Basel I, the original capital adequacy framework of 1988, was based on financial information. By contrast, Basel II has three major components:

- Under Pillar 1, it calls for the analysis of financial information
- Under Pillar 2, it brings the regulators into more detailed supervisory procedures, and
- Under Pillar 3 requires transparency as well as business analytics for reasons of market discipline.

Because of this triple perspective, it is expected that Basel II will significantly increase the need to focus on both financial analysis and business analysis. The former is objective, provided the information included in financial systems is honest and accurate. The latter is rather subjective and brings into play new important factors such as:

- Management risk
- The bank's liquidity
- Leveraging over time
- Type of capital structure, and
- Capital in conjunction to taxation.

The last two bullets oblige senior management to take the proverbial long hard look at cash flow and profitability by product line, as well as re-examine the pattern of sales growth. Leveraging needs to be qualified not only in financial but also in business terms. For instance, too fast sales growth may be as bad as too slow. Also, a steady increase in leveraging eventually leads to bankruptcy, contrary to what some famous professors have stated.[4]

Because many of the issues relating to management risk are cultural, comparisons will need to be done on a country-by-country basis within the framework of a system of standards, as well as through a much greater transparency in financial and business results than is the case today. Take management decisions on credit rating (see Chapter 12) as an example. The principle is that poor judgment gives unreliable results. Also data may be substandard because:

- It is biased (double books)
- It contains creative accounting
- It covers too short a timespan
- It is not detailed enough, and so on.

For a reliable financial analysis of balance sheet and income statement (P&L), data should cover at least 10 years and preferably 20. Other financial information, too, is important on a bank's portfolio in bonds, loans, equities, their price movements, as well as changes in the assets and liabilities ratio and its evolution over time. Such information helps in establishing a time pattern of a likely default point.

Not only should every institution carefully watch its default point, but also the computation of percentiles, quartiles, and median probability of default by major counterparty and correspondent banks has become a 'must'. Notice that not everything is quantitative. Credit risk rating, for instance, also involves subjective judgment, based on business analysis – therefore non-financial factors. This provides the two-channel approach shown in Figure 15.4.

- Compliance to regulatory capital requirements is based on financial data, along criteria already brought to the reader's attention.
- By contrast, economic capital calculation and allocation is primarily based on business data which, as explained, is both qualitative and quantitative or even predominantly qualitative.

A credit risk model based on non-financials is judgmental, involving factors such as: quality of management, compliance to regulations, years the company is in business, nature of products it develops and sells, the degree of satisfaction of its customers, type of market to which it appeals, quality of its competition, delays in paying its debt, industry risk, country risk, and so on. This is business information which complements financial information and serves as proxy to risk evaluation *if*, and only *if*:

- It permits development of a pattern, and
- It can provide an accurate enough picture of company behavior.

In credit risk terms, the result would be a credit rating. Independent rating agencies, and many credit institutions, are experts in this business. They have quantitative and qualitative benchmarks as well as large databases which assist in

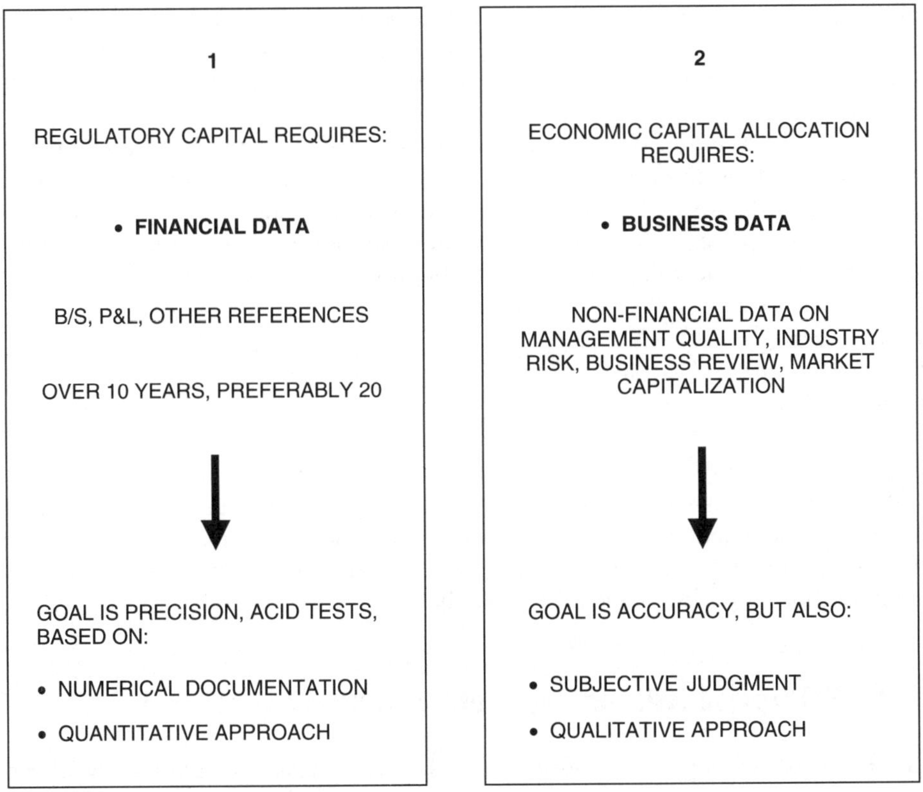

<table>
<tr><th>1</th><th>2</th></tr>
<tr>
<td>REGULATORY CAPITAL REQUIRES:</td>
<td>ECONOMIC CAPITAL ALLOCATION REQUIRES:</td>
</tr>
<tr>
<td>• FINANCIAL DATA</td>
<td>• BUSINESS DATA</td>
</tr>
<tr>
<td>B/S, P&L, OTHER REFERENCES

OVER 10 YEARS, PREFERABLY 20</td>
<td>NON-FINANCIAL DATA ON MANAGEMENT QUALITY, INDUSTRY RISK, BUSINESS REVIEW, MARKET CAPITALIZATION</td>
</tr>
<tr>
<td>↓</td>
<td>↓</td>
</tr>
<tr>
<td>GOAL IS PRECISION, ACID TESTS, BASED ON:

• NUMERICAL DOCUMENTATION

• QUANTITATIVE APPROACH</td>
<td>GOAL IS ACCURACY, BUT ALSO:

• SUBJECTIVE JUDGMENT

• QUALITATIVE APPROACH</td>
</tr>
</table>

Figure 15.4 Accuracy and precision in credit rating call for evaluation along two channels

fairly objective ratings. On the other hand, however, there is a certain amount of subjective judgment involved in business analysis. Therefore, two different independent rating agencies do not need to give the same grade. Most important is that:

■ Estimated probability of default (PD) is based on financial data and, up to a point, it correlates with rating, and
■ The PD trend line establishes the milestones in the watch list, but the trend is also influenced by business data.

Rating by independent agencies and PD trend do not exactly coincide. Furthermore, several experts believe that changes to capital adequacy requirements are more likely to be felt by companies with good ratings, and those able to appeal to high net worth private clients. As a result, already-intensive competition for lower risk business will increase, further forcing banks to continue to improve their efficiency.

Other experts are of the opinion that by requiring higher interest rates for lower quality borrowers, Basel II may well have a negative effect on bank loans – as a risk-adjusted return on capital method will help to apply risk-based pricing. This also

applies to borrowers from structurally weak sectors, where banks will have to determine risk-adjusted credit conditions. My personal opinion is that *risk-based pricing*
will be positive to the economy as a whole, though it might hurt some economically
weak entities.

As value-at-risk did in the mid- to late 1990s at the market risk side, a system of
credit ratings along the preceding lines assists in harmonizing banking supervisory
standards and disclosure requirements in countries that adopt Basel II. Moreover,
with risk-based pricing companies will be more and more assessed on their viability
and future prospects, with corporate financing becoming focused on:

- Risk control,
- Cash flow, and
- Profitability.

The reader should notice that, other things being equal, the more advanced is a
credit institution's risk management, the greater the potential alignment of regulatory
minimum capital requirement with actual risks. Also, the better the prospects of
potential reduction of default probability, which is always present in every enterprise
no matter how good its balance sheet may be.

15.4   Enterprise risk management and internal control

Enterprise risk management addresses itself to risk factors, individual risks, risk
categories, and statements of exposure. The goal is to define and control current
and projected exposures associated to assets and liabilities, including:

- Exposures taken by means of day-to-day business activities, and
- Risks embedded in the inventory of securities, due to investments, trades, and other
  commitments.

Pockets of risk usually include what we are not aware of, but can seriously threaten
our trading book, banking book, investment portfolio, or our company as a whole.
First-class management always aims to position the operations under its control for
short- and long-term market transformation and risks associated to them. Drills,
modeling, and experimentation are a worthy investment because they assist in:

- Determining
- Evaluating, and
- Controlling different types of exposure.

As cannot be repeated too often, this requires considerable skill and high technology. Phil Condit, the CEO of Boeing, says it is the way that information technology
(IT) has changed business processes, rather than IT itself, that makes possible the
rewards manufacturers can reap today.[5] This statement is true for all firms, including
financials.

Boeing's new aircraft, Condit suggests, could not have been developed so quickly without the benefit of investment in up-to-date IT. This focused technological investment sees to it that parts for the plane can be produced more accurately right from the start, eliminating the need for expensive rework, as well as for tools on the assembly floor to hold parts in position while fitters trim to get everything to match.

Similar principles prevail with management information and with risk control. A sound strategy demands that the company's internal accounting management information system, of which we spoke in section 15.2, both works in real time and is kept in compliance with prevailing regulations – because only then does it provide management with information that can be acted upon.

For instance, in the United States IT design should observe and support the Generally Accepted Auditing Standards (GAAS), used for auditing financial statements. GAAS is not to be confused with the Generally Accepted Accounting Principles (GAAP), which regulate the presentation and content of financial statements.

Moreover, IAMIS should be integral part of the entity's *internal control* system,[6] and it must be regularly audited. An assessment of a company's internal control system helps the auditor to better evaluate assertions set forth in financial statements. It also helps to determine the extent of testing to be done – by both internal and external auditors.

In several jurisdictions regulatory authorities are keen to provide auditors with guidance on how to assess an entity's internal control structure during their inspection of financial statements. At the same time, a thorough integration of internal control intelligence is an integral part of enterprise risk management, because it provides evidence on whether or not the board and CEO are in charge.

Given that many of the most important clients of a credit institution are global, successful risk management requires multi-point reporting capabilities, which include accurate knowledge of how much each branch is leveraging the bank's equity and assets. Such results do not come free of cost or effort. The globalization of internal control calls for studies of organizational learning, about:

- *Our* bank, its affiliates and its activities
- All *our* important business partners, and
- The limits reached and exceeded in terms of exposure.

Concentrations of credit risk exist not only with the same counterparty but also with different clients if these are engaged in similar activities, are located in the same geographic region, or have comparable economic characteristics. These clients' ability to meet contractual obligations would be furthermore affected by changes in:

- Economic
- Financial
- Political, or other conditions.

The way to bet is that contrary to common thinking that a global enterprise is more diversified than that which operates in only one country, the global entity faces both a greater number of and more diverse risks. One of the key issues in globalization is how independent business units can cooperate effectively when developing innovative products as well as when evaluating exposure to:

- Clients
- Instruments, and
- Markets.

Headquarters should play a critical role in supporting risk-oriented cooperation. Because a great deal of credit and market information is developed in subsidiaries, companies must, through special task forces, facilitate shared developments of risk control tools, and cross-border transmission of knowledge; also in eliminating complacency and bringing full management attention to troubled spots.

Globalization has also created a market where ten standard deviations (10s) events occur every few years. In this environment, traditional approaches to risk management, like the now classical VAR, are utterly inadequate. New tools are necessary for *extreme events*, and solutions must incorporate the role of:

- Investors
- Traders, and
- Market makers.

A methodology is also needed to model information asymmetries, behavioral biases, and uncertainties in price inference. As mentioned on several occasions, simulation, experimentation, and case studies for risk management purposes should include stress tests. Historical scenarios of extreme events are the crash of:

- The New York Stock Exchange in 1987
- Japan in 1990–2005
- The bond market and Orange County in1994
- Barings Bank in1995
- East Asia and South Korea in 1997
- Dot.coms and telecoms in 2000
- Enron in 2001
- Global Crossing and Worldcom in 2002
- Resona in 2003 (pulled out of the abyss at the eleventh hour through taxpayers' money).

Without the slightest of doubt, the enterprise-wide internal control system should cover not only market risk and credit risk but also operational risk – including settlement risk and legal risk (see section 15.6). In my research, well-managed institutions have underlined the fact that internal control functions are driven from the company's governing body down to operational levels that identify, quantify, report, and manage the risks of the business.

The solution that both supervisory authorities and some of the credit institutions themselves have suggested is that of a risk management group independent of risk-generating functions, such as trading activities, reporting to the executive committee but audited by internal auditing. This risk management function, which some institutions see as the *alter ego* of internal control, is charged with day-to-day responsibility for:

- Risk monitoring
- Measurement, and
- Analytical evaluation.

Its efficiency depends on its ability to ensure that all business activities are being run in accordance with defined top management strategies; that operational controls exist over frontdesk and backoffice; and a real-time information system is on hand to process and visualize the results of risk analysis. Top management directives must explicitly state that internal control should promote:

- Efficient operations within established risk limits
- Reliable financial and regulatory reporting procedures, and
- Compliance with relevant laws, regulations, and institutional policies.

Expanding this paragraph to a global scale, the headquarters should assure that local management policies, by country of operations, pay adequate attention to prudential limits; promote a timely and accurate process for measuring, evaluating, and reporting exposure; put a premium on a strong control culture; and make certain that each independent business unit, as well as the institution as a whole, abides by ethical values. This framework engages the accountability of board members, the CEO, and all senior managers in the affiliates.

15.5   Risks investors take with asset managers

Not only companies but also individual investors take risk of an enterprise type, through the business partnership which they have with asset manager(s). Sometimes, the investor's account is handled by a junior manager who does not have the necessary skill, or even the drive, to pay uninterrupted attention to exposure. In other cases the asset manager assumes too much risk and, contrary to principle, uses the client's securities in repo agreements. In still other cases,

- The investor get the wrong advice, or
- Is being exposed to bad timing.

One of the main mistakes many investment managers made when the NASDAQ dipped at the end of March 2000, was to think that the change in the market's mood would not affect profits. Part of the reason for this illusion has been the fact that, in the S&P Industrial Index, the average company saw its profit margins jump from 4.2% in 1992 to 6.6% in 1999, a level last matched in 1966.

By misjudging the new trend many analysts expected profit margins to hit an all-time high of 7.7% in 2001, in spite of the early 2000 slump. The next hypothesis which went wrong has been that this kind of margin expansion would lift corporate earnings 13% to

14% in each of the next two years. As a result a score of investment advisors projected the S&P 500 would reach 1675 by early 2001, a 10% rise from the April 2000 level – which proved to be wrong.

When it comes to investments, even the pros can make big blunders. As a *Business Week* article had it, right after the NASDAQ rout, Jeffrey M. Applegate, Lehman Brothers' chief investment strategist, whose 'new economy' portfolio had surged 66.6% in a matter of 4 months, believed that growth stocks would again trounce 'old economy' stocks (read value issues). This was expected to happen for the seventh year in a row.

Based on this belief Applegate made big bets on premier names such as America Online, Cisco Systems, IBM, Oracle, Microsoft, and Sun Microsystems, as well as up-and-comers like 'fiber-optics powerhouse' JDS Uniphase. Technology stocks, plus AT&T, Qwest Communications, and Sprint, made up a hefty 75% of the portfolio, versus a 41% weighting in those two sectors in the S&P 500 – and we know what has happened since that time to AT&T, Qwest, AOL, Oracle, Sun Microsystems, JDSU, and the other high techs.[7]

A similar story repeated itself with bonds a few years later. In November 2003 yields were rising and several investment advisors were of the opinion that this was a solid trend. January 2004 saw a reversal which culminated in a minibubble with yields falling sharply and, most importantly, the price of all sorts of junk bonds rising beyond any logic.

- Investors advised to buy debt instruments because yields were falling got burned, and
- From March to May 2004 other better-informed investors and speculators unloaded emerging markets' debt and BB−- and B-rated bonds.

The question these references raise, at least from the investors' viewpoint, is how to make asset managers more responsible, and how to better protect the end investors. An article in *The Economist* responded to this query by stating that there is no clear-cut answer. For instance, in the UK, with the world's largest institutional-investment industry after the United States, a succession of mainly government-sponsored committees have reported on this subject, but these reports lead nowhere.

The latest has been a committee set up by a business-led think-tank: Tomorrow's Company. The key problem identified by this committee centered around a loss of investor trust in the financial services industry. This has been brought about by:

- A series of scandals, and by
- The collapse of the stockmarket.

Neither does it seem that the latest of these committees paid attention to the fact that both in retail finance and institutional investment the pattern of incentive payments and sometimes outrageous commissions can cause serious distortions, harm investors, and accentuate the scandalous practices sometimes hitting the investment industry.

Altogether, there does not seem to be a great deal of imagination in the advice given by the different committees, including the latest one. The key suggestions are better self-regulation, based on an agreed statement of principles, and greater transparency of fees and incentives.[8] *Du déjà vu*, and ineffectual. If self-regulation were the solution to an industry's problems, then regulation would have been superfluous all over the world.

Critics of half-baked measures say that this Committee's report paid little or no attention to improving the way the system works for retail investors. Instead, its recommendations are hollow, except for one on compulsory lessons on basic finance for schoolchildren. Teaching about choosing and managing one's investments, including risk control, is a good concept. What makes the Committee's results deceiving is the lack of any other new ideas, particularly pertaining to:

- The behavior of investment companies, and
- Their advising of clients and of handling their accounts.

'Teaching in schools' is a way of shifting one's responsibilities to the state. To the contrary, *if* self-regulation were the solution, *then* the Committee should have given evidence that asset managers have expertise in the monitoring and measurement of risk. Factual and documented examples on how they are monitoring their own exposure as well as the exposure of their customers, might have been convincing. Just as important would have been evidence about their establishment and observance of risk limits for:

- All products
- All traders, and
- All investment positions.

Asset managers who are worth their salt, and their fees, are setting and monitoring risk limits constantly *as if* they were doing a perpetual inventory control. They are evaluating hedges, informing themselves on market changes and on benefits and risks assumed by their clients; they are also willing and able to recommend *specific risk control action*.

There has been a different, better focused study in the UK, which documented that funds of funds, index funds, and others that provide identical services charge vastly different fees. One of the interesting findings which has come to my attention is that an investor holding a portfolio of the 10% of funds with the lowest historical fees received an extra 10% annually compared to the investor who held the 10% with the highest fees. Paying more, delivers less.

Other interesting information is that investing in funds with high past returns gives an extra 0.97% a year compared to investing in funds with poor past returns. Up to a point, this contradicts the principle that past performance is no prognostication of future performance – but it is always wise to keep in mind a contrary opinion.

Where this leads our discussion is that all investors should learn the basics of risk management and exercise them – including the need for damage control. Government regulation of the investment industry, including hedge funds and funds of funds, is both necessary and urgent, to restore trust. The regulation of hedge funds (see also Chapter 1) will not solve by itself all of the problems, but it will help to restore investment trust.

First and foremost government regulation must close the current divide between heavily regulated public companies and lightly regulated hedge funds. Secondly, all sorts of investment advisors and asset managers must appreciate that their industry will be truly regulated, with capital requirements and stiff penalties for misconduct, unless it changes its ways and pays much more attention to its customers.

A real and present problem is that many funds are being bought by uninformed investors who are swayed by marketing and buy the advice of investment advisors with questionable incentives and even conflicts of interest. Finally, the private investors themselves must become able to see more clearly what risks they are taking, and grasp the fundamental rule of savings: *'Never put your money into anything you do not understand.'*[9]

15.6   The cost of legal risk and reputational risk

Basel II rests on two foundations. The one is prudential capital requirements, and it has been discussed in section 15.3. The other is operational risk control.[10] Operational risk is of many types, which could be effectively classified into three groups, as shown in Figure 15.5. While fraud can cost the company a great deal of money, in the longer run management risk and legal risk can prove to be much more expensive.

The new Basel framework, briefly discussed in section 15.3, establishes an explicit exposure to the risk of losses caused by failures in systems, processes or staff. Or, that are caused by external events like natural disasters affecting the credit institution's ability to continue operating. All told, operational risks can be classified into two main categories:

■ Those that are high frequency but low impact (HF/LI), like petty fraud, and
■ Those that are low frequency but high impact (LF/HI), and may engender not only financial but also brand name and other risks.

Legal risk belongs to the LF/HI class. Even the cost of lawyers fees can be enormous. Mid-May 2004 Microsoft reached a new record: the lawyers who handled the case opposing the software manufacturer to Sun Microsystems, and who seem to have convinced Bill Gates to sign the $1.1 billion settlement, sent in a bill for $258 million for their services.[11] This is a telling example of the cost of legal risk on the lawyers' side alone.

Far more costly can be a legal case that involves the attorney-general and/or the regulators. The case of the 28 April 2003 settlement of ten Wall Street firms with the Securities and Exchange Commission is well known but bears retelling. The bill has been $1.4 billion – one of the largest paid for compliance reasons up to that time.

Another, more recent, example concerns Citigroup's multibillion dollar settlement in a case which became known as 'fraud-on-the-market' (more on this later). On 10 May 2004, the financial conglomerate reached a $2.65 billion settlement with WorldCom shareholders. They had accused the bank's analyst, Jack Grubman, of painting a misleadingly rosy picture of the now-bankrupt telecommunications group's prospects, between 1999 and 2002. A billion dollars here, a billion dollars

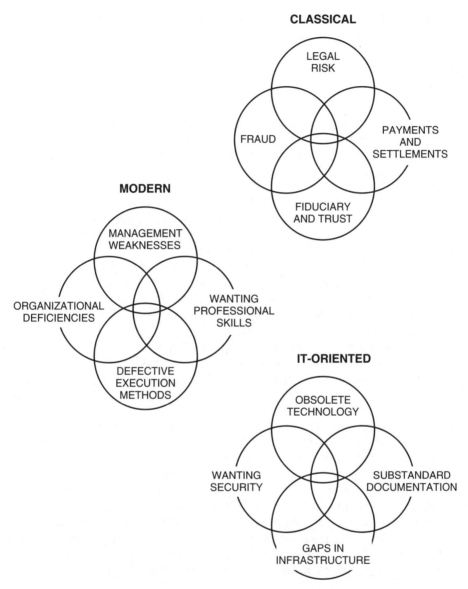

Figure 15.5 Three different groups of operational risk

there, and pretty soon we talk of real money, Everett Dickson the former Republican leader of the US Senate once said. This legal penalty for fraud-on-the-market is enormous, but it might have been even higher, according to informed sources. Special reserves to cover class actions are biting. An example is Citigroup's $4.95 billion special reserve of May 2004, for Enron, WorldCom, and other class actions.[12]

In a way that dramatized the cost of legal risk and management's concern that it might spill over into reputational risk, before the financial markets opened on 10 May, Charles Prince, Citigroup's chief executive, told analysts that his bank, easily the world's biggest by market capitalization, would pay this $2.65 billion to settle class-action litigation accusing it, in essence, of:

- Tainted research in the bubble years of the late 1990s, and
- Fraudulently misleading investors in WorldCom's business prospects.

Nearly $5 billion was put aside as a reserve against hundreds of lawsuits, of which the most significant are tied to Enron and Global Crossing. With this, Citigroup's total bill for stockmarket bubble-related litigation, including the 28 April 2003 SEC settlement, has reached $8 billion. Legal risk will not fade away in the coming years. Instead, no matter where one puts it, it will be in the way.

Most extraordinary about the WorldCom-related settlement sum is that, as Prince insisted, Citigroup has done no wrong. Some analysts said that, though huge, this $2.65 billion is not as much Citigroup *might* have had to pay, as since 2003 courts have become tough places for corporate defendants.

Indeed, the above multibillion settlement was concluded hours before a federal appeals court was due to begin considering an important phase of WorldCom litigation, including, among other things, whether as prominent booster of WorldCom's shares, Citigroup could be held responsible for investors' losses. The court action had been brought by WorldCom shareholders.

Citigroup has not been accused of selling WorldCom bonds to its clients. But the finger has been pointed at other banks for doing just that – including retail depositors. These were bonds of companies throwing themselves over the cliff because of fraud or plain mismanagement – as well as of sovereigns, like Argentina, about to go bust.

Such a scandal, for example, has involved Capitalia, the Italian financial conglomerate and its banks, which sold Parmalat's bonds to retail clients who could ill-afford the losses, just a short time before the hedge fund with a dairy product line on the side went bankrupt.[13] It is to the credit of Matteo Arpe, Capitalia's new CEO, that he took the initiative to refund some of the now worthless bonds to the lower net worth clients to whom Parmalat's rotten debt instruments were sold.

In Citigroup's case, the plaintiffs' lawyers promoted the 'Fraud-on-the-market' theory. This says that since share prices are shaped by information, those who distribute false information are liable for the losses suffered by anyone who bought a company's shares beefed-up in price by unsubstantiated or outright fake financial reports.

- Brokers are liable *when* such information is circulated, and
- It does not matter whether or not the disseminator knew about such information as being fraudulent.

Citigroup's shares plummeted right after this $2.65 billion settlement. This came at an inopportune time because the financial conglomerate had already lost part of its capitalization in the timeframe from 12 April to 9 May 2004. The huge settlement and further special reserves for legal risk accelerated the fall.

At Wall Street, analysts said that it was still unclear whether other banks involved in the WorldCom investment scam – like JP Morgan Chase, Bank of America, and

Deutsche Bank – will be the next targets of class actions. For his part, Alan Havesi, comptroller of the State of New York, who was a principal actor in the Citigroup litigation, stated that this settlement was only a beginning.[14]

Some experts were to suggest that as far as fraudulent information on investments is concerned, a great deal depends on whether the $2.65 out-of-court settlement by Citigroup is seen as part of jurisprudence. Lower courts in the United States have split on whether the fraud-on-the-market theory, which has so far been accepted only for statements made by companies about their own finances, can also be applied to equity research by investment banks. But there may be a spillover.

For his part, Citigroup's CEO said that his bank had been hurt by the Securities and Exchange Commission's submission of a brief supporting the notion that the fraud-on-the-market theory could apply. Some analysts suggested that defeat in court could have cost the bank $54 billion, which would have sunk it. Correctly, Charles Prince preferred to forgo roughly a quarter's earnings than face such a bill.[15] Moreover, because it has chosen to avoid the risk of losing in court,

- Citigroup can continue to say that it has broken no laws, and
- It can also set the cost of the settlement against tax, passing about a third of that bill on to public finances.

For Alan Havesi, the settlement was a wake-up call to those on whom the investing public depends to guard against corporate corruption. The comptroller of the State of New York, who acted as lead plaintiff, is a trustee of the state's public pension fund, which lost $306 million on investments in WorldCom. According to some estimates, if structured according to the same Citigroup formula, settlements with the 17 other underwriters of WorldCom debt could lead to the recovery of an additional $2.8 billion – a windfall that will help cover part of the huge WorldCom losses.

15.7 Operational risk with trusteeship, mutual funds, and hedge funds

When bonds are sold to the general public, as distinguished from direct placement with one or a few big investors, the number of bondholders is usually large and widely scattered. Therefore, it is not practical to deal with each of them individually, and the issuing company appoints a third party as *trustee* to represent the bondholders. The primary function of the trustee, who holds the copy of the bond indenture (see Chapter 3 for the definition), is to act as the bondholder's agent. Possible conflicts of interest come from the fact that the trustee is appointed by the issuer:

- Before any of the bonds are sold, and
- Without consulting the bondholders.

Legally, any competent person may serve as a trustee. Usually, however, a trust company is chosen to discharge most of the duties associated to the debt instrument, capitalizing on the efficiencies that come with a specialized occupation. It is also customary to appoint an ordinary person in addition to the corporate trustee, creating a dual trusteeship which makes it possible to meet the requirements of certain jurisdictions. The trustee's duties are numerous, among the more important being:

- *Certification of the securities issued*, as guaranty of the legal validity of the bond issue
- *Checking of performance*, by examining the terms of indenture, and
- *Action in default*, in which case the trustee is expected to notify the bondholders and take proper action.

It is not necessarily always appreciated that each of these trustee responsibilities, and more, are always subject to operational risk. For instance, the trustee may not perform his or her assigned functions in an able manner, may be misguided by the issuer of bonds, or may have a conflict of interest. In all these cases, the bondholders suffer the consequences of operational risk on the trustee side, issuer side, or may be their own side because of having overlooked issues connected to credit risk and other risks.

Sometimes between the investor on one side, the issuer and trustee on the other, there is an intermediate entity. The mutual funds industry provides an example. This is an industry that between its equity and debt holdings manages $13 billion worldwide. Over the last couple of years, those investors holding a portfolio of funds have been greatly concerned by the fact that the mutual fund industry has gone through turmoil, attacked for various practices:

- From a lack of appropriate corporate governance,
- To violations of fiduciary responsibility for allowing market-timing of its funds, charging excessive fees, and so on.

Some of the reasons for lack of corporate governance structure are historical. In the years immediate after the Second World War virtually *all* fund management companies were small partnerships, or companies closely held by their principals. They looked at themselves as trustees, and were just a step removed from the funds they managed – therefore stewards of the assets entrusted to their care.

By 1960, however, this structure was on the way out. Public offering of management company shares became possible, and numerous management company initial public offers (IPOs) followed. Fund managers began to leverage their entities for greater returns, and focused on the price of their stock. This meant management risk: Their earlier attention to the welfare of their fund shareholders had to compete with other interests such as:

- Building a larger asset base
- Marketing aggressively
- Making as much profit as they could, and
- Charging more up-front and management fees.

Neither shareholders nor bondholders benefited from this twist. Moreover, during the first years of the 21st century, with interest rates at rock bottom and investors desperately looking for higher return, the hedge fund industry skyrocketed – from mastering about $50 billion in 1990, to over $1 trillion by mid-2004. Hedge funds are far more aggressive operators than mutual funds (see Chapter 1).

Not only do institutional investors throw unprecedented amounts of money into hedge funds, but also retail investors run for hedge funds, mainly through funds of funds vehicles sponsored by commercial banks. Because of this, funds of funds have grown at an annual rate of 50% in the years 2001 to 2004, during which time the fund of funds share of hedge-fund assets has risen from 20% to 33%.

Few investors appreciate that funds of funds might be much riskier than they seem, because like the hedge funds in which they invest, they play not only their equity consisting of money placed with them by investors, but also cash borrowed from banks in order to boost returns.[16] More recently, while the risks continue to rise, funds of funds returns have sagged though their managers still hope they will exceed the cost of borrowing. We shall see.

The trusteeship concept discussed in the opening paragraphs of this section and that of gambling with other people's money are in full contradiction to one another. Yet, they seem to live under the same roof with funds of funds, creating an operational risk of major proportions – particularly on the legal side, with fraud-on-the-market the possible aftermath.

15.8 White collar crime hits stakeholders hard

The problems outlined in section 15.7 can get worse with rising interest rates. When hedge funds can borrow at 2%, they might make a profit, depending on the type and amount of risks they assume. But this is no more true when they borrow, for instance, at 8%. And because the funds industry is unregulated, nobody is looking over their shoulders.

In short, hedge funds and funds of funds have a blank check. To make matters worse on the risk side, many investments by hedge funds are hard to value because they are in assets like debt of companies in bankruptcy proceedings. These are not traded, and therefore have no market price.

It looks *as if* the go-go late 1990s are here all over again, but in the meantime both the law and jurisprudence have changed. Adopted in 2002 in America, the Sarbanes–Oxley legislation saw to it that sentencing guidelines for crimes in the executive suit toughened considerably. This is only right; if executives are convicted of crimes, they should be punished, whether the wrongs they did hit bondholders, shareholders, or both. Corporate fraud is not victimless, as is sometimes claimed. It wreaks havoc on all stakeholders:

- Employees
- Customers
- Shareholders, and
- Bondholders.

The effect is particularly destructive if it drives the firm into bankruptcy, as has happened in many cases. In fact, as the Basel Committee points out, there is also the case of *double default*. In its press release of 26 June 2004, Basel says that it believes the recognition of double default effect is necessary in all of its implications, especially those related to:

- Monitoring
- Measurement, and
- Appreciation of the aftermath.

Slowly but surely it is becoming a matter of public conscience that executives holding positions of trust and betraying that trust commit a serious offense.[17] Therefore, the sentencing regime for company executives is justified. The challenge is how to effectively extend the current US practice in the globalized economy to include corporates, sovereigns, and all other entities that betray investor confidence.

As an example on sentencing, in 2004 Martin Grass, a former CEO of Rite Aid, a pharmacy chain whose share price collapsed in 2000 after a $1.6 billion revision to earnings, received an 8-year sentence for fraud. Grass pleaded guilty to fraud but agreed to cooperate with the prosecution of former colleagues. By contrast, Franklin Brown, Rite Aid's ex-chief counsel, made no deal with prosecutors, went to trial and was convicted on ten counts which may carry up to 65 years in prison.[18]

The toughening-up by US government authorities began when, in July 2002, George W. Bush set up a Corporate Fraud Task Force. Since then, the workload of the Department of Justice (DOJ) has soared. Federal prosecutors have charged some 700 defendants in around 300 cases of alleged fraud, including a long list of chief executives. Moreover, through the Sarbanes–Oxley Act, Congress increased significantly the penalties for fraud and the maximum sentence possible nearly quadrupled.

Critics say that as the new regime of punishing white-collar crime is being put in place, sentences are uneven. Carl Cushnie, founder of Versailles, a trade-finance group, was sentenced to just 6 years in jail for his part in what the judge called a 'massive fraud' in 'a grand and evil scheme'. On the other hand, if convicted, seven former executives at Enron Broadband, a subsidiary of the fallen energy firm, whose trial began in September 2004, face the prospect of spending the rest of their lives in prison; so might Jeffrey Skilling, former CEO of Enron. The Enron trial is ongoing and its most juicy parts are, in all likelihood, still to come with the prosecution of Kenneth Ley, the company's former chairman.

Critics add that the new sentencing regime is too tough, stretching the limits of America's legal system. The pros answer that tough sentencing is right; fraud is not a capital offense, but swindles are a serious matter and executives who are wrongdoers can usually afford a good lawyer to defend them – as the trial of Dennis Kozlowski, the former CEO of Tyco, has demonstrated.

One of the cases often cited by critics because of its severity is that of Jamie Olis, a former mid-level finance executive at Dynegy, the Texan energy firm. Olis received a 24-year jail sentence for his part in Project Alpha, whose objective was to inflate Dynegy's cash flow in 2001 by $300 million. The pros point out that the sentence is right because it serves as an example that for financial crime there is punishment.

One of the problems, of course, is how to measure loss by stakeholders. In Jamie Olis' case the judge decided that the loss caused was $100 million. Under the current jurisprudence, this quintupled his sentence. The judge arrived at this number after hearing testimony from an official of the University of California, who stated that the university system's employee-benefits fund lost $100 million due to Dynegy's falling share price at the time of Project Alpha.

Whether the issue of white collar crime concerns debt or equity is immaterial. Material is the fact that a company's executives must be distinguished for their stewardship, not for cooking the books. Investors expect stewards to have and to show special concern in the administration of assets entrusted to them and to demonstrate that they always act in an ethical manner.

Risk control is not only targeting financial exposure, even if this is the most widely considered issue. Management risk is just as important. In this era of questionable corporate governance issues, company directors should think very carefully about board assignments – including the consistent emphasis on the importance of company culture and personal ethics, as well as the fact that business ethics should always be of the highest value.

Notes

1 D.N. Chorafas, *Economic Capital Allocation with Basel II: Cost and Benefit Analysis*, Butterworth-Heinemann, Oxford and Boston, 2004.
2 D.N. Chorafas, *The Real-time Enterprise*, Auerbach, New York, 2005.
3 D.N. Chorafas, *Stress Testing: Risk Management Strategies for Extreme Events*, Euromoney, London, 2003.
4 D.N. Chorafas, *Economic Capital Allocation with Basel II: Cost and Benefit Analysis*, Butterworth-Heinemann, Oxford and Boston, 2004.
5 *The Economist*, 15 November 2003.
6 D.N. Chorafas, *Implementing and Auditing the Internal Control System*, Macmillan, London, 2001.
7 *Business Week*, 10 April 2000.
8 *The Economist*, 19 June 2004.
9 D.N. Chorafas, *The Management of Equity Investments*, Butterworth-Heinemann, Oxford, 2005.
10 D.N. Chorafas, *Operational Risk Control with Basel II: Basic Principles and Capital Requirements*, Butterworth-Heinemann, Oxford and Boston, 2004.
11 *Il Sole 24 Ore*, 13 May 2004.
12 *La Reppublica*, 11 May 2004.
13 D.N. Chorafas, *The Management of Equity Investments*, Butterworth-Heinemann, Oxford, 2005.
14 *Il Sole 24 Ore*, 11 May 2004.
15 *The Economist*, 15 May 2004.
16 D.N. Chorafas, *Alternative Investments and the Mismanagement of Risk*, Macmillan/Palgrave, London, 2003.
17 D.N. Chorafas, *Management Risk: The Bottleneck is at the Top of the Bottle*, Macmillan/Palgrave, London, 2004.
18 *The Economist*, 12 June 2004.

Index